FCE Use of English 2

The "FCE Use of English 2" is a practice book intended mainly for intermediate and post-intermediate students, but it is also useful for more advanced students for revision and consolidation.

The aim of the book is to help students to understand and use English grammar through structurally graded material and full-colour pictures. In addition the book offers preparation for the Cambridge FCE Examination or any other similar examinations.

Oral Development sections

These appear throughout the book and help students practise the grammar structures presented.

Folder sections

Each unit is followed by exercises which provide general practice for the FCE Examination or any other similar examinations. The use of **Phrasal Verbs** is explained in Appendix 2 and the use of **Prepositions** is explained in Appendix 3 at the back of the book. There are also "key" word transformation exercises, collocations and idioms.

Practice test sections

After every unit there is a section which trains students to cope with the Cambridge FCE Examination Paper 3 - Use of English or any other similar examinations.

Pre-test sections

After every four units there is a section which familiarises the students with the format and level of difficulty of the actual tests. These appear in the Teacher's Book and revise all structures taught up to this point.

Further Practice Sections

There are five practice sections, each including exercises on words often confused, open cloze texts, "key" word transformations and multiple choice cloze texts, providing general practice for the FCE examination – Paper 3, Use of English – or any other similar examinations.

A Teacher's Book accompanies the Student's Book. This contains the answers to the exercises in the Student's Book and presents useful grammar tips as well as three tests in two separate versions.

Published by Express Publishing

Liberty House, New Greenham Park, Newbury, Berkshire RG19 6HW
Tel.: (0044) 1635 817 363
Fax: (0044) 1635 817 463
e-mail: inquiries@expresspublishing.co.uk
http: //www.expresspublishing.co.uk

© Virginia Evans, 2001

Design and Illustration © Express Publishing, 1996

First published 1996
New edition 2001

Lay out: *E. Mavragani*

ISBN   1-84216-831-2

1 *Identify the tenses, then match them with the correct description.*

1 They **are getting** married this summer.
2 The robber **waves** his gun and everyone **gets down** on the floor.
3 The sun **rises** in the east and **sets** in the west.
4 The course **starts** on 10th October.
5 Clare **is looking for** a new flat.
6 We'**ve been sharing** a flat for years.
7 They **employ** staff from all over the world.
8 Paula **has become** more independent since starting university.
9 The child **has been missing** since last night.

a fixed arrangements in the near future
b personal experiences/changes that have happened
c actions taking place at or around the moment of speaking; temporary situations
d actions started at a stated time in the past and continuing up to the present
e reviews/sports commentaries/dramatic narratives
f permanent situations or states
g permanent truths or laws of nature
h emphasis on duration of an action that began in the past and continues up to the present
i timetables/programmes (future meaning)

1 ..a..   2 C   3 g   4 i   5 D   6 F   7 E   8 B   9 H

2 *Identify the tenses, then match them with the correct description.*

1 Bill **always stops** to buy milk on his way to work.
2 The new serial **is growing** in popularity.
3 There **goes** the last bus!
4 Scientists **have just discovered** a way to prevent memory loss.
5 Andrea **has phoned** me **every day** this week.
6 Laura **is always criticising** my appearance.
7 I feel exhausted as I **have been working** on my assignment all night.
8 He'**s been asking** to borrow money again.
9 The Kellys **have moved** to Manchester.

a past actions of certain duration having visible results/effects in the present
b changing or developing situations
c recently completed actions
d exclamatory sentences
e frequently repeated actions with "always" expressing the speaker's annoyance or criticism
f actions which happened at an unstated past time and are connected to the present
g emphasis on number, frequency
h repeated/habitual actions
i expressing anger, irritation, annoyance or criticism

1 ..h..   2 C   3 D   4 B   5 E   6 E   7 A   8 G   9 F

3 *Put the verbs in brackets into the correct present forms.*

Dear Mr and Mrs Williams,

I 1) ...*am writing*... (write) to thank you for coming to our wedding last month. I hope you enjoyed yourselves. Sheila and I 2) HAVE JUST RETURN (just/return) from our honeymoon in Kenya and 3) NOW WE ARE LOOKING FORWARD TO (now/look forward to) starting our new life together. We 4) HAVE JUST MOVED (just/move) into our new house and since our honeymoon we 5) spent (spend) all our free time decorating. The house 6) actually .... (actually/begin) to feel like home now and we 7) .... (gradually/settle) into a routine. We 8) .... (have) breakfast together in the morning, but then we 9) .... (not/see) each other until late in the evening when we 10) .... (get) home from work. I hope both of you 11) .... (be) well since we last saw you.

Love,
David and Sheila

Stative verbs express a permanent state rather than an action and do not have continuous forms. These are: **verbs of the senses** (used to express involuntary actions): feel, hear, see, smell, taste etc. *I see someone standing at the front door.* **Verbs of feelings and emotions** : adore, detest, dislike, enjoy, forgive, hate, like etc. *She really enjoys cooking for her friends.* **Verbs of opinion** : agree, believe, suppose, understand etc. *I don't believe he's coming.* **Other verbs** : appear (= seem), belong, concern, contain, depend, fit (= be the right shape and size for sth), **have** (= possess), **know**, mean, owe, own, possess, need, prefer, require, want, weigh, wish, keep (= continue), **seem** etc. *This skirt fits you well.* ~~Lo być wihhym (niewielce) i zawohicie~~

Note: Feel and hurt can be used in continuous or simple forms. *Ann is feeling/feels tired.* **Listen, look** and **watch** express deliberate actions and can be used in continuous forms. *They are looking at some pictures.*

Some stative verbs (be, love, see, smell, taste, think etc) have continuous forms but there is a difference in meaning.

State ~~Stan~~	Action
● I **see** exactly what you mean. (= I understand)	● She **is seeing** a lawyer tonight. (= She's meeting)
● Peter **thinks** he knows everything. (= He believes)	● He **is thinking** of studying Law. (= He is considering)
● They **have** a villa in Portugal. (= They own)	● He **is having** problems. (= He is experiencing)
● A baby's skin **feels** very smooth. (= It has a smooth texture)	● He **is feeling** the engine to see how hot it is. (= He's touching)
● This soup **tastes** of garlic. (= It has the taste of garlic)	● Why are you **tasting** the curry? (= Why are you testing the flavour?)
● The room **smells** of fresh flowers. (= It has the smell of)	● Why **are you smelling** that meat? (= Why are you checking its smell?)
● Most people **love/enjoy** eating out. (= They like in general)	● She **is loving/is enjoying** every minute of her holiday. (= She likes specifically)
● Peter **is** a difficult person to get on with. (= His character is difficult)	● Jane **is being** particularly generous this week. (= She is behaving generously)
● He **looks** as if he's going to faint. (= He appears)	● They **are looking** at the photos. (= They are viewing)
● The patient **appears** to be recovering. (= He seems to be)	● Simply Red **are appearing** on stage next week. (= They are giving a performance)
● Sam now **weighs** more than his father. (= His weight is more)	● The doctor **is weighing** the baby. (= She is finding out its weight)
● My uniform **doesn't fit** me. (= It isn't the right size)	● We **are fitting** a new kitchen next week. (= installing)

4 *Fill in with Present Simple or Continuous.*

1 A: I ...*am seeing*... (see) an old friend tonight.
   B: I .... (see) - so you won't be able to meet me after work, will you?

2 A: Why .... (you/smell) the milk?
   B: It .... (smell) a bit strange. I think it might have gone off.

3 A: .... (you/enjoy) reading Jane Austen's novels?
   B: Not usually, but I .... (enjoy) this particular one.

4 A: Why .... (John/be) so bad tempered today?
   B: I don't know. He .... (be) usually so easy to get on with.

5 A: Carol and I .... (think) of getting married.
   B: .... (you/think) that's a good idea? You haven't known each other for very long.

6 A: .... (you/have) the phone number of a good business consultant?
   B: Why? .... (you/have) problems at work?

7 A: .... (the singer/appear) tonight?
   B: Unfortunately not. She .... (appear) to have lost her voice.

8 A: Why .... (you/taste) the baby's drink?

B: It .... (taste) a little bitter. I think I'll add some more sugar.

9 A: I hear the Fords .... (look) for a bigger house.

B: Yes, it .... (look) as if they are going to move.

10 A: How much .... (the parcel/weigh)?

B: I'm not sure. The assistant .... (weigh) it at the moment.

Have gone to / Have been to / Have been in

- She **has gone to** the bank. *(She's on her way to the bank or she's there now. She hasn't come back yet.)*
- She **has been to** New Orleans. *(She has visited New Orleans but she isn't there now. She has come back.)*
- She **has been in** the Hague for four years. *(She lives in the Hague now.)*

5 *Fill in "has/have been to/in", "has/have gone to".*

1 How long ....*has*..................... she ....*been in*..................... York?

2 Sheila .... Brussels twice this year.

3 Mum .... the supermarket. She'll be back in about an hour.

4 Sam isn't in the office. He .... a meeting.

5 Mr Smith .... Paris for nearly three years.

Since expresses a starting point. *She's been working here* **since** *November.*
For expresses the duration of an action. *They've been in Hawaii* **for** *two weeks.*

6 *Fill in "since" or "for".*

Animals have been a source of help and comfort to humans **1)** ...*since*... history began, and we have known **2)** .... years that animals make people gentler and more relaxed. **3)** .... a long time the question has been exactly how animals can change people. Some researchers believe that stroking a pet helps to relieve anxiety and tension and, **4)** .... the 1960's, therapists have believed that animals' remarkable powers can be used to heal our bodies and minds. This belief has actually been confirmed **5)** .... the discovery that seriously ill people live longer if they have a pet to care for.

7 *Put the verbs in brackets into the appropriate present forms.*

1 George Smith ...*has been training*... (train) for this match for months. He .... (practise) at least four hours a day for the last two weeks and he .... (say) that now he .... (feel) confident. However, he .... (face) a difficult opponent tonight. Palmer .... (win) several games recently, and he .... (look) determined to win this one too. The match .... (be) about to start, so let's watch and see what .... (happen).

2 Louisa usually .... (go) to work by tube, but today she .... (go) there in a chauffeur-driven limousine. The reason for this .... (be) that she .... (just/win) the young business person award, and as part of the prize people .... (treat) her like royalty.

3 Mary .... (dye) her hair for years. She .... (go) to the hairdresser once a week and .... (try) every colour you can imagine. She .... (say) she .... (want) to match her hair with her clothes. I .... (ask) her for ages why she .... (not/keep) her natural colour but she .... (say) she .... (forget) what it is!

4 A: Excuse me, I .... (try) to pay for this shirt for ten minutes. Nobody .... (seem) to want to serve me. I .... (try) complaining but nobody .... (listen). It's the worst service I .... (ever/experience). Something ought to be done!

B: I agree sir, but I .... (not/work) here.

8 *Make all the necessary changes and additions to make a complete letter.*

Dear Sirs,

I write/apply/position of French teacher/advertised /The European. academic qualifications include/ degree in French/Oxford University. I spend several years/Paris/have excellent practical knowledge of French. I work/assistant French teacher/two years/school outside London. I be unemployed/at the moment. I enclose references/former employer and CV. I trust you give/application/serious consideration. I look forward/hear you/earliest convenience.

Yours faithfully,

Dear Sirs,
   I'm writing to apply ...

9 *Identify the tenses, then match them with the correct description.*

1 I **had read** most of his novels by the end of the holiday.

2 I **was enjoying** myself at the party while Tim **was babysitting** at home.

3 We **got up at half past six this morning.**

4 They **were still considering** his proposal **that evening**.

5 She **jogged** five miles every day **when she was young.**

6 She **had** a shower, **got dressed** quickly and **left** for the airport.

7 Reporters **had been telephoning** all morning.

8 A crowd of tourists **were waiting** outside the hotel when the bomb exploded.

9 He **made** his last film in Poland.

10 She **had been going out** with Tony for five years before she decided to marry him.

11 She was upset because she **had** just **heard** the news.

12 The police officer changed her phone number because she **had been receiving** anonymous calls for several weeks.

13 The dancer **had** always **dreamed** of becoming successful.

a action in the middle of happening at a stated past time

b complete action or event which happened at a stated past time

c past actions which happened one immediately after another

d past action in progress interrupted by another past action

e action continuing over a period up to a specific time in the past

f complete past action which had visible results in the past

g past action which occurred before another action or before a stated time

h past habit or state

i Past Perfect Continuous as the past equivalent of the Present Perfect Continuous

j action not connected to the present which happened at a definite past time not mentioned

k Past Perfect as the past equivalent of the Present Perfect

l two or more simultaneous past actions

m past action of certain duration which had visible results in the past

1 .g. **2** .... **3** .... **4** .... **5** ..... **6** .... **7** ..... **8** ..... **9** ..... **10** ... **11** ... **12** ... **13** ...

10 *Put the verbs in brackets into the correct past forms, then match the tenses with the correct description.*

When she **1)** ...*was*... (be) only fifteen Helen **2)** ......*left*............ (leave) school without any qualifications. Nevertheless, she **3)** ...*was*........ (be) very ambitious and **4)** ...*wanted*... (want) to work in the fashion industry. Luckily she **5)** ...*found*...... (find) a job immediately as an assistant in a small fashion company. While she **6)** ...*was working*... (work) there she **7)** ...*was deciding*...... (decide) to go to evening classes to get a qualification in business studies. Once she **8)** ...*successfully completed*...(successfully/complete) the course she **9)** ...*was promoted*...(be/promoted) to the position of assistant manager. After she **10)** ......*did*........ (do) that job for some years she **11)** ...*worked*...... (want) a change. She **12)** ...*thought*.... (think) of moving to London for some time, so she **13)** ...*applied*...(apply) for a job which she **14)** ......*saw*............. (see) advertised in a fashion magazine. Helen **15)** ......*got*........ (get) a job as the manager of a small but prestigious fashion company in central London. She **16)** ...*achieved*...... (achieve) her ambition of becoming a successful businesswoman at last.

a complete past actions not connected to the present with a
stated or implied time reference $1, 5,$

b action in the middle of happening
at a stated past time

c action continuing over a period up
to a specific time in the past

d complete action or event which
happened at a stated past time

e past action which occurred before
another action or before a stated
past time

f the Past Perfect as the past
equivalent of the Present Perfect

11 *Put the verbs in brackets into the correct past forms.*

Christopher Columbus **1)** ...*was born*... (be/born) in Italy in 1451. He **2)** .... (work) as a woollen cloth weaver with his father before he **3)** .... (begin) his nautical career at the age of 22. After several merchant voyages he **4)** .... (settle) in Lisbon, Portugal in 1478. By this time he **5)** .... (teach) himself Portuguese and Latin and **6)** .... (read) many geographical and navigational books. In 1481 he **7)** .... (marry) Felipa Parestrello. They **8)** .... (have) one son, Diego. They **9)** .... (be/married) for two years when his wife **10)** .... (die). At this time he **11)** .... (work) for John II of Portugal. Columbus **12)** .... (always/wish) to sail around the world westward but John II wouldn't agree. Finally King Ferdinand and Queen Isabella of Spain **13)** .... (decide) to finance the voyage. He **14)** .... (set off) for the first time in April 1492. There **15)** .... (be) three ships; the Nina, the Pinta and the Santa Maria and a crew of 90 men. They **16)** .... (have) many false alarms before they finally **17)** .... (spot) the "New World" at 02.00 on Friday the 12th of October, 1492. Columbus **18)** .... (make) another three voyages after this. He **19)** .... (retire) to Valladolid 12 years after his first voyage and in 1517 he **20)** .... (die) there.

12 *Put the verbs in brackets into the Past Simple or Continuous.*

A few years ago a friend of mine, Tom, **1)** ...*was travelling*... (travel) in Java. One day he **2)** .... (decide) to visit an ancient temple. The walls were covered in beautiful old paintings of mysterious-looking faces. While he **3)** .... (walk) around the temple, he **4)** .... (feel) an inexplicable desire to remove one particular face which seemed to be staring at him. Nervously, checking to see that no one **5)** .... (look), he **6)** .... (peel) the face from the wall and **7)** .... (put) it carefully in his bag. Tom **8)** .... (think) no more about the incident until two years later. At that time he **9)** .... (live) in London and **10)** .... (work) in a shop selling old books and manuscripts. One day an extremely old man **11)** .... (walk) slowly through the door. Tom could hardly see him but he **12)** .... (notice) the man's piercing black eyes. He **13)** .... (stare) at Tom, fixing him with his gaze, saying nothing. As the man **14)** .... (stare) at him, Tom **15)** .... (have) an awful, terrifying feeling of shame and fear. Suddenly, the man was gone. When Tom got home that evening he **16)** .... (search) frantically through all his things until he **17)** .... (find) the face from the temple. It was the face of the old man from the shop! He **18)** .... (know) then that he had to return the picture to the temple, or something terrible would happen.

Present Perfect	Past Simple
● *She **has come.*** (unstated time; we don't know when she came)	● *She **came** last Friday.* (stated time - When? Last Friday.)
● *He **has been** in hospital for two months.* (he's still in hospital - action connected to the present)	● *He **was** in hospital for one week.* (he isn't in hospital any more - action not connected to the present)
● *He's **been** out twice this week.* (it's still the same week - action connected to the present)	● *He **went** out twice last week.* (action not connected to the present - it's the next week now)
● *I've **seen** Jessica Lange.* (action connected to the present - she's still alive)	● *I **saw** Richard Burton.* (action not connected to the present - he's dead)
● *The Prime Minister **has decided** to dissolve Parliament.* (announcing news)	● *He **announced** his decision this morning.* (giving details of the news - stated time in the past)

13 *Fill in with Present Perfect or Past Simple.*

1 The president **1)** ...*has announced*... (announce) the introduction of a new set of measures to deal with unemployment. The problem **2)** .... (become) worse in recent months, and yesterday the president **3)** .... (state) that action must be taken now. She actually **4)** .... (sign) the new bill during this morning's session of Parliament.

2 George **1)** .... (arrive) late to work again this morning. He **2)** .... (be) late at least five times this month. The supervisor **3)** .... (speak) to him about it yesterday but he obviously **4)** .... (not/pay) any attention.

3 John Keats, who **1)** .... (die) when he **2)** .... (be) only 26 years old, **3)** .... (write) a lot of beautiful poems. I **4)** .... (read) most of his poetry, but I **5)** .... (never/manage) to get to the end of *Endymion*. It's too long for me!

4 Clare **1)** .... (be) in New York for almost a year now. I **2)** .... (go) to visit her last month and I have to say I **3)** .... (be) very impressed. I **4)** .... (visit) most of the major cities in Europe but I **5)** .... (never/see) any place as exciting as the Big Apple.

5 I **1)** .... (see) five films this month, but I **2)** .... (not/like) any of them very much. Actually, I think the films they **3)** .... (make) ten years ago **4)** .... (be) much better than anything I **5)** .... (see) for ages.

Used to - Be/Get used to + ing form/noun/pronoun - Would - Was going to

- **Used to expresses past habitual actions and permanent states. (Note that stative verbs are not used with "would".)**

  *She **used to wake up** at 6 am every day. (also: would wake up)*
  *They **used to live** in a flat. (not: ~~would~~)*

- **Would expresses past repeated actions and routines - not states.**

  *When I was young, I **would go** for a walk before breakfast. (also: I used to go ...)*

- **Be/Get used to expresses habitual actions and means "be/get accustomed to", "be in the habit of".**

  *She **isn't used to staying up** late at night.*
  *She **is getting used to working** under pressure.*

- **Was going to expresses actions one intended to do but didn't.**

  *She **was going to** buy a new watch but unfortunately she couldn't afford one.*

14 *Complete the sentences using the words in bold. Use two to five words.*

1 Paul lived in Brazil when he was young.
  live Paul ...*used to live*... in Brazil when he was young.
2 When he was in the army, he used to wake up at 5 o'clock in the morning.
  would When he was in the army, ... at 5 o'clock in the morning.
3 Rosa didn't like English food at first, but now she quite likes it.
  used Rosa didn't like English food at first but now... it.
4 He meant to make a cup of tea but they had run out of teabags.
  going He .... a cup of tea but they had run out of teabags.
5 I don't think I'll ever find it easy to eat with chopsticks.
  used I don't think I'll ever .... with chopsticks.
6 My grandmother rarely travels by plane.
  used My grandmother .... by plane.
7 She wanted to call him but she couldn't find his phone number.
  going She .... but she couldn't find his phone number.
8 My mother always gave me a bath every Friday night when I was little.
  would My mother .... a bath every Friday night when I was little.

15 *Make all the necessary changes and additions to make a complete letter.*

Dear Sirs,

Yesterday/I receive/new TV set/I order. However/I be/ very angry/as it arrive/terrible condition. Firstly/delivery men/be rude/refuse/wait/while I/unpack/TV. When I unpack/I see/it be damaged. The control knob/be broken/and there be/ large crack/on the top/TV. I/never before/receive/anything/ in such bad condition. Could you arrange/collect this set/and deliver/a new one/soon/possible? I trust/this matter receive/prompt attention.

Yours faithfully,
L. Rogers (Mr)

Dear Sirs,
 Yesterday I received...

16 *Put the verbs in brackets into the appropriate past forms.*

1 Alexander the Great ...*was born*... (be/born) in 356 BC in Macedonia. He
.... (become) King when he was 20 and .... (continue)
the work that his father .... (begin). In 334 BC he
.... (invade) Persia and by his thirtieth birthday he
.... (conquer) most of south-west Asia. However,
while he .... (plan) the invasion of Arabia he ....
(catch) a fever and .... (die).

2 Last month Albert and I .... (go) on a skiing trip to
Scotland. We .... (save up) for months and so we
.... (be) very excited when the time .... (come) to
leave. We .... (pack) our bags, ... (get) in the car and
.... (set off). We .... (drive) for six hours when
Albert suddenly .... (remember) something - we .... (forget) to pack the skis!

3 George Grimes .... (wake up) feeling very odd. All through the night he ....
(dream) about strange creatures which .... (try) to break in through his window. They
.... (have) horns and big green eyes and they .... (seem) to be threatening him. "Oh well," he .... (think), "at least they aren't real." Just at that moment, however, a big scaly hand .... (come) crashing through the window!

4 When Bob .... (invite) me to go fishing with him I .... (be) excited because I
.... (never/go) fishing before. But as we .... (drive) to the river we
.... (see) the first black clouds and ten minutes later it .... (rain) heavily.
Three hours later, soaking wet, we .... (still/look for) somewhere to get warm and dry.

5 "........................... (you/enjoy) your holiday?" "No, it .... (be) a disaster! As I ....
(get on) the plane, I found I .... (leave) my holiday money at home! I ....
(save) for months to get that money. My father .... (send) me a cheque, but it
.... (take) five days to reach me."

6 Alan .... (work) in the same office for ten years before he .... (apply) for another
post with "Mask Ltd". He .... (wait) for an answer for weeks when he ....
(be/asked) to attend an interview with the Personnel Manager. He .... (go) there dressed
in an expensive suit which he .... (buy) the day before, only to find that they ....
(want) someone to work as a cleaner.

17 *Identify the tenses, then match them with the correct description.*

1 The builders **are going to start** work tomorrow.
2 She'**ll be waiting** outside the station as usual.
3 I forgot to tell Jim the news. I'**ll ring** him now.
4 By Christmas we **will have been working**
together for ten years.
5 Be careful. You're **going to fall off** your bicycle.
6 The meeting **starts** at 9 o'clock.
7 I'm sure things **will work out** in the end.
8 Perhaps your mother **will change** her mind.
9 **Will** many people **be coming** to the wedding?
10 They **will have finished** the plans by the end
of the week.
11 Hospital staff **are beginning** a two-day strike
tomorrow.
12 By the year 2020 more people than ever **will
be moving** to the cities.

a prediction about the future
b asking politely about people's arrangements
c action which may (not) happen in the future
d action which is the result of a routine
e action intended to be performed in the near
future
f action which will be finished before a stated
future time
g action in progress at a stated future time
h evidence that sth will definitely happen
i duration of an action up to a certain time in
the future
j timetable/programme
k fixed arrangement in the near future
l decision taken at the moment of speaking

1 ..*e*.. 2 .... 3 ... . 4 .... 5 ..... 6 .... 7 ..... 8 ..... 9 ..... 10 .... 11 .... 12 ....

Future Forms With Time Words

- We never use future forms after: **as long as, after, before, by the time, if (conditional), unless, in case, till/until, when (time conjunction), whenever, while, once, suppose/supposing, on condition that** etc. *Let's buy more food* **in case** *James* **comes**. *(not: in case ~~James will come~~.)*
- **If** meaning "whether" especially after *I don't know, I doubt, I wonder* etc and **when** used as a question word can be used with future forms. *When will the race take place? I doubt if they will hold their annual anniversary party this year.*

18 *Fill in the correct present or future forms.*

Welcome to Nutfield Valley Health Farm!

After you **1)** *...have settled in...* (settle in), a member of staff **2)** .... (come) and interview you about your specific dietary requirements. Once you **3)** .... (reach) your target weight, you **4)** .... (start) a maintenance diet to make sure you stay slim! To ensure your safety and well-being, our fitness programmes are planned by qualified instructors. Before you **5)** .... (begin), the resident doctor **6)** .... (check) your heart-rate and blood pressure. There is also a fully-equipped medical room in case you **7)** .... (have) any problems - though of course we don't expect you will. At Nutfield Valley you pay only on condition that you **8)** .... (lose) at least 5% of your body weight in two weeks. If not, we **9)** .... (give) you a refund. By the time you **10)** .... (leave), you **11)** .... (feel) like a new person. Of course, we doubt that you **12)** .... (have) any complaints, but our helpful staff are always on hand if there **13)** .... (be) anything you need. Remember, our motto is: "As long as you **14)** .... (be) happy, WE **15)** .... (be) happy!"

19 *Fill in the correct present or future forms.*

Dear Mr Green,

Regarding our telephone conversation last week, here are the details of your forthcoming trip to Thailand. You **1)** *...will be leaving...* (leave) on Saturday 4th December from London Gatwick at 10.00 pm. You **2)** .... (fly) with Thai Air, flight number TA 907. The flight **3)** .... (arrive) in Bangkok at 4.00 pm on 5th December - that **4)** .... (be) 11.00 pm local time. Our tour guide, Jim Smith, **5)** .... (wait) for you at the airport to accompany you to the Imperial Hotel. As soon as you **6)** .... (settle in), you **7)** .... (attend) a welcome dinner party. In the next days you **8)** .... (visit) famous sights. There **9)** .... (be) time for you to do your shopping as well. By the time you **10)** .... (get on) the return flight on 10th December, you **11)** .... (experience) the most traditional aspects of Thai life. Our tour guide **12)** .... (be) with you throughout, so there shouldn't be any problems. If you **13)** .... (need) more information, please contact us.

Yours sincerely,
A. Jones

20 *Fill in "will" or "be going to".*

1 A: There's no sugar left.
B: That's OK. I ...*'ll*... go and buy some.
2 A: Have you got any plans for the evening?
B: Yes, I .... see "The Doll's House" in town.
3 A: Have you bought a dress for the reception?
B: No, but I .... buy one this afternoon.

4 A: Here's £20.
   B: Thank you. I .... pay you back as soon as I can.
5 A: Have you heard that Mrs Potts is ill?
   B: Yes. Actually we .... visit her this afternoon.
6 A: Peter is taking his driving test tomorrow.
   B: Oh, I'm sure he .... pass.
7 A: Is Tom coming tonight?
   B: I don't know. I .... phone him and see.
8 A: Has Helen decided what to study?
   B: Yes. She .... train to be a teacher.
9 A: It's quite cold today.
   B: I think winter .... be here soon.
10 A: We are having a picnic on Sunday.
   B: I hope the weather .... be nice.

21 *Make all necessary changes and additions to make a complete letter.*

Dear Mrs Scott,

I / write / confirm / arrangements / concerning / new nanny Margarita. Margarita's plane / leave Hamburg / 5.30 / arrive/ London Gatwick 6.45, so / it / be /early start / you. As agreed / Margarita / work / 8-10 morning / 3-8 afternoon and evening. She / have / English lessons / every Saturday. As know / by Christmas / Margarita / complete / six months' employment / therefore / expect / pay rise 10%. I / go / holiday / three weeks / Saturday / if / have problems / contact / secretary Elizabeth Hazlett. I hope / things run smoothly / you / Margarita.

Yours sincerely,
Janet Hemsworth

Dear Mrs Scott,
I'm writing to confirm the arrangements concerning your new nanny Margarita...

22 *Put the verbs in brackets into the appropriate present or future forms.*

1 Bill Haynes, author of the immensely popular novel "Black Roses", **1)** .... (write) a new novel. "I **2)** .... (start) next Monday - or at least that's the plan," says Bill. "It's amazing to think that by next year it **3)** .... (be) ten years since I last picked up a pen." Despite his long break, Bill is confident. "I think this book **4)** .... (be) even better than "Roses". I **5)** .... (include) the usual elements of action and adventure but this time there **6)** .... (be) some romance too. I hope it **7)** .... (be) successful." Of course, we **8)** .... (not/know) until it **9)** .... (be/published) next year.

2 The staff of Cottenham Primary School **1)** .... (hold) an open day on August 21st. In the morning you **2)** .... (be able to) meet your child's teachers. At 12.30 the Headmaster, Mr Patterson, **3)** .... (show) the plans for the new adventure playground. We hope that this **4)** .... (finish) by Christmas. If your child **5)** .... (start) school this September, bring him or her along! The programme **6)** .... (begin) at 9 am. See you there!

3 Jeanne and Paul **1)** .... (move) to London next month. Paul is being transferred there and Jeanne hopes she **2)** .... (find) a job by the time they **3)** .... (move) there. They **4)** .... (drive) down next weekend to look for a flat. They hope they **5)** .... (find) something in a nice area, but with prices the way they are, they will have to be satisfied with whatever they **6)** .... (find). Jeanne is afraid she **7)** .... (miss) living in Nottingham, but Paul is convinced that they **8)** .... (be) happier in London because there is so much more to do there.

4 "Where **1)** .... (you/go) on holiday this year Laura? "

"I don't know Sue. What about you?"

"We **2)** .... (probably/go) to Spain again. But as I **3)** .... (get) a pay rise very soon, I'd like to go somewhere more glamorous. I think I **4)** .... (get) some brochures from the travel agent tomorrow, so if you want, I **5)** .... (pick up) a couple for you as well."

"Good idea. With any luck, we **6)** .... (decide) where to go by the time summer **7)** .... (come)!"

5 Dear Anna,

I got the job! I **1)** .... (leave) for Africa in two weeks. It's a shame I **2)** .... (not/see) you before I **3)** .... (go). For the first six months I **4)** .... (work) in a village school, teaching English and Maths. **5)** .... (you/be able) to visit me? If not, by the time I **6)** .... (see) you again, so much **7)** .... (happen) to us both that it'll take us hours to catch up on the news.

Lots of love,
Danielle

Time Words

- **Ago** (= back in time from now) used with Past Simple. *Jill called an hour **ago**.*
- **Before** (= back in time from then) *Phil told me Jill had called an hour **before**.* It can also be used with present or past forms to point out that an action preceded another. *He had been working in the company for two years **before** he was promoted.*
- **Still** is used in statements and questions after the auxiliary verb or before the main verb. *They **can still** walk long distances. She **still works** in the same office.* **Still** comes before the auxiliary verb in negations. *They **still can't** find a solution to the problem.*
- **Already** is used with Perfect tenses in mid or end position in statements or questions. *Sheila had **already** cooked dinner before Liz came home. Has he finished **already**?*
- **Yet** is used with Perfect tenses in negative sentences after a contracted auxiliary verb or at the end of the sentence. *She hasn't **yet** accepted the post. She hasn't accepted the post **yet**.* It can also be used at the end of questions. *Has she phoned **yet**?*

23 *Underline the correct word.*

1 She has gone to Singapore and she's still/yet there.
2 He doesn't want to watch the film as he's seen it already/still.
3 Ann was on a diet five months before/ago. She lost three kilos.
4 She's only been playing the violin for two years and she can already/still play several of Mozart's most difficult pieces.
5 Even after twenty-five years she is still/yet actively involved in the club.
6 Jo's yet/still got a good figure even though she's five months pregnant.
7 "Has Sandra typed up those reports yet/still? I need them now."
8 Peter left the party two hours before/ago because he wasn't feeling well.
9 She had come back ago/before he returned.
10 I can't do the exam - I haven't finished doing all my revision still/yet.

24 *Put the verbs in brackets into a correct tense.*

1 A new addiction **1)** ...*has recently emerged*... (recently/emerge) - to soap operas- and the world's first clinic to treat people obsessed with the soaps **2)** .... (open) next week. Victims **3)** .... (come) from every walk of life - from company directors to cleaners. Symptoms of addiction **4)** .... (include) refusing to miss an episode and watching recorded episodes again and again. One victim **5)** .... (explain) how he **6)** .... (become) addicted five years ago. His obsession **7)** .... (be) so bad that he **8)** .... (be) unable to keep a steady relationship. "When my friends **9)** .... (come round), I was more interested in the soaps. It was almost as if the people on TV **10)** .... (become) my friends instead."

2 A: I **1)** .... (think) of going to that new Chinese restaurant in the city centre to celebrate my birthday. **2)** .... (you/be) there yet?

B: No, I **3)** .... (not/be), but people **4)** .... (say) that the food is fantastic.

A: Would you like to go there next weekend?

B: Yes, that's a great idea. I **5)** .... (write) it in my diary now.

3 John **1)** .... (leave) the house in a rush this morning. As he **2)** .... (drive) to work he suddenly **3)** .... (remember) that he **4)** .... (be/asked) to speak at a conference. He **5)** .... (look) at his watch and **6)** .... (see) that it was nearly time for the conference to begin.

4 Last March Sam **1)** .... (decide) that he **2)** .... (have) enough of working in a bank and that he **3)** .... (ride) around the world on a bicycle. He **4)** .... (leave) England two weeks later with his bike, a rucksack and a tent. He **5)** .... (be) away for six months now, and no one **6)** .... (know) whether he **7)** .... (return) or not.

5 Jan and Paul **1)** .... (argue) in the next room at the moment. It **2)** .... (seem) that Paul **3)** .... (come) in late last night after he **4)** .... (promise) Jan that he **5)** .... (be) home in time for dinner. By the time he **6)** .... (get) home, Jan **7)** .... (give) his dinner to the dog and **8)** .... (wait) by the window for two hours!

6 A: **1)** .... (you/go) on holiday to Germany this year?

B: No, we **2)** .... (go) there every year, so we want a change this year.

A: Where **3)** .... (you/plan) to go instead?

B: Well, we **4)** .... (be/told) that Greece is a beautiful country so we **5)** .... (already/book) a two-week holiday on Corfu.

7 Susan **1)** .... (study) interior design part time for three years and she **2)** .... (get) her diploma next month. Since she **3)** .... (work) in the same company for over ten years she **4)** .... (feel) that she **5)** .... (need) a change, so she **6)** .... (plan) to open her own design business. She **7)** .... (start) looking for an office next week, and she **8)** .... (hope) she **9)** .... (find) something in a good location and at a reasonable price by the end of the month. Her tutors **10)** .... (tell) her that she **11)** .... (be) very talented and they **12)** .... (assure) her that she **13)** .... (make) a success of the business.

8 Jim **1)** .... (walk) along the High Street when he **2)** .... (notice) someone behind him. Actually, he **3)** .... (follow) him since he **4)** .... (get off) the bus. Jim **5)** .... (stop) at a shop window. The man **6)** .... (come) closer to him. Jim **7)** .... (have) the feeling he **8)** .... (see) him before, so he **9)** .... (go) up to him and **10)** .... (ask) : "........................... (not/I/know) you? Why **12)** .... (you/follow) me?" The man **13)** .... (smile) and **14)** .... (say), "Smile! You **15)** .... (be) on Candid Camera!"

9 Julie **1)** .... (always/want) to be famous, ever since she was young. She **2)** .... (take) acting classes for years and last week someone **3)** .... (offer) her a part in an advertisement. They only **4)** .... (need) her voice, though, because it's going to be on the radio. At least her career **5)** .... (start).

10 Tom **1)** .... (save up) to go to France for months, and yesterday when he **2)** .... (count) his savings he **3)** .... (realise) he had enough. Unfortunately as he **4)** .... (drive) to the travel agent's he remembered that he **5)** .... (not/pay) his rent for two months so he **6)** .... (turn) round and **7)** .... (drive) back home again.

11 Next month I **1)** .... (visit) my friend who **2)** .... (live) in Brazil. The flight from London **3)** .... (take) about fifteen hours and I **4)** .... (never/be) on a plane before. I **5)** .... (feel) quite nervous about the journey but my friend **6)** .... (keep) telling me that there **7)** .... (be) nothing to worry about.

In Other Words

- I've never read such a good book.
  It's the best book I've ever read.
- He started studying Spanish two years ago.
  He has been studying Spanish for two years.
- When did he start work?
  How long is it since he started work?
  How long ago did he start work?
- They haven't reached Madrid yet.
  They still haven't reached Madrid.
- He moved to London two months ago.
  He has been in London for two months.
- He hasn't been out for two months.
  The last time he went out was two months ago.
- It's a long time since we went out.
  We haven't been out for a long time.
- I've never eaten Chinese food before.
  It's the first time I've ever eaten Chinese food.
- He started cleaning as soon as the guests (had) left.
  He didn't start cleaning until after the guests had left.
  He started cleaning when the guests (had) left.
  He waited until the guests had left before he started cleaning.
- We joined the club a month ago.
  We've been members of the club for a month.

25 Complete the sentences using the words in bold. Use two to five words.

1 She didn't go out until after Philip had called.
before She waited until Philip ...*had called before she went*... out.
2 She started taking ballet lessons ten years ago.
been She .... for ten years.
3 How long ago did he move to Canada?
moved How long .... to Canada?
4 I've never driven such a fast car!
ever It's the .... driven.
5 We haven't been abroad for two years.
time The last .... two years ago.
6 How long is it since you visited Spain?
visit When .... Spain?
7 She has never eaten lobster before.
time It's the first .... lobster.
8 He hasn't turned up yet.
still He .... up.
9 The last time I saw Emily was six months ago.
for I .... six months.
10 When did Patricia finish writing her essay?
since How long .... writing her essay?
11 She took up knitting five years ago.
been She .... five years.
12 They have never been outside Britain before.
first It's the .... outside Britain.
13 He can't speak Italian yet.
still He .... Italian.
14 How long is it since they met?
ago How .... meet?
15 They waited until sunrise before they got up.
get They .... after sunrise.
16 I haven't smoked a cigarette for six months.
since It's .... a cigarette.
17 I've never seen such a pretty girl.
ever She's the .... seen.

18 She didn't start serving until all the guests had arrived.
before She waited until all the guests .... serving.
19 Geoff hasn't come back from his holiday yet.
still Geoff .... from his holiday.

26 Find the word which should not be in the sentence.

1	being
2	
3	
4	
5	
6	
7	
8	
9	
10	
11	
12	
13	
14	
15	
16	
17	
18	

1 She is being looking for a new job these days.
2 Jerry has been given me a lot of help.
3 Do they know what time does the plane leaves?
4 We have been gone to that restaurant twice this month.
5 He opened the door, switched off the light and had left the house.
6 Tony was used to live on a farm as a young boy.
7 Simon was being happy because he had been offered a scholarship.
8 They had returned from New York late last night.
9 We can leave as soon as we will have the results.
10 I am see what you mean.
11 The Mayor is be going to open the new school tomorrow.
12 Sue has joined our company four years ago.
13 He has to been working as a chef for twelve years.
14 As long as you will promise to be back before ten, you can go out.
15 The workers will have had finished the repairs by Wednesday.
16 He isn't being used to addressing big audiences.
17 Is Fiona will going to get married in June?
18 He is owns a luxurious mansion.

Oral Development 1

Look at the pictures below, then talk about these people. Talk about what they are doing now, what they usually do, what they did/were doing before, and what they will do afterwards. Use a variety of tenses.

eg. The firemen are trying to put out the fire.

27 Look at Appendix 2, then fill in the correct particle(s).

1 Pass me the newspaper I want to see what's ...*on*... at the cinema tonight.
2 Mercian diplomats have **broken** .... all relations with Northumbrio.
3 According to the police report, the thieves **broke** .... through the back door.
4 Please have a seat - the meeting **is** .... to start.
5 Scientists have **broken** .... in their fight against TB.
6 There was mass panic when cholera **broke** .... in the city.
7 You aren't allowed to leave the auditorium until the concert **is** ....
8 They became annoyed with Sam, who kept **breaking** .... their conversation.
9 I'm not surprised Sally and Jim **broke** ....; they kept quarrelling all the time.
10 Thousands of villagers fled when war **broke** .... in the north of the country.
11 On seeing the pictures he **broke** .... and confessed to his crimes.
12 Can you **break** the report .... into five separate sections?
13 By 1980, flared trousers **were** .... Nobody seemed to like them any more.
14 He took a deep breath before **breaking** the bad news .... Mrs Jones.
15 This is a difficult task - do you think he will **be** .... it?
16 We may **be** .... a cold winter this year.

28 Look at Appendix 3, then fill in the correct preposition.

1 Helen was absent ...*from*... school for more than a week.
2 John is bad .... algebra.
3 The money we owe the bank amounts .... over £100,000.
4 I've been acquainted .... Norman for many years now.
5 I wish Vince wouldn't boast .... winning the lottery.
6 Beware .... holes in the pavement when you walk round this city.
7 Paul was ashamed ...... himself after his unfair attack .... his friend.
8 Peter blamed Alan .... losing so much money in bad deals.
9 When the broken window was discovered Sam put the blame .... his brother.
10 The police blamed the fire .... people smoking in the building.
11 Let's agree .... the best way to solve this problem.
12 Helen's so argumentative! She never agrees .... anything I say.
13 Very few people believe .... ghosts.
14 George is busy .... his homework right now.
15 What time is the train due to arrive .... St. Petersburg?
16 When he arrived........................... school the gates were locked.
17 Both families approved .... the marriage.
18 John was angry .... Anne's attitude towards the children.
19 She was angry .... Pete .... not ringing her.
20 I was angry .... George .... his behaviour on the school trip.
21 Ben was anxious .... Amanda to pass her driving test.
22 Sheila was anxious ..... her impending French test.
23 You must take all the tablets if you are to benefit .... them.
24 You mustn't let people take advantage .... you like that.
25 There's no advantage .... rushing through your work if you are going to make a lot of mistakes.
26 Albert Einstein was brilliant .... physics.
27 This film begins .... the hero running to catch the 8 o'clock train.

29 Complete the sentences using the words in bold. Use two to five words.

1 She took a month to decorate the flat.
  her   It ...*took her a month*... to decorate the flat.

2 Shall I call the office for you?
   me   Would .... the office for you?

3 "I'm sorry I broke your window," he said.
   breaking He .... my window.

4 He plays tennis skilfully.
   skilful   He .... player.

5 Kevin doesn't mind working long hours.
   used   Kevin .... long hours.

6 They cancelled the match because of the hail.
   off   The match .... because of the hail.

7 She didn't hire him until she had seen his references.
   hired   She waited until she had seen his references .... him.

8 The summit meeting will be held in Berlin.
   place   The summit meeting .... Berlin.

9 She has a good relationship with her colleagues.
   gets   She .... her colleagues.

10 It was difficult for her to connect the new dishwasher.
   found   She .... the new dishwasher.

11 They moved to Rome two years ago.
   in   They .... two years.

12 The lift isn't working; use the stairs instead.
   out   The lift ....; use the stairs instead.

30 *Match the following idioms with the correct definition, then make sentences using them.*

1	a night owl	a	someone who says very little about themselves
2	a fly-by-night	b	someone who likes to get up early
3	a lame duck	c	someone who spends all their free time in front of the TV
4	a dark horse	d	someone who is lively and energetic
5	a cold fish	e	someone who you are extremely fond of
6	an early bird	f	someone who prefers to do things at night
7	a couch potato	g	someone who is weak and depends on others for help
8	a live wire	h	someone who is unreliable
9	the apple of one's eye	i	someone who is lively and entertaining at parties
10	the life and soul of the party	j	someone who is unfriendly and unemotional

1 ......*f*....... | 3 .... | 5 .... | 7 .... | 9 ....
2 .... | 4 .... | 6 .... | 8 .... | 10 ....

31 *Choose the correct word from the verbs in brackets.*

1 The teacher won't ...*let*... you use a dictionary during the test. (allow, leave, let)
2 Since it's getting late I suggest we .... it as it is and start working on it tomorrow. (allow, leave, let)
3 They won't .... you to enter unless you're a club member. (allow, leave, let)
4 I think I'll .... my hair grow long. (allow, leave, let)
5 I don't think she'll ever .... from the shock. (heal, improve, recover)
6 He's still ill but I think his condition will .... soon. (heal, improve, recover)
7 It will take a long time for his injuries to .... completely. (heal, improve, recover)
8 He went for a holiday by the sea to help him .... from his illness. (heal, improve, recover)

Part 1

For questions 1 - 15, read the text below and decide which word A, B, C or D best fits each space. There's an example at the beginning (0).

Counterfeits

The art of counterfeiting is an **(0)** ... one. Nowadays it is a million dollar business, especially in France. Seventy percent of products **(1)** ...throughout the world are produced in France. The problem has **(2)** ... so serious that a French organisation, which was **(3)** ... in 1872 to protect the rights of manufacturers, has just opened a museum to draw **(4)** ... to this industry. It is hoped that the museum will also show **(5)** ... buyers what harm they can **(6)** ... by purchasing imitation products. Counterfeiting is not confined to forged money and watches. The museum has more than 300 exhibits **(7)** ... from luxury items through to toys, foods, computers, electrical appliances, cutlery and even flowers. While luxury bargain-hunters may enjoy the thrill of snapping up a fake Gucci handbag at the market, imitations are not **(8)** ... to such extravagant products. For **(9)** ..., a Cartier watch may be **(10)** ... a luxury while a **(11)** ... of Nike basketball shoes is not; nevertheless, counterfeit versions of both can be found. Counterfeiting causes more problems than just the **(12)** ... of revenue and jobs. Some products such as medicines, food and toys can be dangerous, and all are illegal. So the **(13)** ... time you are tempted to go on a shopping trip to Paris, **(14)** ... that under French law anyone knowingly purchasing a counterfeit product is **(15)** ... a crime.

	A		B		C		D		
0	A antique	**B** archaic	**C** old	**D** antiquated	**0**	A B **C** D
1	A followed	**B** copied	**C** repeated	**D** reproduced	**1**	A B C D
2	A developed	**B** turned	**C** become	**D** changed	**2**	A B C D
3	A formed	**B** made	**C** consisted	**D** installed	**3**	A B C D
4	A warning	**B** notice	**C** interest	**D** attention	**4**	A B C D
5	A potential	**B** probable	**C** evident	**D** supposed	**5**	A B C D
6	A make	**B** cause	**C** create	**D** offer	**6**	A B C D
7	A prolonged	**B** ranging	**C** extending	**D** varied	**7**	A B C D
8	A fixed	**B** set	**C** limited	**D** bounded	**8**	A B C D
9	A example	**B** once	**C** long	**D** short	**9**	A B C D
10	A held	**B** recognised	**C** seen	**D** considered	**10**	A B C D
11	A twin	**B** couple	**C** set	**D** pair	**11**	A B C D
12	A missing	**B** lack	**C** loss	**D** failure	**12**	A B C D
13	A after	**B** following	**C** future	**D** next	**13**	A B C D
14	A retain	**B** remember	**C** keep	**D** remind	**14**	A B C D
15	A committing	**B** doing	**C** causing	**D** having	**15**	A B C D

Practice Test 1 ....

For questions 16 - 30, read the text below and think of the word which best fits each space.
Use only one word in each space. Write your answers in the answer boxes provided.

Caravanning in Wales

The sea cliffs and sandy beaches of Wales are hard **(0)** .... beat. Add to **(16)** .... wild, romantic scenery, ancient castles, modern theme parks and cheap accommodation and you've got a great family holiday. Of course **(17)** .... makes Wales so green is the rain. Even in mid-summer, you can expect a couple of wet and windy days. But don't let that **(18)** .... you off. There are **(19)** .... of indoor activities, so you can enjoy **(20)** .... whatever the weather. For **(21)** .... people Wales is a caravan country. If you haven't stayed in a caravan **(22)** .... you were little, it's **(23)** .... you tried it again. Standards of comfort are much higher **(24)** .... a decade ago, with facilities such **(25)** .... laundries and kids' play areas. A good example is the Fontygary Holiday Park. You can stay in a spacious caravan equipped **(26)** .... TV, shower, separate bedrooms and fridge, **(27)** .... works out to be less expensive when compared **(28)** .... a guesthouse or self-catering cottage. And you won't even need to leave the site to **(29)** .... fun. The kids can swim in the 25-metre indoor pool, or join **(30)** .... the games organized by the entertainment staff. Meanwhile you can take a sauna, go to the gym, have your hair styled, or just sit on the cliff top and enjoy the view.

0	to	0
16		16
17		17
18		18
19		19
20		20
21		21
22		22
23		23
24		24
25		25
26		26
27		27
28		28
29		29
30		30

Part 3

For questions 31 - 40, complete the second sentence so that it has a similar meaning to the first sentence. Use the word given and other words to complete each sentence. You must use between two and five words. Do not change the word given. Write your answers in the answer boxes provided.

0 I'm sure it wasn't Jim who did it.
have
It .... Jim who did it.

0	*can't have been*	0 0 1 2

31 The First World War began in 1914.
broke
The First World War .... in 1914.

31		31 0 1 2

32 When did she decide to apply for the post?
since
How long .... to apply for the post?

32		32 0 1 2

33 She could hardly absorb all the new information.
difficulty
She .... all the new information.

33		33 0 1 2

34 Is he expected to return soon?
back
Is .... soon?

34		34 0 1 2

35 I've never spoken to him before.
first
It's the .... spoken to him.

35		35 0 1 2

36 It was her intention to call you, but she forgot.
going
She .... but she forgot.

36		36 0 1 2

37 They began interviewing candidates two weeks ago.
for
They .... two weeks.

37		37 0 1 2

38 He managed to break the world record after trying twice.
breaking
He .... the world record after trying twice.

38		38 0 1 2

39 "You've spoilt my party," she said to him.
spoiling
She .... party.

39		39 0 1 2

40 They haven't decided on a date yet.
still
They .... a date.

40		40 0 1 2

Part 4

For questions 41 - 55, read the text below and look carefully at each line. Some of the lines are correct and some have a word which should not be there. If a line is correct, put a tick (✔) by the number in the answer boxes provided. If a line has a word which should not be there, write the word in the answer boxes provided.

Springtime in Paris

0	✓	0
00	*which*	00
41		41
42		42
43		43
44		44
45		45
46		46
47		47
48		48
49		49
50		50
51		51
52		52
53		53
54		54
55		55

0 Last April I spent a week in Paris.
00 I stayed in a small hotel which with a
41 little garden behind of it. Every morning I
42 had breakfast in the garden. Afterwards
43 I went out for to explore Paris. All day,
44 every one day I walked around the
45 city. Paris in April is very much beautiful,
46 with trees and flowers in everywhere. Luckily
47 for me it was unusually sunny.
48 Despite of this, it was still quite cold.
49 More than once I got lost. This was
50 a little frightening as I do not speak much French.
51 However, I soon discovered that too many people
52 in Paris speak the English. During my evenings there
53 I relaxed myself at my hotel by taking a
54 hot bath. At the end of the week I was that sorry to leave,
55 but I promised to myself I would go back one day.

Part 5

For questions 56 - 65, read the text below. Use the word given in capitals at the end of each line to form a word that fits in the space in the same line. Write your word in the answer boxes provided.

Moving House

Moving house is said to be the third most **(0)** .... experience you can have (coming after the **(56)** .... of a close relative, or a divorce). The reason for this is partly the **(57)** .... involved, but also the feeling of **(58)** .... caused by completely changing your environment. Of course, a **(59)** .... approach can help ease the difficulties, especially on the day of **(60)** .... . Plan your packing carefully or, better, employ a **(61)** .... company to pack and move your things. This will **(62)** .... lessen the amount of damage to your **(63)** .... . It's also a good idea to take out **(64)** .... . Some worry is, of course, **(65)** .... but try to keep calm and look forward to life in your new home.

STRESS			
DIE	**0**	*stressful*	0
	56		56
ORGANISE	**57**		57
SECURITY	**58**		58
SYSTEM	**59**		59
	60		60
REMOVE	**61**		61
RELY	**62**		62
CERTAIN	**63**		63
POSSESS	**64**		64
INSURE	**65**		65
AVOIDABLE			

The Infinitive/-ing form/Participles

Forms of the Infinitive   Forms of the -ing form

	Active Voice	Passive Voice	Active Voice	Passive Voice
Present	(to) type	(to) be typed	typing	being typed
Pres. Cont.	(to) be typing		—	—
Perfect	(to) have typed	(to) have been typed	having typed	having been typed
Perf. Cont.	(to) have been typing		—	—

* Passive Present Continuous and Perfect Continuous Infinitives are rarely used.

Forms of the infinitive corresponding to verb tenses

- **Present Simple/Future Simple → Present Infinitive**
  he drives/he will drive → (to) drive
- **Present Continuous/Future Continuous → Present Continuous Infinitive**
  he is driving/he will be driving → (to) be driving
- **Past Simple/Present Perfect/Past Perfect/Future Perfect → Perfect Infinitive**
  he drove/he has driven/he had driven/he will have driven → (to) have driven
- **Past Cont./Present Perfect Cont./Past Perfect Cont./Future Perfect Cont. → Perfect Cont. Infinitive**
  he was driving/he has been driving/he had been driving/he will have been driving → (to) have been driving

32 *Rewrite the sentences using the verb in brackets. Mind the tense of the infinitives.*

1 She has lost her job. (seem)   ....*She seems to have lost her job.*..........
2 Ann was accepted to work there. (seem) ....
3 He is working hard. (appear) ....
4 They have been watching TV all afternoon. (seem) ....
5 Tom missed the train. (appear) ....
6 They are moving house. (seem) ....
7 She found the solution. (claim) ....
8 It has been raining hard. (appear) ....
9 She is reading a magazine. (pretend) ....
10 Sharon tells lies. (tend) ....

33 *Fill in the correct form of the infinitive.*

1 The weather seems ...*to have improved*... (improve). Let's go out.
2 She appears .... (work) on her composition for hours.
3 She has decided .... (accept) my offer.
4 I'm hoping .... (leave) by then so I won't be able to come with you.
5 This carpet is filthy; it really needs .... (clean) soon.
6 The waste from the power station is said .... (pollute) the atmosphere for months.
7 It will be much too hot .... (wear) a coat.
8 You must have been thirsty .... (drink) all that water.
9 He appears .... (injure) as a result of the fight.
10 You're not expected .... (pay) the whole amount today.
11 The report was supposed .... (finish) two hours ago.
12 It was very cold earlier on today but it seems .... (warm up) now.
13 He claims .... (discover) a cure for the common cold.
14 Can I trust you .... (keep) this a secret?
15 She seems .... (work) too hard these days.

The to-infinitive is used

- **to express purpose** *She lied **to avoid** being punished.*
- **after certain verbs** (agree, appear, decide, expect, hope, plan, promise, refuse etc) *He **promised to be** back at 11.00.*
- **after certain adjectives** (difficult, glad, happy, obliged, sorry, unable etc) *He was **happy to hear** he had been promoted.*
- **after "I would like/would love/would prefer"** to express specific preference. *I'd **prefer to stay** in tonight.*
- **after certain nouns.** *It's my **privilege to present** the winner of the competition.*
- **after "too/enough" constructions.** *It's **too late to go** now. She's **experienced enough to be** appointed Sales Manager. He's got **enough patience to cope** with children.*
- **after: be + the first/second etc/next/last/best etc.** *You'll be **the first to break** the news.*
- **with: it + be + adjective** (+of + noun/pronoun) *It was **rude of him to speak** like that.*
- **with: so + adjective + as** *Would you be **so kind as to help** me with the washing?*
- **with "only"** expressing an unsatisfactory result. *She went there **only to find** the meeting had been called off.*
- **in the expression: for + noun/pronoun + to-inf.** ***For Mary to behave** like that was very unusual.*
- **in the expressions: to tell you the truth, to begin with, to be honest, to start with, to sum up etc.** ***To begin with**, I'd like to introduce our new manager, Mr Jones.*

- Note that if two infinitives are joined by "and" or "or", the "to" of the second infinitive can be omitted. *I'd like to go to an island **and swim and sunbathe** all day long during my holidays.*
- **Dare** expressing lack of courage is used with an infinitive with or without to. *I don't **dare (to) tell** him the truth.* **Dare** expressing anger, threat or warning is used with an infinitive without to. ***Don't** you **dare come** back late.* **Dare** expressing challenge is used with a to-infinitive. *I **dare** you **to jump** over the fence.*

The infinitive without to is used

- **after modal verbs** (can, may, will, would etc) *You **may use** the phone.*
- **after had better/would rather/would sooner.** *I'd **rather have** an early night.*
- **after feel/hear/let/make/see in the active.** *Will you **let** me **play** in the garden?*
  But: be heard/be made/be seen, all take a to-inf. *She **was made to work** overtime.*
- **"Let"** turns into "was/were allowed to" in the passive. *He **wasn't allowed to play** in the garden.*

The -ing form is used

- **as a noun.** ***Collecting** stamps is his favourite hobby.*
- **after prepositions.** *He left **without being** seen.*
- **after certain verbs** (anticipate, appreciate, avoid, consider, continue, delay, deny, discuss, detest, escape, excuse, explain, fancy, finish, forgive, go (physical activities), imagine, it involves, keep (= continue), it means, mention, mind (= object to), miss, pardon, postpone, practise, prevent, quit, recall, recollect, report, resent, resist, risk, save, stand, suggest, tolerate, understand etc) *She **doesn't mind working** long hours.*
- **after: detest, dislike, enjoy, hate, like, love, prefer to express general preference.** *I **enjoy snorkelling**. (in general)* [like + to-inf = it's a good idea *John **likes to walk** long distances.*]
- **after: I'm busy, it's no use, it's no good, it's (not) worth, what's the use of, can't help, can't stand, feel like, there's no point (in), have difficulty (in), in addition to, as well as, have trouble, have a hard/difficult time.** *Tom **had difficulty (in) driving** on the left when he first came here.*
- **after: look forward to, be/get used to, be/get accustomed to, admit (to), object to, what about...?, how about ...?** *He **admitted (to) stealing** the old woman's jewels.*
- **after: spend/waste (money, time etc)** *She **spent** a fortune **redecorating** her house.*
- **after: hear, listen, notice, see, watch to express an incomplete action, an action in progress or a long action.** *I **saw** her **window-shopping** as I drove by. (I saw **part** of the action.)* but: hear, listen, see, watch + infinitive without to express a complete action, something that one saw or heard from beginning to end. *I **saw** the car **crash** into the shop window. (I saw **all** the action.)*

34 **Put the verbs in brackets into the correct form of the infinitive or the -ing form.**

1 I suggest ...*calling*... (call) the cinema to find out what time the film begins.
2 It's no use .... (try) to make excuses. She won't believe you.
3 I look forward .... (see) the artwork in the museum's latest exhibition.
4 She spent a long time .... (talk) on the telephone so she didn't finish her chores.
5 Fred enjoys .... (listen) to classical music as it helps him relax.
6 To tell you the truth, I don't know how .... (dance).
7 We were happy .... (hear) that Mary is coming to visit us.
8 The couple plan .... (announce) their engagement later today.
9 Will you let me .... (read) you some parts to tell me if you like them?
10 We saw him .... (paint) the fence as we walked past his house.
11 I would have preferred .... (change) my clothes before we went out to dinner.
12 It was so nice of him .... (send) me flowers.
13 Sandra was the last .... (perform) at the dance recital.
14 For Bob .... (retire) at such a young age was unexpected.
15 It's raining. There's no point in .... (go) out now.
16 Would you be so helpful as .... (carry) this heavy bag for me?
17 You should .... (speak) to her when you saw her.
18 He seems .... (work) hard on a solution to the problem. Don't interrupt him.
19 He was the first runner .... (finish) the marathon.
20 We rushed to the station only .... (arrive) as the train was leaving.

35 **Put the verbs in brackets into the -ing form or the infinitive without to.**

1 I saw her ...*turn*... (turn) the corner and .... (disappear).
2 Can you hear the dog .... (bark) outside?
3 I watched the plane .... (take off) and then I left.
4 He was listening to the rain .... (patter) on the roof.
5 Paul noticed a woman .... (stare) at him while he was waiting at the station.
6 When she opened the door she saw someone .... (try) to steal her car.

36 **Fill in the blanks with the correct form of the infinitive or -ing form.**

1) ...*Ordering*... (order) your own meal in a restaurant may soon be a thing of the past. In Brussels, at an Italian restaurant, the waiter, Tony, claims to be able 2) .... (choose) the right dish for each customer. After 3) .... (work) for many years in Italian restaurants, Tony noticed that different people prefer certain types of food. "Women appear 4) .... (like) milder foods and rich, creamy sauces while men seem 5) .... (enjoy) spicier foods cooked in olive oil and served with juices from the meat," he reports. Tony makes his choices by 6) .... (chat) to his customers - but not about their tastes in food. What he does first is 7) .... (find out) what

kind of personality the customer has. After 8) .... (serve) an Englishman a salad of red tuna with garlic and parsley, Tony was happy 9) .... (see) that his customer was very satisfied. One Italian particularly enjoyed 10) .... (munch) on wild mushrooms stuffed with Mediterranean anchovies which Tony had served with black olives, spicy olive oil and lime. Tony spends a lot of time 11) .... (observe) his customers. Once, a young French couple argued throughout the meal. Tony avoided 12) .... (give) them a sour dessert. He served them a sweet dessert instead, and after that they couldn't stay angry with each other. People aren't accustomed 13) .... (be/served) meals that are not of their own choice, but Tony seems 14) .... (know) exactly what people will like. This restaurant is certainly worth 15) .... (visit).

2 The Infinitive / -ing form / Participles ······························

37 *Fill in the blanks with the correct form of the infinitive or -ing form.*

Steam trains were replaced by electric ones years ago, so when the newspaper I work for heard that the "Black Admiral" steam engine had been restored, they decided **1)** ...*to send*... (send) me on its first trip. I didn't object to **2)** .... (go) even though I generally dislike **3)** .... (travel) by train. In fact I was looking forward **4)** .... (see) something I had never seen before. When I arrived at the station I saw lots of people **5)** .... (celebrate) the rebirth of the Admiral, and I was glad **6)** .... (be) part of the party. At 2 o'clock everyone was ready **7)** .... (board) the train. I settled myself into a compartment where I was soon joined by an old man who claimed **8)** .... (be) one of the original workers on the Admiral. He claimed **9)** .... (work) for a penny a day, and told me how much he had hated **10)** .... (be/covered) in coal dust all the time. His family had been too poor **11)** .... (buy) more than the basic necessities. It was a sad story, but it was a pleasure **12)** .... (listen) to him. At every station people were waiting **13)** .... (greet) the train, and it was exciting **14)** .... (see) the spectators' faces as the past seemed **15)** .... (come) alive again. If all trains were as appealing as the Black Admiral, I would choose **16)** .... (travel) by train all the time.

Verbs taking to-infinitive or -ing form without a change in meaning

● **begin, continue, intend, start + to-inf or -ing form. We don't normally have two -ing forms together.** *She began **dancing**/**to dance**. not: She is **beginning dancing**.*
● **advise, allow, encourage, permit, require + object + to-inf.** *He **advised me to stay** indoors.*
● **advise, allow, encourage, permit, require + -ing form.** *He **advised staying** indoors.*
● **be advised, be allowed, be encouraged, be permitted, be required + to-inf.** *We **were advised to stay** indoors.*
● **need, require, want + to-inf/-ing form/passive inf.** *You **need to prune** the trees. The trees **need pruning**. The trees **need to be pruned**.*

---

38 *Complete the sentences using the words in bold. Use two to five words.*

1 We are allowed to take a one-hour lunch break.
   allow   They ...*allow us to take*... a one-hour lunch break.
2 They require employees to work on Saturdays.
   required Employees .... on Saturdays.
3 You need to improve your handwriting considerably.
   needs   Your handwriting .... considerably.
4 She has been learning German since last year.
   began   She .... last year.
5 They advised not drinking the water.
   were   We .... the water.

39 *Fill in the blanks with the correct form of the infinitive or -ing form.*

For Thomas **1)** ...*to agree*... (agree) to go on a walking holiday was very surprising. He usually hated **2)** .... (do) outdoor activities of any kind. We thought we'd have difficulty in **3)** .... (persuade) him but it was his idea **4)** .... (set off) the very next day. We suggested **5)** .... (go) to the Lake District as it would be the best place **6)** .... (find) hotel rooms each night. Though we'd have preferred **7)** .... (take) the coach, Thomas encouraged us **8)** .... (travel) by train. We decided **9)** .... (meet) at the station early the next morning as we wanted **10)** .... (be) in Carlisle by midday. Imagine the look on our faces when Thomas arrived on a huge, brand-new motorbike. "Do you think I'll be allowed **11)** .... (take) it on the train?" he said. "It needs **12)** .... (run in) and this holiday's the ideal time **13)** .... (do) it!"

Verbs taking to-infinitive or -ing form with a change in meaning

1 **forget + to-inf** (= fail to remember to do sth)
*He **forgot to turn off** the radio.*
forget + -ing form (= not recall a past event)
*I'll never **forget seeing** the Eiffel Tower for the first time.*

2 **remember + to-inf** (= not forget to do sth)
*Please, **remember to feed** the dog before leaving.*
remember + -ing form (= recall a past event)
*I don't **remember seeing** him at the party last night.*

3 **mean + to-inf** (= intend to) *She **means to study** art in Paris this summer.*
mean + -ing form (= involve) *I won't go if it **means taking** the train during rush hour.*

4 **go on + to-inf** (= finish doing sth and start doing sth else; then; afterwards) *He pruned the hedges, then **went on to mow** the lawn.*
go on + -ing form (= continue)
*We **went on dancing** until we got tired.*

5 **regret + to-inf** (= be sorry to) *I **regret to inform** you that there are no seats on the 12.30 flight.*
regret + -ing form (= have second thoughts about sth already done) *He **regrets buying** such an expensive sports car.*

6 **would prefer + to-inf** (specific preference)
*I'd **prefer to eat** at this restaurant.*
prefer + -ing form (in general)
*I **prefer reading** spy stories.*
prefer + to-inf + rather than + inf without to
*I **prefer to drive** to work **rather than take** the bus.*

7 **try + to-inf** (= do one's best; attempt)
***Try to throw** the ball into the basket.*
try + -ing form (= do sth as an experiment)
***Try cooking** with olive oil, you might find it improves the taste.*

8 **want + to-inf** (= wish) *I **want to go** home.*
want + -ing form (= sth needs to be done)
*These windows **want cleaning**.*

9 **stop + to-inf** (= pause temporarily). *Can we **stop** here **to admire** the view?*
stop + -ing form (= finish; cease)
*He **stopped studying** and switched on the TV.*

10 **be sorry + to-inf** (= regret) *I **was sorry to hear** he failed his exam.*
be sorry for + -ing form (= apologise for)
*She **was sorry for yelling** at him.*

11 **hate + to-inf** (= not like what one is about to do)
*I **hate to argue**, but you are definitely wrong.*
hate + -ing form (= feel sorry for what one is doing) *I **hate bothering** you at such a late hour.*

12 **be afraid + to-inf** (= be too frightened to do sth; hesitate) *She **was afraid to jump** into the pool.*
be afraid of + -ing form (= be afraid that what is referred to by the -ing form may happen) *When driving in the rain, I'm **afraid of skidding** on the wet road.*

40 *Put the verbs in brackets into the infinitive or -ing form.*

1 A: I'll never forget ...*travelling*... (travel) across America.
  B: Yes, but you forgot .... (send) me a postcard, didn't you?
2 A: I hate .... (ask) you, but can you help me with the housework?
  B: Sure, but remember I hate .... (do) the vacuuming.
3 A: The door wants .... (fix).
  B: I know. I wanted .... (ask) the carpenter to come and have a look but I forgot.
4 A: I'm sorry .... (put) you in such a difficult position.
  B: It's OK. I'm sorry for .... (shout) at you.
5 A: I'd prefer .... (spend) this weekend at home.
  B: Really? I prefer .... (go out) whenever I've got free time.
6 A: Did he go on .... (talk) about the same boring topics all night?
  B: No, he went on .... (show) us his holiday photos.
7 A: Don't be afraid .... (talk) to her in French.
  B: I can't. I'm afraid of .... (make) mistakes.
8 A: I meant .... (tell) you there's a job vacancy at the chemist's.
  B: Well, I won't apply if it means .... (work) at the weekend.

9 A: Why don't you try .... (take) a different medicine if you're still ill?
   B: I think I'll just try .... (get) some more sleep.
10 A: Let's stop .... (have) something to eat.
   B: Again? I wish you'd stop .... (eat) so much!
11 A: The notice says the gallery regrets .... (inform) us that the Picasso exhibition has finished.
   B: Oh, no! Now I regret .... (not/go) last week.
12 A: Did you remember .... (post) the letters?
   B: I remember .... (take) them but I think I've left them on my desk.

41 **Fill in the correct form of the infinitive or the -ing form.**

Eli Bilston always enjoyed **1)** ...*telling*... (tell) us about his life, and we were always afraid **2)** .... (interrupt) him because he had a very hot temper. He had left school at thirteen, and he had managed to avoid **3)** .... (look for) a real job by **4)** .... (work) for his father in the family scrapyard. He was supposed **5)** .... (check) the weight of scrap metal leaving the yard, but he always preferred **6)** .... (sit) around and **7)** .... (make) cups of tea for the other workers instead. You won't be surprised **8)** .... (hear) that eventually Eli's father noticed him **9)** .... (waste) time **10)** .... (do) nothing, and asked him **11)** .... (find) another job. Eli never regretted **12)** .... (have) to leave the scrapyard, because his next job was even easier! He was employed at Dudley Zoo as a nightwatchman, where he found it a pleasure just **13)** .... (sit) and **14)** .... (watch) the monkeys **15)** .... (play) in their cages. His only duty was **16)** .... (feed) the jaguars at dawn - something which he claims he only forgot **17)** .... (do) once in his time there. He said that he would never forget **18)** .... (see) the zookeeper's face after the poor man had tried **19)** .... (give) them their lunch - they had nearly eaten him alive! After **20)** .... (work) in the zoo for six years, war broke out in Europe and Eli went on **21)** .... (join) the army in the hope of finding some adventure.

42 **Fill in the correct form of the infinitive or the -ing form.**

1 I used to love ...*visiting*... Santorini so much that I finally bought a house there.
2 He couldn't bear ....his mother the truth because he didn't want to upset her.
3 I'm sorry, I don't remember ....you before.
4 I'll have to go to Belgium by train - I'm afraid of ....
5 You are required ....this form before you can start the job.
6 Before you leave, don't forget ....the plants.
7 I regret ....you that your house must be demolished.
8 If we want to catch the early train, it means .... up early tomorrow morning.
9 I would prefer ....to the cinema for a change - we always go to the theatre.
10 There's no point .... ! It was your decision after all.
11 The explorer escaped from the lion only ....himself surrounded by savages.
12 As a child, I spent so much time .... that people used to call me "the Fish".
13 If you can't get the stain out of your shirt, you could try .... salt on it.
14 He regretted .... lies to his parents.
15 Try .... some more pepper to the soup. It might taste better.
16 Please stop ....! There's a meeting in progress next door.
17 The thief got into the manager's office by pretending .... a cleaner.
18 You must complete this exercise without .... a dictionary.
19 Acid rain is said .... many trees all over Europe.
20 What do you mean Bob's a vegetarian? I saw him .... a chicken sandwich only yesterday!

Santorini - Greece

43 *Fill in the correct form of the infinitive or the -ing form.*

1   I advise you ...*to take*... (take) some money in case the banks are shut.
2   My mother used .... (encourage) us to eat lots of vegetables.
3   Don't forget .... (lock) the door when you leave the office.
4   Do you remember .... (swim) in Lake Langaron last summer?
5   When you finish this exercise go on .... (do) the composition on page 11.
6   Would you mind .... (turn) the radio down? I've got a headache.
7   Why don't we try .... (eat) some Thai food for a change?
8   They stopped running .... (have) a rest.
9   He put off .... (tell) her the bad news.
10 I really regret .... (spend) so much money at the weekend.
11 I suggest .... (look) this word up in a dictionary.
12 David was too afraid .... (swim) in the rough sea.
13 He doesn't look old enough .... (be/married).
14 I couldn't stop .... (wonder) whether I had done the right thing.
15 In general I prefer .... (watch) films on the big screen rather than on TV.
16 I'm sorry, I didn't mean .... (hurt) you.
17 Don't you dare .... (be) late again.
18 I need to get a job. I'm tired of .... (have) to rely on my parents for money.
19 Have you considered .... (learn) another language?
20 I can't stand .... (listen) to you complaining all the time.

Participles

- **Present participles (verb + ing) describe what somebody or something is.** *It was a **fascinating** story. (What kind of story? Fascinating.)*
- **Past participles (verb+ ed) describe how somebody feels.** *We were **fascinated** by his story. (How did we feel about his story? Fascinated.)*

 44 *Underline the correct participle.*

On Saturday, I took my children to the circus. I thought I would have a **1)** boring/bored time, but actually I was quite **2)** astonishing/ astonished by the **3)** amazing/amazed acts. We were **4)** stunning/stunned by the acrobats. They balanced on top of each other with incredible ease. We were really **5)** impressing/impressed by their performance. The children found the lion-tamer's act **6)** exciting/excited. I felt **7)** terrifying/terrified when he put his hands into the lion's mouth, but the children were **8)** amusing/amused and they clapped loudly. A magician performed many incredible tricks; it was **9)** fascinating/fascinated to watch him make various objects disappear and reap-

pear. The children were more **10)** interesting/interested in the elephant act. When the huge animals came into the arena, the audience cheered. The elephants were well-trained and their tricks were **11)** entertaining/entertained. Some children from the audience were invited to ride on the elephants' backs. My children were **12)** disappointing/disappointed when they were not chosen, but their disappointment faded when the clowns took the centre ring. It was quite a **13)** captivating/captivated show. By the time we got home we all felt **14)** exhausting/exhausted.

In Other Words

- It's too hot for him to go jogging.
  It isn't cool enough for him to go jogging.
  It's so hot that he can't go jogging.
- It's dangerous to exceed the speed limit.
  Exceeding the speed limit is dangerous.
- They allowed us to enter the room.
  We were allowed to enter the room.
- It took him two hours to reach London.
  He took two hours to reach London.
  Reaching London took him two hours.
- She made him carry the bags.
  He was made to carry the bags.

- I prefer listening to music to dancing.
  I prefer to listen to music rather than dance.
- We were interested in the lecture.
  We found the lecture interesting.
- Could you do the washing?
  Would you mind doing the washing?
- He had difficulty (in) concentrating on his work.
  It was difficult for him to concentrate on his work.
  He could hardly concentrate on his work.
  He found it difficult to concentrate on his work.
- She let them use the spare room.
  They were allowed to use the spare room.

45 *Complete the sentences using the words in bold. Use two to five words.*

1   We were allowed to take our dog inside.
     allowed   They ...*allowed us to take*... our dog inside.
2   We found what she said shocking.
     were   We .... she said.
3   Going swimming after eating is dangerous.
     go   It is dangerous .... after eating.
4   Could you turn the volume up?
     mind   Would .... the volume up?
5   He prefers walking to riding a bicycle.
     walk   He prefers .... a bicycle.
6   It was difficult for her to understand what he was talking about.
     difficulty   She .... what he was talking about.
7   The box was too heavy for him to lift.
     enough   The box .... for him to lift.
8   The dress is so long that she can't wear it.
     her   The dress is .... wear.
9   They made him wait for an hour.
     was   He .... for an hour.
10 She could hardly do the exercises.
     difficult   She .... the exercises.
11 He made her promise that she would come back.
     was   She .... that she would come back.
12 The audience found the performance amusing.
     were   The audience .... the performance.
13 The film was so interesting that I saw it twice.
     was   I .... the film that I saw it twice.
14 It was difficult for him to understand the instructions.
     hardly   He .... the instructions.
15 Could you move a bit please?
     mind   Would .... a bit please?
16 The headmaster let the boys leave the school.
     were   The boys .... the school.
17 She prefers working to staying at home.
     than   She prefers .... at home.
18 They took three days to finish the project.
     them   It .... to finish the project.

46 *Find the word which should not be in the sentence.*

1	*to*
2	
3	
4	
5	
6	
7	
8	
9	
10	
11	
12	
13	
14	
15	
16	
17	
18	

1 She let me to use her computer.
2 The Persian rug was too expensive for us to buy it.
3 Taking regular exercise it is beneficial to your health.
4 In addition to be losing her purse, Joan also lost her passport.
5 We saw the Queen to welcome the British Olympic winners.
6 It was enough too late to find accommodation elsewhere.
7 We would sooner to renew our contract than move somewhere else.
8 The archaeologist is believed to have being found the tomb of the ancient King.
9 He might to be given a more responsible position in future.
10 To making promises you do not intend to keep is dishonest.
11 Those curtains want being dry-cleaning.
12 She prefers working out than to sitting at home doing nothing.
13 I would like entertaining people at home at the weekends.
14 We enjoy going for fishing from time to time.
15 It's no use you spending money on impractical household items.
16 She'll never forget to meeting Bruce Springsteen.
17 He was afraid of to tell his parents that he had damaged the car.
18 Shirley won't accept their offer if it means that working at the weekend.

Oral Development 2

A group of people went fishing last Sunday. Use the list below and your own ideas to say what happened using infinitives or -ing form.

decide, look forward to, try, manage, continue, stop, notice, begin, have a difficult time, be afraid, appear, happen help, be relieved, regret

eg. Bob and his friends decided to go fishing last Sunday. All of them ...

47 *Look at Appendix 2, then explain the phrasal verbs in bold.*

1 The company is planning to **bring out** a new perfume in the summer. *launch; produce*
2 The situation **calls for** immediate action.
3 The director's death **brought about** the collapse of the company.
4 Do **carry on with** your work while I'm away.
5 Heavy smoking **brought on** his death.
6 John **was** completely **carried away** by the music and lost track of time.
7 The nurse **brought** the patient **round** by putting cold water on his face.
8 They managed to **carry** the task **through** despite opposition.
9 This tune **brings back** memories of my childhood.
10 The sale of the paintings will **bring in** several thousand pounds.
11 We need to **carry out** some tests to find out what's wrong with you.
12 She was nervous about chairing the meeting, but she **carried** it **off** without any problems.
13 Please don't **bring up** the subject of politics in class.
14 The meeting was **called off** due to the President's sudden illness.
15 When fire broke out we **called out** the fire brigade.
16 They tried to **bring down** the government by starting a revolution.

48 *Look at Appendix 3, then fill in the correct preposition.*

1 She applied ...*to*... the manager .... the post of editor of the magazine.
2 He is crazy .... all kinds of fast cars.
3 I wouldn't bet .... it being warm tomorrow.
4 The manager of the bank had to account .... all the money that was missing.
5 I didn't realise there would be a charge .... using this telephone.
6 The police announced that they were going to charge someone .... the murder of the priest.
7 Nobody seems to care .... what is happening in the world today.
8 James' mother told him to take care .... himself during the journey.
9 Mark was very clever .... figuring out how machines worked.
10 It was very clever .... you to remember to bring an umbrella.
11 If you apply now, you're assured .... getting a place on the course.
12 You can't compare Elvis Presley .... Michael Jackson. Elvis is the king.
13 Compared .... winters in Moscow, this isn't really cold at all.
14 The Police Inspector wasn't able to comment .... the case as they had no new evidence.
15 I'm going to have to stop eating chocolate. I think I'm addicted .... it.
16 Michael's been asked to contribute .... this new science fiction magazine.
17 I couldn't get into the museum because it was crowded .... tourists.
18 Scientists are still trying to find a cure .... AIDS.
19 You have to comply .... these rules or you will lose your job.
20 Brian's been accused .... cheating in his exams.
21 Maria should go and see a doctor. She has been complaining .... back pains for weeks now.
22 I'm going to complain .... the manager .... this meal. It was terrible.
23 It upsets me when people are cruel .... their pets.
24 He doesn't seem to be aware .... what's going on around him.
25 This new book I'm reading is based .... the life of Jackie Onassis.

49 *Complete the sentences using the words in bold. Use two to five words.*

1 When did George give up his job?
  since   How long ...*is it since George gave*... up his job?

2 The machine stopped working so we asked someone to check it.
   down The machine .... asked someone to check it.
3 The soup is so hot that she can't eat it.
   hot The soup .... to eat.
4 Could you water the flowers?
   mind Would .... the flowers?
5 The film was quite boring.
   were We .... the film.
6 She prefers watching TV to listening to music.
   rather She'd .... to music.
7 We left early to avoid the traffic.
   out We .... to avoid the traffic.
8 They made the children study for five hours a day.
   were The .... for five hours a day.
9 He finds driving on the left difficult.
   used He .... on the left.
10 He thought she was his aunt.
   for He .... his aunt.
11 The tiles on their roof need replacing.
   need They .... the tiles on their roof.
12 He doesn't want her to work as a waitress.
   objects He .... as a waitress.
13 We haven't had any news from him for a month.
   heard We .... for a month.

50 *Complete the sentences below with a suitable word from the list below.*

a bell	**a fox**	**a cucumber**	**a lamb**	**a picture**
a pancake	**a bee**	**a peacock**	**the grave**	**a sheet**

1 The bride looked as pretty as ...*a picture*... in her white silk wedding gown.
2 Mr Bayer looks a rather rough type but he is really as gentle as ....
3 Her voice rang out as clear as ....
4 When Jenny came top of the class she was as proud as ....
5 The land around town is as flat as .... There isn't a hill in sight.
6 When Mr Jenkins heard the news he went as white as ....
7 Her mother has been as busy as .... all day making all the last minute preparations for the wedding.
8 John remained as silent as .... as he listened to my plans for the future.
9 Mary stayed as cool as .... and gave not even the slightest sign that she had met him before.
10 You can be sure he has an ulterior motive for inviting us to dinner; he is as cunning as ....

51 *Tick the correct boxes.*

	of scissors	of men	of false teeth	of cutlery	of questions	of shoes
couple						
pair	✔					
set						

Practice Test 2 ···

For questions 1 - 15, read the text below and decide which word A, B, C or D best fits each space. There's an example at the beginning (0).

Bicycles

Why don't the British cycle? Only a quarter of the **(0)** ... twenty million bicycles in the country are thought to be in **(1)** ... use. In Denmark, which is flatter but no darker or rainier than Britain, twenty per cent of all journeys are made by bicycle, while in Britain the **(2)** ... is only 5%. The government are trying to **(3)** ... this. It is hoped that a grant of millions of pounds from the National Lottery will **(4)** ... more people to use their bikes. The money will be used to **(5)** ... for a 6,500 mile national network of cycle tracks. Britain needs to **(6)** ... environmentally friendly schemes such as this. The southern third of the country is one of the most **(7)** ... areas of the world. Environmentalists make it **(8)** ... to build new roads, and **(9)** ... roads are very overcrowded. One official committee described the growth of motor transport as "possibly the **(10)** ... environmental threat to the UK". The **(11)** ... of building the cycle tracks is to motivate people to use their bicycles instead of their cars. However, the new tracks are being built **(12)** ... cities and not through them. This **(13)** ... that only long distance journeys may be easier and safer. Those cyclists who want to **(14)** ... inside cities will still be in danger of **(15)** ... their lives on busy roads every time they use their bicycles.

	A		B		C		D	
0	A	counted	B	numbered	C	estimated	D	guess
1	A	right	B	regular	C	normal	D	proper
2	A	size	B	portion	C	figure	D	part
3	A	improve	B	succeed	C	excel	D	help
4	A	support	B	activate	C	boost	D	encourage
5	A	cost	B	give	C	pay	D	afford
6	A	do	B	introduce	C	commence	D	make
7	A	full	B	loaded	C	occupied	D	crowded
8	A	rough	B	uneasy	C	stiff	D	difficult
9	A	existing	B	prevailing	C	living	D	left
10	A	hardest	B	greatest	C	grandest	D	strongest
11	A	aim	B	function	C	design	D	course
12	A	from	B	in	C	among	D	between
13	A	tells	B	says	C	means	D	defines
14	A	travel	B	wander	C	tour	D	follow
15	A	expiring	B	losing	C	missing	D	terminating

0	A	B	C■	D
1	A	B	C	D
2	A	B	C	D
3	A	B	C	D
4	A	B	C	D
5	A	B	C	D
6	A	B	C	D
7	A	B	C	D
8	A	B	C	D
9	A	B	C	D
10	A	B	C	D
11	A	B	C	D
12	A	B	C	D
13	A	B	C	D
14	A	B	C	D
15	A	B	C	D

Part 2

For questions 16 - 30, read the text below and think of the word which best fits each space.
Use only one word in each space. Write your answers in the answer boxes provided.

Travel Insurance

When going **(0)** .... holiday, it is always a good idea to take **(16)** .... travel insurance. This is just in **(17)** .... something goes **(18)** .... along the way. You could lose your luggage, you could **(19)** .... robbed, or even become ill and need expensive medical treatment. For millions of holiday makers, travel insurance is just a precaution **(20)** .... will help them have an enjoyable and worry-free holiday. But for **(21)** .... , travel insurance is a way of earning money **(22)** .... making false claims against insurance companies. For **(23)** ...., some people pretend that they have had expensive equipment stolen which in **(24)** .... never even existed, and then claim large sums **(25)** .... compensation. Such claims cost insurance companies a total **(26)** .... £50 million per year. But the cheats' luck is about to run **(27)** .... **(28)** .... to a new computer system, companies will be able to tell at a glance **(29)** .... someone has made a claim within the last three years. Honest travellers will no **(30)** .... have to pay through the nose for other people's dishonesty.

0	on	0 ▭ ▬
16		16 ▭ ▭
17		17 ▭ ▭
18		18 ▭ ▭
19		19 ▭ ▭
20		20 ▭ ▭
21		21 ▭ ▭
22		22 ▭ ▭
23		23 ▭ ▭
24		24 ▭ ▭
25		25 ▭ ▭
26		26 ▭ ▭
27		27 ▭ ▭
28		28 ▭ ▭
29		29 ▭ ▭
30		30 ▭ ▭

Part 3

For questions 31 - 40, complete the second sentence so that it has a similar meaning to the first sentence. Use the word given and other words to complete each sentence. You must use between two and five words. Do not change the word given. Write your answers in the answer boxes provided.

0 I'm sure it wasn't Jim who did it.
have
It .... Jim who did it.

| 0 | *can't have been* | 0 0 1 2 |

31 He proposed some interesting ideas at the meeting.
put
He .... at the meeting.

| 31 | | 31 0 1 2 |

32 He made us wait two hours before he called us in.
were
We .... two hours before he called us in.

| 32 | | 32 0 1 2 |

33 Kevin doesn't work as hard as he did in the past.
used
Kevin .... he does now.

| 33 | | 33 0 1 2 |

34 He was about to leave when the phone rang.
point
He was .... when the phone rang.

| 34 | | 34 0 1 2 |

35 Dad let us stay up late last night.
were
We .... late last night.

| 35 | | 35 0 1 2 |

36 I like studying arts more than sciences.
to
I prefer .... sciences.

| 36 | | 36 0 1 2 |

37 He paid £50 for the answerphone.
him
The answerphone .... £50.

| 37 | | 37 0 1 2 |

38 We met Ann while we were in Florida.
across
We .... we were in Florida.

| 38 | | 38 0 1 2 |

39 Sophie hasn't been to a party for a month.
last
It's a month .... a party.

| 39 | | 30 0 1 2 |

40 Shall we have dinner together tonight?
about
How .... tonight?

| 40 | | 40 0 1 2 |

Part 4

For questions 41 - 55, read the text below and look carefully at each line. Some of the lines are correct and some have a word which should not be there. If a line is correct, put a tick (✔) by the number in the answer boxes provided. If a line has a word which should not be there, write the word in the answer boxes provided.

Winter Visits to London

0	Every year at Christmas time my parents	
00	pay on a short visit to London.They like	
41	to fly there on a Friday morning and	
42	return on a Sunday evening. While been in London	
43	they always stay in an expensive hotel	
44	close to the Marble Arch. Christmas time may	
45	seem a strange time for to visit London.	
46	After it all, England in the wintertime can be	
47	cold, wet and foggy itself. Sometimes it even	
48	snows. However, my parents like going	
49	because, despite of the cold weather,	
50	there is a lots to do. My mother goes	
51	in order that to visit the shops and buy	
52	presents, my father does enjoys visiting the	
53	museums and art galleries, and they	
54	both like to visiting the theatre in the evening	
55	when the streets are being lit with Christmas lights.	

0	✓	0
00	*on*	00
41		41
42		42
43		43
44		44
45		45
46		46
47		47
48		48
49		49
50		50
51		51
52		52
53		53
54		54
55		55

Part 5

For questions 56 - 65, read the text below. Use the word given in capitals at the end of each line to form a word that fits in the space in the same line. Write your word in the answer boxes provided.

Collecting Things

Nowadays, you are more likely to hear **(0)** .... than serious comment when stamp-collecting is mentioned because it's no longer **(56)** .... . But lots of people are **(57)** .... about collecting things and find it a **(58)** .... way to spend their time.
Souvenirs from holiday **(59)** ...., whatever the country, are **(60)** .... popular with collectors. So are household items with something special in common which makes them **(61)** ...., such as sugar spoons with engraved pictures, scarfs or **(62)** .... mugs. Collecting things is a **(63)** .... activity - great for meeting new people - which may be why it is said to have **(64)** .... benefits. It is a relaxing and interesting **(65)** .... .

LAUGH

FASHION
ENTHUSIASM
CREATE
LOCATE
PARTICULAR

ATTRACT

COLOUR
SOCIAL
PSYCHOLOGY
OCCUPY

0	*laughter*	0
56		56
57		57
58		58
59		59
60		60
61		61
62		62
63		63
64		64
65		65

3 *Modal Verbs*

The modal verbs are: **can, could, may, might, must, ought to, will, would, shall, should.**
They take **no -s** in the third person singular and are followed by an infinitive without to except for
"ought to". *He **must be** at work. He **ought to do** what you asked him to.* **They come before the subject in
questions and are followed by "not" in negations.** *"**Could you** help me with the dishes?" "I'm sorry, I
can't."* **Certain verbs or expressions can be used with the same meaning as modals. These are: need
(= must), had better (= should), have (got) to (= must), be able to (= can), used to (= would) etc.**
*I've **got to go** to the library.*

Summary of Functions of Modal Verbs and Synonymous Expressions

Ability

She **can** dance well.
She **could/was able to** dance well
when she was young. (repeated
action - ability in the past)
She**'s able to** type 120 words
per minute.
They **were able to** buy a car after
saving for years. (single action in
the past)
He **couldn't/wasn't able to** save
the patient.

Obligation

I **must** cut down on fats. (I **need** to;
I say so)
I **have to** cut down on fats. (I**'m
obliged** to; the doctor says so)
I **had to** cut down or else I would
have got overweight. (past)
We **ought to stay** within the speed
limit. (It **is** the right thing to do, but
we **don't** always do it.)
We **ought to have** stayed within the
speed limit. (It **was** the right thing to
do but we **didn't** do it.)

Requests

Can I see the Manager? (informal)
Could I see the Manager? (polite)
May I see the Manager, please?
(formal)
Might I see the Manager? (very
formal)
Will you do my shopping? (infor-
mal)
Would you mind working overtime?
(polite; formal)

Possibility

He **can't** still be at home. (90%
certain)
He **could/may** be tired. (50%
certain; it's possible he is tired)
He **might** come later. (40% certain;
perhaps he will come later)
He **could have** killed her. (luckily
he didn't - past)
He **may/might have** sold his
house. (perhaps he sold it - past)
It **is likely that** Ann will offer to
help.
Ann **is likely to** offer to help.
It **was likely that** she had missed
the bus. (past)
She **was likely to** have missed
the bus. (past)

**Note: to express possibility in
questions we use:** Is he likely to ...?
Is it likely that he ...? Can he ...?
Could he ...? Might he ...?
*Could he still be at work? (not:
~~may~~)*

Necessity

I **must** see a doctor soon. (I say so)
I **had to** see a doctor. (I was
obliged to; past)
He **has to** wear an overall at work.
(necessity from outside the speaker)
He **had to** wear an overall when
he was at school. (past)
We**'ve got to** move house. (informal)
They **had to** move house. (past)
The cat **needs** feeding. **or** The cat
needs to be fed. (it **is** necessary)
The cat **needed** feeding. **or** The
cat **needed to be** fed. (it **was**
necessary)
You **ought to** behave yourself. (it
is necessary)
She **doesn't have to/doesn't need
to** come. (it **isn't** necessary -
absence of necessity)
She **didn't have to/didn't need to**
come. (it **wasn't** necessary for her to
come and we don't know if she did)
She **needn't have** come so early.
(it **wasn't** necessary for her to
come but she did)

Prohibition / Duty

You **can't** enter this area. (prohibition - you **aren't allowed to**)
They **couldn't** enter that area.
(prohibition - they **weren't
allowed to**)
You **mustn't** touch the statues.
(prohibition - it is forbidden)
You **may not** smoke in the
corridors. (prohibition - formal)
All applicants **must** fill in this
form. (duty)
All applicants **had to** fill in that
form. (duty - past)
People **ought to** respect
the environment. (It **is** the right
thing to do but people **don't**
always do it.)
He **ought to have** notified the
police of the burglary. (It **was**
the right thing to do but he **didn't**
do it.)

Summary of Functions of Modal Verbs and Synonymous Expressions

Criticism	Logical Assumptions	Probability
You **could** at least call her. (present) You **could** at least **have** called her yesterday. (past) He **should** let us know. He **should have** let us know before. (but he **didn't**) You **ought to** be more helpful. You **ought to have** been more helpful. (It **was** the right thing to do, but you didn't do it.)	He **must** be tired. (90% certain - positive; I'm sure he **is** tired.) He **must have** arrived by now. (positive; I'm sure he **has arrived**.) It **can't/couldn't** be a fake. (negative; I'm sure it **isn't** a fake.) She **can't/couldn't have** killed him. (negative; I'm sure she **didn't kill** him.)	He **will** come tomorrow. (100% certain; prediction) He **should/ought to** come by later. (90% certain; future only; it's probable) He **should/ought to have** reached Rome by now. (He has probably reached Rome.)

Permission	Offers / Suggestions	Advice
You **can/can't** take my car. (giving or refusing permission; informal) He **wasn't allowed to/couldn't** take my car. (past) He **was allowed to** take my car. (not: could; past) **Could** I go out for a minute? (more polite; asking for permission) You **may** go out for a minute. (formal; giving permission) **Might** I have the pleasure of your company? (very formal; asking for permission) I'm sorry, but you **can't/mustn't** make long distance phone calls. (informal; refusing permission) Visitors **may not** take pictures of the statues. (formal; refusing permission - written notice) You **are allowed to** see the patient. (permission)	**Can I/we** carry your bags? (offer - informal) **Shall I/we** collect your laundry? (offer - informal) **Would you like** to stay with me for a couple of days? (offer) **Would you like** me to give you a lift? (offer) **Shall we** have a break? (suggestion) **I/We can** watch TV. (suggestion) We **could go** to the theatre tonight. (suggestion) We **could have** stayed longer if you'd wanted. (suggestion - past) **Let's** play football! (suggestion) **Why don't we** play football? (suggestion) **How about** playing football? (suggestion) **What about** playing football? (suggestion)	You **should** stop smoking. (general advice; I advise you) You **should have** stopped smoking. (but you **didn't**) You **ought to** comply with the regulations. (I advise you; most people believe this.) You **ought to have** contacted a lawyer earlier. (but you **didn't**) You **had better** not lie to her. (It **isn't** a good idea; advice on a specific situation) It **would have been better if** you hadn't lied to her. (but you **did**) **Shall** I enter the competition? (asking for advice)

52 Read the following sentences, then identify the use of each verb in bold.

1   They **can't** have lied.   ......*logical assumption - negative*.......
2   You **must** tell them the truth.   ....
3   He **was able to** run the Marathon.   ....
4   **Can** you help me with my homework?   ....
5   He **should** have seen a doctor.   ....
6   You**'d better** admit to your guilt.   ....
7   They **don't have to** employ more staff.   ....
8   **Shall** I speak to the Manager about my problem?   ....
9   People **ought to** treat animals with respect.   ....
10   She isn't at home. She **may** be at the supermarket.   ....
11   He **had to** wear glasses.   ....
12   She **could** at least **have** told me in advance.   ....

53 *Identify the use of the verbs in bold, then say the same sentence in as many ways as possible.*

1 She **can** cook Chinese food.   ......ability...... ..She's able to cook Chinese food..
2 Tim **may** come over today.   ....
3 He **should** be at the party tonight.   ....
4 They **must have** gone out; the lights are off.   ....
5 I **need** to call my mother.   ....
6 You **ought to** take an umbrella; it's raining.   ....
7 You **could** at least **have** driven her to work.   ....
8 I **have to** help Mum clean the house.   ....
9 **Can I** have a look at your newspaper?   ....
10 **Would** you like me to carry that for you?   ....
11 We **can** go to the beach tomorrow.   ....
12 You **may not** smoke in the hospital.   ....
13 All employees **must** attend the meeting.   ....
14 The dogs **need** to be fed at 12:00.   ....
15 You **should** go to Pam's party.   ....
16 **Shall** we go out tonight?   ....
17 People **ought to** drive more carefully.   ....
18 She **can't** be feeling well.   ....

Must (affirmative logical assumption) - May/Might (possibility) - Can't/Couldn't (negative logical assumption)

Present Infinitive	*I'm sure he **works** overtime.* *Perhaps he **will work** overtime.*	*He must **work** overtime.* *He may/might **work** overtime.*
Present Cont. Infinitive	*I'm sure he **is working**.* *Perhaps he **will be working**.*	*He must **be working**.* *He may/might **be working**.*
Perfect Infinitive	*I'm sure he **didn't work**.* *I'm sure he **hasn't worked** before.* *I'm sure he **hadn't worked**.*	*He can't **have worked**.* *He can't **have worked** before.* *He can't **have worked**.*
Perfect Cont. Infinitive	*Perhaps he **was working**.* *Perhaps he **has been working**.*	*He may/might **have been working**.* *He may/might **have been working**.*

54 *Complete the sentences using the words in bold. Use two to five words.*

1 I'm sure she lost the race.
  have   She ...*must have lost*... the race.
2 Perhaps she will phone us sometime today.
  may   She .... sometime today.
3 I don't think the Rogers have been living here long.
  been   The Rogers .... here long.
4 I'm sure he has spent all his money.
  have   He .... all his money.
5 I'm sure James won't be seeing the boss tomorrow.
  be   James .... the boss tomorrow.
6 Perhaps he is feeling ill.
  be   He .... ill.

7 I'm sure Alan wasn't driving carelessly.
been Alan .... carelessly.
8 Perhaps he had left before you called.
have He .... before you called.
9 I'm sure she is considering your offer.
be She .... your offer.
10 Perhaps they rented the flat.
may They .... the flat.

Mustn't - Needn't

- **mustn't (= it's forbidden)** *You **mustn't** park on the double yellow lines.*
- **needn't / don't have to (= it isn't necessary)** *You **needn't** do the ironing. I'll do it tonight.*

55 *Complete the sentences using the words in bold. Use two to five words.*

1 It's forbidden to feed the animals.
not You ...*must not feed*... the animals.
2 It isn't necessary to cut the grass; it's still quite short.
have You .... the grass; it's still quite short.
3 It's prohibited to take dogs into the restaurant.
not You .... into the restaurant.
4 It isn't necessary to dust the furniture; I'll do it later.
need You .... the furniture; I'll do it later.
5 Children aren't allowed to run in the corridor.
not Children .... in the corridor.
6 Sixth formers needn't wear school uniforms.
have Sixth formers .... school uniforms.

Needn't - Didn't need to - Needn't have

- **don't have to / don't need to / needn't + present infinitive (It is not necessary in the present or future.)** *Citizens of EU countries **don't have to** /**don't need to**/**needn't** have a visa to go to England.*
- **didn't need to / didn't have to (It was not necessary in the past and we may not know if the action happened or not.)** *She **didn't need to**/**didn't have to** go out last night. (It wasn't necessary for her to go out, and we don't know if she went or not.)*
- **needn't + perfect infinitive (We know that something happened in the past although it was not necessary.)** *He **needn't have** given the waiter such a big tip. (He did, although it was not necessary.)*

56 *Complete the sentences using the words in bold. Use two to five words.*

1 Tim went on a two-day trip. He took more clothes than necessary.
have Tim ...*needn't have taken*... so many clothes on a two-day trip.
2 He decided not to take his passport because it wasn't necessary.
need He .... his passport.
3 We bought more food than was necessary for the party.
have We .... so much food for the party.
4 It wasn't necessary for Gloria to iron the clothes because Sue had already done it.
have Gloria .... the clothes because Sue had already done it.
5 It isn't necessary to have a visa to visit Australia.
need You .... a visa to visit Australia.
6 It wasn't necessary for Jim to accept the offer.
have Jim .... the offer.

be supposed to - be to

- **be supposed to (= should)** expresses the idea that someone else expects something to be done. *You **are supposed to** be helpful to customers. (Your boss expects you to.) You **should** be helpful to customers. (It's a good idea because it makes a good impression.)*
- **be to + infinitive** expresses the idea that someone else demands something. *You **are to** be in my office at 12 sharp. (You must be in my office at 12 sharp.)*
- **be supposed to** and **be to** are used to express what someone expects about a previously arranged event. *The shop assistant **was supposed to** give me a receipt.*

 57 *Read the following sentences and explain their meaning.*

1 You **were supposed to** eat your salad. ...*Your mother wanted you to eat your salad.*...
2 You **should** clean your room. ....
3 You **are to** finish your homework. ....
4 All students **are supposed to** do their homework. ....
5 You **are supposed to** wear running shoes. ....
6 You **should** wear running shoes. ....
7 I **was to** walk the dog twice a day. ....
8 I **was supposed to** walk the dog twice a day. ....

58 *Rewrite the sentences using the words in brackets.*

1 Let's go jogging. (shall) ...*Shall we go jogging?*....
2 Please turn the TV off. (could) ....
3 Am I allowed to sit here? (may) ....
4 Please answer the phone. (will) ....
5 Don't bite your nails. (must) ....
6 Do you mind if I use your pen? (can) ....
7 I wish I had checked the tyres. (ought) ....
8 These curtains don't have to be ironed. (need) ....
9 It's not polite to speak with your mouth full. (should) ....
10 Why don't we visit Mark and Jane? (shall) ....
11 Is there any chance that he'll phone? (likely) ....
12 It's advisable to brush your teeth after meals. (should) ....
13 There's a possibility that he'll arrive a little late. (might) ....
14 Do you know how to ice-skate? (can) ....
15 It wasn't necessary to show any identification but he did. (need) ....
16 Why didn't you tell me there was no one in? (could) ....
17 It wasn't necessary for us to wait because there was no queue. (need) ....
18 Let's go to the cinema tonight. (shall) ....
19 It's important that you be here at 9.00. (must) ....
20 I'm sure he is a millionaire. (must) ....
21 Perhaps he'll change his mind. (may) ....
22 Please, help me carry these! (could) ....
23 I don't believe she paid so much for that dress. (can) ....
24 It's a good idea to lock the door at night. (should) ....
25 Is there any chance we'll get a pay rise? (likely) ....
26 Why didn't they inform us of the delay? (could) ....
27 We could try to mend it ourselves. (Let's) ....
28 It wasn't necessary for you to go to so much trouble. (need) ....
29 It's a good idea to show more respect. (ought to) ....
30 You have to inform the bank of any change of address. (must) ....

59 *Fill in the blanks with a suitable word or phrase practising modals. Identify the use of the modal verb and/or the expressions used.*

1   She ...*must have worked*... (work) late last night; she looks exhausted.   ...*logical assumption*...
2   When we emigrated to Australia, we .... (leave) our pets behind.   ....
3   .... (we/go)? It's getting late.   ....
4   You .... (start) learning Spanish if you're going to live in Madrid.   ....
5   You .... (be) kinder to her; she's only a baby.   ....
6   .... (you/collect) my parcel for me?   ....
7   You .... (not/smoke) cigars on an aeroplane.   ....
8   You .... (not/pay) by cheque without a cheque guarantee card.   ....
9   The doctor says I .... (lose) weight before my operation.   ....
10 .... (I/paint) my room a different colour, please?   ....
11 You really .... (not/eat) so much red meat.   ....
12 He .... (take) your car since he had the keys.   ....
13 I'm sorry to bother you but .... (you/help) me?   ....
14 Call them later; they .... (sleep) now.   ....
15 You .... (write) to your grandfather more often.   ....
16 She types very fast. Actually she .... (type) 150 words per minute.   ....
17 You .... (confirm) your resignation in writing.   ....
18 Ian .... (tell) her the truth; she now feels betrayed.   ....
19 Ann .... (play) the piano at the age of six.   ....
20 They .... (sell) their flat and buy a bigger one.   ....

60 *Read the following situations, then write how you would respond to each using modals.*

1   Your friend has won £10,000 in the lottery. What do you advise her to do?
    ...*"You should go to Venice." "Why don't you go to Venice?"*...
2   Your friend cannot sleep at night. What do you suggest he does? ....
3   It is snowing. Tom said he would be home early and he still hasn't arrived. What do you think? .....
4   Some children are playing football in the flower beds. What do you say to them? ....
5   It is your birthday. Your friend gives you a very expensive present. What do you say?......................
6   You are at a train station. An old lady is carrying a heavy suitcase. How do you offer to help her? ..
7   You are in a train. The window is open and you are cold. What do you say to the other passengers?
8   You see your windowcleaner with a broken arm. What do you say to your friend?...........................
9   You are looking after your young cousin. It is after midnight and he is still running around the
    house. What do you say to him?   ....
10 Your friend hurt her leg a week ago. She still hasn't seen her doctor. What do you tell her to do?...
11 Your friends are late for your dinner party. What do you say as you impatiently look at your watch?
12 Your friends arrive three hours late for the dinner party. They say they were delayed by an
    unexpected visitor. How do you reply? ....

In Other Words

- Perhaps he is sleeping now.
  He may be sleeping now.
- I'm sure he hasn't finished yet.
  He can't have finished yet.
- I'm sure he has left.
  He must have left.
- Shall I help you with the dishes?
  Would you like me to help you with the dishes?
- It's forbidden to take pictures in this museum.
  You mustn't take pictures in this museum.
  You aren't allowed to take pictures in this museum.
- It isn't necessary for you to take the bus.
  You don't have to/don't need to/needn't take the bus.

- It wasn't necessary for her to take so much money with her.
  She needn't have taken so much money with her.
- He is likely to perform in the concert.
  It is likely that he will perform in the concert.
  He'll probably perform in the concert.
- Let's go for a ride.
  Shall we/Why don't we go for a ride?
  What/How about going for a ride?
- It would be a good idea to stop smoking.
  You should stop smoking.
  You'd better stop smoking.
- Would you mind if I used your phone?
  May/Might I use your phone?

61 *Complete the sentences using the words in bold. Use two to five words.*

1 Perhaps the car needs a new engine.
   need   The car ...*may/might need*... a new engine.
2 Why don't you go to Canada for a holiday?
   could   You .... for a holiday.
3 Shall I get you a cup of tea?
   me   Would .... you a cup of tea?
4 Sue will probably go to see her aunt.
   is   Sue .... to see her aunt.
5 It wasn't necessary for them to buy such a big car as they did.
   have   They .... such a big car.
6 It's forbidden to smoke in this building.
   not   You .... in this building.
7 It would be a good idea to change your hairstyle.
   better   You .... your hairstyle.
8 Why didn't anybody warn me about the bus strike?
   have   You .... about the bus strike.
9 It isn't necessary for you to attend the meeting.
   need   You .... the meeting.
10 Let's go to the cinema.
   going   What .... the cinema?
11 I'm sure he is seeing Ruth.
   be   He .... Ruth.
12 It isn't necessary for you to come early tonight.
   have   You .... early tonight.
13 I'm sure he didn't send you this letter.
   sent   He .... this letter.
14 May I read your newspaper?
   mind   Would .... your newspaper?
15 I'm sure she wasn't lying to you.
   been   She .... to you.
16 She is likely to fail her exams.
   that   It is .... her exams.
17 It's forbidden to talk to the driver while he is driving.
   must   You .... the driver while he is driving.

18 It wasn't necessary for him to give me the money back so soon.
given He .... the money back so soon.

19 Perhaps she went to her uncle's.
have She .... to her uncle's.

20 Shall I help you lengthen your dress?
me Would .... you lengthen your dress?

62 *Find the word which should not be in the sentence.*

1	*to*
2	
3	
4	
5	
6	
7	
8	
9	
10	
11	
12	
13	
14	
15	
16	
17	
18	
19	
20	

1 You needn't to repeat the course.
2 Mick was being able to change the faulty fuse on his own.
3 Maeve might have been helped you if you had asked her.
4 Fortunately, we didn't have needed to walk the whole distance.
5 Would it you like me to pick up the laundry?
6 He should have must known better than to trust her.
7 Jeremy would like that to study nuclear physics.
8 She had has to work overtime every day last month.
9 They ought to have had given us more instructions.
10 Let's not to argue about this any more.
11 The Prime Minister is being supposed to leave for the USA tonight.
12 Were you allowed it to take photos inside the museum?
13 They can't have had spent all that money in just one week.
14 Children are may not to be left unattended at any time.
15 Would they mind if my bringing a friend along?
16 They must have pack all their things before noon.
17 You should have try to treat customers more politely.
18 Might I to ask you for a favour?
19 You needn't have to invited so many people.
20 Let's we go to Ann's.

Oral Development 3

Make speculations for the following pictures as in the example:

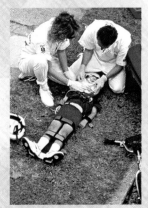   

S1: ***There must have been an accident.***
S2: ***The boy may not have seen the car coming.***

45

63 *Look at Appendix 2, then fill in the correct particle(s).*

1 While I was walking down Oxford Street I **came** ...*across*... a good record shop.
2 You should try to **cut** .... the number of cigarettes you smoke a day.
3 After the death of his father the young man **came** .... a lot of money.
4 I wonder how she **came** .... that expensive car.
5 We were driving slowly enjoying the countryside, when a police car **cut** .... and stopped us.
6 The writer's new book **came** .... in time for Christmas.
7 This necklace **came** .... me from my grandmother.
8 The stain **came** .... of the shirt when it was washed.

9 Tim **isn't cut** .... such a high-pressure job.
10 The performance **came** .... well.
11 Nothing about the accident **came** .... in the news.
12 You are always **cutting** .... our conversations!
13 You'd better **come** .... a good excuse or you'll be in trouble.
14 Our electricity was **cut** .... because we forgot to pay the bill.
15 After playing football in the rain he **came** .... a bad cold.
16 Do **come** .... anytime. We can have a cup of coffee together.

64 *Look at Appendix 3, then fill in the correct preposition.*

1 Your diet is deficient ...*in*... iron.
2 The TV programme was aimed .... teenagers.
3 She had to beg .... money on the street.
4 He is very careless .... his clothes.
5 There was a long delay .... the completion of the road.
6 As it was icy he lost control of his car and crashed .... a wall.
7 The couple took great delight .... their new-born baby.
8 I was delighted .... the news of their engagement.
9 Sue is very attached .... her pet dog.
10 She couldn't concentrate .... what she was doing because the television was on.
11 The holiday was different .... the one they had last year.
12 The only difference .... the twins is in their characters; one is shy while the other is outgoing.
13 There is a great demand .... economical cars.

14 The Manager demanded an explanation .... his assistant.
15 A policeman arrested the woman .... stealing from a shop.
16 Contrary .... what the newspaper said, the minister had agreed to sign the treaty.
17 Babies are dependent .... their mothers for everything.
18 The doctor told the woman that she was allergic .... dairy products.
19 The young actress could never dream .... starring in such a film.
20 Although her husband has been dead for years, she still dreams .... him.
21 Are you conscious .... the fact that you have caused us a lot of trouble?
22 In the desert you can die .... thirst.
23 A lot of people died .... the accident.
24 The boy was bored .... his computer game after having played it all day.
25 We were doubtful .... whether we should sign the contract or not.

65 *Complete the sentences using the words in bold. Use two to five words.*

1 Perhaps he got caught in the traffic.
have He ...*may have got caught*... in the traffic.
2 You should continue practising daily.
keep You should .... daily.
3 It wasn't necessary for Julie to buy him a present but she did.
bought Julie .... him a present.

4   She took a month to reorganise the office.
    her   It .... reorganise the office.
5   Is there any chance of his coming to the party?
    likely   Is he .... to the party?
6   When did he start his own business?
    set   When .... his own business?
7   They made us wait two hours before boarding the plane.
    were   We .... two hours before boarding the plane.
8   They have been discussing the new law for a week.
    discussion   The new law .... for a week.
9   People believe Sarah was responsible for the accident.
    believed   Sarah .... responsible for the accident.
10 He prefers cycling to walking.
    prefer   He would .... walk.
11 This new project is very interesting.
    interested   We are .... this new project.
12 We haven't seen Jean for a long time.
    since   It's a long time .... Jean.

66 Explain the idioms in bold.

1   I'm surprised he wasn't killed - it was **a really close shave**.
2   We have to pay for a new roof. That's a thousand pounds **down the drain**.
3   I'm afraid we'll have to give him the sack - his missing the meeting **was the last straw**.
4   That man thinks too much of himself - he **is always blowing his own trumpet**.
5   I must have offended her somehow - she **is looking daggers** at me.
6   As she said, he's a total idiot - that's his character **in a nutshell**.
7   Since you have no proof to show us, I'm afraid your theory just **doesn't hold water**.
8   He's so sensitive to criticism that if you even make a suggestion he **flies off the handle.**
9   He's obsessed with environmental problems; where they are concerned he **has got a real bee in his bonnet.**
10 I've never seen two people make friends so quickly - from the first day they **got on like a house on fire**.
11 I'm very suspicious about his making that offer - in fact, I **smell a rat**.
12 It's impossible to ignore him in a meeting - he really knows how to **make his presence felt.**
13 I wouldn't book a holiday with that company - they'll make you **pay through the nose**.

67 Fill in the blanks with the words from the lists below in their correct form.

a. bring - carry - fetch - take

1   The baby is too young to walk so he has to be .... everywhere.
2   You may borrow this book as long as you .... it back tomorrow.
3   Bob .... his dog for a walk by the canal last night.
4   I bought so much shopping I couldn't .... it all home.
5   My dog has been trained to .... my slippers from the bedroom.

b. anxiety - nuisance - problem - trouble

1   The woman was full of .... when her daughter was late home.
2   That boy is a(n) .... - he's always disturbing the class.
3   Can you speak up, please? I have a(n) .... with my hearing.
4   If you don't revise, you'll have a lot of .... answering the questions.
5   I left my glasses at home - what a(n) .... !

Practice Test 3 ·······························

For questions 1 - 15, read the text below and decide which word A, B, C or D best fits each space. There's an example at the beginning (0).

Living a healthier life

Keeping fit and healthy may (0) ... difficult, but there are a few easy-to-follow (1) ... . Firstly, a balanced diet is absolutely essential. This (2) ... selecting food that is (3) ... in salt and sugar. Experts recommend (4) ... the amount of fat in our diet, as too much can lead to heart problems. They also suggest increasing the (5) ... of high fibre food we eat. This comes in the (6) ... of fresh fruit, vegetables, wholemeal bread and pasta. As well as being packed (7) ... vitamins and minerals, they are delicious too. Secondly, it's important to fit exercise into your daily (8) ... . This can be done by simply walking as much as (9) ... and climbing stairs instead of (10) ... the lift. Exercise is necessary to (11) ... a healthy body, as well as increasing energy levels and (12) ... you feel generally fitter and happier. Finally, staying relaxed is important for good health. Too much stress can (13) ... to a variety of illnesses, from headaches to high blood pressure. (14) ...possible, do things you enjoy and treat yourself occasionally. So the message is (15) ... - enjoy yourself but learn to respect your body too. It's all a question of getting the balance right.

	A		B		C		D	
0	A have	B	seem	C	find	D	happen
1	A laws	B	guides	C	orders	D	guidelines
2	A contains	B	points	C	means	D	suggests
3	A poor	B	short	C	small	D	low
4	A declining	B	dropping	C	cutting	D	reducing
5	A bulk	B	amount	C	number	D	mass
6	A form	B	way	C	look	D	means
7	A by	B	with	C	of	D	in
8	A routine	B	custom	C	time	D	practice
9	A possible	B	probable	C	able	D	capable
10	A catching	B	having	C	taking	D	going
11	A keep	B	maintain	C	support	D	manage
12	A providing	B	doing	C	assisting	D	making
13	A bring	B	direct	C	guide	D	lead
14	A Whichever	B	Whenever	C	However	D	How
15	A ordinary	B	natural	C	simple	D	casual

	A	B	C	D
0	☐	■	☐	☐
1	☐	☐	☐	☐
2	☐	☐	☐	☐
3	☐	☐	☐	☐
4	☐	☐	☐	☐
5	☐	☐	☐	☐
6	☐	☐	☐	☐
7	☐	☐	☐	☐
8	☐	☐	☐	☐
9	☐	☐	☐	☐
10	☐	☐	☐	☐
11	☐	☐	☐	☐
12	☐	☐	☐	☐
13	☐	☐	☐	☐
14	☐	☐	☐	☐
15	☐	☐	☐	☐

Part 2

For questions 16 - 30, read the text below and think of the word which best fits each space.
Use only one word in each space. Write your answers in the answer boxes provided.

Laughter

You not only laugh more **(0)** .... you are relaxed, but you **(16)** .... relax when you laugh, and it has **(17)** .... found that when you're **(18)** .... holiday it is easier to do both.

But for **(19)** .... people laughter is not just a pleasure, it is a **(20)** .... of fighting illness. Some hospitals have begun to bring in clowns to relieve the silent, depressing atmosphere, especially in children's wards.

This scheme is called "Medical Smile" and it helps sick children in a **(21)** .... that doctors, with all **(22)** .... knowledge, can't do. The effect of the clowns is more **(23)** .... psychological. Laughter helps strengthen the immune system - **(24)** .... is, the part of our bodies **(25)** .... fights off disease. We take **(26)** .... more oxygen when we laugh, and our heartbeat slows **(27)** ....

Hospital clowns are becoming more **(28)** .... more popular because **(29)** .... the positive effect they have. They both relieve depression, which tends to **(30)** .... illnesses worse, and give people the will to fight their illnesses themselves.

0	when	0
16		16
17		17
18		18
19		19
20		20
21		21
22		22
23		23
24		24
25		25
26		26
27		27
28		28
29		29
30		30

Practice Test 3 ....

Part 3

For questions 31 - 40, complete the second sentence so that it has a similar meaning to the first sentence. Use the word given and other words to complete each sentence. You must use between two and five words. Do not change the word given. Write your answers in the answer boxes provided.

0 I'm sure it wasn't Jim who did it.
   have
   It .... Jim who did it.

0	*can't have been*	0 **0** 1 2 ☐☐■

31 Smoking on buses isn't allowed.
   are
   You .... on buses.

31		31 **0** 1 2 ☐☐☐

32 Shall I do the washing up?
   me
   Would .... the washing up?

32		32 **0** 1 2 ☐☐☐

33 He promised me he would be back before midnight.
   word
   He .... he would be back before midnight.

33		33 **0** 1 2 ☐☐☐

34 It wasn't necessary for her to get up early as it was Sunday.
   need
   She .... up early as it was Sunday.

34		34 **0** 1 2 ☐☐☐

35 They made the girl take her medicine.
   was
   The girl .... her medicine.

35		35 **0** 1 2 ☐☐☐

36 I'll try as hard as I can to finish in time.
   best
   I .... finish in time.

36		36 **0** 1 2 ☐☐☐

37 I suppose they are ready to go now.
   be
   They .... now.

37		37 **0** 1 2 ☐☐☐

38 Sheila hasn't been to a disco for months.
   since
   It's months .... to a disco.

38		38 **0** 1 2 ☐☐☐

39 You can call me any time you want.
   give
   You .... any time you want.

39		39 **0** 1 2 ☐☐☐

40 Skiing in the Swiss Alps thrills me.
   ski
   It's .... the Swiss Alps.

40		40 **0** 1 2 ☐☐☐

Part 4

For questions 41 - 55, read the text below and look carefully at each line. Some of the lines are correct and some have a word which should not be there. If a line is correct, put a tick (✔) by the number in the answer boxes provided. If a line has a word which should not be there, write the word in the answer boxes provided.

Satellite TV

0	The arrival of satellite TV has brought up a whole new	**0**	*up*
00	world of viewing into our living rooms - if we can afford	**00**	✓
41	to pay for it, that this is. Major sporting events can now	**41**	
42	be seen live. Besides of this, a wider variety of sports	**42**	
43	is now available. The viewer can choose anything	**43**	
44	from dog-racing up to sumo wrestling. Certain channels	**44**	
45	show 20 films every day. Again, the choice is enormous-	**45**	
46	from old classics or to the latest Hollywood releases.	**46**	
47	For those ones who like to keep informed, 24-hour	**47**	
48	news it is available at the touch of a button. Children	**48**	
49	are not forgotten either. A special for junior channel	**49**	
50	broadcasts out cartoons and children's films. But do we really	**50**	
51	need all this choice? The most danger is that we will become	**51**	
52	a population of passive couch-potatoes with square	**52**	
53	eyes and fingers glued to the remote-control. Of course	**53**	
54	the choice is a good thing, but viewers should use their	**54**	
55	ability to select the best and disregard of the rest.	**55**	

Part 5

For questions 56 - 65, read the text below. Use the word given in capitals at the end of each line to form a word that fits in the space in the same line. Write your word in the answer boxes provided.

Easter Island

Although Easter Island is **(0)** .... for its
(56) .... stone statues, very little is known
about the **(57)** .... which produced them.
(58) .... believe that the statues were
first put up by **(59)** .... who arrived between
the first and seventh centuries AD from **(60)** ....
islands to the north-west. They continued to make
these **(61)** .... for over a thousand years, possibly
for **(62)** .... reasons. The statues became larger
and more **(63)** .... until about 1500, when
(64) .... suddenly stopped. By the time
European **(65)** .... arrived in 1722, the statue -
making civilisation had died out.

FAME	
ASTONISH	
CIVILISE	
ARCHAEOLOGY	
COLONY	
DISTANCE	
CONSTRUCT	
RELIGION	
DECORATE	
PRODUCE	
SAIL	

0	*famous*
56	
57	
58	
59	
60	
61	
62	
63	
64	
65	

4 Adjectives / Adverbs / Comparisons

Adjectives tell us what something is like. They are the same in singular and plural. They can be used before a noun or after a linking verb (appear, be, become, get, feel, look, seem, smell, sound, stay, taste). *She's got **long** hair. These roses smell **nice**.* Adjectives can be **factual** (*big, square, blue* etc) **or express an opinion** (*nice, beautiful* etc).

Order of Adjectives

- When two or more adjectives are used before a noun, they normally go in the following order:

	Opinion			Fact Adjectives					noun
	adjectives	size	age	shape	colour	origin	material	used for/ be about	noun
It's a	lovely	small	old	square	brown	Chinese	wooden	writing	table.

- When there are two or more adjectives of the same type, the more general adjective goes before the more specific. *a kind, gentle lady*
- **Afraid, alike, alive, alone, ashamed, asleep, content, ill, glad** etc are never followed by a noun. *The students were **ashamed** of what they had done. (not: the ashamed students)*
- **Chief, eldest, former, indoor, inner, main, only, outdoor, outer, principle, upper** can only be used before nouns. *This is an **indoor** swimming pool. (not: This swimming pool is indoor.)*
- **Present and past participles** can be used as adjectives. *The film was **amusing**. We were **amused**.*

68 *Rewrite the sentences putting the adjectives into the correct place, then identify what kind of adjectives they are.*

1 I love ice-cream. (strawberry, Italian, tasty) ...*I love tasty Italian strawberry ice-cream.... (opinion, origin, material)*
2 They have a sofa. (leather, navy-blue, modern)
   ....
3 He loves his bike. (new, red, expensive, mountain)
   ....
4 She has a voice. (lovely, singing, pure)
   ....
5 He's just sold that suit to a woman. (beautiful, slim, tall, French, young) ....
6 She bought curtains. (brown and orange, dining-room) ....
7 She bakes cakes. (chocolate, delicious, birthday, round) ....
8 June has a puppy. (tiny, brown, fluffy) ....
9 She was given a dress. (black, spectacular, Italian, evening) ....
10 He bought a racquet. (tennis, graphite, new) ....
11 He has a grandfather. (French, ninety-year-old, wonderful) ....
12 We watched a film. (boring, German, black and white) ....
13 She wears lipstick. (pink, horrible, glossy) ....
14 We used to have a teacher. (strict, old, biology, American) ....
15 It was a dress. (wedding, antique, cream, stunning, lace) ....
16 Yesterday we went to the club. (huge, sports, modern) ....
17 Mary has a job. (sales, demanding, new) ....
18 The house has a kitchen. (large, well-equipped, white, modern) ....
19 It was a pool. (marble, huge, white, swimming) ....
20 He has a bag. (black, big, school) ....
21 I have rarely seen such a film. (American, well-made, detective)
   ....

- **Nouns of material, purpose** or **substance can be used as adjectives.** *(a summer suit, a television series)*
- **Certain adjectives can be used metaphorically:** *silky skin (soft and smooth, like silk),* but **a silk dress** *(a dress made of silk),* **stony look** *(disapproving look)* but **a stone wall** *(a wall made of stone),* **golden eagle** *(a bird with gold-brown feathers)* but **a gold ring** *(a ring made of gold),* **feathery snowflakes** *(soft and delicate like feathers)* but **a feather pillow** *(a pillow containing feathers),* **metallic paint** *(paint which looks like metal)* but **metal-rimmed glasses** *(glasses with a rim made of metal),* **leathery meat** *(too firm and difficult to cut)* but **a leather coat** *(a coat made of leather),* **a leaden sky** *(dark sky; the colour of lead)* but **lead pipes** *(pipes made of lead),* **a steely character** *(a hard, strong, unkind character)* but **a steel-plated tank** *(a vehicle with a steel covering).*

 69 *Underline the correct adjective.*

1 A gold/golden eagle glided gracefully across the sky.
2 She ruined her silk/silky suit by washing it.
3 We had to climb over a low stone/stony wall.
4 He approached the task with steel/steely determination.
5 This soap will leave your skin feeling silk/silky and soft.
6 Leathery/Leather coats never seem to go out of fashion.
7 This plant has soft feather/feathery leaves.
8 We spotted the metal/metallic blue car speeding into the tunnel ahead.
9 The manager's stone/stony expression showed that all was not well.
10 She was given an expensive gold/golden watch for her twenty-first birthday.

70 *Put the adjectives in the correct order.*

Rent our house in Italy for your holidays!

It's a **1)** ...*beautiful large stone*... (stone, beautiful, large) villa on the coast, with spectacular views of the sea. You will love the **2)** .... (old, huge, marble) swimming pool we have in our **3)** .... (mountainside, terraced, colourful) garden. There is a **4)** .... (sunny, stone, rectangular) patio at the front with many **5)** .... (terracotta, flower-filled, circular) pots. The house has five **6)** .... (elegant, white, medium-sized) bedrooms and three marble bathrooms - each with its own **7)** .... (antique, little, wonderful) wall-painting. The living room has a **8)** .... (cool, lovely, marble) floor with **9)** .... (expensive, Persian, antique) rugs and comfortable sofas. You can eat in the many **10)** .... (Italian, excellent, traditional) restaurants nearby and enjoy using the facilities in the new sports centre.

Compound adjectives are formed with:
- **present participles.** *a smart-looking man, a sharp-cutting knife*
- **past participles.** *a much-liked colleague, a well-known singer*
- **cardinal numbers + nouns.** *a one-month holiday, a seventy-mile speed limit, a three-year degree*
- **prefixes and suffixes.** *anti-social behaviour, a part-time worker*
- **badly, ill, poorly, well + past participle.** *a badly-treated animal, a well-established firm*

71 *Make compound adjectives to describe the following.*

1 A student who has been taught well. ...*a well-taught student*....
2 A letter that you have been waiting for for a long time. ....
3 A person who loves having fun. ....
4 A garden which is tended perfectly. ....

5 A life that is free of trouble. ....

6 A visit that was not timed well. ....

7 An action that is not advisable. ....

8 A journey of seven days. ....

● Most common adjectives do not have a particular ending. However there are certain common endings for adjectives which are formed from nouns and verbs. These are: **-able** *(predictable)*, **-al** *(practical)*, **-ant** *(observant)*, **-ar** *(polar)*, **-ary** *(reactionary)*, **-ate** *(passionate)*, **-ial** *(racial)*, **-ent** *(dependent)*, **-esque** *(grotesque)*, **-ful** *(remorseful)*, **-ian** *(Albanian)*, **-ible** *(sensible)*, **-ic** *(dramatic)*, **-ical** *(economical)*, **-ious** *(vicious)*, **-ish** *(selfish)*, **-ist** *(racist)*, **-ive** *(reactive)*, **-less** *(mindless)*, **-like** *(man-like)*, **-ly** *(warmly)*, **-ory** *(celebratory)*, **-ous** *(glamorous)*, **-some** *(lonesome)*, **-y** *(sunny)*.

● The most common prefixes used with adjectives are:

a- *(asocial)*, **ab-** *(abnormal)*, **anti-** *(anticlockwise)*, **dis-** *(discontent)*, **hyper-** *(hypersensitive)*, **il-** *(illegal)*, **im-** *(immortal)*, **in-** *(incredible)*, **ir-** *(irrational)*, **mal-** *(malnourished)*, **non-** *(non-violent)*, **over-** *(overactive)*, **pre-** *(prepacked)*, **pro-** *(pro-industry)*, **sub-** *(subterranean)*, **super-** *(superconfident)*, **un-** *(unappreciated)*, **under-** *(underfed)*.

---

72 *Use the words in capitals to form a word that fits in the space in the same line.*

Taking a break

Choosing a holiday can be an **(0)** .... and
(1) .... experience. Imagining all the places you
might visit can add a **(2)** .... touch to the
(3) .... routine of everyday life. Long,
(4) .... beaches and a hotel room with a
(5) .... view is what many of us expect of an
(6) .... holiday. Some people prefer a calm,
(7) .... time, while to others a more active,
(8) .... holiday is more
(9) .... . Whatever you choose, if you plan carefully,
you're bound to have an **(10)** .... time.

EXCITE
ENJOY
MAGIC
REPEAT
SUN
SPECTACLE
ENJOY
RELAX
ADVENTURE
APPEAL
FORGET

0	exciting	
1		
2		
3		
4		
5		
6		
7		
8		
9		
10		

Some adjectives can be used with **the** as nouns to talk about groups of people in general. These are: **the blind, the deaf, the disabled, the elderly, the homeless, the hungry, the living, the middle-aged, the old, the poor, the rich, the sick, the strong, the unemployed, the weak** etc. *Disabled people* need help and understanding. **The disabled** need help and understanding. *(refers to disabled people in general).* **The disabled people** over there are training for the "Paraplegic Olympics." *(refers to a specific group of disabled people.)*

---

73 *Fill in "the" where necessary.*

1 He takes ...*the*... disabled children in his area riding on Friday afternoons.

2 When the government decided to raise taxes .... rich people were unhappy and .... poor were devastated.

3 Christmas can be a very sad time for .... lonely people and .... homeless.

4 We were relieved to hear that all .... injured were recovered from the wreckage before the plane exploded.

5 .... survivors carried .... injured people to the ambulances.

6 .... deaf communicate by using sign language.

- **Adverbs** normally describe verbs, adjectives, other adverbs or whole sentences. *He swims very* **fast**. They tell us **how** (adverbs of manner - *carefully*), **where** (adverbs of place - *there*), **when** (adverbs of time - *tomorrow*), **how often** (adverbs of frequency - *always*), or **how much** (adverbs of degree - *completely*) **something happens. There are also relative adverbs** (when, where, why) **and sentence adverbs** (maybe).

Order of Adverbs

- Adverbs can be used in **front, mid** or **end** position in a sentence.

Front	Mid	End
All afternoon *they played* ***quietly in the sitting room***.		

- **Adverbs of manner** can be used in any position; in front position they give emphasis. *She opened the letter* **carefully**. **Carefully**, *she opened the letter. (emphasis)*
- **Adverbs of manner, place** and **time**, when used in the same sentence, are usually placed as follows:

subject + verb	manner	place	time
He was working	*quietly*	*in the shed*	*all day*.

Note that when there is a verb of movement, the order is **place - manner - time**.

subject + verb	place	manner	time
She went	*there*	*by bus*	*yesterday*.

- **Adverbs of time** usually go in end position. They also go in front position to emphasise the time.

subject + verb	place	manner	time		time	subject+ verb	place	manner
She goes	*to the gym*	*on foot*	*every day*.		*Every day*	*she goes*	*to the gym*	*on foot*.

- **Adverbs of frequency** (always, ever, occasionally, seldom, sometimes, usually etc) go after the auxiliary but before the main verb. *She* **is always** *complaining*. *She* **always comes** *on time*. In short answers, however, adverbs of frequency go before the auxiliary. *"Is he always so bad tempered?"* *"Yes, he* **always** *is."*
- **Adverbs of degree** (almost, hardly, quite etc) go before the words they modify. *I've* **almost finished**.

74 *Rewrite the sentences putting the adverbs in the correct place and making any other necessary changes.*

1 Ferries sail to the island. (weekly, twice, only, during the winter)
...*Ferries sail to the island only twice weekly during the winter.* ...
2 He does the shopping. (reluctantly, at the supermarket, every week)
....
3 She waited for her test results. (worriedly, in the hospital, all day)
....
4 The clock strikes twelve times. (exactly, in the hall, at midday)
....
5 My mother used to read to me. (aloud, always, in the evenings)
....
6 The soldiers marched. (to the battlefield, bravely, yesterday)
....
7 They go by car. (at weekends, to the leisure centre, sometimes)
....

8   We arrived after a bumpy flight. (in Scotland, eventually, safely, extremely)

....

9   The detective had been following the suspect. (all day, carefully)

....

10 She walks. (quickly, every morning, to the station)

....

11 The little boy ran. (excitedly, from the room, suddenly)

....

12 She turned up looking annoyed. (at the party, unexpectedly, terribly)

....

13 He studied. (hard, all morning, in his bedroom)

....

14 She looked at her reflection. (for ten minutes, carefully, in the mirror)

....

15 The children sit and play. (in their room, for hours, happily)

....

16 He waved goodbye. (to his friend, at the airport, sadly)

....

17 The old boat sailed into the harbour. (slowly, through the water, this afternoon)

....

18 He ran to answer the phone. (down the stairs, to the hall, quickly)

....

19 She sat reading a book. (all day, lazily, by the fire)

....

20 He looked to see if anyone was there. (out the window, nervously, this morning)

....

75 *Rewrite the text putting the adverbs in the correct place.*

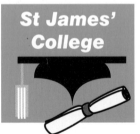

St James' College

Have you thought about your child's future? (carefully) Have you thought about sending your child to boarding school, but have been worried about how your child would react to being away from you? (particularly) On the 22nd and 23rd of this month, we at St James are opening our doors to parents like you. St James is located near Chatwick main train station and sits on a mountainside overlooking the Menta Lakes. (conveniently / picturesquely) Students sleep in twin rooms that have been redecorated and are designed to be as comfortable as possible. (tastefully / specially) Students work hard and are supervised by experienced teachers. (all day) In the evening they can sit in our comfortable canteen for a very nutritious meal prepared by our resident chef who selects only fresh ingredients. (daily / expertly) Once you've spent the day with us, we can guarantee you and your child will want to reserve a place. (at once)

...Have you thought carefully about your child's future?...

There are certain adverbs which have the same form as their adjectives. These are: best, better, big, cheap*, clean*, clear*, close*, cold, daily, dead, dear*, deep, direct, dirty, early, easy, extra, far, fast, fine*, free, further, hard, high, hourly, inside, kindly, last, late, long, loud*, low, monthly, past, quick*, quiet*, right, slow, straight, sure, thin*, thick, tight, weekly, well, wide, wrong, yearly etc. *She was an **early** riser. She woke up **early**.* **Those adverbs with an asterisk (*) can be found with -ly ending without a difference in meaning, but then they are more formal.** *I bought it **cheap**. (informal) ALSO I bought it **cheaply**. (formal)*

76 *Identify the highlighted words as adjectives or adverbs.*

This year's road race was the **1)** best I've ever seen. The event is held **2)** yearly, and entrance to the main stand is **3)** free. The race is always a **4)** sure exhibition of exceptionally **5)** fine driving. It was a **6)** cold morning, and the teams had woken up **7)** early to get their cars ready. They had trained **8)** long and **9)** hard to get here. The race was due to start at 11 o'clock, but started **10)** late as the track wasn't **11)** clean. There was a **12)** loud roar when all the drivers started their cars, then they proceeded **13)** quickly to the starting line. The gun went off, and the cars moved, as if in **14)** slow motion. They drove **15)** past the stands, and turned a

16) tight corner onto the main circuit. On the fifth lap one driver made a **17)** wrong decision, and his car stopped **18)** dead as it collided with a safety-barrier. The race was **19)** fast, and all the drivers drove **20)** well, but it was **21)** clear from the beginning who was going to win: an Australian driver had taken the **22)** inside lane and overtaken everybody in only the second lap. Over the rest of the race he managed to distance himself **23)** further from all the other cars. It was an **24)** easy victory for him, and he continued round the track for an **25)** extra lap to celebrate his win.

Adverbs with two forms and differences in meaning

deep = a long way down	**full** = exactly; very	**late** = not early	**sure** = certainly
deeply = greatly	**fully** = completely	**lately** = recently	**surely** = without a doubt
direct = by the shortest route	**hard** = intently; with effort	**near** = close	**wide** = off-target
directly = immediately	**hardly** = scarcely	**nearly** = almost	**widely** = to a large extent
easy = gently and slowly	**high** = at / to a high level	**pretty** = fairly	**wrong** = incorrectly
easily = without difficulty	**highly** = very much	**prettily** = in a pretty way	**wrongly** = unjustly (wrongly
free = without cost	**last** = after all others	**short** = suddenly	goes before verbs/past part. -
freely = willingly	**lastly** = finally	**shortly** = soon	wrong/wrongly go after verbs)

77 *Underline the correct item.*

1 I managed to get to New York easy/easily by flying there directly/direct.
2 She has been deeply/deep upset by his behaviour late/lately.
3 Lately/Late the cost of living has been increasing; things generally are not nearly/near as cheap as they used to be.
4 It is wide/widely believed that she was wrong/wrongly accused.
5 Laura is a very shy person who rare/rarely goes out and she does not mix free/freely with the other students.
6 She is highly/high regarded in the school as people can get on with her easily/easy.
7 I was not full/fully satisfied with the doctor as he had wrong/wrongly diagnosed my previous illness.
8 "Do you intend to leave shortly/short?" "I think so. I've nearly/near finished."
9 He'll surely/sure get a good grade; he's been studying very hardly/hard for the past year.
10 I was prettily/pretty embarrassed when I realised that I had hardly/hard enough money to pay the bill.
11 He came last/lastly in the race and was pretty/prettily disappointed by his performance.
12 The train goes direct/directly to Edinburgh without stopping so it will probably be full/fully.
13 She free/freely admitted that she had not been working very hard/hardly recently.
14 It is wide/widely believed that politicians are people who can't be full/fully trusted.
15 Sure/Surely we must be near/nearly there by now.

- **Quite** (= fairly, to some degree) is used in **favourable comments**. *He's **quite** good at tennis.* **It is used before a/an**. *He's **quite** a successful businessman.* **Quite** (= completely) is used with adverbs, some verbs and adjectives such as: alone, amazing, brilliant, certain, dead, dreadful, different, exhausted, extraordinary, false, horrible, impossible, perfect, ridiculous, right, sure, true, useless etc. *It's **quite certain** he committed the crime. I'm **quite sure** he hasn't told us the truth.*
- **Rather** is used: a) in **unfavourable comments**. *She's **rather bad** at Maths.* b) in **favourable comments** meaning "to an unusual degree". *The meeting was **rather** interesting. (it was more interesting than we expected)* and c) with **comparative degree**. *She's **rather taller** than me.* **Rather** is used before or after **a/an**. *It's **a rather** cold day. It's **rather a** cold day.*
- **Fairly/Pretty** are synonymous with **quite** and **rather**. They can be used after **a**. *She's **a fairly/pretty** hard working person.*

78 *Underline the highlighted word(s) which can be used. In some sentences all words might be possible.*

1 Ann has four children, and they're all quite/rather/fairly/pretty well behaved.
2 That was quite/rather/fairly/pretty an interesting speech Jane gave. I was quite/rather/fairly/pretty impressed.
3 Life is quite/rather/fairly/pretty more difficult now than it was in the past.
4 It was quite/rather/fairly/pretty obvious that he was lying.
5 Ken is quite/rather/fairly/pretty a good painter and quite/rather/fairly/pretty imaginative too.
6 The supermarket stocks quite/rather/fairly/pretty a wide variety of imported products but they are quite/rather/fairly/pretty expensive.

7 It's quite/rather/fairly/pretty colder today than it was yesterday. Be quite/rather/fairly/pretty sure to dress up well.
8 She's quite/rather/fairly/pretty an arrogant woman. I find her quite/rather/fairly/pretty difficult to get on with.
9 Can we stop for a bite to eat soon? I'm feeling quite/rather/fairly/pretty hungry.
10 The exercise took quite/rather/fairly/pretty longer than I expected.
11 This exercise is quite/rather/fairly/pretty difficult but I'm quite/rather/fairly/pretty sure you can do it.
12 The journey takes quite/rather/fairly/pretty a long time but the ticket is quite/rather/fairly/pretty cheap.

Regular Comparative and Superlative Forms

Adjectives	Positive	Comparative	Superlative
of one syllable add -(e)r/-(e)st to form their comparative and superlative forms	tall close sad	taller (than) closer (than) sadder (than)	the tallest (of/in) the closest (of/in) the saddest (of/in)
of two syllables ending in -ly, -y, -w also add -er/-est	silly narrow	sillier (than) narrower (than)	the silliest (of/in) the narrowest (of/in)
of two or more syllables take more/most	modern beautiful	more modern (than) more beautiful (than)	the most modern (of/in) the most beautiful (of/in)

Note: clever, common, cruel, friendly, gentle, narrow, pleasant, polite, shallow, simple, stupid, quiet form their comparative and superlative forms with -er/-est or more/most.
narrow - narrower - narrowest. ALSO narrow - more narrow - most narrow

79 *Put the adjectives in brackets into the correct form.*

Kinsale may be one of **1)** ...*the smallest*... (small) towns in Southern Ireland but it's also one of **2)** .... (famous). It is well known for its **3)** .... (wonderful) fish restaurants. Some of **4)** .... (good) known chefs in the world have trained in the restaurants there. The town itself is one of **5)** .... (picturesque) in Southern Ireland. It's situated by the sea, which ensures that it is **6)** .... (cool) in the summer than other inland towns. A **7)** .... (huge) cathedral overlooks the town and it is one of **8)** .... (breathtaking) in the whole area. To the north of the town lies one of **9)** .... (high) mountain ranges in the country. The town is very **10)** .... (beautiful), with its many craft shops and narrow cobbled streets. Most tourists visit Kinsale for its fish restaurants, which are family owned. This means that the service there is **11)** .... (good) than in other restaurants. The staff are **12)** .... (welcoming) there than anywhere else. The food may be **13)** .... (expensive) but you'll have one of **14)** .... (pleasurable) evenings of your life there. So go ahead and visit Kinsale.

Adverbs	Positive	Comparative	Superlative
adverbs having the same forms as their adjectives add **-er/-est**	slow	slower	the slowest
early drops **-y** and adds **-ier/-iest**	early	earlier	the earliest
two syllable or compound adverbs take **more/most** (Compound adverbs are adjectives + **-ly.** *useful - usefully*)	often comfortably	**more** often **more** comfortably	the **most** often the **most** comfortably

Irregular Forms

Positive	Comparative	Superlative
good / well	better	best
bad / badly	worse	worst
much	more	most
many / a lot of	more	most
little	less	least
far	farther	farthest
far	further	furthest

Well is the adverb of **good**. *He is a good cook. He cooks* **well**.

a) **further/farther** (adv) = longer (in distance)
   His office is **further/farther** *away than mine.*
   further (adj) = more
   I need **further** *information on this.*
b) **very + positive degree** *I'm* **very** *happy in my job.*
c) **even/much/far/a bit + comparative degree**
   The working conditions were **even worse than we** *expected.*
d) **most + adj/adv of positive degree = very**
   She was waiting **most patiently** *to see the doctor.*
e) **any + comparative (used in negatives and questions)**
   Can't you drive **any** *faster?*

80 *Change the words in brackets into adverbs and put them into the correct form.*

Finally, a new washing powder that gets rid of stains **1)** ...*effectively*... (effective) and leaves your clothes **2)** .... (brilliant) white. New "All-bright" cleans **3)** .... (powerful) than any other product on the market. It gets the dirt out **4)** .... (quick) and **5)** .... (thorough) than any ordinary powder. Indeed, in no time at all new "All-bright" will be selling **6)** .... (good) than any other brand at your supermarket. With a prize-winning formula that has been researched **7)** .... (extensive) by our scientists than any other product, success is guaranteed. With new "All-bright" your money will go **8)** .... (far) than it's ever gone before. So pick up your box of new "All-bright" today!

81 *Underline the correct item.*

I am writing to request **1)** farther/<u>further</u> information on the climbing holidays you run. I am **2)** most/much interested in climbing, but fear that I will be **3)** most/much older than the other participants. Also, I am **4)** far/very less fit than I used to be. Nonetheless, I am **5)** even/very keener on the sport than ever. So my question is, will there be climbs which are **6)** a bit/most easier for older ones like me? In addition, do you do discounts for pensioners? Your holidays are **7)** very/even expensive for someone on a low income. I look forward to hearing from you and receiving **8)** any/more details.

Types of Comparisons

● **as ... (positive degree) ... as** **not so/as ... (positive degree) ... as** **such a(n)/so ...as**	*He is **as** handsome **as** everyone says he is!* *She **isn't as** tall **as** her sister.* *Mrs Jones is **not so** friendly **as** she looks.*
● **twice/three times etc/half as ... (positive degree) ... as**	*She puts **four times as** much sugar in her tea **as** me.* *If he was **half as** lucky **as** you, he'd be extremely rich.*
● **the same as**	*He has **the same** views **as** his father.*
● **look, sound, smell, taste + like**	*That dress **looks like** an old sack.*
● **less ... (positive degree) ... than** **the least ... (positive degree) ... of/in**	*This chocolate has **less** fat **than** that one but the Swiss chocolate **has the least** fat **of** all.*
● **the + comparative ..., the + comparative**	***The easier** the exam, **the higher** your marks will be.* ***The more** people who use buses, **the better** it is for the environment.*
● **comparative + and + comparative**	*It's getting **colder and colder** every day.*
● **prefer + -ing form/noun + to + -ing form/noun** (general preference)	*I **prefer** eating healthily **to** eating junk food.* *Men usually **prefer** beer **to** milk.*
● **would prefer + to-inf + rather than + inf without to** (specific preference)	*I **would prefer** to go swimming **rather than** watch television all day.*
● **would rather/sooner + inf without to + than + inf without to**	*I'd **rather** walk **than** drive.*
● **clause + whereas/while + clause** (comparison by contrast)	*This book says the battle was in 1066, **whereas** that book says it was in 1166.*

82 *Complete the sentences using the words in bold. Use two to five words.*

1 As he gets older, he seems to become more sensible.
  the   The older he becomes, ...*the more sensible*... he seems.
2 The students would rather start early than finish late.
  than   The students would prefer .... finish late.
3 Wouldn't you rather have juice than water?
  to   Wouldn't you .... water?
4 I spent half as much money as my brother.
  twice   My brother spent .... I did.
5 Riding a bike is easier than riding a horse.
  as   Riding a horse is .... a bike.

6 Wouldn't you prefer to come out instead of staying at home alone?

rather   Wouldn't you .... at home alone?

7 I didn't think it would be so difficult.

more   It was .... I thought.

8 This building is older than the church.

so   The church .... this building.

9 His job is getting more hectic all the time.

and   His job is .... all the time.

10 David and I have sent the same number of Christmas cards.

many   I have sent .... David.

11 I'd weigh a ton if I ate all you do.

as   If I ...., I'd weigh a ton.

12 The post office was nearer than we thought.

far   The post office .... we thought.

13 If you work hard, the exam will be easy.

the   The harder you work, ... will be.

14 The party will be better if many people come.

more   The ...., the better the party will be.

15 I would rather eat chocolate than apples.

eating   I prefer .... apples.

16 My husband likes a cooked breakfast but I prefer just toast.

whereas   I .... my husband likes a cooked breakfast.

17 Today I feel happier than ever.

as   I've never felt .... today.

18 That dress is a third of the cost of the blue one.

much   The blue dress is .... that one.

19 Chris finds mathematics easier than physics.

not   Physics is .... for Chris.

20 I'm sorry but this is the fastest I can go.

any   I'm sorry but I .... than this.

Like - As

- **Like is used: a) for similarities.** *She works like a slave. (she isn't a slave),* **b) after feel, look, smell, taste, sound + noun.** *It feels like velvet. It looks like Turner is going to win the race.* **and c) with nouns, pronouns or the -ing form to express similarity.** *It's like walking on a tightrope.*
- **As is used: a) to say what somebody or something really is (jobs/roles).** *She works as a clerk. (she's a clerk),* **b) after accept, be known, class, describe, refer to, regard, use.** *He's known as an expert on antiques.* **c) in the expressions: as usual, as ... as, as much, the same as.** *Certain items such as scissors, knives etc should be kept out of reach of children.* **and d) in clauses of manner to mean "in the way that".** *Do it as I showed you.*

83 *Fill in "as" or "like".*

1 Although it lives in the sea, the whale is classed ...*as*... a mammal. It may look *like*.. a dangerous beast, but it is really ..*as*.. gentle ..*as*.. a lamb.

2 My friend George describes himself ..*as*... a great singer. He thinks he has a voice *like*.. an angel, but when he sings it sounds *like*. a cat wailing! He works ..*as*.. a taxi driver and everybody keeps telling him not to give up his job!

3 McTaverty's Tavern has been described ...*as*... the best restaurant in Perthshire, with dishes that smell delicious and taste ..*like* they have been made with only the finest ingredients. Surprisingly, the prices are not ..*as*.. high ...*as*.. you might expect.

4 *Adjectives / Adverbs / Comparisons*

4 Majorie works ..*as*.. a criminal lawyer and is regarded *as*.. an expert in her field. She works extremely hard and at the end of a long day in court all she feels .*like*.. doing is collapsing in front of the TV.

5 If you want to go on a diet, do ..*as*... your doctor tells you. There are some foods such ..*as*.. vegetables which you can eat ..*as*... much of *as*... you want. Why not try soya meat? It tastes just *like*. real meat and can be used in the same way ..*as*.. mince, but is a low-fat food.

6 ..*As*. I was saying, you look exactly .*like*.. my cousin Hilary - you know, the one who works ..*as*... an air hostess.

7 Fred was known ..*as*.. an unpunctual person and ..*as*... usual, he was late again. After standing in the rain *like*. an idiot for half an hour, gradually getting wetter and wetter, I decided to go home before I began to look *like*. a drowned rat. – *otrzpiony sczuv to po PL mokra kura*

8 Howard and Hugh aren't related but they look almost exactly the same ..*as*. each other. They are referred to ..*as*.. "The Twins". When they walk into a room, it's *like* seeing double.

9 For ..*as*. long *as*.. I live, I'll never forget my first holiday in Hawaii. It was ..*like* paradise. I intend to return there ..*as*.soon ..*as*.. I can afford the air fare.

10 Trying to make sense of the written word is a bit *like*. being lost in a forest: all the trees look the same, just ..*as*. for a young child all the words look the same ..*as*.. each other.

In Other Words

- Kate is more intelligent than Ruth.
  Ruth isn't as intelligent as Kate (is).
  Ruth is less intelligent than Kate.
- I've never seen such a cute baby.
  It's the cutest baby I've ever seen.
- As he gets richer, he becomes more selfish.
  The richer he gets, the more selfish he becomes.
- He's the best dancer of all.
  No one else dances as well as he does.
  He dances better than any other dancer.
  He's a better dancer than anyone else.
  He's better than any other dancer.

- Can't you find a faster car than this?
  Is this the fastest car you can find?
- I prefer (eating) olives to (eating) pickles.
  I like olives more than pickles.
  I'd prefer to eat olives rather than (eat) pickles.
  I'd rather eat olives than pickles.
- He's a good basketball player.
  He plays basketball well.
- Ann is very motherly to her child.
  Ann behaves in a motherly way to her child.
- That shirt is similar to this one.
  That shirt and this one are alike.

84 *Complete the sentences using the words in bold. Use two to five words.*

1 Samantha is prettier than Julia.
as   Julia ...*is not as pretty as*... Samantha.

2 He's the most amusing person I've ever met.
than   He is .... I've ever met.

3 John can be a very good cook when he is in the right mood.
well   John .... when he is in the right mood.

4 As I get older, I become happier.
the   The .... I become.

5 Why didn't you find a cheaper restaurant?
cheapest   Is this .... you could find?

6 Laura has been a professional dancer for five years.
professionally   Laura .... for five years.

7 Caroline is the meanest woman I've ever met.
never   I've .... woman as Caroline.

8 We have got the same number of brothers.
many   I have got .... you.

9 Charlotte and Elizabeth look very much alike.
   similar   Charlotte .... Elizabeth.
10 Doctor Doyle is caring to all her patients.
   way   Doctor Doyle .... to all her patients.
11 We've never had such a wonderful holiday.
   most   This is ......the....most... we've ever had.
12 He plays snooker very well.
   good   He ....is....a....very.....good....sn.. snooker player.
13 Tracy eats more cheese than I do.
   less   I ....eat....less....cheese.........less............................ Tracy does.
14 He likes reading more than watching TV.
   rather   He ......prefer.to.read.........rather....than.......................... watch TV.
15 Jane is more artistic than I am.
   less   I .... Jane.

                 PREFER DOING STH TO DOING STH ELSE
                 PREFER TO DO RATHER THAN DO STH ELSE.

85 *Find the word which should not be in the sentence.*

1 The lions are noble animals.
2 The author's latest novel wasn't any more better than his previous one.
3 Your version of the incident is as very confusing as Peter's.
4 This soup tastes like as porridge.
5 They hardly not understood where all their money had gone.
6 I'd sooner than go now.   S - RAT
7 I always feel more safer when I'm wearing a seat-belt.
8 His offer was many more generous than we had expected.
9 Your behaviour is getting the worse and worse.
10 She prefers wholemeal bread than to white bread.   PFENOZIARNISIY
11 Their car cost three times as much more as ours.
12 He is known as like "the living legend" of his time.
13 I'd rather buy a second-hand car than to spend so much on a new one.
14 It was the most best offer I could ever have had.
15 Your sofa is much similar to the one in my living room.

1	The
2	MORE
3	VERY
4	AS
5	NOT
6	THAN
7	MORE
8	MANY
9	THE
10	THAN
11	MORE
12	LIKE
13	TO
14	MOST
15	MUCH

Oral Development 4

Look at the pictures below, then talk about the animals using comparative and superlative forms. Use the suggestions given as well as your own ideas.

expensive to feed, intelligent, difficult, friendly, beautiful, useful, good companion etc.

eg. A goat is less expensive to feed than a chimpanzee.

86 *Look at Appendix 2, then fill in the correct particle(s).*

1 The death penalty should be **done** *away with*. .
2 The car **drew** .... at the side of the road.
3 You shouldn't spend all your money as you may need something to **fall** .... in the future.
4 It was after midnight when the train finally **drew** .... at the station.
5 If you **fall** .... your rent, you'll be evicted.
6 The soldiers **fell** .... the oncoming army and defeated them.
7 You shouldn't **do** .... your parents. They do care for you.
8 Joan is crying because she **fell** .... her best friend.
9 **Do** .... your shoe laces or you'll trip.
10 The house was so badly built that two walls **fell** .... after three months.
11 Peter went to the bank to **draw** .... £300 to pay for his new computer.
12 Our holiday plans **fell** .... due to lack of money.
13 When the man approached her, she **drew** .... in fear.
14 He wants to save up to buy a car so he'll have to **do** .... a holiday this year.
15 She **fell** .... his story and gave him all her money, only to find he was a conman.
16 After a long discussion she **fell** .... our plan.

87 *Look at Appendix 3, then fill in the correct preposition(s).*

1 She's experienced ...*in*... restoring paintings.
2 He was doubtful .... passing his physics tests.
3 The athlete failed .... his attempt to break the world record.
4 Tom failed .... pass his driving test for the fourth time.
5 London is famous .... its museums.
6 Mary found it difficult to cope .... two children and a full-time job.
7 Diane argued .... Sally .... who would do the ironing.
8 After such a hard winter we are all eager .... summer to come.
9 Now that Jane is 9, she is capable .... crossing the street on her own.
10 He didn't accept the job because he was dissatisfied .... the wages offered.
11 I don't think there is any excuse .... such bad behaviour.
12 The boss was furious .... me .... the mix-up in travel arrangements.
13 The receptionist had a little difficulty .... understanding the foreign tourist.
14 She is an expert .... cooking Japanese food.
15 Professor Davidson is an expert .... Sociology.
16 He's an expert .... this type of machinery.
17 She's an expert .... Greek history.
18 The memory of this computer is equal .... that one.
19 All the children are fond .... their new teacher.
20 She remained faithful .... her beliefs.
21 Most people believe that experiments .... animals should be stopped.
22 Everybody congratulated him .... his success.
23 This music is familiar .... me.
24 A literature student should be familiar .... Jane Austen's novels.
25 All the students were enthusiastic .... the school trip.
26 She was envious .... my diamond engagement ring.

88 *Complete the sentences using the words in bold. Use two to five words.*

1 I'm sure she is planning to quit her job.
   be   She ...*must be planning*... to quit her job.
2 I've never read such an exciting story.
   the   It's ...*the most exciting story*.................................I've ever read.
3 They seem to have a friendly relationship with each other.
   get   They seem .... each other.

4 Her mother doesn't like her working as a waitress.
   disapproves   Her mother .... as a waitress.
5 Perhaps they haven't told him the truth yet.
   may   They .... the truth yet.
6 She'll probably look for another flat.
   likely   She .... another flat.
7 He was so embarrassed that he couldn't think of anything to say.
   too   He was .... of anything to say.
8 I'll take care of this matter at once.
   see   I'll .... at once.
9 Martha is the most efficient typist in the office.
   as   No other typist in the office .... is.
10 He is proud of his collection of French impressionists.
   pride   He .... of French impressionists.
11 When did the earthquake happen?
   is   How long .... happened?
12 Train tickets aren't as expensive as plane tickets.
   less   Train tickets .... plane tickets.

89 *Complete the sentences below with a suitable word or words from the box, then explain the idioms.*

a brush	**brass**	**a bat**	**a feather**	**a church mouse**
life	**gold**	**a fiddle**	**clockwork**	**two peas in a pod**

1 Old Mr Higgins is as fit as ...*a fiddle*... . He still jogs ten miles every morning.
2 She gets up at six every morning as regular as ...... *CLOCK WORK* .
3 My suitcase feels as light as .... I must have forgotten to pack something.
4 I wouldn't take any notice of anything he says. He's as daft as ....
5 My dad is as blind as .... without his glasses.
6 I thought John was abroad, but he turned up at the meeting as large as ....
7 The twins are as alike as .... Nobody can tell them apart.
8 She marched to the front of the queue as bold as .... and demanded to be served at once.
9 The children were as good as .... I didn't hear a peep out of them all night.
10 Even though Mrs Kelly is as poor as .... she still gives money to charity regularly.

90 *Put a tick in the appropriate boxes.*

a.

	experience	a living	a prize	a salary	possession	weight	a game	sb's heart
win								
earn								
gain	✔							

b.

	life	a passport	disease	rumours	a road	the agony	a building
spread							
extend							
prolong	✔						

Practice Test 4 ....

For questions 1 - 15, read the text below and decide which word A, B, C or D best fits each space. There's an example at the beginning (0).

Water

Water is one of our most **(0)** ... resources; to **(1)** ... it simply, without water there would be no life. Unfortunately many of us seem to have **(2)** ... this fact, and as a result the world is **(3)** ... the danger of running **(4)** ... water. The actual **(5)** ... of water on earth has changed little since the time of the dinosaurs. The problem has been **(6)** ... by people's misuse of our water supply. This not only **(7)** ... that we have polluted our rivers and seas, but also that we are **(8)** ... a great deal of this precious resource. Unfortunately, the destruction of the rain forests has **(9)** ... this problem worse since much of the rain that falls is **(10)** ... because it runs off into the sea. The population of the earth is increasing daily, so it is vital that we **(11)** ... a solution to this problem before it is too late. The first step is to educate people, especially by reminding them of the **(12)** ... of water. For most of us it is available whenever we **(13)** ... it, whether to bathe in or to drink, so we seldom bother to think about it. People then need to be taught how to reuse or recycle water. One of the simplest ways of doing this is to reuse bath or shower water for **(14)** ... cleaning or watering the garden. Ponds which filter used water are also becoming popular. Whatever methods we might decide to use, we must **(15)** ... the worth of water and how we can conserve it.

	A	B	C	D			A	B	C	D
0	valid	precious	worthy	superior		**0**	☐	■	☐	☐
1	show	make	write	put		**1**	☐	☐	☐	☐
2	looked over	omitted	forgotten	missed		**2**	☐	☐	☐	☐
3	facing	witnessing	viewing	noticing		**3**	☐	☐	☐	☐
4	out of	into	off	away with		**4**	☐	☐	☐	☐
5	sum	total	number	amount		**5**	☐	☐	☐	☐
6	brought out	caused	done	happened		**6**	☐	☐	☐	☐
7	underlines	says	means	proves		**7**	☐	☐	☐	☐
8	exploiting	wasting	spending	throwing		**8**	☐	☐	☐	☐
9	caused	done	created	made		**9**	☐	☐	☐	☐
10	missed	fallen	lost	given up		**10**	☐	☐	☐	☐
11	recover	work	come up	find		**11**	☐	☐	☐	☐
12	value	cost	price	tag		**12**	☐	☐	☐	☐
13	ask	require	command	open		**13**	☐	☐	☐	☐
14	housing	household	housekeeping	housework		**14**	☐	☐	☐	☐
15	comprehend	estimate	perceive	realize		**15**	☐	☐	☐	☐

Part 2

For questions 16 - 30, read the text below and think of the word which best fits each space.
Use only one word in each space. Write your answers in the answer boxes provided.

Coping with Shyness

Shyness is a problem that is common **(0)** .... many people. In **(16)** ...., according to Mr Zimbardo, a distinguished psychologist at Stanford University, eight **(17)** .... of ten people are reported to **(18)** .... been shy at some **(19)** .... in their lives. Most people **(20)** .... have this condition, suffer feelings of discomfort and anxiety at the **(21)** .... of meeting others, especially at social gatherings **(22)** .... parties. Keeping away from such situations is not really a solution, of course, and if a shy person can manage to overcome their fears they **(23)** .... gain a feeling of self-satisfaction as **(24)** .... as improving their social life. However, if the case of shyness is severe, when important occasions are missed or a person's social, educational or professional life is affected, **(25)** .... the label "shyness" is inappropriate. **(26)** .... this stage, it is termed "social phobia". Those suffering **(27)** .... this condition are very often bright, talented and sensitive people. But feelings of social isolation, resulting **(28)** .... loneliness, can lead to additional problems **(29)** .... as alcohol abuse or addiction to medication. Fortunately, a number of treatments are available and come in the form of individual **(30)** .... group therapy and training. Therefore, a person who has social phobia has an excellent chance of recovery.

0	to	0
16		16
17		17
18		18
19		19
20		20
21		21
22		22
23		23
24		24
25		25
26		26
27		27
28		28
29		29
30		30

Part 3

For questions 31 - 40, complete the second sentence so that it has a similar meaning to the first sentence. Use the word given and other words to complete each sentence. You must use between two and five words. Do not change the word given. Write your answers in the answer boxes provided.

0 I'm sure it wasn't Jim who did it.
have
It .... Jim who did it.

0	*can't have been*	0 **0 1 2** ☐☐■

31 Debbie and Ann went to the same school.
as
Debbie went .... Ann did.

31		31 **0 1 2** ☐☐☐

32 Can't you think of a better excuse?
best
Is that .... think of?

32		32 **0 1 2** ☐☐☐

33 He was still looking for a solution when I left him.
search
He was still .... when I left him.

33		33 **0 1 2** ☐☐☐

34 She's decided to enter the beauty contest.
go
She's decided .... the beauty contest.

34		34 **0 1 2** ☐☐☐

35 They looked for a new nanny for a week.
spent
They .... for a new nanny.

35		35 **0 1 2** ☐☐☐

36 I'm sure he was trying to be kind.
been
He .... to be kind.

36		36 **0 1 2** ☐☐☐

37 They made everyone leave through the back exit.
was
Everyone .... through the back exit.

37		37 **0 1 2** ☐☐☐

38 I wonder if you know how I can reach her.
happen
Do .... how I can reach her?

38		38 **0 1 2** ☐☐☐

39 He hasn't worked for six months.
was
The last time .... six months ago.

39		39 **0 1 2** ☐☐☐

40 She speaks Spanish fluently.
a
She .... speaker.

40		40 **0 1 2** ☐☐☐

Part 4

For questions 41 - 55, read the text below and look carefully at each line. Some of the lines are correct and some have a word which should not be there. If a line is correct, put a tick (✔) by the number in the answer boxes provided. If a line has a word which should not be there, write the word in the answer boxes provided.

Flight Disaster

0	I had always been lucky with the holiday flights	**0** the ⬜ 0 ⬛
00	until I went on a package holiday to Hawaii. The	**00** ✓ ⬜ 00 ⬛
41	journey out to there was fine, but coming	**41** ⬜ 41 ⬜
42	back was a different story. To start it with, the return flight	**42** ⬜ 42 ⬜
43	was delayed in two days which was not really a problem	**43** ⬜ 43 ⬜
44	as I was having a good time. Unfortunately, when I finally	**44** ⬜ 44 ⬜
45	left from Honolulu, the capital, on the first part	**45** ⬜ 45 ⬜
46	of the journey, I landed in Los Angeles instead of	**46** ⬜ 46 ⬜
47	Chicago. I was taken off the plane and had to stay	**47** ⬜ 47 ⬜
48	all overnight in a hotel. The next day I got on a direct	**48** ⬜ 48 ⬜
49	flight to London, but only to end up in Minneapolis.	**49** ⬜ 49 ⬜
50	I got on another plane where a woman she began	**50** ⬜ 50 ⬜
51	to run around wildly and we all had to	**51** ⬜ 51 ⬜
52	leave off the plane because we thought she had	**52** ⬜ 52 ⬜
53	a bomb. Then there was a storm, so we landed	**53** ⬜ 53 ⬜
54	in Boston. I finally got to home, but without one	**54** ⬜ 54 ⬜
55	suitcase which was been lost somewhere en route.	**55** ⬜ 55 ⬜

Part 5

For questions 56 - 65, read the text below. Use the word given in capitals at the end of each line to form a word that fits in the space in the same line. Write your word in the answer boxes provided.

Good News for Baldies

Finnish **(0)** .... believe they have discovered a **SCIENCE**
(56) .... substance that helps hair growth. Although **NATURE**
not a medical condition, baldness has **(57)** .... **REPEAT**
attracted promises of cures, most of them false.
But this new formula has proved particularly
(58) .... . The treatment was discovered accidental- **SUCCESS**
ly and involves a **(59)** .... of tablets and the **COMBINE**
(60) .... of a lotion on the affected areas. The **APPLY**
(61) .... of the product have made **MANUFACTURE**
(62) .... to the effect that the preparation may **SUGGEST**
correct a vitamin **(63)** .... . However, there is no **DEFICIENT**
(64) .... evidence to back up such a claim. Longer **DEFINE**
trials need to be done to provide **(65)** .... that this **PROVE**
cure really works.

0	scientists	⬜ 0 ⬛
56		⬜ 56 ⬜
57		⬜ 57 ⬜
58		⬜ 58 ⬜
59		⬜ 59 ⬜
60		⬜ 60 ⬜
61		⬜ 61 ⬜
62		⬜ 62 ⬜
63		⬜ 63 ⬜
64		⬜ 64 ⬜
65		⬜ 65 ⬜

1 Pre-Test

A *Choose the correct item.*

1 He greeted us and went on .... for the delay.
A **have apologised**   C **to apologise**
B **apologise**   D **apologising**

2 Sheila stopped .... the medicine, as it wasn't doing any good.
A **to take**   C **take**
B **have taken**   D **taking**

3 I don't look .... my mother at all.
A **as**   C **alike**
B **similar** D **like**

4 He was made .... the name of his accessory.
A **revealing**   C **to reveal**
B **having revealed** D **reveal**

5 It's .... cold today to go surfing.
A **much** C **very**
B **far**   D **too**

6 I'd rather buy a silk dress .... a cotton one.
A **of**   C **than**
B **from** D **rather than**

7 The more carefully you read, ... you'll understand the book.
A **the better** C **the best**
B **best**   D **better**

8 Mr Smith is as fit as a .... despite his age.
A **bat**   C **fiddle**
B **glove** D **hat**

9 Is it worth .... so much money on space travel?
A **have spent** C **spend**
B **to spend**   D **spending**

10 We saw a great film at the cinema two weeks ....
A **yet** C **before**
B **ago** D **still**

11 I regret .... you that you haven't passed.
A **informing**   C **inform**
B **have informed** D **to inform**

12 Do you fancy .... a pizza tonight?
A **to order**   C **ordering**
B **have ordered**   D **order**

13 My exam results are nearly the same .... yours, that's a real coincidence.
A **as** C **of**
B **in** D **like**

14 Most children prefer watching TV .... reading a book.
A **to**   C **from**
B **but** D **than**

15 She would prefer to go out .... stay at home.
A **of**   C **from**
B **rather than** D **to**

16 The little girl admitted .... some sweets from the shop.
A **take**   C **to take**
B **to having taken** D **taken**

17 She was dissatisfied .... her exam results.
A **from** C **of**
B **with** D **about**

18 Don't forget to congratulate Robin .... passing her driving test.
A **on**   C **of**
B **about** D **in**

19 She hasn't enrolled for the course ....
A **until** C **already**
B **yet**   D **still**

20 Brian hates ....; he likes swimming instead.
A **to jog**   C **jogging**
B **to jogging** D **been jogging**

21 It was .... an uninspiring speech and we were very disappointed.
A **fairly** C **very**
B **rather** D **pretty**

22 I'd sooner .... to university than get a job.
A **to go** C **having gone**
B **go**   D **going**

23 My father objects .... my mother with the housework.
A **to help** C **have helped**
B **help**   D **to helping**

24 The journey was .... longer than I thought it would be.
A **farther** C **very**
B **any**   D **even**

B **Put the verbs in brackets into the correct tense.**

My father was very pleased when he **1)** .... (buy) this house because he **2)** .... (always/want) to own a house by the sea. My parents **3)** .... (live) here for twenty years now and they **4)** .... (never/regret) leaving the city. I **5)** .... (stay) here at the moment because I **6)** .... (need) some sea air. It's wonderful. I **7)** .... (walk) on the beach every day. I'm sure I **8)** .... (be) sad to leave this earthly paradise.

C **Put the verbs in brackets into the correct tense.**

Next month John **1)** .... (start) a new job. He **2)** .... (decide) to leave his old job when his aunt, who **3)** .... (own) a company, asked him to join her. He is sure that he **4)** .... (enjoy) the new job as he **5)** .... (always/want) to work in business. At the moment he **6)** .... (go) through the company files so he can learn as much as possible. He **7)** .... (work) next to an experienced accountant for the first two weeks. He hopes he will not let his aunt down as he **8)** .... (not/work) in a similar post before.

D **Complete the sentences using the words in bold. Use two to five words.**

1 Shall I bring your meal now?
   me   Would .... bring your meal now?
2 It is forbidden to walk on the grass.
   must   You .... the grass.
3 His wife is the loveliest woman I've ever met.
   never   I .... lovely woman as his wife.
4 She hasn't been to the gym for six months.
   last   The .... to the gym was six months ago.
5 It was hard for him to hear you as he was standing so far away.
   found   He .... hear you as he was standing so far away.
6 Bob hasn't got his results yet.
   still   Bob .... his results.
7 Barbara hasn't had a break for six hours.
   since   It's .... a break.
8 Could you open the window?
   mind   Would .... the window?
9 It was her intention to come but she had some important business to attend to.
   going   She .... but she had some important business to attend to.
10 She is likely to be at work.
   will   It is .... at work.
11 Johnnie is the nicest man I've ever met.
   anyone   Johnnie .... I've ever met.
12 He found the strenuous work tiring.
   was   He .... the strenuous work.
13 They were about to leave when the phone rang.
   point   They were .... when the phone rang.
14 The policeman let the prisoner make one phone call.
   was   The prisoner .... one phone call.
15 His jokes were so amusing that we laughed for hours.
   were   We .... his jokes that we laughed for hours.
16 Mike finds working on a word processor difficult.
   used   Mike .... on a word processor.
17 Your watch and mine look very much alike.
   similar   Your .... mine.
18 Jenny spent more than was necessary on Bill's wedding present.
   have   Jenny .... so much on Bill's wedding present.

19 I'm sure the Smiths are on holiday this week.
   must   The Smiths .... this week.
20 I'm sure he didn't forget to invite them.
   have   He .... to invite them.

E *Fill in the correct particle(s).*

1 It is not nice to do people .... when they can't defend themselves.
2 The woman was brought .... by having water splashed on her face.
3 An epidemic of measles has broken .... at the local primary school.
4 Several villages were cut .... by the deep snow.
5 This situation calls .... immediate action.
6 *Sleeping Beauty* will be .... at the Theatre Royal for three weeks.
7 If we fall .... the rent, the landlord has the right to evict us.
8 He bought a mansion after he came .... a lot of money.

F *Fill in the correct preposition(s).*

1 We took advantage .... the fine weather and went for a picnic.
2 She's always dreamed .... becoming a famous singer.
3 English people always comment .... the weather. It's in their nature.
4 My boss has given me more work than I can cope ....
5 Demand .... sugar has fallen dramatically over the past decade.
6 The government has no choice but to comply .... the workers' demands.
7 The school boy put the blame .... his friend so he wouldn't be punished.
8 Rio de Janeiro is famous .... its carnival which takes place every February.

G *Correct the following sentences by taking out the inappropriate word.*

1 The car who they had rented broke down after half an hour.
2 Tom has two brothers as the well as three sisters.
3 My aunt she has lived in America for the past ten years.
4 This car cost to my parents a lot.
5 My school it is so far away that I have to travel two hours to get there.
6 Sharon did has met many famous film stars.
7 He likes driving a second hand cars.
8 Since she got married, Judy is the most happiest person I know.
9 He has an uncle who he likes fishing.
10 Jack thought of the film was boring, but I enjoyed it.
11 The hotel is furnished with antiques which they have been restored.
12 Mary's parents did took her to the zoo for her birthday.

1	
2	
3	
4	
5	
6	
7	
8	
9	
10	
11	
12	

H *Fill in the correct word derived from the words in bold.*

1 Drivers should drive slowly in bad weather, ... if there is fog.   **PARTICULAR**
2 Mr Travers is retiring after a .... career in advertising.   **SUCCESS**
3 Traffic jams are almost .... during the rush hour.   **AVOID**
4 The .... of the new office block will be in central London.   **LOCATE**
5 The refugees fled the country with all their .... in a single suitcase.   **POSSESS**
6 A new .... has been formed to combat air pollution.   **ORGANISE**
7 The .... of her name from the list was an unexpected shock.   **REMOVE**
8 John's father .... won't let him use the car again after he crashed it.   **CERTAIN**
9 His job is very .... as it involves a lot of responsibility.   **STRESS**
10 Everyone at the meeting made .... about how to raise money.   **SUGGEST**
11 My grandfather was born in a .... village high in the mountains.   **DISTANCE**
12 Because there was no ...., the suspect was found not guilty.   **PROVE**

Sentences can consist of main and subordinate clauses. Subordinate clauses can be: a) **noun clauses** (*I suppose **that he'll be back in an hour.***), b) **relative clauses** (*I saw the man **who stole your ring.***) and c) **adverbial clauses** i.e. clauses of manner, time, place, reason, concession, purpose, result, comparison, condition (***Although she is well-trained,*** *she didn't get the job.*).

Relative Clauses

They are introduced by: a) relative pronouns i.e. **who, whom, whose, which, that** or b) relative adverbs i.e. **when, where, why.**

Relative Pronouns

	Subject of the verb of the relative clause (cannot be omitted)	Object of the verb of the relative clause (can be omitted)	Possession (cannot be omitted)
used for people	who/that *That's the girl **who/that** lives next door.*	who/whom/that *The boy **(who/whom/that)** he waved to is my cousin.*	whose *That's the man **whose** wife was killed in an accident.*
used for things/ animals	which/that *I saw a film **which/that** was directed by Polanski.*	which/that *The dog **(which/that)** you saw outside is my neighbour's.*	whose/of which *That's the table the leg **of which/whose** leg is broken.*

- **Whom, which, whose** can be used in expressions of quantity with **of** (some of, many of, half of etc)
  *She received a lot of presents for her birthday. Most of them were from her family. She received a lot of presents for her birthday, **most of which** were from her family.*
- **That** can be used instead of **who, whom** or **which** but it is never used after commas or prepositions.
  *She's the girl **who/that** got a very good degree. The girl in the back, **who** is sitting next to Mary, is my niece.* ("that" is not possible)

Relative Adverbs

Time	**when** (= in/on/at which)	*1995 was the year **(when)** I finished my studies.*
Place	**where** (= in/at/on/to which)	*That's the place **(where)** we went last week.*
Reason	**why** (= for which)	*That's the reason **(why)** I moved house.*

 91 *Fill in: where, whose, who, which, when and why.*

Buying a present for someone is often a tricky business. The first thing **1)** ...*(which)*... you have to decide is what to buy and the shop **2)** .... you should go to buy it. Then you might want to buy a joint present with a friend, so you have to find a time **3)** .... you are both free. It is probably most difficult buying a present for someone **4)** .... you don't know very well and **5)** .... tastes you know little about. You have to try to find something **6)** .... you think they would like. However, it is also no easy job buying a present for a close member of your family, such as your

mother. I never know what excuse to tell my mother when I go out. I can't tell her the reason **7)** .... I'm going out because I want to surprise her on the big day. Still, it is worth all the trouble just to see the look of pleasure on someone's face the moment **8)** .... they receive your gift.

92 *Fill in: who, which, whose, when, where or why.*

1993 was the year **1)** ...*(when)*... I took my first holiday abroad. We were students at the time, with very little money, which is the reason **2)** .... we decided to go to Spain. We booked through the local travel agent, **3)** .... went to a lot of trouble to find us a resort **4)** .... was quiet by day but **5)** .... had a lively night life. I went with my friend Cynthia, **6)** .... has been my friend for nearly six years now. The flight to Malaga, **7)** .... took over five hours, was very comfortable. Cynthia, **8)** .... was a little nervous, was comforted by an air stewardess **9)** .... was very courteous and helpful. The hotel **10)** .... we stayed was just a 10-minute walk from the centre. It had a swimming pool and a gym **11)** .... we used every morning. We spent the first day of our holiday on the beach, **12)** .... was beautiful. Unfortunately, when we got back to the hotel that night my friend, **13)** .... skin is very pale, realised that she had got badly burned. The suncream **14)** .... she had applied was simply not strong enough. I explained the situation to the hotel manager, **15)** .... was very helpful. He telephoned the local doctor, **16)** .... arrived shortly afterwards. He advised my friend to stay in bed for at least three days. After these three days, my friend, **17)** .... had fully recovered, was ready to go out for the evening. We found a lovely restaurant **18)** .... we tried some local dishes. We had a great time for the rest of our holiday. We found some very good discos **19)** .... we spent many of our evenings. We also went to some places **20)** .... had live Spanish music. We made some good friends **21)** .... we are still in contact with. Cynthia has learned her lesson, too. Whenever we go on holiday in a country **22)** .... climate is hotter than ours, she remembers to bring a high factor suncream with her.

Prepositions in Relative Clauses

We do not normally use prepositions before relative pronouns.
*The office **in which** she works is in the town centre. (formal - not usual)*
*The office **which** she works **in** is in the town centre. (usual)*
*The office she works **in** is in the town centre. (more usual)*

93 *Rewrite the sentences in as many ways as possible.*

1   The hotel where we stayed was in the mountains.
   ...*The hotel in which we stayed was in the mountains*....
   ...*The hotel we stayed in was in the mountains*....
2   That's the box where we keep the books.
   ....
   ....

3   The girl to whom John was talking is my sister.
   ....
   ....
4   The house where I spent my childhood has been demolished.
   ....
   ....
5   That's the man to whom he spoke on the day of the murder.
   ....
   ....
6   The friend I was travelling with spoke German.
   ....
   ....

Defining / Non-defining Relative Clauses

- A **defining relative clause** gives necessary information and is essential to the meaning of the main clause. It is not put between commas. *People **who drive carelessly** should be banned from the roads.*
- A **non-defining relative clause** gives extra information which is not essential to the meaning of the main clause. It is put between commas. *Mr Jones, **who helps me with the garden** , was taken to hospital last night.*
  Note how the commas change the meaning of a sentence. *The players, who were involved in the fight, were sent off the pitch. (All the players were sent off.) The players who were involved in the fight were sent off the pitch. (Only the players who were involved in the fight were sent off.)*

94 *Fill in the relative pronoun, adding commas where necessary. Write D for defining, ND for non-defining and whether the relative can be omitted or not.*

1 The woman ...*who/that*... bought the house next door is very friendly. ..*D*.. ....*not omitted*.....
2 Ann .... is a generous person took us all on holiday. ....
3 The hospital .... he was treated is a very good one. ....
4 People .... don't eat meat are called vegetarians. ....
5 The house .... they live is very small. ....
6 The book .... I am reading at the moment is very interesting. ....
7 The hotel .... is opposite the museum is very expensive. ....
8 People .... speak two languages equally well are called bilingual. ....
9 Dublin .... has a population of one million is a very beautiful city. ....
10 People .... mug other people should be punished. ....
11 My best friend .... name is Sarah is living in Poland now. ....
12 Greece .... has many beautiful islands is a great place for holidays. ....
13 People .... drink and drive should be heavily fined. ....
14 Women .... are pregnant should not smoke. ....
15 The flat .... she lives in is very cold. ....
16 Majorca was the first place .... we went on holiday together. ....
17 The man .... the police arrested last night was charged with murder. ....
18 The newspaper .... I buy is always full of interesting articles. ....
19 The velvet dress .... she wore to the party was very expensive. ....
20 The students .... were involved in the march were arrested. ....

95 *Combine the following sentences using relatives.*

1 This is the house. Shakespeare lived here.
  ...*This is the house where Shakespeare lived*....
2 She bought a new dress. She wore it to my party. ....
3 That's the woman. She won the lottery last week. ....
4 This is the vase. He bought it at an auction. ....
5 My friend has a new cat. Its name is Riley. ....
6 This is the cinema. It was built in 1945. ....
7 This is Mary. I'm sharing a flat with her. ....
8 The cheque only arrived today. He posted it last week. ....
9 I'm reading *Wuthering Heights*. It was written by Emily Brontë. ....
10 Paul's new car has broken down. This car cost him £10,000. ....
11 Here's a photograph of the hotel. We stayed there last summer. ....

In Other Words

- That's the village I grew up in.
  That's the village where I grew up.
  That's the village which I grew up in.
- March is the month when she was born.
  March is the month in which she was born.
- I've got some letters; two of them are yours.
  I've got some letters, two of which are yours.
- We missed most of the film, which was a pity.
  It was a pity that we missed most of the film.

- This is Joan; her son is a footballer.
  This is Joan whose son is a footballer.
- That woman helped me find the way.
  That's the woman who helped me find the way.
- They released some men; three of them are Polish.
  They released some men, three of whom are Polish.

96 *Complete the sentences using the words in bold. Use two to five words.*

1 We met many people on holiday - many of them were from England.
   whom   We met many people ...*on holiday, many of whom*... were from England.
2 That customer refused to pay his bill.
   who   That's .... pay his bill.
3 We went to a very expensive restaurant.
   which   The restaurant .... was very expensive.
4 We had some visitors - three of them were Chinese.
   whom   We had some visitors, ... Chinese.
5 Many tourists stay at Jury's Hotel.
   where   Jury's Hotel .... stay.
6 Members of the AA can ring this number when their cars break down.
   whose   Members of the AA .... ring this number.
7 There are eighty people working here - many of them are Irish.
   whom   There are eighty people .... are Irish.
8 I lost my favourite earrings, which is a pity.
   that   It is .... my favourite earrings.
9 My twenty-three year old brother is in India.
   who   My brother .... in India.
10 Matthew, with whom I went out, is from Wales.
   who   Matthew, ..., is from Wales.

Clauses of Manner

- **Clauses of manner are introduced by: as if/as though (after act, appear, be, behave, feel, look, seem, smell, sound, taste), as, how, (in) the way, (in) the way that, the way in which, (in) the same way, (in) the same way as.** *Try to do it as I showed you.*
- **In clauses of manner introduced with as if/as though we can use were instead of was in all persons in formal English.** *She acts as if she were/was in charge of the project.*
  Note how the tense forms are used after as if/as though:
- **as if/as though + any tense form (showing probability/similarity - how sb/sth seems)**
  She feels as if she has got a temperature. (She may have a temperature.) She sounded as if she had a cold. (She may have had a cold.)
- **as if/as though + Past Simple/Past Continuous (unreal in the present)** *She acts as if she knew everything. (but she doesn't)*
- **as if/as though + Past Perfect (unreal in the past)** *She felt as if they had misjudged her. (but they hadn't)*

97 *Put the verbs in brackets into the correct tense.*

1 He talked about Denmark as though he ...*had been*... (be) there but we know he never has.
2 She looks as if she .... (be) really ill.
3 It looks as though it .... (rain).
4 She behaves as if she .... (be) in trouble.
5 The weather here is so bad, it looks as though we .... (have to) holiday abroad.
6 It smells as if you .... (put) lots of herbs in the stew.
7 Maeve looked as though she .... (have) little sleep the night before, but she had gone to bed quite early.
8 When he speaks, it sounds as if English .... (not/be) his first language.
9 She spoke about university as though she .... (spend) years there but in fact she'd only spent a month there.
10 I spoke to Simon last night and he sounded as though he .... (be) really upset about something.
11 She sounded as if she .... (be) French.
12 This sauce tastes as if you .... (put) too much pepper in it.
13 My sister isn't rich but she spends money as though she .... (have) loads of it.
14 She acts as though she .... (be) very confident, but in fact she's quite shy.
15 She treats me as though I .... (be) her child.
16 He talks about karate as if he .... (have) a black belt but we know he's only just started lessons.
17 Little Tommy was trembling as though he .... (see) a ghost.
18 She behaved as if nothing .... (happen).
19 When Moira broke off their relationship, John behaved as if the world .... (end).
20 That woman looks as though she .... (faint). Bring her some water.

Copenhagen - Denmark

98 *Complete the sentences using the words in bold. Use two to five words.*

1 Someone must have used too much garlic in the sauce.
 if   The sauce tasted ...*as if someone had used*... too much garlic.
2 You look like you need a holiday.
 if   You look .... a holiday.
3 He seems to have lost weight since I last saw him.
 as   He looks .... weight since I last saw him.
4 She had a feeling she had met Gary before.
 though She felt .... Gary before.
5 She behaves like a beauty queen.
 as   She behaves .... a beauty queen.
6 She seems to need a rest.
 if   She looks .... a rest.
7 I mowed the lawn as he had told me to.
 way   I mowed the lawn .... told me to.
8 She isn't rich but she acts like a millionairess.
 if   She acts .... a millionairess.
9 I taught the class as she had instructed me to.
 way   I taught the class .... instructed me to.
10 My grandfather seems to have got much thinner since I last saw him.
 as   My grandfather looks .... much thinner since I last saw him.
11 I polished the silver like she told me to.
 way   I polished .... told me to.
12 He orders me like his slave.
 as   He orders .... his slave.

Clauses of Time

- Clauses of time are introduced by: **after, as, as long as, as soon as, before, by the time** (= before, not later than), **every time, immediately, just as, once, the moment (that), until/till** (= up to the time when), **when, while** etc. *The castaway had to wait five years **until** he was rescued.*
- Clauses of time follow the rule of the sequence of tenses; that is, when the verb of the main clause is in a present or future form, the verb of the time clause is in the present form, and when the verb of the main clause is in a past form, the verb of the time clause is in a past form too. Note that **will/would** are never used in a clause of time. *I'll cook dinner as soon as I**'ve finished** washing up. (not: as soon as I will finish) She **left** her job **as soon as** she **got** married. (not: as soon as she gots)*
- When the time clause precedes the main clause, a comma is used. When the time clause follows, no comma is used. *By the time he arrived, she had left.* but: *She had left by the time he arrived.*

99 *Underline the appropriate time phrase and put the verbs into the correct tense.*

Dear Friend,

The World Wildlife Fund is currently launching its most important campaign ever to help protect our vanishing species of wildlife from extinction. 1) (Before/As soon as) the turn of the century there 2) .... (be) more than 40,000 tigers in India, while now there are around 3,750. 3) (Before/Until) twenty years ago the numbers of Black Rhinos 4) .... (exceed) 60,000. Now, less than 2,500 remain. 5) (As long as/As soon as) animal habitats continue to be burned, polluted and destroyed, species 6) .... (continue) to disappear. 7) (While/When) there 8) .... (be) still a demand for illegal rhino horns and tiger bones, the hunting of wildlife will continue. 9) (By the time/Every time) people 10) .... (become) aware of the situation, it may be too late. We must act now 11) (before/until) these animals 12) .... (disappear) forever. That's why WWF is urging all governments to get tough on illegal traders. 13) (Every time/While) a crime against wildlife 14) .... (be/exposed), we are one step closer to our goal. If, like me, you believe that we must do all we can to stop this destruction, join the fight today and support the WWF campaign. Your gift will go directly to our vanishing species programme. Please support this crucial work. WWF can't fight alone.

- **When (time conjunction) + present tense.** *When I **arrive**, I'll call you.*
  When (question word) + will/would. *When **will he arrive**?*
- **When is used for things which are sure to happen.** *When he gets promoted, he'll be given more money.*
  If is used for things which may happen. *If he works hard, he'll be promoted.*

100 *Fill in "if" or "when" and put the verbs in brackets into the correct tense.*

1 I will visit you ...*when*... I ...*finish*... (finish) work today.
2 The aeroplane will take off without us .... we .... (arrive) late at the airport.
3 .... you .... (not/reach) a decision yet, I'll call back tomorrow.
4 .... (you/finish) this report?
5 .... John .... (return) from work, we can go shopping.
6 .... Jack .... (ring) while I am out, tell him to be here at 12.00.
7 .... I .... (be) ready, I'll give you a call.
8 .... we can't come up with the money soon, the deal .... (fall through).
9 .... the star .... (arrive) at the hotel, she will be greeted by crowds of fans.
10 .... (you/stop) lying about your age?

101 *Complete the sentences in any meaningful way using an appropriate time word.*

1 The shop had closed ...*before/by the time they got there*....
2 She went into the classroom ....
3 The baby cried for its mother ....
4 I recognised him ....
5 The cake must be left to cool down ....
6 I will meet you ....
7 She couldn't walk properly ....
8 I want to see you ....

Clauses of Place

Clauses of place are introduced by: where, wherever, everywhere, anywhere etc. *She'll follow him* **wherever** *he goes.* **Will/Would are never used in clauses of place.** *Everywhere Joan* **goes** *she gets into trouble. (not: Everywhere Joan will go...)*

102 *Fill in: where, wherever, everywhere or anywhere.*

1 ...*Wherever/Everywhere*... I looked, people were dancing.
2 .... Ruth goes, she always misses England.
3 Now that Hilary has a car she can go .... she wants.
4 David tends to be happy .... he is living.
5 I don't mind .... we go to eat, as long as it's cheap.
6 Have you seen my watch .... in the house?
7 You can see these advertisements .... you go.
8 I couldn't find a parking space .... close to the office.

Clauses of Reason

- **Clauses of reason are introduced by: as, because, for, on the grounds that, the reason for, the reason (why) etc.** *As they had no money to buy a ticket, they hitchhiked.*
- **Because usually answers a why-question.** *"Why didn't you invite him?" "**Because** I don't like him."* **For (= because) always comes after a comma in written speech or a pause in oral speech.** *I didn't invite him,* **for** *I don't like him. (very formal)*
- **Because of/Due to + noun/-ing form.** *Because of the train strike, no one could get to work last Tuesday.* **Because of/Due to + the fact that ... Due to the fact that** *he had no money, he was unable to buy any Christmas presents.*

103 *Join the sentences using the words in brackets.*

1 It was raining. The match was called off. (due to) ...*Due to the rain, the match was called off*....
2 He left her. He couldn't put up with her complaints. (for) ....
3 We can't go on holiday. There's too much work to do. (since) ....
4 I can't come with you. I have to visit my uncle. (as)..
5 She made mistakes. She wasn't experienced. (because)..
6 I didn't know that she had been married. She seldom talks about herself. (since)
    ....
7 She took a break. She wasn't feeling well. (because) ....
8 She was soaked to the skin. It was raining very hard. (as) ....
9 He is in debt. He will have to reduce his spending a lot. (on the grounds that) ....
10 They turned back. They didn't want to get stuck in the traffic. (for) ....

Clauses of Result

- Clauses of result are introduced by: **that** (after **such/so ...**), **(and) as a result, (and) as a consequence, consequently, so** etc. *It was **such bad weather that** we stayed in.*
- **such a(n) + (adjective) + singular countable noun.** *He is **such a rude person that** nobody likes him.*
- **such + (adjective) + uncountable/plural noun.** *It was **such lovely scenery that** we took lots of photos.*
- **such + a lot of + noun.** *There were **such a lot of people** on the train **that** we couldn't get on.*
- **so + adjective/adverb.** *She drives **so carelessly that** she's bound to have an accident.*
- **so + few/little/many/much + noun.** *He had **so much luggage that** he couldn't carry it.*
- **so + adjective + a(n) + noun.** *It's **so hot a day that** everyone is going to the beach. (not usual)*
- **as a result/therefore/consequently/so + clause.** *The cinema was crowded **so we left**.*

104 *Fill in: so, such or such a(n).*

A few years ago, I spent my holiday on the Greek island of Santorini. I was **1)** ...so... worried about travelling alone that I became quite nervous. However, about five minutes after the ferry had left I met **2)** .... nice American couple that I stayed with them for the whole holiday. When we docked, we were pushed onto a bus that was filled with **3)** .... a lot of people that we felt as if we couldn't breathe. At the bus station there were **4)** .... many people waiting to offer us accommodation that we decided to ignore them, preferring to walk along the main road to find somewhere to stay ourselves. After an hour or so we started to think that not accepting any of the men's offers of accommodation had been **5)** .... bad idea that we decided to ask someone for help. We asked an old man if he knew of anywhere we could stay. He led us to a lovely little apartment on the edge of a cliff. It was **6)** .... gorgeous a flat, and the view was **7)** .... good that we took it immediately. We had brought **8)** .... few things with us, and it took us **9)** .... short time to unpack that we were on the famous black sand beach in no time. We had **10)** .... nice time together and we became **11)** .... good friends that we still keep in touch, sending letters and Christmas cards. This year Scott and Arianne are coming to Scotland to spend Christmas with me. It will be great to see them again.

105 *Rewrite the text using such/so ... that.*

There were <u>many people in the station. I was unable to</u> find the friend I had arranged to meet. It had also <u>been a long time since I'd seen her. I barely</u> remembered what she looked like. Then, suddenly I heard a familiar voice behind me. "Marilyn, is that really you?" Rachel smiled at me. "<u>It's been terribly long. I've got</u> an awful lot of things to tell you. Come on! Let's go somewhere for coffee." I took her to a lovely café I know. It was <u>a very nice day so we decided</u> to sit outside in the sun. <u>We had a lot to say to each other. We didn't notice</u> the time fly. We <u>used to spend a lot of time together.</u> I always knew what she was thinking. We had never kept secrets from each other. Now, she seemed happy enough, but <u>her eyes looked really sad. I was sure</u> that there was something she wasn't telling me. When I confronted her, she said that everything was fine. "Don't try to pretend, Rachel," I said. "We've been <u>very good friends for many years now. You can't possibly think</u> I can't tell that you're upset."

In Other Words

- She was so upset that she couldn't stop crying.
  She was too upset to stop crying.
- It's such a heavy box that I can't lift it.
  The box is too heavy for me to lift.
  It's so heavy a box that I can't lift it.
- No one knows the reason for his leaving.
  No one knows (the reason) why he left.

- He missed the train so he was late for the meeting.
  He missed the train and as a result/consequently /therefore he was late for the meeting.
- The workers went on strike because they weren't paid enough.
  The workers went on strike, for they weren't paid enough.

106 *Complete the sentences using the words in bold. Use two to five words.*

1 The town was so unfriendly that we left immediately.
  an It was ...*such an unfriendly town that*... we left immediately.
2 He couldn't eat the food because it was very spicy.
  for He couldn't eat .... very spicy.
3 Do you know the reason for her being so upset?
  why Do you .... upset?
4 It was such a lovely summer in England that we stayed at home.
  so It .... in England that we stayed at home.
5 The trip abroad was cancelled due to lack of interest.
  of The trip abroad was cancelled .... interest.
6 She was rushing to the office so she couldn't talk to me.
  consequently She was rushing to the office and .... to me.
7 It was such an interesting book that I stayed up all night to finish it.
  so It was .... I stayed up all night to finish it.
8 No one knows what caused his illness.
  why No one knows .... ill.
9 She lost her ticket so she had to buy another one.
  result She lost her ticket and .... to buy another one.

Oral Development 5

Use the notes below and your own ideas to talk about Jasmin Rogers. Try to link your ideas together using relative pronouns/adverbs, time words and words introducing clauses of reason, place or result.

Jasmin Rogers (Wales)

- was fascinated by the sea
- joined the National diving team
- keen on protecting endangered species
- participated in many expeditions
- hard working - gained her colleagues' respect
- found treasure on a ship - became famous
- no time for a husband and family

eg. Jasmin Rogers, who comes from Wales, was so fascinated ...

Expressing Purpose - Clauses of Purpose

Purpose is expressed with:

● to/in order to/so as to + inf	She is studying **to be** a doctor.
● so that + can/will (present/future reference)	We'll have an early night **so that** we **won't be** tired tomorrow.
● so that + could/would (past reference)	He employed a detective **so that** he **could** find the murderer.
● with a view to/with the aim of + -ing form	They started saving up **with a view to buying** a car.
● for + noun/-ing form	She bought some cream **for polishing** silver.
● in case + Present (present/future reference) ● in case + Past (past reference)	I'll phone him **in case** he**'s forgotten** the appointment. He took a torch **in case** there **was** no light in the attic.

Negative Purpose is normally expressed with:

● so as not/in order not + to -inf	They spoke in whispers **so as not to wake** the children.
● so that + can't/won't (present/future reference) ● so that + couldn't/wouldn't (past reference)	I'll invite her **so that** she **won't** feel lonely. They hid the letter **so that** he **wouldn't** find out the truth.
● for fear/lest + might/should ● for fear of sth/doing sth	They put on their life jackets **for fear** they **might** drown. He left his money in the hotel safe **for fear of losing** it.
● prevent + noun/pronoun + (from) + -ing form	They put up notices to **prevent people (from) walking** on the grass.
● avoid + -ing form	He took a map to **avoid getting** lost.

● **Clauses of purpose follow the rule of the sequence of tenses.** She **trains** every day **so that** she **can** enter the competition. She **trained** every day **so that** she **could** enter the competition.

107 *Join the sentence in as many ways as possible as in the example:*

1 We took some food. We might get hungry on the journey. ...*We took some food so that we ...... wouldn't get hungry on the journey. We took some food in case we got hungry on the journey. We took some food to avoid getting hungry on the journey. We took some food so as not to get hungry on the journey. etc...*

2 She studies hard. She wants to get a good job when she finishes university. ....
....

3 We flew direct to Rome. We didn't want to get stuck in London. ....
....

4 He has joined a gym. He wants to be healthy and fit for the summer. ....
....

5 She didn't go to town yesterday. She didn't want to spend any money. ....
....

108 *Join the sentences using the words in brackets.*

1 He's taking driving lessons. He wants to be able to drive to work. (so that)
...*He's taking driving lessons so that he'll be able to drive to work....*

2 She left her jewellery in a safe deposit box. It may be stolen. (fear) ....

3 The beekeeper put on a veil and helmet. He didn't want to be stung by the bees. (avoid) ....

4 She is on a strict diet. She wants to fit into her black dress for the party. (as) ....

5 He left home early. He wanted to be at the restaurant on time. (in order to) ....

6 I'll bring something for dessert. We may want to eat something sweet later. (in case)

....

7 This is a bread bin. You use it to keep bread fresh. (for) ....

8 I brought my umbrella. The weather forecast said it would rain later. (in case) ....

109 *Complete the sentences using the words in bold. Use two to five words.*

1 He had taken an anorak so he wouldn't get wet.
    avoid   He had taken an anorak ...*to avoid getting* ... wet.

2 Travellers are advised to take out insurance. Their luggage may go astray.
    case   Travellers are advised to take out insurance .... astray.

3 Lynn has just bought a new car. She plans to drive around Europe this summer.
    aim   Lynn bought a new car .... around Europe this summer.

4 There are ramps in the road so that motorists won't drive too fast.
    prevent   There are ramps in the road .... too fast.

5 John took up karate. He wanted to become fitter.
    view   John took up karate .... fitter.

6 I'll pack some juice for the picnic. We may be thirsty later.
    case   I'll pack some juice for the picnic .... later.

7 I went to the market early. I wanted to buy some fresh fish.
    in   I went to the market early .... some fresh fish.

8 This is a hammer. You use it to bang in nails.
    for   A hammer is .... nails.

9 Mary did her Christmas shopping early. She didn't want to do it on Christmas Eve.
    avoid   Mary did her Christmas shopping early .... on Christmas Eve.

10 Dennis is saving money. He wants to go to Australia.
    order   Dennis is saving money .... to Australia.

11 She started an art and design course last year. She plans to open her own business.
    view   She started an art and design course last year .... her own business.

110 *Fill in an appropriate purpose word and put the verbs into the correct form.*

Dear Sir/Madam,

    We have produced this information sheet **1)** ...*with a view*... to ...*making*... (make) the registration procedure easier for you. Read it carefully **2)** .... (familiarise) yourself with the procedure.

    Each faculty must register at a certain time so please do come on time **3)** .... (not/make) the process more difficult. You must report to the registrar's office **4)** .... (give) her your personal details. You must also bring your passport with you **5)** .... they .... (verify) these details. After this you must go to the main section **6)** .... (have) your photograph taken. You will then be given your student identification card which may be used **7)** .... (take out) books. We have included a map of the campus **8)** .... you .... (not/get) lost.

    We look forward to seeing you on registration day.

                               Yours faithfully,
                               Jane Smith

Clauses of Concession

Concession is expressed with:

- **Although/Even though/Though + clause.** *Although it snowed heavily*, he came to the meeting. **Though** can also be put at the end of the sentence. *It snowed heavily. He came to the meeting, **though**.*
- **Despite/In spite of + noun/-ing form. Despite his illness/being ill,** *he went to the party.*
- **Despite/In spite of the fact + that -clause. In spite of the fact that he was ill,** *he went to the party.*
- **while/whereas/but/on the other hand/yet + clause.** *He worked hard, **yet he failed to meet the deadline.***
- **nevertheless/however + clause.** *He has lots of experience; **however, he didn't get the job.***
- **However/No matter how + adj/adv + subject (+ may) + verb. However fast he runs,** *he can't beat Tom.*
- **adj/adv + though + subject + verb/(may + bare inf). Clever though he is,** *his laziness caused him to fail the exam. **Much though I may want it,** I can't afford a holiday this year.*
- **adj/adv + as + subject + verb. Skinny as he is,** *he eats a lot.*

A comma is used when the clause of concession either precedes or follows the main clause.
Even though he was tired, he went to the party. He went to the party, even though he was tired.

111 *Underline the correct item.*

1 Yet/No matter what he does to please her, she always finds something to complain about.
2 Although/However I set my alarm clock for 7.00 am, it didn't go off.
3 Despite/Even though the bad weather forecast, Susan and Jim went climbing.
4 She tries hard, although/yet she makes little progress.
5 Tom's wife drives better than he does, whereas/although he won't admit it.
6 Lots of people drive fast although/in spite of police warnings.
7 Bad mannered though/yet he is, he has got lots of friends.
8 She is a brilliant singer; while/nevertheless, she refuses to sing in public.
9 Rich as/even though they are, they never buy expensive things.
10 However/While much she denies it, she does dye her hair blonde.
11 She speaks Japanese fluently, yet/despite she has never visited the country.
12 In spite of/However all the bad publicity, the film became a box office success.
13 Janine turned up at the wedding even though/despite she wasn't invited.
14 However/Though hard he tries, he'll never outsmart Pat.
15 Much as/yet I admire her, I can't accept her point of view on this matter.
16 The northwest of the country gets a lot of rain whereas/as the east gets more snow.

112 *Fill in: although/though/even though, despite, while/whereas, but, however/no matter how, or nevertheless.*

Your Stars

"... And now for a quick look at what's in store for Librans this month. It may seem like all work and no play at the moment. **1)** ...*Nevertheless*..., if you apply yourself, you'll feel satisfied with a job well done. And don't worry! **2)** .... difficult things may be right now, you'll soon have a chance to relax. **3)** .... having a lot on your mind, you must be careful not to neglect your partner. **4)** .... you are probably feeling confident and secure in your relationship, he/she is likely to be in need of some extra love and attention. There will be a lot of demands on your time this weekend **5)** .... the situation will ease by the end of the month. And **6)** .... there may be lots of changes in store for you, there's nothing you can't cope with."

113 *Rephrase the sentences in as many ways as possible in order to express concession.*

1 The weather was cold. They enjoyed the picnic. ...*Despite the weather being cold, they enjoyed the picnic. Although the weather was cold, they enjoyed the picnic. Cold as the weather was, they enjoyed the picnic. In spite of the fact that the weather was cold, they enjoyed the picnic. The weather was cold. They enjoyed the picnic, though. etc...*

2 She is young. She is sensible. ....
....
....

3 He is thin. He went on a diet. ....
....
....

4 He had no money. She married him. ....
....
....

5 He is wealthy. He never spends money on himself. ....
....
....

114 *Complete the missing parts of the sentences using words expressing concession.*

1 ...*No matter what he says*..., you mustn't believe him.
2 ...., he lost the election.
3 He didn't get the job. ....
4 ...., he can't get over his divorce.
5 He wants to buy a new car, ...
6 ...., the shop wouldn't replace it.
7 ...., he insulted her.
8 The film was boring; ....

115 *Complete the sentences using the words in bold. Use two to five words.*

1 Diamonds are expensive but people buy them.
though   Even ...*though diamonds are expensive*..., people buy them.
2 The weather is so warm that we're wearing T-shirts, even though it's almost Christmas.
yet   It's almost .... so warm that we're wearing T-shirts.
3 He tried to solve the problem but he couldn't find the solution.
how   No .... to solve the problem he couldn't find the solution.
4 He got a well paid job even though he didn't have much experience.
of   In .... experience, he got a well paid job.
5 He read the book, although he found it boring.
fact   He read the book, ... it boring.
6 You can say what you like but I don't think he'll win.
matter   No ...., I don't think he'll win.
7 Although she dislikes pets, she allowed her children to get a dog.
nevertheless   She .... her children to get a dog.
8 John is interested in computers. His wife enjoys gardening.
while   John is interested in computers .... gardening.
9 You can try all you want, but you'll never convince him to help you.
matter   You'll never convince him to help you, ... try.
10 She was very upset but she managed to behave cheerfully.
as   Upset .... to behave cheerfully.
11 I like horror films; they frighten me though.
even   I like horror films .... me.

Oral Development 6

Look at the pictures and notes below, then talk about them using words expressing concession. You may use your own ideas.

Gymnastics

good body, patience, long hours of work, fame, little time for personal life, control over one's body/mind, injuries

Rafting

strong nerves, adventurous spirit, strong swimmer, accidents, contact with nature, willing to take risks, leisure activity

eg. Gymnastics takes long hours of hard work whereas rafting is a leisure activity. etc

116 *Complete the sentences using the words in bold. Use two to five words.*

1 She was very tired and as a result she fell asleep at the wheel.
   that She was ...*so tired that she*... feel asleep at the wheel.
2 The player was disqualified because he had been caught cheating.
   due The player was disqualified .... he had been caught cheating.
3 She received three letters this morning. All of them were from Tony.
   which She received three letters this morning, ... from Tony.
4 The way she behaves, you'd think she was the director.
   as She .... the director.
5 You are advised to book early so that you can be sure of a place.
   order You are advised to book early .... of a place.
6 The match had already finished when I got there.
   by The match had already finished .... there.
7 It was an exciting match, even though our team lost.
   despite It was an exciting match, ... lost.
8 The film got several reviews; none of them were favourable.
   which The film got several reviews, ... favourable.
9 The children ran away to avoid being bitten by the dog.
   fear The children ran away .... bite them.
10 The mountain was too high for us to climb in one day.
   such It was .... we couldn't climb it in one day.
11 She is good natured; she loses her temper easily, though.
   as Good natured ...., she loses her temper easily.
12 He didn't get the job because he did badly in the interview.
   his He didn't get the job .... badly in the interview.
13 Be sure to arrive early if you don't want to miss the beginning of the play.
   as Be sure to arrive early .... the beginning of the play.

Exclamations

Exclamations are used to express anger, fear, shock, surprise etc. They always take an exclamation mark (!). Some exclamations are: Oh dear!, Ah!, Oh!, Good gracious! etc.

- **What + a(n) + (adjective) + singular countable noun** *What a* sweet baby!
- **What + (adjective) + uncountable/plural noun** *What utter* nonsense! *What* beautiful paintings!
- **How + adjective/adverb** *How tall* he is! *How quickly* she walks!
- **How + adjective + a(n) + noun** *How clever* a boy! *(not common)*
- **You + (adjective) + noun** *You* lucky girl!
- **such (a/an) + (adjective) + noun** She's *such an arrogant* person!
- **so + adjective/adverb** She's *so arrogant*!
- **adverb/adverbial particle + subject + verb of movement** *Off* the competitors went!
- **Here/There + subject + verb** *Here* she is! *(*But when the subject is a proper noun, it follows the verb. We say: *Here* is Ann!)
- **Interrogative - negative question at the beginning of the sentence** *Aren't they* nice children!

117 *Fill in: what (a/an), how, so or such (a/an).*

1	...*What a*... strange man he is!	11	.... awful day I had!
2	.... inconsiderate of you!	12	.... tasty biscuits!
3	It was .... lovely meal!	13	.... high he jumps!
4	.... sweet she is!	14	Her pies are .... delicious!
5	.... shiny hair she has!	15	They are .... noisy neighbours!
6	The film was .... boring!	16	.... warm the sea is!
7	.... cold it is!	17	.... odd thing to do!
8	.... nice eyes he's got!	18	They had .... wonderful holiday!
9	The journey was .... long!	19	.... dirty Tommy is!
10	He's .... interesting person!	20	.... nice weather we're having!

118 *Rephrase the following as in the example:*

1 It was such an exciting match! ...
*Wasn't the match exciting!/What an exciting match!/
How exciting a match!/Wasn't it an exciting match!/
The match was so exciting!...*

2	How expensive a coat!	7	What cold hands!
3	Isn't she clever!	8	How lucky John is!
4	It was such a waste of time!	9	He's so forgetful!
5	The water is so dirty!	10	She cooks so well!
6	Wasn't it a terrible storm!	11	Doesn't he talk nonsense!

119 *Fill in: what (a/an), how, so or such (a/an).*

John: Did you see that film last night? I've never seen anything as good as that!
Simon: The one with Harrison Ford? Yes, It was **1)** ...*so*... well-made!
John: And I couldn't believe **2)** .... funny it was in places!
Simon: And **3)** .... lot of special effects!
John: Yes. The whole thing had **4)** .... strong effect on me! Actually, I couldn't stop thinking about it.
Simon: I wonder how long it will be before there's a sequel.
John: I don't know. Very soon, I imagine, as the film was **5)** .... good!

Linking Words

Linking words show the logical relationship between sentences or parts of a sentence.

120 *Rewrite the sentences from the table in as many ways as possible. Whenever this is not possible, make up a new sentence so that other linking words can be used.*

eg. *He is both rich and good looking. He's not only rich but also good looking. etc*

Positive Addition	and, both...and, not only...(but also/as well), too, moreover, in addition to, furthermore, further, also, not to mention the fact that, besides	He is rich **and** good-looking.
Negative Addition	neither...nor, nor, neither, either	**Neither** Tracy **nor** Maeve speaks Spanish.
Contrast	but, not...but, although, while, whereas, despite, even if, even though, on the other hand, in contrast, however, (and) yet, at the same time	I can't cook, **whereas** my husband can. Nick doesn't like pop music, **but** he loves opera.
Similarity	similarly, likewise, in the same way, equally	Cyclists should wear helmets; **similarly,** horse riders should, too.
Concession	but, even so, however, (and) still, (and) yet, nevertheless, on the other hand, although, even though, despite/in spite of, regardless of, admittedly, considering, whereas, while, nonetheless	London is a very noisy city **but** still I like it. London is a very noisy city **and yet** I like it.
Alternative	or, on the other hand, either...or, alternatively	We could **either** go to a restaurant **or** get a take away.
Emphasis	besides, not only this but...also, as well, what is more, in fact, as a matter of fact, to tell you the truth, actually, indeed, let alone, not only that	She never even made the bed, **let alone** cleaned the house.
Exemplification	such as, like, for example, for instance, particularly, especially, in particular	I enjoyed all Charlotte Brontë's books, **especially** "Jane Eyre".
Clarification	that is to say, specifically, in other words, to put it another way, I mean	Fiona finds learning French very difficult, **specifically,** remembering the grammar rules.
Cause / Reason	as, because, because of, since, on the grounds that, seeing that, due to, in view of, owing to, for, now that, so	The factory workers asked for a pay rise **on the grounds that** the cost of living had risen.

Manner	as, (in) the way, how, the way in which, (in) the same way (as), as if, as though	He behaves **as if** he owned the place, but he's only a waiter.
Condition	if, in case, assuming (that), on condition (that), provided (that), providing (that), unless, in the event (that), in the event of, as/so long as, whether, whether...or (alternative condition), only if, even if, otherwise, or (else), in case of	Allen told the children they could stay up late **provided that** they didn't watch too much TV.
Consequence of a condition	consequently, then, under those circumstances, if so, if not, so, therefore, in that case, otherwise, thus	I'm hoping that John will let us have the car tonight. **If not**, I'm afraid we won't be able to go out.
Purpose	so that, so as (not) to, in order (not) to, in order that, for fear (that), in case	Louise went to bed early **so as not to** be tired during the exam.
Effect / Result	such/so...that, consequently, for this reason, as a consequence, thus, therefore, so	It rained all day, and **therefore** we couldn't go to the zoo.
Comparison	as...as, (more) ... than, half as...as, nothing like, the...the, twice as...as, less...than	Even though they are twins, they are **nothing like** each other.
Time	when, whenever, as, while, now (that), before, until, till, after, since	I will leave **when** I'm ready.
Place	where, wherever	Richard tends to make friends **wherever** he goes.
Exception	but (for), except (for), apart from	When I was at school I was good at most subjects **except for** maths.
Relative	who, whom, whose, which, what, that	That woman over there is the one **who** owns the hotel by the sea.
Chronological	**beginning:** initially, first..., at first, to start/begin with, first of all **continuing:** secondly ..., after this/that, second.., afterwards, then, next, before this **concluding:** finally, at last, in the end, eventually, lastly, last but not least	**Firstly** heat the oil in a pan. **Then** break the eggs and beat them. **Finally,** pour the eggs into the pan and stir them gently.
Reference	concerning, regarding, with respect/ regard/reference to, in respect/regard/ reference to this/to the fact that	Write the report **with reference to** the points we discussed last week.
Summarising	in conclusion, in summary, to sum up, as I have said, as (it) was previously stated, on the whole, in all, all in all, altogether, in short, briefly, to put it briefly	**All in all** I enjoyed the book, although I found the plot hard to follow in places.

5 Clauses / Linking Words ....

121 *Join the sentences, then identify the function of the linking words in brackets.*

1 Claire is reliable. She is conscientious too. (in addition to)
   ...In addition to being reliable Claire is also conscientious. (positive addition). ...

2 There have been severe snowstorms all over Britain. Scotland has been the worst hit. (specifically)
   ....

3 Peter can't afford a holiday this year. Dick can't either. (neither ... nor)
   ....

4 Many famous people supported the cause. Princess Diana and Michael Jackson did, for example.
   (such as) ....

5 My nephew likes to wear a watch. He can't tell the time yet though. (even though)
   ....

6 The film was good. The ending was a bit of a disappointment, though. (except for)
   ....

7 The firefighter rushed into the blazing building. He didn't think of the danger. (regardless of)
   ....

8 Colin's mother is French. He can't speak a word of the language, though. (and yet)
   ....

9 The elderly woman walked very slowly and hesitantly. She was probably in great pain. (as if)
   ....

10 I would like to make an appointment with the bank manager. It's about my application for a loan.
   (concerning) ....

11 I suppose I can tell you. You mustn't tell anyone else. (providing) ....

12 I always have a hot chocolate before I go to bed. It helps me to sleep. (in order to) ....

13 Yesterday I found a wallet. It contained over a hundred pounds. (which) ....

14 I really enjoy surfing. It's difficult. (although) ....

122 *Complete the sentences using the words in bold. Use two to five words.*

1 I haven't worn my blue dress for a long time.
   since   It's a long time *...since I last wore...* my blue dress.
2 There was a queue at the supermarket so I was late home.
   due   I arrived home late .... there was a queue at the supermarket.
3 James has decided to buy a motorbike; we can't stop him.
   prevent   We can't .... a motorbike.
4 She studied biology because she wanted to be a nurse.
   view   She studied biology .... a nurse.
5 He was hard-working but he couldn't find a job.
   though   Hard-working .... not find a job.
6 She left all her money in the bank because she was afraid of being burgled.
   fear   She left all her money in the bank .... burgled.
7 I cashed a cheque because I might need more money.
   case   I cashed a cheque .... money.
8 Take some sandwiches. There may not be a café at the station.
   in   Take some sandwiches .... a café at the station.
9 My little brother is very different from me.
   like   My little brother is .... me.

10 He was the only one who didn't enjoy the film.

except Everyone .... him.

11 Always drive carefully if you don't want to have an accident.

avoid Always drive carefully .... an accident.

12 He won't agree to modernising the office, not even to hiring more staff.

alone He won't agree to modernising the office .... more staff.

13 Whatever you say, I will never marry him.

what I will never marry him .... you say.

14 You can come with me but only if you promise to behave yourself.

provided You can come with me .... to behave yourself.

15 Once everybody had arrived, the teacher began the lesson.

had The teacher waited .... she started the lesson.

16 I used to work in that shop.

where That's the shop .... work.

17 She was so worried that she couldn't concentrate on her work.

too She was .... on her work.

18 I didn't tell him what I thought because I didn't want to upset him.

so I didn't tell him what I thought .... him.

19 It was such a loud bang that we all jumped.

so It was .... we all jumped.

20 The music was too loud; I got a headache.

such It was .... I got a headache.

123 *Find the word which should not be in the sentence.*

1	*as*
2	
3	
4	
5	
6	
7	
8	
9	
10	
11	
12	
13	
14	
15	
16	
17	
18	
19	
20	
21	
22	
23	
24	
25	

1 He was promoted as because of his exceptional performance at work.

2 As a result of his being waking up late, he missed the meeting.

3 The woman who greeting the crowd is the Duchess of Kent.

4 The star hired a bodyguard for fear of she might be kidnapped.

5 A pen is used for to writing.

6 Despite of being pressed for time, he listened to her complaints.

7 Brilliant though his proposals as were, they were not accepted.

8 Those whose houses were damaged by the flood they will be compensated.

9 I'll collect the tickets before I will go to the office.

10 Nobody knows the reason for his being absence.

11 She crossed the street to avoid from meeting him.

12 How so considerate of you to give us a call!

13 The man that arrested for arson will appear in court today.

14 When they will finish rehearsing, they are planning to give a press conference.

15 They introduced new measures in order that to control the situation.

16 She has got so little of information that she can't possibly help us.

17 They're planning to record the match in case they will miss it.

18 Theirs was such a nice furniture that we all admired it.

19 What an awful weather!

20 This is the fireman who he risked his life to save the girl.

21 We were running out of time so that we had to make haste.

22 He decided to visit the place where Monet spent his life there.

23 The MP, whose his speech made such an impression, is leaving for Paris tonight.

24 He left early so that as to be sure of getting to work on time.

25 John acts as if he were been in charge of the whole department.

124 Look at Appendix 2, then explain the phrasal verbs in bold.

1 They managed to **get along** despite their difficulties. *have a good relationship*
2 I don't understand what you're **getting at** by saying such things.
3 She **gets on with** all her colleagues; she's such a nice person.
4 He tried to **get through to** Ann but the phone was engaged.
5 Although he caused the accident, he **got away with** a small fine.
6 She's good at **getting** her ideas **across**; everyone understands her.
7 She **gives away** all her old clothes to charity.
8 The people couldn't **get on** the bus because it was already full.
9 It took him three weeks to **get over** his chest infection.
10 The student failed to **get through** the whole exam in the time allowed.
11 The Indians had to **give in** when the cavalry surrounded them.
12 She tried hard to **give up** smoking.
13 The food supplies **gave out** after three days so they had nothing but water.
14 The engine was dirty so the car **gave off** a lot of fumes.

125 Look at Appendix 3, then fill in the correct preposition(s).

1 He was very jealous ...*of*... his friend's success.
2 The old lady was generous .... her grandchildren.
3 The little boy was very frightened .... the dog next door.
4 To make a good impression .... his employer he volunteered to work late.
5 The actress was not impressed .... the role she was offered.
6 The watch he bought from the man was identical .... the one I had lost.
7 The key .... his success is his decisiveness.
8 The students were dismissed .... class at the end of the lesson.
9 The doctor was intent .... helping the patient.
10 The baby had no intention .... eating its food.
11 He is very keen .... playing computer games.
12 They were keen .... do something different at the weekend.
13 The girl had heard .... the accident from an old friend.
14 He has not heard .... his penfriend in Russia for ages.
15 I've heard .... him but I haven't met him.
16 He forgave me .... insulting him.
17 The man was found guilty .... murder.
18 The woman felt guilty .... leaving her dog outside all night.
19 The boy was expelled .... school for hitting his teacher.
20 There has been an increase .... the price of fuel recently.
21 She was good .... everything at school.
22 She's good .... her dog because it keeps her company.
23 The man was not involved .... the fight.
24 She was afraid .... jump from the building even though it was on fire.
25 That student was hopeless .... getting her work in on time.
26 The ice-cream consisted .... chocolate, bananas, coconut and cream.

126 Complete the sentences using the words in bold. Use two to five words.

1 You mustn't reveal anything to the press.
   allowed   You ...*aren't allowed to reveal*... anything to the press.
2 They stole jewellery worth £2,000,000.
   ran   They .... worth £2,000,000.
3 She was too young to travel on her own.
   old   She .... travel on her own.

4 Josh emigrated to Britain. He wanted to start a new life there.
view Josh emigrated to Britain .... a new life there.
5 Whatever you say, you won't change his mind.
what You won't change his mind .... you say.
6 Don't you hate people taking you for granted?
taken Don't you .... for granted?
7 May I take this chair?
mind Would you .... this chair?
8 Although she had a headache, she carried on with her work.
having Despite ...., she carried on with her work.
9 It took ten minutes to revive him after he hit his head.
bring It took ten minutes .... after he hit his head.
10 Perhaps you'll see him later.
may You .... later.
11 Hungry as I was, I refused the dinner invitation.
though Even ...., I refused the dinner invitation.
12 If you exercise more, you'll be fitter.
the The .... you'll be.

127 *Complete the idioms below using an appropriate word from the box, then explain the meaning of the idioms.*

dogs	cows	goat	bear	pig	elephant	cat	rat	horse	fish

1 I felt like a ...*pig*... in the middle caught between the two rivals.
2 My sister drinks like a .... She got through two bottles of wine last night.
3 The extension turned out to be a white .... as nobody needed the extra space.
4 You're flogging a dead .... trying to persuade me to come with you. You'll never get me to change my mind.
5 I wouldn't mind lending him money but what gets my .... is that he never pays me back.
6 Karen is like a .... with a sore head this morning. What has made her so bad tempered?
7 The man told me he had come to mend the photocopier but I began to smell a .... when I found him in the director's office.
8 The deal was supposed to be secret. Who let the .... out of the bag?
9 Since the new manager took over the business is really going to the .... The service is not up to standard and the staff are inexperienced.
10 I could stay and talk to you till the .... come home, but I really must leave now.

128 *Underline the correct item.*

rise - rose - risen (int) = get higher; move upward
raise - raised - raised (tr) = cause to rise; make higher or greater
arise - arose - arisen = (of problems) appear

lie - lied - lied = not to tell the truth
lie - lay - lain (intr) = be in a horizontal position
lay - laid - laid (tr) = cause to place down (also: lay the table; lay eggs)

1 You should raise/rise/arise your hand to get the teacher's attention.
2 She always lies/lays about her age so no one knows how old she really is.
3 We'll have to put off making a decision because a problem has arisen/risen/raised.
4 It's not good for you to lie/lay in bed all day.
5 I always wake up just after the sun has arisen/risen/raised.
6 They lied/laid/lay the unconscious man on the bed.
7 Everyone arose/rose/raised to their feet when the judge entered the courtroom.
8 She laid/lied/lay on the floor groaning in pain.

Practice Test 5 ....

For questions 1 - 15, read the text below and decide which word A, B, C or D best fits each space. There's an example at the beginning (0).

Saving Europe's Woodlands

Hidden in almost every European country there are ancient and untouched forests. These forests are often **(0)** ... in wildlife and are **(1)** ... to many endangered species. One example is a small patch of Scottish forest which **(2)** ... a variety of coniferous trees **(3)** ... for a wide range of birds and insects. Although many of the ancient **(4)** ... of Europe worshipped trees, there is **(5)** ... respect for them today. The World Wildlife Fund has decided to **(6)** ... attention to the importance of Europe's ancient woodlands. They are asking for the remaining forests to be protected by controlling the trade in wood. **(7)** ..., governments are being asked to regenerate forests where **(8)** ..., and manage them in a more nature-friendly way. At present almost a third of western Europe is **(9)** ... by trees. Unfortunately, many of these were only **(10)** ... recently. This means they can't support such a(n) **(11)** ... variety of plant and animal life. If we destroy the ancient forests, we will cause many species to **(12)** ... extinct. The decline of ancient forests began thousands of years ago. Yet, with the growing awareness of the **(13)** ... of ancient woodlands, it is hoped those remaining will be **(14)** ... . By the year 2000 the W.W.F. hopes to have **(15)** ... many forest reserves across Europe. It isn't too late to do something for our ancient trees.

	A		B		C		D	
0	A	full	B	wealthy	C	prosperous	D	rich
1	A	house	B	place	C	home	D	shelter
2	A	contains	B	includes	C	embraces	D	holds
3	A	capable	B	suitable	C	able	D	plenty
4	A	humans	B	peoples	C	beings	D	persons
5	A	small	B	tiny	C	little	D	few
6	A	draw	B	bring	C	carry	D	move
7	A	As well as	B	In addition	C	Too	D	Plus
8	A	necessary	B	important	C	urgent	D	vital
9	A	loaded	B	packed	C	full	D	covered
10	A	placed	B	put	C	plotted	D	planted
11	A	deep	B	wide	C	excessive	D	extreme
12	A	come	B	end	C	become	D	get
13	A	value	B	advantage	C	gravity	D	seriousness
14	A	released	B	endured	C	survived	D	saved
15	A	done up	B	set up	C	brought on	D	made out

	A	B	C	D
0	▭	▭	▭	▬
1	▭	▭	▭	▭
2	▭	▭	▭	▭
3	▭	▭	▭	▭
4	▭	▭	▭	▭
5	▭	▭	▭	▭
6	▭	▭	▭	▭
7	▭	▭	▭	▭
8	▭	▭	▭	▭
9	▭	▭	▭	▭
10	▭	▭	▭	▭
11	▭	▭	▭	▭
12	▭	▭	▭	▭
13	▭	▭	▭	▭
14	▭	▭	▭	▭
15	▭	▭	▭	▭

Part 2

For questions 16 - 30, read the text below and think of the word which best fits each space.
Use only one word in each space. Write your answers in the answer boxes provided.

Wake Up, It's Summer!

The summer season makes **(0)** .... of us feel good, and scientists believe that they **(16)** .... discovered the reason for this. "Bright light makes you feel more awake and helps you sleep better," says Dr. Arendt, from the University of Surrey, **(17)** .... is studying the effect of light **(18)** .... the human body. Light travels through the eye and sends a message to the part of the brain that controls sleep and appetite. So in the summer months **(19)** .... sunlight is increased, your energy level goes **(20)** ...., thus decreasing the need to eat and sleep. **(21)** .... addition, the heat from the sun also **(22)** .... a calming effect as it reduces blood pressure, producing a feeling of relaxation. Sea and mountain air are also beneficial in summer as they make you breathe **(23)** .... deeply, increasing the **(24)** .... of oxygen in your blood. For **(25)** .... people, however, there is a negative side **(26)** .... summer. Those suffering **(27)** .... low blood pressure may experience feelings of tiredness and anxiety at this **(28)** .... of year. Experts advise such people to **(29)** .... up exercise and to add more salt **(30)** .... their diet. So, if you can, enjoy the benefits of bright light, warm days and seaside air and you'll feel completely refreshed.

0	all/most	0
16		16
17		17
18		18
19		19
20		20
21		21
22		22
23		23
24		24
25		25
26		26
27		27
28		28
29		29
30		30

Part 3

For questions 31 - 40, complete the second sentence so that it has a similar meaning to the first sentence. Use the word given and other words to complete each sentence. You must use between two and five words. Do not change the word given. Write your answers in the answer boxes provided.

0 I'm sure it wasn't Jim who did it.
have
It .... Jim who did it.

0	*can't have been*	0 0 1 2

31 They rejected his offer.
down
They .... his offer.

31		31 0 1 2

32 He couldn't think of a better solution.
the
It was .... think of.

32		32 0 1 2

33 The figures showed a drop in sales.
according
There was a drop .... the figures.

33		33 0 1 2

34 He quarrelled with her about the computer.
fell
He .... the computer.

34		34 0 1 2

35 Although she is rich, she is extremely mean.
her
Despite ...., she is extremely mean.

35		35 0 1 2

36 He is less domineering than his brother.
not
He is .... his brother.

36		36 0 1 2

37 His parents won't allow him to stay out late.
let
His parents .... out late.

37		37 0 1 2

38 They were greatly surprised when he won the election.
aback
They .... he won the election.

38		38 0 1 2

39 Laura was so excited that she couldn't keep still.
to
Laura was .... still.

39		39 0 1 2

40 The house in which I grew up is being demolished.
where
The house .... is being demolished.

40		40 0 1 2

Part 4

For questions 41 - 55, read the text below and look carefully at each line. Some of the lines are correct and some have a word which should not be there. If a line is correct, put a tick (✔) by the number in the answer boxes provided. If a line has a word which should not be there, write the word in the answer boxes provided.

Toys

0	Toys are tools that they help children to
00	enjoy that vital activity, play. Play is the
41	means of by which children learn about the
42	world and how to be use their bodies. Toys
43	also help children develop the ability
44	to use up their imagination. It is not always
45	the most expensive a toy that they find most
46	fascinating. The most best toys for young
47	children include jigsaws and pull-along toys
48	on a string. Balls and climbing frames help children
49	to develop movement skills. The children really
50	like to playing in paddling pools or sandpits.
51	They also like to copy after their parents,
52	so they enjoy small versions of kitchen and
53	garage equipment. In the fact, almost anything
54	can be turned into a toy. Children love
55	playing and will use whatever is at their hand.

0	*they*	0
00	✓	00
41		41
42		42
43		43
44		44
45		45
46		46
47		47
48		48
49		49
50		50
51		51
52		52
53		53
54		54
55		55

 Part 5

For questions 56 - 65, read the text below. Use the word given in capitals at the end of each line to form a word that fits in the space in the same line. Write your word in the answer boxes provided.

Cars on Display

At a recent **(0)** .... auto show, several **JAPAN**
(56) .... cars were displayed. They are designed to **EXPERIMENT**
be smaller, lighter and to be powered by new,
(57) .... advanced engines. Few of these cars will **TECHNOLOGY**
go into **(58)** .... since they are only concept cars. **PRODUCE**
Other new ideas include using **(59)** .... to power **ELECTRIC**
cars. It is the most **(60)** .... promising fuel. The **ECONOMIC**
(61) .... of electric cars is their heavy batteries and **ADVANTAGE**
their need to be **(62)** .... recharged. Another new **FREQUENT**
concept is a computer system which helps the **(63)** .... **DRIVE**
with **(64)** .... . Cars of the future will change the **NAVIGATE**
way we drive **(65)** .... . **CONSIDER**

0	*Japanese*	0
56		56
57		57
58		58
59		59
60		60
61		61
62		62
63		63
64		64
65		65

6 Reported Speech

Direct Speech gives the exact words someone said. We use inverted commas in Direct Speech. *"It's a nice song,"* he said.	**Reported Speech** gives the exact meaning of what someone said but not the exact words. We do not use inverted commas in Reported Speech. He said **it was a nice song**.

Say - Tell - Ask - Speak - Talk

- **Say** is used in Direct Speech. It is also used in Reported Speech when it is not followed by the person the words were spoken to. *"She won't come,"* he **said.** ➡ He **said (that)** she wouldn't come.
- **Tell** is used in Reported Speech when it is followed by the person the words were spoken to. *"She won't come,"* he said to me. ➡ He **told me (that)** she wouldn't come.
- **Ask** is used in reported questions and commands or in direct questions.
  He said to me, *"Please leave."* ➡ He **asked me** to leave.
  "He asked, "Have you got any money?" ➡ He **asked me if** I had any money.
- We use **say + to - infinitive** but never ~~say about~~. We use **tell sb, speak/talk about** instead.
  Ann **said to call** her at 12.00. He **told them/spoke/talked about** the incident.

Expressions with say, tell and ask

Expressions with say	say good morning/evening etc, say something, say one's prayers, say a few words, say so, say no more, say for certain, say for sure etc
Expressions with tell	tell the truth, tell a lie, tell (sb) the time, tell sb one's name, tell a story, tell sb a secret, tell sb the way, tell one from another, tell sb's fortune, tell sb so, tell the difference etc
Expressions with ask	ask a favour, ask the time, ask a question, ask the price etc

129 *Fill in: say, tell or ask in the correct form.*

1 Tony ...*said*... he enjoyed the performance.
2 I can't .... for sure, but I think she's divorced.
3 Never .... me a lie again.
4 The teacher .... she was happy with our results.
5 She .... me for a loan of £50.
6 Don't .... the secret to anybody else.
7 My neighbour always .... "hello" whenever he sees me.
8 Please .... me if I look okay in this dress.
9 She .... the doctor how long she would have to stay in hospital.
10 He .... he had never seen such a ridiculous film before.
11 "Of course I'll help you," she .... to me.
12 Can you .... me the way to the nearest bank?
13 Don't .... I didn't .... you they were coming.
14 Mum promised to .... us a story before we go to bed.
15 I wish she'd stop .... favours.
16 She stopped to .... a passer-by the time.
17 The twins look alike. I can't .... one from another.
18 She .... me to meet her at the cinema at 8 o'clock.
19 I remember her .... something, I just can't remember exactly what.
20 And now I would like to .... a few words about this year's competition.
21 To .... you the truth, this is the first time I've tasted blackberries.
22 She did .... me her name but I can't remember it now.
23 I don't feel like arguing so we'll .... no more about the subject.

There are three types of Reported Speech: statements, questions and commands/requests/ suggestions.

A. Statements

- Reported statements are usually introduced with say or tell. That is optional in the reported sentence. Inverted commas are omitted in Reported Speech.
  "He is rich," Ann said. ➡ *Ann* **said (that)** *he was rich.*
- Personal pronouns and possessive adjectives change according to context.
  "I like **your** *car," he said to Mary.* ➡ *He told Mary that* **he** *liked* **her** *car.*
- Tenses change as follows:

	Direct Speech		Reported Speech
Present Simple	*"She* **works** *hard," he said.*	➡	*He said (that) she* **worked** *hard.*
Present Cont.	*"She* **is working** *hard," he said.*	➡	*He said (that) she* **was working** *hard.*
Past Simple	*"She* **worked** *hard," he said.*	➡	*He said (that) she* **had worked** *hard.*
Past Cont.	*"She* **was working** *hard," he said.*	➡	*He said (that) she* **had been working** *hard.*
Future Simple	*"She* **will work** *hard," he said.*	➡	*He said (that) she* **would work** *hard.*
Future Cont.	*"She* **will be working** *hard," he said.*	➡	*He said (that) she* **would be working** *hard.*
Present Perfect	*"She* **has worked** *hard," he said.*	➡	*He said (that) she* **had worked** *hard.*
Present Perf. Cont.	*"She* **has been working** *hard," he said.*	➡	*He said (that) she* **had been working** *hard.*

- Past Perfect and Past Perfect Continuous do not change in Reported Speech.
- Past Simple changes to Past Perfect or remains the same. When the reported sentence contains a time clause, the tenses of the time clause remain unchanged. *"She came round to my house* **while I was doing** *my shopping," he said.* ➡ *He said (that) she* **had come**/**came** *round to his house* **while he was doing** *his shopping.*
- If the reported sentence is out of date, the tenses change, but if it is up to date, the tenses can remain the same. *"She* **called** *last week," he said.* ➡ *He said (that) she* **had called** *the week before. (speech reported after she had called - out of date) He* **is seeing** *the dentist tonight," she said.* ➡ *She said he* **is seeing** *the dentist tonight. (speech reported before he sees the dentist - up to date)*

Tenses do not change in Reported Speech when:

- the reporting verb (said, told etc) is in the Present, Future or Present Perfect.
  "I can't drive," he **says**. ➡ *He* **says** *(that) he* **can't** *drive.*
- the speaker expresses general truths, permanent states or conditions.
  "The sun rises in the East," the teacher said. ➡ *The teacher said (that) the sun* **rises** *in the East.*
- the reported sentence deals with conditionals type 2/type 3, wishes or unreal past.
  "I wish I **was flying** *to Brazil," he said.* ➡ *He said (that) he wished he* **was flying** *to Brazil.*
- the speaker is reporting something immediately after it was said (up to date).
  "The food **is** *delicious," he said.* ➡ *He said (that) the food* **is** *delicious. (up to date)*
  Note: If the speaker expresses something which is believed to be true, the tenses may change or remain the same. *"She likes seafood," he said.* ➡ *He said (that) she* **likes**/**liked** *seafood.* However, if the speaker expresses something which is believed to be untrue, the tenses change. *"India is a rich country," he said.* ➡ *He said (that) India* **was** *a rich country.*
- Time words can change or remain the same depending on the time reference.

Direct Speech		Reported Speech
tonight, today, this week/month/year	➡	that night, that day, that week/month/year
now	➡	then, at that time, at once, immediately
now that	➡	since
yesterday, last night/week/month/year	➡	the day before, the previous night/week/month/year
tomorrow, next week/month/year	➡	the following day/the day after, the following/next week/month/year
two days/months/years etc ago	➡	two days/months/years etc before

"The report **is** *due in* **next week**," the lecturer said.* ➡ *The lecturer said (that) the report* **was** *due in* **the following week**. (out-of-date reporting) "I* **went** *to a party* **last night**," she said.* ➡ *She said (that) she* **went** *to a party* **last night**. (up-to-date reporting)*

6 Reported Speech ....

- certain words change depending on the context: this/these ➡ that/those, here ➡ there, come ➡ go
  etc *"He isn't coming to the meeting,"* she said. ➡ *She said he wasn't **going** to the meeting.*

130 *Turn the following sentences into Reported Speech.*

1 "They will have arrived in Bali by now," he said. .. (out-of-date reporting) ...*He said they would have arrived in Bali by then*....

2 "I've always hated the music they play at this disco," he said. (out-of-date reporting) ....

3 "He'll repair the car next Friday," she said. (up-to-date reporting) ....

4 "I'll be travelling home this time next week," she said. (out-of-date reporting) ....

5 "He left last Monday," she says. ....
....

6 "I haven't decided what type of car I'll buy," he said. (up-to-date reporting) ....
....

Bali - Indonesia

7 "It's time we went out," she said. ....

8 "The earth is round," he said. ....

9 "When they were fishing they caught a trout," he said. ....

10 "Your reports are all typed up," the secretary said. (up-to-date reporting) ....

11 "Dinosaurs are extinct," the teacher said. ....

12 "Paris is a small city," said Lucy. ....

13 "I've been sunbathing all afternoon," he said. (out-of-date reporting) ....

14 "She looks very pretty today," said Paul. ....

15 "If I were you, I'd enter the competition," he said. ....

16 "If they had played well, they'd have won," the coach said. ....

17 "She doesn't seem to be enjoying herself," he said. (up-to-date reporting) ....

18 "Water freezes at 0°C," the professor said. ....

19 "She ought to see a doctor,"he said. ....

20 "Mum is making a cake now," said Tom. (out-of-date reporting) ....

21 "We went to Australia two years ago," she said. (out-of-date reporting) ....

22 "He can't possibly be serious," Tim said. (up-to-date reporting) ....

23 "We were watching television when we heard the news," her father said. ....

24 "I am meeting Terry tomorrow," she said. (up-to-date reporting) ....

25 "Next time you'll have to do better than that," my boss said. (out-of-date reporting)
....

Reported Questions - Indirect Questions

- **Reported Questions** are introduced with **ask, wonder, inquire, want to know** etc. In reported
  questions we use affirmative word order and the question mark becomes a full stop. Inverted commas are omitted. To report a question we use: a) **ask + question word** (who, where, which, how
  etc) when the direct question begins with a question word, and b) **ask + if/whether** when the direct
  question begins with an auxiliary verb (can, do, have etc). Tenses, personal pronouns, possessive
  adjectives, time words etc change as in statements.

Direct Speech	Reported Speech
"What time is it?" she asked him.	*She asked him **what time it was**.*
"Do you eat meat?" she asked him.	*She asked him **if/whether he ate meat**.*

131 *Turn the following sentences into Reported Speech.*

1 "Will you take the dog out for a walk?" he asked me. ...*He asked
    me if/whether I would take the dog out for a walk....*
2 "How much money have you got?" he asked me. ....
3 "Did you really write this poem?" she asked Tim. ....
4 "How did the operation go?" they asked the doctor. ....
5 "Will you be going on holiday next Easter?" he asked her. ....
6 "Is that your daughter walking along the pier, Mary?" Joan asked.

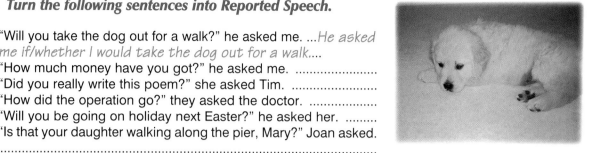

    ....
7 "Why is he acting this way?" she asked me. ....
8 "Can you let Joan know I'll be late?" she asked me. ....
9 "Which of these dresses suits me best?" she asked Lynn. ....
10 "Does this bicycle belong to anyone?" he asked. ....
11 "Who used my toothbrush?" he asked. ....
12 "Do you want to join us at 6.00?" he asked me. ....
13 "Why didn't you tell me about the party?" he asked me. ....
14 "Have you been to York before?" she asked Sue. ....

● **Indirect questions** are used to ask for advice or information. They are introduced with: **Could you tell me...?, Do you know...?, I wonder..., I want to know..., I doubt ...,** etc and the verb is in the affirmative. If the indirect question starts with "**I want to know ...**", "**I wonder...**" or "**I doubt ...**", the question mark is omitted. Question words (**what, where, who** etc) or **whether** can be followed by an infinitive in the indirect question if the subject of the question is the speaker.

Direct questions	Indirect questions
"Where is Joan?" he asked me.	*Do you know **where Joan is**?*
"Did he tell you the truth?" she asked me.	*She wondered **if/whether he had told** me the truth.*
"What shall I do next?" he asked me.	*He wanted to know **what he should do** next/**what to do** next.*

---

132 *Turn the following sentences into Indirect questions. Omit question marks where necessary.*

1 Where are you going? (I want to know ...) ...*I want to know where you are going....*
2 Did he steal the money? (I doubted ...) ....
3 Has she told anyone about our engagement? (He wondered ...) ....
4 What time does the train leave? (Could you tell me ...) ....
5 Who did it? (She wondered ...) ....
6 Where have you been? (He wanted to know ...) ....
7 Does he speak French fluently? (I wonder ...) ....
8 Will she be on time? (I doubt ...) ....
9 How long has he been working here? (Do you know ...) ....
10 Are they moving house? (I want to know ...) ....

Reported Commands/Requests/Suggestions

● **Reported Commands / Requests / Suggestions** are introduced with a special introductory verb (**advise, ask, beg, suggest** etc) (see pages 103-104) followed by a **to-infinitive**, an **-ing form** or a **that-clause** depending on the introductory verb.

"Watch out," he said to me.	➡ *He told me **to watch out**. (command)*
"Please, don't move," he said to me.	➡ *He asked me **not to move**. (request)*
"Let's play chess," he said.	➡ *He **suggested playing** chess. (suggestion)*
"You'd better see a doctor," he said.	➡ *He **suggested that I (should) see** a doctor. (suggestion)*

133 *Turn the following sentences from Direct to Reported Speech.*

1 "Put out your cigarettes please!" he said to us. ...*He asked us to put out our cigarettes.*....
2 "Wipe your feet on the mat!" mother said. ....
3 "Please forgive me!" she said. ....
4 "Could you babysit for me tonight?" he said to me. ....
5 "You shouldn't eat so much meat," she said to me. ....
6 "Be here on time in future," Tom's boss said. ....
7 "Could you pass me the salt?" Barry said to her. ....
8 "Let's buy some new curtains!" Sally said. ....
9 "You'd better go to bed early," Henry said. ....
10 "Don't be horrible to your little sister!" his father said. ....

Modal Verbs in Reported Speech

Note how the following modal verbs change in Reported Speech when the reported sentence is out of date. **will/shall** ➡ **would**, **can** ➡ **could** (present reference)/**would be able to** (future reference), **may** ➡ **might/could**, **shall** ➡ **should** (asking for advice) / **would** (asking for information) / **offer** (expressing offers), **must** ➡ **must/had to** (obligation) (* "**must**" remains the same when it expresses possibility or deduction), **needn't** ➡ **didn't need to** / **didn't have to** (present reference) / **wouldn't have to** (future reference). **Would, could, used to, mustn't, should, might, ought to** and **had better** remain unchanged in Reported Speech.

Direct Speech	Reported Speech
He said, "*I will always love you.*"	➡ He said (that) he **would** always love me.
He said, "*I can't help you.*"	➡ He said (that) he **couldn't** help me.
He said, "*We can come soon.*"	➡ He said (that) they **would be able** to come soon.
He said, "*It may snow.*"	➡ He said (that) it **might** snow.
He said, "*What time shall we leave?*"	➡ He asked what time we **would** leave. (information)
He said, "*Shall I buy a red one?*"	➡ He asked (me) if he **should** buy a red one. (advice)
He said, "*Shall I help you?*"	➡ He **offered** to help me. (offer)
He said, "*You must tell the truth.*"	➡ He said (that) I **had to** tell the truth. (obligation)
He said, "*She must have got lost.*"	➡ He said (that) she **must** have got lost. (deduction)
He said, "*They should try a little harder.*"	➡ He said (that) they **should** try a little harder.
He said, "*She had better pay me back.*"	➡ He said (that) she **had better** pay him back.
He said, "*You needn't hurry.*"	➡ He said (that) I **didn't have to/didn't need to** hurry.
He said, "*You needn't come to work on Friday.*"	➡ He said (that) I **wouldn't have to** go to work on Friday.

134 *Turn the following sentences into Reported Speech.*

1 She said, "You needn't pay until Christmas." ...*She said (that) I wouldn't have to pay until Christmas.*....
2 She said, "When shall we let them know?" ....
3 She said, "Shall I carry your suitcase?" ....
4 She said, "I can't play chess very well." ....
5 She said, "We must finish the work today." ....
6 She said, "You needn't wear formal clothes." ....
7 She said, "You should take more exercise." ....
8 She said, "Shall I get you an aspirin?" ....
9 She said, "Tony must have missed his bus." ....
10 She said, "We'll go to the zoo tomorrow." ....
11 She said, "I may take up skiing." ....
12 She said, "What shall I buy him for his birthday?" ....
13 She said, "They won't arrive on time." ....
14 She said, "They needn't be at the meeting next week." ....

Special Introductory Verbs

Introductory verb	Direct Speech	Reported Speech
agree + to-inf	*"Yes, I'll come with you."*	➡ He **agreed to come** with me.
demand	*"Tell me everything!"*	➡ He **demanded to be told** everything.
offer	*"Would you like me to carry it?"*	➡ He **offered to carry** it.
promise	*"I'll study more."*	➡ He **promised to study** more.
refuse	*"No, I won't come with you."*	➡ He **refused to come** with me.
threaten	*"Behave yourself or I'll punish you."*	➡ He **threatened to punish** me if I didn't behave myself.
claim	*"I heard her say that."*	➡ He **claimed to have heard** her say that.
advise + sb + to-inf	*"You should take a coat."*	➡ He **advised me to take** a coat.
allow	*"You can use my phone."*	➡ He **allowed me to use** his phone.
ask	*"Please, put it away."*	➡ He **asked me to put** it away.
beg	*"Please, please help me."*	➡ He **begged me to help** him.
command	*"Fire!"*	➡ He **commanded the soldiers to fire.**
encourage	*"Go ahead, phone her."*	➡ He **encouraged me to phone** her.
forbid	*"You mustn't eat sweets."*	➡ He **forbade me to eat** sweets.
instruct	*"Insert your card and wait for the machine to open."*	➡ He **instructed me to insert** my card and **wait** for the machine to open.
invite sb	*"Would you like to come to my house?"*	➡ He **invited me to go** to his house.
order	*"Sit down immediately."*	➡ He **ordered me to sit down** immediately.
permit	*"You may speak now."*	➡ He **permitted me to speak** .
remind	*"Don't forget to pay the bill."*	➡ He **reminded me to pay** the bill.
urge	*"Finish your work."*	➡ He **urged me to finish** my work.
warn	*"Don't touch that switch."*	➡ He **warned me not to touch** that switch.
want	*"I'd like you to go out."*	➡ He **wanted me to go** out.
accuse sb of + -ing form	*"You broke the vase."*	➡ He **accused me of breaking** the vase.
apologise for	*"I'm sorry I upset you."*	➡ He **apologised for upsetting/having upset** me.
admit (to)	*"Yes, I lied to her."*	➡ He **admitted (to) lying/having lied** to her.
boast about	*"I am better than you."*	➡ He **boasted about being** better than me.
complain to sb about	*"You never tidy up."*	➡ He **complained to me about my** never **tidying** up.
deny	*"No, I didn't steal the car."*	➡ He **denied stealing/having stolen** the car.
insist on	*"You must wear warm clothes."*	➡ He **insisted on me/my wearing** warm clothes.
suggest	*"Let's go to the theatre."*	➡ He **suggested going** to the theatre.
agree + that-clause	*"Yes, that is a beautiful hat."*	➡ He **agreed that** it was a beautiful hat.
boast	*"I'm a brilliant dentist."*	➡ He **boasted that** he was a brilliant dentist.
claim	*"I know the answer."*	➡ He **claimed that** he knew the answer.
complain	*"You never listen to me."*	➡ He **complained that** I never listened to him.
deny	*"I've never spoken to her."*	➡ He **denied that** he had ever spoken to her.
exclaim	*"It's wonderful!"*	➡ He **exclaimed that** it was wonderful.
explain	*"It's an easy recipe to follow."*	➡ He **explained that** it was an easy recipe to follow.
inform sb	*"You will be called for an interview."*	➡ He **informed me that** I would be called for an interview.
promise	*"I won't lie to you again."*	➡ He **promised that** he wouldn't lie to me again.
suggest	*"You ought to take the other road."*	➡ He **suggested that** I take the other road.
explain to sb + how	*"This is how you make it."*	➡ He **explained to me how** to make it.

6 Reported Speech ....

Introductory verb	Direct Speech	Reported Speech
wonder where/what why/how + clause (when the subject of the introductory verb is **not the same** as the subject in the reported question)	He asked himself, "How can she reach the top?" He asked himself, "Where is Joan?" He asked himself, "Why is she crying?" He asked himself, "What is she doing?"	➡ He **wondered how** she could reach the top. ➡ He **wondered where** Joan was. ➡ He **wondered why** she was crying. ➡ He **wondered what** she was doing.
wonder + whether + to-inf or clause **wonder where/what/ how + to-inf** (when the subject of the infinitive is the **same** as the subject of the verb)	He asked himself, "Shall I buy that car?" He asked himself, "Where am I going?" He asked himself, "What should I tell her?" He asked himself, "How can I fix it?"	➡ He **wondered whether** to buy that car. ➡ He **wondered whether** he should buy that car. ➡ He **wondered where** he was going. ➡ He **wondered what** he should tell her. ➡ He **wondered how** to fix it.

135 *First write an appropriate introductory verb, then report the following sentences.*

1	"I'll be home early."	*...promise...*	*He promised to be home early.*
2	"Press the button first."	....	....
3	"I didn't copy John's work."	....	....
4	"He never tells the truth."	....	....
5	"I'm so good at maths."	....	....
6	"She's so beautiful!"	....	....
7	"Peter is unable to attend the meeting tomorrow."	....	....
8	"No, I won't tell you what happened."	....	....
9	"I think you should go home."	....	....
10	"That's how you fix it."	....	....
11	"You really ought to go home."	....	....
12	"This is how I began my career."	....	....
13	"Yes, I told them everything."	....	....
14	"I'm sorry I shouted."	....	....
15	"You lied to me."	....	....
16	"I'd like you to carry the bag."	....	....
17	"Don't forget to ask Janet."	....	....
18	"Don't touch this wire."	....	....
19	"You may go now."	....	....
20	"Come on, try it again!"	....	....
21	"She really must attend more frequently."	....	....
22	"Would you like to go to the theatre?"	....	....
23	"You mustn't talk during the exam."	....	....
24	"Go ahead, enter the race!"	....	....
25	"Run immediately!"	....	....
26	"Please, please tell me the truth!"	....	....
27	"James never told me he was working undercover."	....	....
28	"You can take my car."	....	....
29	"I won't do it again."	....	....
30	"Give me the money or I'll shoot you."	....	....
31	"Would you like me to help?"	....	....
32	"Give me everything."	....	....
33	"I'm sorry I was late."	....	....
34	"Yes, he is very handsome."	....	....
35	"I know that musician well."	....	....
36	"Please, explain once more."	....	....
37	"You are never on time."	....	....

Reporting conversations or dialogues

- Everyday conversations and dialogues are a mixture of statements, commands and questions. To report these we use: **and, as, adding that, and he/she added that, explaining that, because, but, since, so, and then he/she went on to say, while, then** etc or the introductory verb in the present participle form. Exclamations such as: Oh!, Ouch!, Oh no! etc are omitted in Reported Speech.

Direct Speech	Reported Speech
"Oh, it's a lovely evening. Shall we go for a walk?" he said.	➡ *He said that it was a lovely evening* **and** *suggested going for a walk.*
"I can't wear it," she said. "It's too tight."	➡ *She said that she couldn't wear it* **because** *it was too tight.*
"Let's take a taxi," he said. "I want to arrive on time."	➡ *He suggested that they should take a taxi,* **explaining that** *he wanted to arrive on time.*

Exclamations - "Yes/No" short answers - Question tags

- **Exclamations** are replaced in Reported Speech with **exclaim, thank, wish, say, cry out in pain** etc, **give an exclamation of surprise/horror/disgust/delight** etc. The exclamation mark becomes a full stop. Exclamatory words such as Oh!, Eek!, Wow!, Oh!, Oh dear!, Well! etc are omitted in Reported Speech. *"Aggh!" she said at the sight of the syringe.* ➡ *She* **gave an exclamation of horror** *at the sight of the syringe.*
- **Yes/No short answers** are expressed in Reported Speech with **subject + appropriate auxiliary verb** or **subject + appropriate introductory verb**. *"Will you tell me?" he said. "No," she said.* ➡ *He asked her if she would tell him but she said* **she wouldn't.** *or He asked her if she would tell him but she* **refused.**
- **Question tags** are omitted in Reported Speech. An appropriate introductory verb can be used if we want to retain their effect. *"She is still at work, isn't she?" he said.* ➡ *He* **wondered** *if she was still at work.*

136 *Turn the following conversations into Reported Speech using special introductory verbs.*

A   "Carter, when are you taking your holidays this year?" said the manager.

"Actually, I've already been on holiday, sir. Don't you remember? I went on safari in Kenya," said Carter.

"Oh yes, of course. You went in March, didn't you?"

"That's correct, sir," said Carter.

"Did you enjoy it?" the manager asked.

"Well, I didn't manage to see many animals. It was very disappointing," Carter replied.

"Have you got any plans to go back there?" the manager said.

"Well, yes, actually I've already booked tickets for next year. I'm going in February. I think it will be a better time for seeing the animals," said Carter.

"So, we'll be looking for a new accountant then, if you come face to face with a lion," said the manager.

...The manager asked Carter when he was taking his holidays that year. ....

....

....

B   "Let's spend the weekend in Scotland," said Andrea. "We can find a cheap bed and breakfast in the Highlands."

"And just what are we going to do all weekend with nothing but sheep for company!" Cathy said.

"I'll teach you to ski," said Andrea.

...Andrea suggested spending ....

....

C "James, have you written to the University of Madrid yet?" Mr Mills said.

"No, I'm sorry," said James. "I haven't had time."

"There's no point in apologising to me, James," said Mr Mills. "You see, you must apply early because they fill their places very quickly."

"The thing is that I'm afraid I won't pass my Spanish exam," said James.

"Well, have you been working hard?" said Mr Mills.

"Yes, I have," said James, "but I'm much better at French, and I had hoped to apply to Paris."

"Yes, it's true you are better at French," said Mr Mills. "If I put your name down for the Sorbonne, will you write tonight?"

"Yes sir, I'll write as soon as I get home," James promised.

...Mr Mills asked James if he ....

....

....

....

Punctuation in Direct Speech

- **We capitalise the first word of the quoted sentence. The full stop, the question mark, the exclamation mark and the comma come inside the inverted commas. The comma comes outside the inverted commas only when "he said/asked" precedes the quoted sentence.** *"She went out," he said. He said, "She went out." "She," he said, "went out."* **We do not use a comma after the question mark.** *"Can I speak to you?" I asked.* but: *I asked, "Can I speak to you?"*
- **When the subject is a pronoun, it comes before the reporting verb (said, asked etc) but when the subject is a noun, it often comes after "said", "asked" etc at the end or in the middle of the quoted sentence.** *"He moved house," she said. "He moved house," said Sarah. "He," said Sarah, "moved house."* but: *She/Sarah said, "He moved house."* (not: ~~Said Sarah,~~ *"He moved house."*)
- **Each time the speaker changes, we normally start a new paragraph.**

 Rewrite the following as a conversation. Mind the punctuation.

A Stephen denied having got them lost and refused to take responsibility for their situation. Catherine accused him of not knowing how to read a map, and threatened to leave him if he didn't get them out of the mess. Stephen complained that she always made him do all the work. Catherine apologised for not helping but begged him to do something, adding that she didn't want to spend the night in the open. Stephen promised that they would find somewhere to stay, and urged her to keep calm. He eventually asked her to help him with the map reading. She laughed and suggested that perhaps he should try holding the map the right way up. ...*"It's not my fault we got lost," Stephen said*...

....

....

....

B The diver boasted about having found a shipwreck full of treasure on the ocean floor. His friend accused him of lying as that part of the sea had been explored thoroughly, yet the diver still insisted, claiming that only he had searched that particular area. Then his friend went on to tell him that if that was the case, he should notify the authorities as soon as possible in order to lay claim to the treasure. She warned him that if he failed to do this someone else might claim the treasure for themselves. It was at this stage that the diver admitted that the wreck wasn't that old and that the treasure consisted of Monopoly money! ...*"I have found* ....

....

....

....

Subjunctive

● The bare infinitive form of the subjunctive is used after certain verbs and expressions to give emphasis. These are: **advise, ask, demand, insist, propose, recommend, request, suggest, it is essential, it is imperative, it is important, it is necessary, it is vital** followed by **(that) + subject. In British English we normally use "should + simple form" instead of the bare infinitive form of the subjunctive.** *It is vital (that) you **deliver** the parcel today. (less usual) It is vital **that you should deliver** the parcel today. (more usual)*

138 *Rewrite the following sentences using the words in brackets.*

1 "I would eat only the fish," he said. (suggest) ...*He suggested that I (should) eat only the fish*....
2 "Let's go to the beach," he said. (propose) ....
3 "Why not paint the room blue?" said Dad. (recommend) ....
4 "Please bring me a cup of tea," she said. (request)...
5 "You must do your homework," said Mr Smith. (insist) ....

139 *Turn the following dialogue into Reported Speech.*

Joan: Mmm, I'm really going to enjoy this sandwich. I'm so hungry. I haven't eaten anything since breakfast. Are you sure you don't want anything?
Geoffrey: Yes. I've eaten too much already today. I can't eat another thing.
Joan: Why not just have a glass of milk then?
Geoffrey: Good idea.
Joan: I really enjoyed the visit to the aquarium this morning. What shall we do this afternoon?
Geoffrey: Let's go to the folk museum. It looks very interesting.
Joan: Yes, but don't forget we have to be back at the hotel by six.
Geoffrey: We definitely have enough time, don't worry.
Joan: Oh no! I can't find my purse. I must have dropped it in the car park.
Geoffrey: I'll go back and look for it if you like.

...*Joan said that she was going to enjoy her sandwich because*...

140 *Turn the following sentences into Reported Speech using special introductory verbs.*

1 "Don't go near the bull." ...*She warned me not to go near the bull*....
2 "What a brilliant idea!" ....
3 "I'll definitely take you to the park tomorrow." ....
4 "Let's have the wedding in the spring." ....
5 "Please, please don't tell my father what happened." ....
6 "You are always late." ....
7 "I'm sorry I wasn't there when you needed me." ....
8 "You switched the reports, didn't you?" ....
9 "No, I won't lend you the money." ....
10 "You can't go to the party tonight." ....
11 "Shall I hang out the washing?" ....
12 "Don't forget to send Mum a birthday card." ....
13 "This is how you switch on the machine." ....
14 "I'm the best tennis player in the club." ....
15 "Go ahead, propose to her." ....

6 Reported Speech

141 Turn the following text into Direct Speech.

Daniel asked the bank manager for a loan. The bank manager asked him exactly what he wanted the money for. Daniel explained that he wanted to set up his own cleaning business. The bank manager agreed that it was a good idea but urged him to be very careful before investing a lot of money. Daniel admitted that he'd never had his own business before. The bank manager apologised for being unable to promise Daniel a loan immediately. He suggested that Daniel write a business plan and come back in a week. Daniel agreed to return the following Thursday. ..."*I was wondering if it was possible for me to apply for a loan,*" *Daniel said to the bank manager.*..

142 Rewrite the following sentences in Reported Speech.

1 "I'm learning French," he said. "I'm going to Paris for my holidays."
   ...*He said he was learning French, adding that he was going to Paris for his holidays....*
2 "Can you take the dog for a walk?" he said to her. "I'm busy." ....
3 "You shouldn't smoke," she said. "It's bad for your health." ....
4 "Can I borrow your pen, please?" he said to her. "I need to write something." ....
5 "Please don't talk," said the teacher. "This is a test." ....
6 "Why don't you turn off the TV?" she said to him. "You aren't watching it." ....
7 "Come to our house tonight, Mary," he said. "Jim wants to see you." ....
8 "Have you read your newspaper?" he asked her. "I want to look at it." ....
9 "The baby should be asleep," she said. "It's ten o'clock." ....
10 "I don't want any more cake," she said. "I've had enough." ....
11 "Don't play near the road," their mother said. "It's too dangerous." ....
12 "I like Susan," he said. "She's very friendly." ....
13 "I'm teaching Jane's class," she said. "She's on holiday this week." ....
14 "Sarah would like to have the house," he said. "She's lived here a long time." ....
15 "You could become famous, June," he said. "You're a very good singer." ....
16 "Are you going to take the job?" he asked her. "Or will you wait for a better one?" ....
17 "Can you phone Julie?" she asked me. "I heard she has had a fight with Mark." ....
18 "Do you know when May will be back?" she asked. "She's been away all week." ....
19 "Do you think we should try this new restaurant tonight?" he asked his wife. "I've heard it's very good." ....
20 "If anyone phones," she said, "tell them I won't be here until tomorrow." ....
21 "I'd love to go to Venice," she said. "I've never been there." ....
22 "Don't ask Simon how to use the computer," she said. "He doesn't know a thing about them." .....
   ....
23 "I must go now," said Samantha, "or I might miss the bus." ....
24 "I'm sorry I didn't phone you yesterday," said Charlotte. "I had to visit my aunt." ....

143 Complete the sentences using the words in bold. Use two to five words.

1 "You should go to the dentist Tina," he said.
   advised   He ...*advised Tina to go*... to the dentist.
2 "Try to remember your books tomorrow," she said.
   urged   She .... our books the next day.

3 "You took my pencil!" Mark said to Mandy.
   of   Mark .... his pencil.
4 "Don't forget to take your keys," said Dad.
   me   Dad .... my keys.
5 "I hate the English weather," said Celine.
   about   Celine .... the English weather.
6 "You must have another piece of apple pie, Laura," said Grandad.
   on   Grandad .... piece of apple pie.
7 "I'll never let you down," Ian told Elizabeth.
   promised   Ian .... Elizabeth down.
8 "You never put the cap on the toothpaste, John," said Mary.
   complained   Mary .... the cap on the toothpaste.
9 "I'm the best-looking boy in the class," said Greg.
   that   Greg .... the best-looking boy in the class.
10 "Would you like to come to lunch next Friday?" Bill said to me.
   invited   Bill .... the following Friday.
11 "I did not eat the biscuits," said Alex.
   eating   Alex .... the biscuits.
12 "Let's go out for dinner," said Amanda.
   going   Amanda.. for dinner.
13 "You must not touch these ornaments," said Lisa to us.
   to   Lisa .... the ornaments.
14 "He knows where the stolen paintings are," said Sue.
   claimed   Sue .... the stolen paintings were.
15 "You may now kiss the bride," said the priest to David.
   permission   The priest .... the bride.
16 "Don't drive the car; the brakes aren't working," Dad said to me.
   not   Dad .... the car because the brakes weren't working.
17 "It's a boy!" said the midwife.
   exclaimed   The midwife .... a boy.
18 "Please, please don't hurt me," she cried.
   not   She .... her.
19 "Do give me the money!" she said to me.
   urged   She .... the money.
20 "Yes, I think you are right to complain," said Lorna to me.
   agreed   Lorna .... to complain.
21 "Please leave me alone," Clare said to them.
   asked   Clare .... alone.
22 "I'm sorry I hurt your feelings, Jane," I said.
   hurting   I .... her feelings.
23 "OK, it was me. I tore Mum's new dress," she said.
   having   She .... Mum's new dress.
24 "Call an ambulance immediately!" said Bob to the passer-by.
   to   Bob .... an ambulance immediately.
25 "Would you like me to do the washing up?" said Dan.
   offered   Dan .... the washing up.
26 "No, I won't go to the party with you," said Lena.
   refused   Lena .... the party with me.
27 "You can use my credit card," Jake said to me.
   me   Jake .... his credit card.
28 "Go ahead, join the expedition," he said to her.
   encouraged   He .... the expedition.
29 "Go away or I'll lose my temper," he said to me.
   his   He .... if I didn't go away.
30 "Yes, I'll paint the bathroom," said Catherine.
   agreed   Catherine .... the bathroom.

6 Reported Speech

144 Find the word which should not be in the sentence.

1 He claimed that to have met the Queen of Spain.
2 Sophia wanted to know what time did they returned home the previous night.
3 The players complained of to the coach about having to play in the hail.
4 Margaret promised to will be careful with the money given to her.
5 The boy asked to his mother if he could play with his friends.
6 He said about that he was feeling under the weather.
7 She said she was ready to go, but adding that the taxi was waiting.
8 The manager told us do not to misuse office equipment.
9 Did he tell to you what happened?
10 She demanded that to be given his name and address.
11 They suggested to buying her a nice wedding present.
12 It is important that he to attend the conference.
13 He told me that I would not have had to leave early the next day.
14 She apologised for having keeping us waiting.
15 Jack wondered whether that to go ahead with his plan.
16 He asked me if he could use my computer and I said he could to.
17 The manager insisted that we are put an advertisement in the papers.
18 Do you know what time do the children finish school?
19 My sister encouraged me how to try once more.
20 They accused him of having been falsified the documents.

1	that
2	
3	
4	
5	
6	
7	
8	
9	
10	
11	
12	
13	
14	
15	
16	
17	
18	
19	
20	

Oral Development 7

In pairs, students look at the first picture and make up a short dialogue based on the situation given. Next, a pair of students act out the dialogue while the rest of the class take notes. The students report the conversation. Do the same with the other picture.

Last month Monica and Philip went on a cruise. What could they have been talking about?

Sharon met her uncle last Monday. What could they have been talking about?

145 Look at Appendix 2, then fill in the correct particle(s).

1 Even though the police **went** ...*after*... the criminals they didn't catch them.
2 "His line is engaged at the moment. Do you want to **hold** .... or ring back later?"
3 John won't be at work today; he's **gone** .... the flu.
4 Sorry for being late but I was **held** .... in the traffic.
5 Melanie is going to **go** .... the dancing competition.
6 The fire will **go** .... if you don't put more wood on it.

7 The robbers **held** .... the bank and escaped with thousands of pounds.
8 Yes, of course - bring some friends with you. There should be plenty of food to **go** ....
9 She **held** .... some very important information which she refused to reveal.
10 Even though Joe was very angry he managed to **hold** .... his anger.
11 Even though the police **went** .... the evidence many times, they didn't find anything.
12 The villagers fear that the supply of water will not **hold** .... for the summer.

146 Look at Appendix 3, then fill in the correct preposition(s).

1 The surgeon is going to operate ...*on*... my father tomorrow.
2 Ireland qualified .... the World Cup Finals in1990.
3 He insisted .... having his lawyer present.
4 Mary is married .... John.
5 If he persists .... coming to work late every day, I'll have to speak to him.
6 He was criticised for his neglect .... his duties.
7 Frank is a very mean person. He finds it very difficult to part .... his money.
8 There were many objections .... the council building another shopping centre.
9 Mary was very nervous .... having a blood test.
10 Many people are ignorant .... the long-term effects of pollution.
11 He wrote a cheque .... £250.
12 His arguments are lacking .... logic.
13 John takes great pride .... his new car.
14 Sally prides herself .... being very honest.

15 Carmel is very proud .... her daughter's achievements.
16 She paid .... her new dress .... cheque.
17 As the shop didn't accept credit cards, I had to pay .... cash.
18 You can't expect Joe to know everything. He's still relatively new .... the job.
19 He presented the new employee .... the manager.
20 He was presented .... a gold watch on his retirement.
21 I sometimes mistake Clare .... her sister on the phone.
22 I'm hoping .... a second interview next week.
23 John is notorious .... telling lies.
24 He's fortunate .... having many good friends.
25 She quarrelled .... Andrew .... which television programme to watch.

147 Complete the sentences using the words in bold. Use two to five words.

1 It would be a good idea to lose some weight.
   better   You ...*had better lose*... some weight.
2 You didn't need to buy me this ring.
   have   You .... this ring.
3 I don't think I can finish all this work by tomorrow.
   get   I don't think I can .... by tomorrow.
4 One of the three students he examined was Italian.
   whom   He examined three students, ... Italian.
5 He lost his job because he was extremely disorganised.
   result   He was extremely disorganised .... lost his job.
6 Sue is probably going to the cinema tonight.
   likely   Sue .... the cinema tonight.

7 They didn't want to spend a lot of money so they booked a self-catering holiday.

avoid They booked a self-catering holiday .... a lot of money.

8 We were disconnected halfway through our conversation.

cut We .... halfway through our conversation.

9 "OK, I'll take you to the funfair," Father said to us.

to Father .... to the funfair.

10 He is an expert but he couldn't answer my question.

being In .... he couldn't answer my question.

11 "Of course I didn't give them your name," he said to me.

having He .... my name.

12 She was so irritated by his attitude that she felt like screaming.

irritating His .... she felt like screaming.

148 *Explain the meaning of the idioms in bold.*

1 Mary has agreed to help us raise the money but **her heart isn't in it**.

2 The students were told to **learn the poem by heart** as they would be asked to recite it in class the next day.

3 That's the third glass she's broken this morning. She's **all fingers and thumbs**.

4 I don't know how Carla manages with two small children and a husband who **never lifts a finger** to help.

5 My grandmother never looks at a recipe. She prefers to cook **by rule of thumb**.

6 It had been so long since I'd had a drink that the wine **went straight to my head**.

7 Max has been drawing up contracts for so long that he can now do it **standing on his head**.

8 Sue is looking very **down in the mouth** this morning. Has she had bad news?

9 Larry never had to advertise his business as people heard about him **through word of mouth**.

10 The employee was stealing company property right **under our noses**.

Expressions with "Do"	Expressions with "Make"
one's best/worst, business with sb, a crossword, damage to, one's duty, an exercise, an experiment, somebody a favour, good, one's hair, harm, homework, housework, a job, lessons, sth for a living, miracles (for), research, right/wrong, a service, the shopping, a good turn, a translation, the washing up, wonders, work etc	allowances for, an appointment, an acquaintance, an arrangement, a bargain, the beds, the best of, a cake, certain, changes, coffee, a deal with sb, a decision, a difference, a discovery, an effort, an enemy of, ends meet, an excuse, friends with, a fortune, haste, fun of, a fool of sb, an impression, improvements, a joke, a mess, a mistake, money, a note, a nuisance, (a) noise, an offer, peace, preparations, a profit, progress, sure, a translation, trouble, war, a will etc

149 *Fill in "do" or "make" in the correct form.*

1 I enjoy ..*doing*.. the crossword in *The Guardian*.

2 It's not a good idea to ..... an enemy of Clare.

3 We had better start .... preparations for the christening.

4 Pete .... a great deal of damage already.

5 It's your turn to .... the washing up tonight.

6 The boy promised to ...... his best in the test.

7 She .... her exercises every morning before work.

8 Pat doesn't appreciate .... a fool of.

9 I .... friends with some people from Germany while I was travelling to Budapest.

10 They find it difficult .... ends meet.

11 Mum has promised to .... a cake for the party.

12 A man phoned earlier to .... an appointment.

13 He asked me what I .... for a living.

14 Our neighbours are always .... noise.

15 Can't you at least .... an effort?

16 It appears that she .... a fortune when she was living in Japan.

Practice Test 6

Part 1

For questions 1 - 15, read the text below and decide which word A, B, C or D best fits each space. There's an example at the beginning (0).

The American Eagle

America's national symbol is that great bird which is **(0)** ... as the bald eagle. However, the number of this species has dropped from 50,000 in the 1940's to about 300 today. Fortunately, America has taken **(1)** ... by starting to breed these eagles. This takes place at a research centre in Oklahoma, where 300 have been bred and then released into the wild. The eggs are **(2)** ... from wild eagles' nests, found **(3)** ... the country, and are flown straight to the centre by aeroplane. During the **(4)** ..., they are kept **(5)** ... in a special container which **(6)** ... them from sunlight, which could easily kill them. Once they are at the centre, they are continually **(7)** ... until they hatch. Eight hours after the birds emerge, they are given their first meal, **(8)** ... of little pieces of a special meat. At 6 weeks old, they are taken outside to get used **(9)** ... the cooler temperature. The **(10)** ... stages of the bird's introduction to the wild take place at the top of a(n) **(11)** ... tower, where they are kept in a big cage and fed on fish. As time goes by, the cages are removed and they eventually **(12)** ... to fly. All would agree that the **(13)** ... of these beautiful birds flying high in the southern skies **(14)** ... all the **(15)** ... worthwhile.

0	**A** regarded	**B** called	**C** referred	**D** known				
1	**A** measure	**B** move	**C** action	**D** step				
2	**A** assembled	**B** concentrated	**C** piled	**D** collected				
3	**A** throughout	**B** all	**C** at	**D** through				
4	**A** journey	**B** cruise	**C** travel	**D** expedition				
5	**A** certain	**B** safe	**C** sure	**D** harmless				
6	**A** avoids	**B** prevents	**C** hinders	**D** protects				
7	**A** controlled	**B** checked	**C** seen	**D** noted				
8	**A** consisting	**B** making	**C** having	**D** including				
9	**A** of	**B** from	**C** to	**D** in				
10	**A** end	**B** final	**C** latest	**D** finished				
11	**A** eminent	**B** deep	**C** outstanding	**D** high				
12	**A** learn	**B** train	**C** teach	**D** practise				
13	**A** vision	**B** picture	**C** sight	**D** view				
14	**A** creates	**B** makes	**C** does	**D** has				
15	**A** attempts	**B** effort	**C** trial	**D** experiment				

	A	B	C	D
0	☐	☐	☐	■
1	☐	☐	☐	☐
2	☐	☐	☐	☐
3	☐	☐	☐	☐
4	☐	☐	☐	☐
5	☐	☐	☐	☐
6	☐	☐	☐	☐
7	☐	☐	☐	☐
8	☐	☐	☐	☐
9	☐	☐	☐	☐
10	☐	☐	☐	☐
11	☐	☐	☐	☐
12	☐	☐	☐	☐
13	☐	☐	☐	☐
14	☐	☐	☐	☐
15	☐	☐	☐	☐

Part 2

For questions 16 - 30, read the text below and think of the word which best fits each space.
Use only one word in each space. Write your answers in the answer boxes provided.

Tasty Snacks

We **(0)** .... love to eat between meals, **(16)** .... it's a bar of chocolate after breakfast or a packet of crisps before dinner. But when we think **(17)** .... it, most of these "snack" foods are **(18)** .... of fat, salt and sugar and thus contain a **(19)** .... of calories. Another disadvantage is that after **(20)** .... consumed these foods, there is a temptation to eat **(21)** .... as they still leave you feeling hungry. But who says snack foods have to be bad **(22)** .... you? They can, in **(23)** ...., be very good for you if you just choose carefully.

One of the best and healthiest snack options is dried fruit. It's really tasty and makes a brilliant, easy-to-eat snack, as **(24)** .... as leaving you satisfied. **(25)** .... is also a great variety to choose **(26)** ...., with dried bananas, apricots, grapes and apples available at **(27)** .... supermarkets. You can enjoy dried fruit for morning and afternoon breaks, at school or at work, in the car or **(28)** .... watching television. Dried fruit also makes the perfect fast food for late-night homework sessions. So next time you fancy **(29)** .... sweet, try the healthy option and you'll **(30)** .... pleasantly surprised.

0	*all*	0 ▬
16		16
17		17
18		18
19		19
20		20
21		21
22		22
23		23
24		24
25		25
26		26
27		27
28		28
29		29
30		30

Part 3

For questions 31 - 40, complete the second sentence so that it has a similar meaning to the first sentence. Use the word given and other words to complete each sentence. You must use between two and five words. Do not change the word given. Write your answers in the answer boxes provided.

0 I'm sure it wasn't Jim who did it.
have
It .... Jim who did it.

0	*can't have been*	0 **0** 1 2

31 He hasn't finished packing yet.
still
He .... packing.

31		31 **0** 1 2

32 It was foolish of her to give up her job.
should
She .... her job.

32		32 **0** 1 2

33 He couldn't run fast because of his swollen ankle.
prevented
His swollen ankle .... fast.

33		33 **0** 1 2

34 It's pointless to argue about it any more.
worth
It's .... any more.

34		34 **0** 1 2

35 They finished sooner than we had expected.
take
They didn't .... we had expected to finish.

35		35 **0** 1 2

36 "I'm sorry I spoilt your plans," he said.
for
He .... my plans.

36		36 **0** 1 2

37 We should go to bed; it's past eleven.
turn
We ....; it's past eleven.

37		37 **0** 1 2

38 She raised two children while working at the same time.
up
She .... while working at the same time.

38		38 **0** 1 2

39 The doctor won't let him take any strenuous exercise.
be
He won't .... any strenuous exercise.

39		39 **0** 1 2

40 I'm sure he knew all along.
have
He .... all along.

40		40 **0** 1 2

Practice Test 6 ....

For questions 41 - 55, read the text below and look carefully at each line. Some of the lines are correct and some have a word which should not be there. If a line is correct, put a tick (✔) by the number in the answer boxes provided. If a line has a word which should not be there, write the word in the answer boxes provided.

Exploring France

0	Every October I like to go to the France for my holidays.	
00	Last year I visited the Loire Valley and I had the best	
41	two weeks of my life. I had got such good fun I cried when	
42	it was time to leave. When I was arrived in Calais	
43	the sun was shining and I was glad I had decided to	
44	go for camping. There are lots of campsites in the Loire,	
45	and I found a small one near of a beautiful castle. King	
46	Louis XIV had the castle built in order that to impress a	
47	princess he wanted her to marry, but she rejected him for an	
48	English Duke. I fell in love with the place at once. The campsite	
49	was superb. Although October is late for camping, there	
50	were quite a lot of people staying in there. It was	
51	highly recommended in my guidebook and a friend of	
52	mine had also suggested I go to that particular one site.	
53	Most of the other campers were at around my age and I	
54	made friends with several of them. Six of us have agreed	
55	to meet there again next year for another more great holiday.	

0	the	___0___
00	✓	___00___
41		___41___
42		___42___
43		___43___
44		___44___
45		___45___
46		___46___
47		___47___
48		___48___
49		___49___
50		___50___
51		___51___
52		___52___
53		___53___
54		___54___
55		___55___

For questions 56 - 65, read the text below. Use the word given in capitals at the end of each line to form a word that fits in the space in the same line. Write your word in the answer boxes provided.

The Planet Jupiter

Jupiter is the (0) .... planet in order of distance from the sun. It takes almost twelve years to complete a whole (56) .... of the sun. When viewed through telescopes from Earth's (57) ...., the "great red spot" is Jupiter's most (58) .... feature. This oval spot is (59) .... 28,000 miles long. It was pale pink in early (60) .... drawings but, in recent decades, astronomers have recorded a (61) .... towards a red grey colour. The spot changes position from time to time - sometimes drifting as far as 20,000 miles from where it is (62) .... seen. Spacecrafts have sent back (63) .... views of Jupiter's orbiting moons. Jupiter's nearest moon is called "Io" and has (64) .... volcanoes which are (65) .... erupting.

FIVE

REVOLVE
OBSERVE
NOTICE
ROUGH
ASTRONOMY
DEVELOP

NORMAL
FASCINATE
ACT
CONTINUE

0	fifth	___0___
56		___56___
57		___57___
58		___58___
59		___59___
60		___60___
61		___61___
62		___62___
63		___63___
64		___64___
65		___65___

Passive Voice / Causative Form 7

Passive Voice

The **passive** is formed with the appropriate tense of the verb **to be** + past participle. Only transitive verbs (verbs which take an object) can be put into the passive.

	Active Voice	Passive Voice
Present Simple	He **gives** lectures.	Lectures **are given**.
Present Continuous	He **is giving** a lecture.	A lecture **is being given**.
Past Simple	He **gave** a lecture.	A lecture **was given**.
Past Continuous	He **was giving** a lecture.	A lecture **was being given**.
Future Simple	He **will give** a lecture.	A lecture **will be given**.
Present Perfect	He **has given** a lecture.	A lecture **has been given**.
Past Perfect	He **had given** a lecture.	A lecture **had been given**.
Future Perfect	He **will have given** a lecture.	A lecture **will have been given**.
Present Infinitive	He should **give** a lecture.	A lecture should **be given**.
Perfect Infinitive	He should **have given** a lecture.	A lecture should **have been given**.
-ing form	She remembers him **giving** a lecture.	She remembers a lecture **being given**.
Perfect -ing form	**Having given** the lecture, ...	The lecture **having been given**, ...
modal + be + p.p.	He **must give** a lecture.	The lecture **must be given**.

- **Present Perfect Continuous, Future Continuous and Past Perfect Continuous are not normally used in the passive.**
- **Get is used in colloquial English instead of be to express something happening by accident.**
  She'**ll get** killed if she goes on driving like that.

Use

The passive is used: **a) when the person who performs the action (agent) is unknown, unimportant or obvious from the context** Her flat **was broken into** yesterday. (by a burglar - obvious agent) **b) to emphasise the agent** Her wedding dress was delivered to her **by the dressmaker herself** yesterday. **c) to make statements more formal or polite** My dress **has been ruined**. (more polite than saying "You have ruined my dress.) **and d) when we are more interested in the action than the agent, such as in news reports, formal notices, instructions, processes, headlines, advertisements** etc. A Christmas bazaar **will be held** tomorrow.

150 *Put the verbs in brackets into the correct passive form.*

1 Holland ...*is said*... (say) to be one of the prettiest countries in Europe.
2 I hate .... (tell) lies.
3 My television .... (deliver) tomorrow.
4 Their telephone .... (install) yesterday.
5 Teachers ought .... (pay) a higher salary.
6 Hotel rooms must .... (vacate) by 12 noon.
7 The villa .... (sell) by public auction next week.
8 She hopes her home .... (build) by May.
9 *Heartbreak House* .... (write) by George Bernard Shaw.
10 My car .... (respray) at the moment.
11 Hopefully, she .... (promote) by the end of next month.
12 I wish I .... (teach) how to type when I was at school.
13 Your application should .... (hand in) last Monday. It's too late now I'm afraid!
14 The wedding reception must .... (book) a month before the wedding.
15 The building .... (evacuate) ten minutes before the explosion took place.

Changing from Active into Passive

- The object of the active verb becomes the subject in the passive sentence. The active verb changes into a passive form and the subject of the active verb becomes the agent, which is either introduced with "by" or is omitted.

Active Voice		
subject	verb	object
John	posted	the letters.

Passive Voice		
subject	verb	agent
The letters	were posted	by John.

- **By + agent** is used to say who or what did the action. *She was knocked over by a car.* **With + instrument /material** is used to say what the agent used or after past participles such as coloured, crammed, crowded, filled, flavoured, packed etc. *She was killed with a hammer.* **By + agent** is omitted when the agent is **unknown, unimportant, obvious from the context** or referred to by words such as: **someone, people, I, etc.** *They revealed the truth.* ➡ *The truth was revealed.* ("by them" is omitted)
- **Verbs which take who objects** *(give, offer etc)* form their passive in two ways; it is more usual to start the sentence with the person object, not the thing object. *They offered Ann a bunch of flowers.* ➡ *Ann was offered a bunch of flowers.* (more usual than: *A bunch of flowers was offered to Ann.*)
- **Verbs followed by a preposition** *(accuse of, take down etc)* take the preposition immediately after them when turned into the passive. *She took down the minutes of the meeting.* ➡ *The minutes of the meeting were taken down.*
- In **passive questions** with **who, whom** or **which** we do not omit **by**. *Who gave you this information?* ➡ *Who were you given this information by?*
- **Hear, help, make, see** are followed by a **to-infinitive** in the passive. *She made me work overtime.* ➡ *I was made to work overtime.* **Note that hear, see, watch** can be followed by a **present participle** in the active and passive. *We saw her crying.* ➡ *She was seen crying.*

151 *Change the sentences from the active into the passive. Omit the agent where it can be omitted.*

1 Santa Claus will leave your presents in the stocking. ...*Your presents will be left in the stocking by Santa Claus.*...
2 Bad organisation spoiled their holiday. ....
3 Teachers mark hundreds of exam papers every year. ....
4 Who wrote *Romeo and Juliet?* ....
5 You should dry your hair before you go out. ....
6 You mustn't tell him the truth. ....
7 She likes people taking her to the theatre. ....
8 Why didn't they give her the job? ....
9 She told them not to tell anyone. ....
10 They should have given us a bonus. ....
11 The doctors will bring him in for an examination. ....
12 Fog has delayed all flights. ....
13 She didn't send me any parcels. ....
14 She had cleaned the house before I got there. ....
15 When we arrived at the hotel, they had filled all the rooms. ....
16 Why haven't you invited Mary to the party? ....
17 Paula will help you finish your project. ....
18 The mayor is opening the new community centre next week. ....
19 We heard her complaining strongly to the manager. ....
20 You can leave your bags at the left-luggage office. ....
21 Workmen found some antique vases in the old house. ....
22 The architects have drawn up plans for the new library. ....
23 Who gave him the new car? ....
24 They are going to set the lion free next week. ....
25 What time do you expect him to arrive? ....

152 *Change the sentences from the passive into the active.*

1 Who was the Mona Lisa painted by? ...*Who painted the Mona Lisa?*...
2 The old barn has been pulled down. ....
3 The results will be published in July. ....
4 The trip was ruined by bad weather. ....
5 The letter should have been posted last week. ....
6 Who was the money raised by? ....
7 Why hasn't the house been painted yet? ....
8 She was heard shouting. ....
9 How much were you paid? ....
10 His car has been stolen. ....
11 I can't bear being cheated. ....
12 A famous actress will be chosen to advertise the product. ....
13 John was made to do the washing up. ....
14 The ozone layer is gradually being destroyed by pollution. ....
15 A bring-and-buy sale is being held next month. ....
16 Our house was done up by a famous interior decorator. ....
17 The cracks in the wall were caused by the earthquake. ....
18 Thousands of rare birds are killed by hunters every year. ....
19 Her purse was stolen on the bus. ....
20 When will we be told the time of his arrival? ....
21 An ancient village has been uncovered by archaeologists. ....
22 Why hasn't the dishwasher been repaired yet? ....
23 A new drug is being developed by scientists. ....
24 A new breed of cow is to be introduced into the country by farmers. ....
25 The furniture will have been removed by noon. ....
26 Who were you going to be replaced by? ....
27 The island is being ruined by tourists. ....
28 Two rooms had been booked for her by her travel agent. ....
29 She was seen to leave the building. ....
30 Seats should have been reserved a week ago. ....

153 *Fill in "by" or "with".*

1 *The Magus* was written ...*by*... John Fowles.
2 Who was the radio invented ....?
3 The cyclist was knocked down .... a bus.
4 Soup is eaten .... a spoon.
5 The car was fixed .... a mechanic.

6 The glass was cut .... a special tool.
7 Her hair is coloured .... henna.
8 "Born in the USA" was sung .... Springsteen.
9 The roast was flavoured .... wine.
10 Music will be played .... the local band.

154 *Change into the passive.*

A Police are investigating a series of break-ins in the Hattersby area. Residents have heard noises, but nobody has actually seen anything suspicious. The recent rise in crime in the neighbourhood has shocked residents. Locals are discussing matters of security with the police and they have requested greater police presence in the area.

...*A series of break-ins*..
....
....
....
....

B A wealthy businessman has just bought the Black Swan Hotel. The Barrett family owned it for many years, and they should have restored the building many years ago, but they couldn't find enough money. The new owner is closing the hotel for a few months for redecoration. At the moment workmen are polishing the floors and redecorating all the rooms.

The verbs **believe, expect, feel, hope, know, report, say, think** etc are used in the following passive patterns in personal and impersonal constructions.

- **subject (person) + passive verb + to -inf** (personal construction)
- **it + passive verb + that -clause** (impersonal construction)

The police report that she is in France.
She is reported to be in France.
It is reported that she is in France.

155 *Turn the following sentences into the passive as in the example:*

1 They think he is lying.
   He ...*is thought to be lying*....
   It ...*is thought that he is lying*....
2 They believe he got lost in the forest.
   He ....
   It ....
3 They say she has been very ill.
   She ....
   It ....
4 They said the president had been shot.
   The president ....
   It ....
5 They believe she was taking drugs.
   She ....
   It ....

6 They expect he will pass his driving test.
   He ....
   It ....
7 They said she was wrongly accused.
   She ....
   It ....
8 They believe he is leaving soon.
   He ....
   It ....
9 They say his health is very poor.
   His health ....
   It ....
10 They report that some papers have been stolen.
   Some papers ....
   It ....

156 *Complete the sentences using the words in bold. Use two to five words.*

1 Many people believe that eating too fast causes indigestion.
   believed It ...*is believed that eating*... too fast causes indigestion.
2 The teacher will send you out if you keep on talking.
   be You .... if you keep on talking.
3 They are going to transfer him to Portugal.
   be He .... to Portugal.
4 They will have completed the construction by September.
   been The .... by September.
5 They are holding the caretaker responsible for the problems.
   is The .... for the problems.
6 A journalist is going to cover the story.
   be The story .... by a journalist.
7 They will have appointed a new director by the end of the week.
   been A new .... by the end of the week.
8 They gave him a gold watch when he retired.
   was He .... when he retired.
9 The mother told her son off for shouting.
   was He .... by his mother for shouting.
10 They are opening the new restaurant this evening.
   is The new restaurant .... this evening.

157 *Rewrite the following text in the passive.*

Mr Owen Gibbon has discovered a valuable oil painting in the attic of his house in Rochester. George Stubbs, the famous animal artist, painted the work in 1760. Mr Gibbon's great-grandfather bought the picture in the 1890's, but after his death the family stored it away in the attic. Art historians are examining the painting, and have valued it at £500,000. Mr Gibbon has offered the work to the National Gallery, where experts will restore the picture to its former beauty. They will have finished the restoration work by June.

....

....

....

158 *Rewrite the following texts in the passive.*

A The Winter Production Company has finally released the film which the public has been waiting for for so long: *The Hawk*. The Winter Company was originally going to release the film in August but they decided to wait until October, as they know that fewer people go to the cinema in the summer. Richard Able directed *The Hawk* and critics are encouraging people to see it. Cinemas report that British audiences have bought a lot of tickets and that they are sure *The Hawk* will be a success.

....

....

....

B Over the past ten years oil spills have polluted the seas surrounding Britain. The tankers spill oil onto the coast and this harms many forms of wildlife. Environmentalists say that they need a lot of volunteers if they are to minimise the damage. In future, the government has promised that it will prosecute the owners of any tankers that pollute the North Sea in this way. The government also hopes that they can prevent such incidents by building more lighthouses along the coastline.

....

....

....

Oral Development 8

A fire broke out yesterday at Chelsey. Look at the notes below, then report the incident. You may use ideas of your own. Use passive forms.

- fire - department store - 11.00 pm last night
- passer-by notice flames 2nd floor
- call firefighters - try to put it out
- 2 night-watchmen trapped - taken to hospital
- now treated for 3rd degree burns
- half building destroyed
- reason for fire: electrical fault

eg. A fire broke out at 11.00 pm last night. Flames were noticed on the 2nd floor by a passer-by ...

Causative Form (have sth done)

- We use **have + object + past participle** to say that we arrange for someone to do something for us.
  *He asked Sally to type the letters. He **had the letters typed**. (He didn't do it himself - Sally did it.)*

Present Simple	*She **makes** dresses.*	*She **has** dresses made.*
Present Continuous	*She **is making** a dress.*	*She **is having** a dress made.*
Past Simple	*She **made** a dress.*	*She **had** a dress made.*
Past Continuous	*She **was making** a dress.*	*She **was having** a dress made.*
Future Simple	*She **will make** a dress.*	*She **will have** a dress made.*
Future Continuous	*She **will be making** a dress.*	*She **will be having** a dress made.*
Present Perfect	*She **has made** a dress.*	*She **has had** a dress made.*
Present Perf. Cont.	*She **has been making** dresses.*	*She **has been having** dresses made.*
Past Perfect	*She **had made** a dress.*	*She **had had** a dress made.*
Past Perfect Cont.	*She **had been making** dresses.*	*She **had been having** dresses made.*
Infinitive	*She can **make** dresses.*	*She can **have** dresses made.*
-ing form	*She likes **making** dresses.*	*She likes **having** dresses made.*

- The verb **to have**, used in the causative, forms its **negations** and **questions** with **do/does** (Present Simple) or **did** (Past Simple). *He **doesn't have** his shirts ironed. **Did he have** the brakes checked?*
- **Get** is often used in the causative instead of **have**. *Did you **have/get** your nails polished?*
- The **causative** can be used instead of the passive to express **accidents** and **misfortunes**. *He **had** his nose broken in a fight. (= His nose was broken in a fight.)*

159 *Write the sentences in the causative as in the example:*

1 Their wedding reception was organised by caterers.
   ...They had their wedding reception organised by caterers....
2 I'll ask her to make the appointment for Friday. ....
3 He was mending the table for Sophie. ....
4 He took his boots to be re-heeled. ....
5 Has your leg been X-rayed? ....
6 I will tell James to cancel the meeting tomorrow. ....
7 Don't ask them to post the letters. ....
8 I'll get the men to move this for you by this evening. ....
9 The mechanic is repairing her car. ....
10 They renovated the Smiths' house last year. ....
11 They are going to clean our swimming pool. ....
12 Where do they take their photographs to be developed? ....
13 He doesn't mind the barber cutting his hair short. ....
14 You should ask someone to water your plants while you're on holiday. ....
15 Will she get someone to deliver the computer? ....
16 She prefers sending her clothes to the dry-cleaner's. ....
17 My father likes people taking his photograph. ....
18 Our cooker was being repaired when the lights went off. ....
19 Would you like someone to do the shopping for you? ....
20 The beautician polished the model's nails. ....

160 *Write sentences in the causative as in the example:*

1 The doctor examined Paul's ankle. What did Paul do? *...He had his ankle examined....*
2 Someone delivers her groceries once a week. What does she do?
   ....
3 A hairdresser has cut and styled Pamela's hair. What has she done?
   ....

4 Someone will repair our leaking roof. What will we do?

....

5 Someone cut the lawn for them while they were away. What did they do?

....

6 Somebody had serviced their car before they went on holiday. What had they done?

....

7 A builder will do up Jan's attic. What will Jan do?

....

8 Someone is designing some furniture for him. What is he doing?

....

9 A detective investigated the case for her. What did she do?

....

10 Someone has written the actor's life story for him. What has he done?

....

11 Someone is organising a birthday party for her. What is she doing?

....

12 The secretary had prepared the minutes for him before the meeting. What had he done?

....

13 He was building their swimming pool. What were they doing?

....

14 He had someone paint his daughter's portrait. What did he do?

....

- **Make/Have + object + bare infinitive** are used to express that someone **causes** someone else to do something, but their meaning is slightly different. *She **made John do** the shopping. (She insisted that John should do the shopping.) She **had John do** the shopping. (She asked John to do the shopping.)*
- **Get + object + to -inf** shows that someone **persuades** someone else to do something. *She **got Ann to tidy** her room. (She persuaded Ann to tidy her room.)*

161 *Rephrase the following using have, get or make as in the example:*

1 She insisted that they go to the meeting. ...*She made them go to the meeting.*...
2 We are going to ask the plumber to install a new shower. ....
3 We persuaded Paul to lend us some money. ....
4 The teacher asked Sam to open the window. ....
5 The dentist insisted that George sit still. ....
6 Mrs Jones will ask the attendant to fetch her car. ....
7 The doctor persuaded her to go to hospital. ....
8 My brother insisted that I give him back his book. ....
9 She persuaded her friend to help her with the cleaning. ....
10 We'll ask the receptionist to give him his key. ....
11 He insisted on them keeping quiet. ....
12 My father persuaded me to help him wash his car. ....
13 Mr Smith insisted that Jane stay late at work. ....
14 I'll ask Pam to turn down the radio. ....
15 Sue persuaded the caretaker to fix the door. ....

162 *Complete the sentences using the words in bold. Use two to five words.*

1 The hairdresser will have to cut your hair.
   have   You'll ...*have to have your hair*... cut.
2 A large dog has attacked my cat.
   been   My cat .... a large dog.
3 Her mother insisted that she buy a new dress for the party.
   her   Her mother .... a new dress for the party.

4 Someone will steal your purse if you don't look after it.
   be   Your purse .... if you don't look after it.
5 Jane insisted that I have some more cake.
   made   Jane .... some more cake.
6 They are resurfacing our drive tomorrow.
   resurfaced We .... tomorrow.
7 Our furnace will need servicing soon.
   have   We will need .... soon.
8 Someone cleans my house every week.
   have   I .... every week.
9 How did he persuade you to do it?
   get   How .... do it?
10 She got a friend to make her an evening dress.
   made   She .... by a friend.
11 Their house had been burgled when I last saw them.
   had   They .... when I last saw them.
12 I asked my parents to pay for my flight home.
   had   I .... for my flight home.
13 Hooligans attacked Barney outside the stadium.
   got   Barney .... outside the stadium.
14 She doesn't like ironing so the cleaner does it for her.
   done   She doesn't like ironing so .... by the cleaner.
15 He arranged for a friend to bring his books over from England.
   had   He .... from England.

Oral Development 9

The local council has decided to improve the children's park. Read the notes below, then make sentences using the causative. You can also use your own ideas.

things already done

build swimming pool, put up climbing frame, plant lawn

things being done

put up swings, install benches, paint roundabout

things to be done

tile toilets, paint walls, hire supervisors

things that will have been done by the end of the month

complete first-aid room, put in drinking fountain

eg. They have had the swimming pool built.

163 *Complete the sentences using the words in bold. Use two to five words.*

1 Lucy persuaded Andrew to take her out to dinner.
   got   Lucy ...*got Andrew to take her*... out to dinner.
2 Our heater needs repairing.
   have   We'll .... repaired.
3 A beautician does her nails every week.
   done   She .... by a beautician every week.
4 The dentist is extracting her tooth now.
   extracted   She .... now.

5 I'll ask Mark to fetch my laundry.
   have   I .... my laundry.
6 His car was badly damaged in an accident.
   had   He .... in an accident.
7 The shopkeepers were forced to work on Christmas Eve.
   made   The shopkeepers .... on Christmas Eve.
8 He got someone at the office to send the fax.
   sent   He .... by someone at the office.
9 She insisted that we come home early.
   made   We .... early.
10 Someone had dented her car when she came out of the shop.
   had   She .... when she came out of the shop.
11 They can get someone to groom the dog next week.
   have   They can .... next week.
12 He used to pay someone to do his accounts once a month.
   done   He used .... once a month.
13 Why did he insist that I buy this dress?
   make   Why .... this dress?
14 Did he ask the nurse to dress the wound?
   get   Did he .... the wound?
15 The boxer broke his arm in a fight.
   broken   The boxer .... in a fight.
16 I must have someone look at this painting - it might be valuable.
   looked   I must .... - it might be valuable.
17 The contract will have been drawn up for you by the time you get back.
   had   We will .... up for you by the time you get back.
18 The police ordered him to tell them what had happened.
   made   The police .... what had happened.
19 Margery dealt with the new client for him.
   got   He .... the new client for him.

164 *Find the word which should not be in the sentence.*

1 She has been had her house repainted.
2 Did he make you to stay at home?
3 He was been knighted for his service to the country.
4 Liz has had her hair be done.
5 The bankrobbers were been arrested at the airport yesterday.
6 The pictures they were donated to the gallery by the Queen.
7 She did got him to cook dinner for her.
8 He was been stopped at customs.
9 Charlotte had Bill to mend her TV.
10 The symphony was being written by Sibelius.
11 Could you have someone to repair the fax machine?
12 He paid a lot to have had the engine rebuilt.
13 They have their taxes be done by an accountant.
14 The goods will have be shipped to you tomorrow.
15 He likes to having his autograph asked for.
16 Those faxes have to be had sent today.
17 They have had central heating installed last Monday.
18 Jo was been given a beautiful necklace for Christmas.
19 All the windows were being broken in last night's explosion.
20 She had her nose be broken while playing cricket.

1	been
2	
3	
4	
5	
6	
7	
8	
9	
10	
11	
12	
13	
14	
15	
16	
17	
18	
19	
20	

165 *Look at Appendix 2, then substitute the underlined words with keep, let or look and the appropriate particles.*

1 Mary had <u>to stay away</u> from school as she was ill.   *...to be kept away...*

2 You should <u>stay away from</u> fattening foods.   ....

3 They <u>continued</u> climbing despite the heavy snowfall.   ....

4 He had to run to <u>move at the same speed as</u> the boys.   ....

5 You have to <u>continue to be informed of</u> the latest news.   ....

6 It was raining so heavily that I thought it would never <u>become less strong</u>.   ....

7 We thought we would be fined but fortunately the policeman <u>didn't punish us</u>.   ....

8 Sarah is growing so chubby that I have to <u>make her clothes bigger</u>.   ....

9 He really <u>disappointed us</u> by not keeping his promise.   ....

10 Can you <u>take care of</u> my children this afternoon?   ....

11 My grandfather <u>fondly remembers</u> the days of his youth.   ....

12 She <u>looked quickly at</u> her notes before entering the office.   ....

13 Do <u>visit</u> us some day!   ....

14 She <u>despises</u> people who don't have a university degree.   ....

15 They <u>examined</u> the flat before they rented it.   ....

16 She <u>carefully examined</u> the contract before she signed it.   ....

17 If you don't understand a word, <u>look for it</u> in a dictionary.   ....

166 *Look at Appendix 3, then fill in the correct preposition.*

1 Ireland relies ...*on*... tourism to boost its income and provide employment.

2 My teeth are very sensitive .... cold things such as ice-cream.

3 Her family have always abstained .... drinking.

4 Several diseases may result .... not getting enough vitamin C.

5 The quarrel resulted .... Catherine leaving the house.

6 The results .... the competition were announced yesterday.

7 Carrots are rich .... vitamin A.

8 Everyone joins .... with the choir at the end of the service.

9 Doctors are meant to be sympathetic .... their patients' fears.

10 Sally was able to sympathise .... my situation as she'd been through something similar before.

11 Has it ever occurred .... you that you need more interests in your life?

12 The reason .... the closure of the club was lack of membership.

13 I tried to reason .... David but he was just too upset to listen.

14 I decided to leave the club rather than submit .... its new rules.

15 The builders have submitted their plans .... approval by the council.

16 Joe succeeded .... reaching the airport on time despite the heavy traffic.

17 Jim is such a horrible person - he's rude .... everyone.

18 I had to lean .... the wall as I felt as if I was going to faint.

19 The police searched the premises .... weapons.

20 The burglars ransacked the house in search .... valuables.

21 Although they spoiled our plans, they weren't a bit sorry .... it.

22 Don't say you're sorry .... annoying me if you don't mean it.

23 I'm really counting .... all the family being there.

24 I don't think they're going to offer her the job. I feel her age may count .... her.

25 The relationship .... a mother and her baby is a very special one.

26 John has got such a great relationship .... Clare.

27 Spain is very popular .... British holiday makers.

28 Children are prone .... illnesses such as chickenpox, mumps and measles.

167 *Complete the sentences using the words in bold. Use two to five words.*

1 She is too poor to buy a house.
   not   She ...*isn't rich enough to buy*... a house.
2 Can't you get a better picture on the TV?
   the   Is this .... get on the TV?
3 He asked his mum to shorten his trousers.
   shortened He .... by his mum.
4 Always beware of pickpockets while shopping.
   look   Always .... while shopping.
5 The coffee is so hot I can't drink it.
   too   The coffee .... to drink.
6 He left one morning and we still don't know where he is.
   day   He left one morning and .... we don't know where he is.
7 He hates his mother telling him off.
   told   He hates .... his mother.
8 There's a meeting going on next door.
   progress   There's .... next door.
9 George is the most boring person I've ever met.
   such   I've .... person as George.
10 She spent all morning decorating the flat.
   doing   She spent all morning .... the flat.
11 "No, I won't accept your apology," she said to me.
   to   She .... apology.
12 She was ninety-two when she died.
   age   She .... ninety-two.

168 *Choose the correct verb to complete the sentences.*

1 I don't like doing business with him because he ...B... such a hard bargain.
   A makes B drives C leads D arranges

2 The audience .... their breath until the acrobat was safely down from the highwire.
   A took B caught C wasted D held

3 I don't think Robert is responsible enough to .... a business on his own.
   A run B do C bear D make

4 They're trying to .... their child out of the habit of telling lies.
   A finish B end C change D break

5 Don't .... heart - I'm sure you'll succeed if you keep trying.
   A take B cross C lose D sink

6 We have enough problems without you .... trouble all the time.
   A falling B getting C being D making

7 The doctor may be able to help you, but don't expect him to .... miracles.
   A create B work C turn D develop

8 Surely you know it's rude to ..... people names?
   A shout B call C insult D give

9 I think we ought to .... a party for Tim's birthday.
   A drop B put C throw D cast

10 Just because Louise makes a lot of money, everyone expects her to .... all the bills.
   A foot B stand C run D carry

11 He was found guilty of burglary and had to .... time in prison.
   A have B make C do D take

12 I don't mind if you come home late, but I .... the line at your staying out all night.
   A mark B draw C rule D colour

Practice Test 7 ....

Part 1

For questions 1 - 15, read the text below and decide which word A, B, C or D best fits each space. There's an example at the beginning (0).

Art Goes Audio

Visitors to the **(0)** ... Tate Gallery in London can now **(1)** ... the British artist David Hockney talk about one of his paintings, which is **(2)** ... *The Bigger Splash*. Following the example of the French, who have **(3)** ... such a system in the Louvre in Paris, technology is coming to both the Tate and the National Gallery, two of Britain's **(4)** ... prestigious art institutions. The Tate is now offering Tateinform, a personal audio **(5)** ... to the paintings and sculptures **(6)** ... show, and to the themes of **(7)** ... displays. At the **(8)** ... of a button visitors can listen to artists, art critics and gallery curators explaining any work that **(9)** ... their interest; they can stop, start, rewind or fast-forward their cassette machines **(10)**

... they want. Many of the commentaries on works of art **(11)** ... several layers of information. Style, content and symbols may be explained, or you may even be given details of particular paints the artist has used. Some of the artists **(12)** ... on the inspiration for their own works. David Hockney, for **(13)** ..., talks about his interest in the surface and movement of water in his commentary for *The Bigger Splash*. The **(14)** ... of audio guides is a great help to people wanting to **(15)** ... a better understanding of art.

0	A	known	B	familiar	C	famous	D	accustomed
1	A	hear	B	listen	C	attend	D	observe
2	A	told	B	said	C	announced	D	called
3	A	brought in	B	brought on	C	brought about	D	brought along
4	A	much	B	wholly	C	most	D	great
5	A	instruction	B	guide	C	plan	D	map
6	A	in	B	at	C	on	D	to
7	A	sure	B	definite	C	secure	D	certain
8	A	switch	B	touch	C	press	D	push
9	A	catches	B	opens	C	turns	D	fills
10	A	that	B	however	C	where	D	whenever
11	A	offer	B	say	C	propose	D	tell
12	A	aim	B	focus	C	look	D	direct
13	A	illustration	B	sample	C	instance	D	case
14	A	start	B	introduction	C	presentation	D	discovery
15	A	earn	B	take	C	gain	D	win

	A	B	C	D
0			▬	
1				
2				
3				
4				
5				
6				
7				
8				
9				
10				
11				
12				
13				
14				
15				

Part 2

For questions 16 - 30, read the text below and think of the word which best fits each space.
Use only one word in each space. Write your answers in the answer boxes provided.

Dinner Parties

Organising a dinner party can **(0)** .... a stressful business. Firstly you have to decide **(16)** .... you are going to invite and make **(17)** .... the guests are going to mix well. It's **(18)** .... good inviting people that are either going to sit around **(19)** .... small groups and only speak to each **(20)** .... or people that are going to hide behind the furniture and not talk at **(21)** .... Also you have to ensure they can get to and from your home **(22)** .... any problems. Next is organising the food. You want to prepare a meal that is above average standard, but doesn't **(23)** .... the earth. It is also wise to ask the guests about their likes and dislikes **(24)** .... you invite them, as you don't want to serve up a meal nobody **(25)** .... eat. Cooking the meal is important as **(26)** ...., because you want it ready at the time you stated. Seating arrangements are important too. You don't want **(27)** .... the quiet guests at one end of the table and the talkative **(28)** .... at the other. Serving drinks before, during and **(29)** .... the meal is always a good way to **(30)** .... people to relax and chat. And remember to shut the cat in another room, as you don't want it jumping onto the table searching for a snack!

0	be	0 ▭ ▬
16		16 ▭ ▭
17		17 ▭ ▭
18		18 ▭ ▭
19		19 ▭ ▭
20		20 ▭ ▭
21		21 ▭ ▭
22		22 ▭ ▭
23		23 ▭ ▭
24		24 ▭ ▭
25		25 ▭ ▭
26		26 ▭ ▭
27		27 ▭ ▭
28		28 ▭ ▭
29		29 ▭ ▭
30		30 ▭ ▭

Practice Test 7 ....

Part 3

For questions 31 - 40, complete the second sentence so that it has a similar meaning to the first sentence. Use the word given and other words to complete each sentence. You must use between two and five words. Do not change the word given. Write your answers in the answer boxes provided.

0 I'm sure it wasn't Jim who did it.
have
It .... Jim who did it.

0	*can't have been*	0 **0** 1 2

31 I'm looking forward to the summer holidays.
longing
I .... the summer holidays.

31		31 **0** 1 2

32 Is it OK if I park my car here?
objection
Is there .... my car here?

32		32 **0** 1 2

33 "I didn't cheat in the exam," he said.
cheating
He .... in the exam.

33		33 **0** 1 2

34 Since no one was interested, the meeting was cancelled.
interest
Due ...., the meeting was cancelled.

34		34 **0** 1 2

35 Isn't it a wonderful painting!
such
It .... painting!

35		35 **0** 1 2

36 Liz has got the flu.
gone
Liz .... the flu.

36		36 **0** 1 2

37 Get some more money; you might need it.
in
Get some more money .... it.

37		37 **0** 1 2

38 My parents don't want me to go to France.
object
My parents .... to France.

38		38 **0** 1 2

39 People believed the earth was flat.
believed
The earth .... flat.

39		39 **0** 1 2

40 She spent two weeks writing her essay.
her
It took .... her essay.

40		40 **0** 1 2

Part 4

For questions 41 - 55, read the text below and look carefully at each line. Some of the lines are correct and some have a word which should not be there. If a line is correct, put a tick (✔) by the number in the answer boxes provided. If a line has a word which should not be there, write the word in the answer boxes provided.

Caribbean Paradise

0	St Lucia has always been on one of my all-time favourite	**0** on
00	holiday destinations. I first discovered its dramatic	**00** ✓
41	scenery on my honeymoon before twelve years ago	**41**
42	and have been back such many times since. I generally	**42**
43	stay in the north of the island at where there are	**43**
44	many well-equipped villas situated in acres of private	**44**
45	tropical grounds along stretches of a white sandy beaches.	**45**
46	The food is excellent too, and combining traditional	**46**
47	local cooking with European sophistication.	**47**
48	During the day there is plenty to do so,	**48**
49	including watersports such like as windsurfing and	**49**
50	snorkelling and beach games like volleyball. Entertainment	**50**
51	is also being provided at night with steel bands and	**51**
52	limbo dancing. However, you can spend on many hours	**52**
53	just sitting up outside looking at the spectacular	**53**
54	sunsets and listening to the gentle lapping	**54**
55	of the waves on the shore. This is a real island paradise.	**55**

Part 5

For questions 56 - 65, read the text below. Use the word given in capitals at the end of each line to form a word that fits in the space in the same line. Write your word in the answer boxes provided.

Healthy Teeth for Life

With the latest **(0)** .... advances and a little	**TECHNOLOGY**	**0** technological
(56) .... care there's no reason why you shouldn't	**LOVE**	**56**
have **(57)** ...., healthy teeth for life. In fact, figures	**ATTRACT**	**57**
show that children now have healthier teeth than		**58**
ever before. All you need to do is follow these sim-		
ple guidelines **(58)** .... . Remove plaque by brush-	**CARE**	**59**
ing your teeth twice **(59)** .... . It is	**DAY**	**60**
(60) .... important to clean them before you go to	**PARTICULAR**	**61**
sleep as **(61)** .... against acid damage, since the	**PROTECT**	**62**
(62) .... of saliva declines during sleep. Have your	**PRODUCE**	**63**
teeth checked **(63)** .... by your dentist, and take	**REGULAR**	
extra care of your teeth during **(64)** .... . Some	**PREGNANT**	**64**
dental **(65)** .... are free if you're pregnant - so	**TREAT**	**65**
make the most of it!		

8 Conditionals / Wishes / Unreal Past

Conditionals

	If-clause (hypothesis)	Main clause (result clause)	Use
Type 1 **real present**	**If + any present form** **(Present S., Present Cont.** **or Present Perfect)**	**Future/Imperative** **can/may/might/must/should** **+ bare inf/Present Simple**	**true or likely to** **happen in the** **present or future**
	*If you **play** with matches, you **will burn** yourself.* *If you **have taken** the books, you **can start** working on your essay.* *If you **see** him, **tell** him to come immediately.*		
Type 2 **unreal** **present**	**If + Past Simple** **or Past Continuous**	**would/could/might + bare** **infinitive**	**untrue in the** **present; also used** **to give advice**
	*If I **were** you, I **wouldn't feel** sorry at all. (advice)* *If she **was working** more, she **would be** paid more.* *(but she isn't working much - untrue in the present)*		
Type 3 **unreal** **past**	**If + Past Perfect or** **Past Perfect Continuous**	**would/could/might + have** **+ past participle**	**imaginary situation** **contrary to facts in** **the past; also used** **to express regrets** **or criticism**
	*If he **had followed** his parents' advice, he **wouldn't have lost** all his money.*		

- **Conditionals are usually introduced by if. Other expressions are: unless (= if not), providing, provided (that), as long as, on condition (that), but for + -ing form/noun, otherwise, or else, what if, supposing, even if, only if.** *Unless she stops eating like that, she'll have heart problems.* *Get up now **or else** you'll be late for school.* **Note that when only if begins a sentence, the subject and the verb of the main clause are inverted.** *Only if you have a ticket **will you be** allowed in.*
- **When the if-clause precedes the main clause, we separate the two clauses with a comma.** *If you are ill, you must stay in bed. but: You must stay in bed if you are ill.*
- **In conditionals type 2 in formal English we normally use were instead of was after if for all persons.** *If he **were**/**was** rich, he would travel round the world.*
- **We do not normally use will, would or should in if-clauses.** *If you **like** this, you can have it. (not: if you will like.)* **However, will, would or should can be used in if-clauses to make a request or express annoyance, doubt/uncertainty or insistence.** *If she **should** call, put her through to me. (doubt/uncertainty - I doubt that she will call ...) If you **will**/**would** be quiet, we'll watch the video. (request - Please be quiet.)*

169 *Put the verbs in brackets into the correct tense, then identify the types of conditionals.*

1 If you ...*don't do*... (not/do) your homework, you won't be allowed to go out. ...*(Type 1)*...
2 If he .... (take out) a loan, he'd be able to buy a car.
3 Keep the noise down or else someone .... (hear) us.
4 The state of the economy .... (improve) provided that there is a change of government.
5 I won't go on holiday unless you .... (come) with me.
6 If you .... (talk) less, you would be able to concentrate on your work.
7 If she .... (read) the newspaper, she would have known about the earthquake.
8 If the food .... (not/be) so good, we wouldn't have eaten so much.
9 If you .... (stop) complaining, we would be able to get some work done today.
10 Even if I .... (phone) them, it would have been too late to change their minds.
11 Unless you .... (turn down) the music, I won't be able to concentrate on what I'm doing.

12 Unemployment will decrease provided the government .... (take) appropriate measures.
13 If you continue to threaten me, I .... (have to) seek legal advice.
14 I .... (speak) to her if she apologised for her appalling behaviour.
15 I wouldn't have been able to sit the exam if you .... (not/help) me.
16 What .... (he/say) if you told him the truth?
17 If you watch this film, you .... (get) an idea of how difficult life is for these tribes.
18 If you .... (cancel) within the time limit, we would have given you a full refund.
19 If she had realised how late it was, she .... (not/ring) us.
20 We could have some fresh air if you .... (open) the window.

170 *Complete the text by putting the verbs in brackets into the correct tense.*

Einstein is reported to have said, "If I **1)** ...*had known*... (know) the destruction I would cause, I **2)** .... (become) a watch-maker." If we **3)** .... (continue) to use nuclear energy as a means of defence, we **4)** .... (make) our planet uninhabitable. If the public **5)** .... (be) more aware of the dangers, they **6)** .... (demand) the right to live in a safer society. If the Cold War had developed into World War III, the human race **7)** .... (be/wiped out) forever. Unless we **8)** .... (discover) a way to prevent nuclear war, by the 21st century we **9)** .... (face) major disaster. Some scientists claim that if we **10)** .... (tap into) the natural energy in the universe, we **11)** .... (provide) ourselves with a never-ending, pollution-free source of power. Only if we **12)** .... (put) more money into research and less into defence **13)** .... (we/be able to) discover other forms of energy. As long as we **14)** .... (continue) to abuse knowledge and power, the earth **15)** .... (remain) an insecure planet to inhabit.

171 *Rewrite the following as conditional sentences.*

1 You have to go to Athens to see the Acropolis.
   ...*If you go to Athens, you can see the Acropolis*....
2 You need to pass your driving test before you can drive.
   Unless ....
3 You must study harder to pass your exams.
   If ....
4 As long as the rain continues we can't play football.
   Unless ....
5 Tom had to ask for a pay rise or he wouldn't have got one.
   Unless ....
6 You need all the right spices to make an authentic Indian meal.
   If ....
7 Going there by bus will be cheaper than going by train.
   If ....
8 Entering this competition could win you a mountain bike.
   If ....
9 We will have to leave without him if he doesn't arrive in the next 10 minutes.
   Unless ....
10 We will be able to go swimming if the weather improves.
   Unless ....

172 *Read the following situations, then write as many conditional sentences as possible.*

1 As long as it rains, I'll stay at home.
   ...*If it rains, I'll stay at home. Only if it rains will I stay at home. I won't stay at home unless it rains*....
2 I'll save money, then I'll go to France on holiday.
   ....
   ....

3 Wait five minutes and I'll give you a lift.

....

....

4 I'll cook and you can do the washing up afterwards.

....

....

Omission of "if"

If can be omitted in if-clauses. In this case should (conditionals type 1), were (conditionals type 2) and had (conditionals type 3) come before the subject.
If he should win the race, he will receive £1,000. ➡ ***Should he win*** *the race, he will receive £1,000.*
If I were him, I wouldn't eat meat. ➡ ***Were I*** *him, I wouldn't eat meat.*
If I had seen her, I would have spoken to her. ➡ ***Had I seen*** *her, I would have spoken to her.*

173 *Rewrite the following sentences omitting "if".*

1 If I were you, I wouldn't apply for the post of firefighter.
....*Were I you, I wouldn't apply for the post of firefighter.* ...

2 If you should go to the post office, could you buy me some stamps?

....

3 If anyone should ring, will you take a message?

....

4 If you had turned off the oven sooner, the pizza wouldn't have burnt.

....

5 If I were younger, I'd accept his offer.

....

Mixed Conditionals

All types of conditionals can be mixed. Any tense combination is possible if the context permits it.

	If-clause	Main clause	
Type 2	*If she **was sleeping** all day,* (She was sleeping all day	*she **will feel** better now.* so she feels better now.)	**Type 1**
Type 2	*If I **were** rich,* (I'm not rich *If you **paid** more attention,* (You don't pay attention	*I **would have bought** a new car.* so I didn't buy a new car.) *you **wouldn't have made** such a mess.* so you made a mess.)	**Type 3**
Type 3	*If I **had been invited**,* (I wasn't invited	*I **would go** tonight.* so I'm not going tonight.)	**Type 2**

174 *Rewrite the following as mixed conditionals.*

1 He's not a good worker, so he wasn't promoted.
...*If he were a good worker, he would have been promoted.*...

2 They walked 40 kilometres, so they're exhausted now.

....

3 You didn't make an appointment, so we can't see you tomorrow.

....

4 She didn't take the medication and now she's ill again.

....

5 The flight left on time, so they will be in Moscow by now.

....

6 They were working in the rain all day, so they're soaking wet now.

....

7 She didn't study at all so she'll do badly in the test.

....

8 He's so gullible that he believed everything you said.

....

9 She was talking all day, so her throat is sore now.

....

10 He doesn't listen to anyone's advice, so he didn't do what you suggested.

....

175 *Complete the following sentences with an appropriate conditional clause.*

1 If you want an exotic holiday, ...*you should go to Thailand*...
2 Unless you give him enough notice, ...
3 If you hadn't overfed the cat, ...
4 Had I known she was in trouble, ...
5 Only if he apologises ....
6 The argument wouldn't have started if ....
7 If I had more time, ...
8 You wouldn't have had so much trouble if ....
9 Should I meet her again, ...
10 Had I known how late I was going to be, ...
11 Only if we start recycling ....
12 If you had tried harder, ...
13 Had he given me clearer instructions, ...
14 If we leave at six o'clock, ...
15 Should she ring while I'm out, ...

176 *Complete the sentences using the words in bold. Use two to five words.*

1 You'd better cut down on sugar.
   were   If I ...*were you, I would*... cut down on sugar.
2 Tom got lost because we didn't give him clear directions.
   have   Tom .... if we had given him clear directions.
3 If you don't criticise his work, he'll never improve.
   unless   He'll never improve .... his work.
4 She doesn't have many friends because she is shy.
   were   If she .... have many friends.
5 We'll only sign the contract if he changes that clause.
   will   Only if he changes that clause .... the contract.

6 He's afraid of heights, so he won't come climbing.
were If he ...., he would come climbing.

7 Lucy can prepare the report, but she'll have to be given instructions.
only Lucy can prepare the report .... instructions.

8 As long as you give it back by Friday, you can borrow my book.
provided You can borrow my book .... by Friday.

9 If you don't lend us some money, we won't be able to go to the theatre.
unless We won't be able to go to the theatre .... some money.

10 She missed the meeting because her car broke down.
broken She wouldn't have missed the meeting if .... down.

11 I need to get this to her, but I haven't got her fax number.
had If ...., I could get this to her.

12 He forgot about the invitation so he didn't go to the dinner.
not Had .... the invitation, he would have gone to the dinner.

13 I think Bill should look for a better job.
were If .... look for a better job.

14 We didn't take a map so we got lost.
taken If ...., we wouldn't have got lost.

15 Mark didn't tell her it was a secret so she told Pam.
have If Mark had told her it was a secret, ... Pam.

Wishes

Form		Use
I wish (if only) (wish/regret about the present)	+ Past tense	wish/regret about a present situation we want to be different
	*I wish we **were** on holiday. (It's a pity we aren't.)*	
I wish (if only) (wish/regret about the present)	+ could + bare infinitive	wish/regret in the present concerning lack of ability
	*I wish I **could** speak French. (but I can't)*	
I wish (if only) (regret about the past)	+ Past Perfect	regret that something happened or didn't happen in the past
	*I wish you **had listened** to me. (but you didn't)*	
I wish (if only) (impossible wish for a future change)	+ subject + would + bare inf (a. "wish" and "would" should have a different subject. We never say: I wish I would, He wishes he would etc b. wish + inanimate subject + would is used to express the speaker's disappointment or lack of hope	wish for a future change unlikely to happen or wish to express dissatisfaction; polite request implying dissatisfaction or lack of hope

*I wish he **would stop** lying. (But I don't think he will - wish for a future change unlikely to happen.)*
*I wish they **would take** this more seriously. (dissatisfaction)*
*I wish it **would stop** snowing.(But I'm afraid it won't stop snowing - wish implying disappointment)*
*I wish you **wouldn't throw** litter on the floor. (Please, don't throw litter on the floor - request implying lack of hope)*

● **After I wish we can use were instead of was in all persons.** *I wish he **were/was** more helpful.*

177 Put the verbs in brackets into the correct tense.

I've had a long career. If I **1)** ...*hadn't been chosen*... (not/be/chosen) to play the lead in my school play, I **2)** .... (not/become) what I am today. I was only nine and I'm sure I **3)** .... (feel) nervous if I **4)** .... (not/have) my parents' support. They encouraged me to take dancing classes after that. If only I **5)** .... (not/refuse)! I love dance now and if I **6)** .... (be) younger, I **7)** .... (study) ballet. Apart from that, I don't have many regrets about my career. I wish I **8)** .... (perform) more in the theatre, but I suppose if I **9)** .... (have), I **10)** .... (not/have) time to do so many film roles.

178 Write sentences as in the example:

1 You didn't watch the news so you didn't know there was a train strike.
   ...*I wish I had watched the news. If I had watched the news, I would have known there was a train strike.*...

2 You work long hours and you can't spend much time with your family.
   ....

3 You wanted to travel abroad but you forgot to renew your passport.
   ....

4 You can't drive a car so you can't get around easily.
   ....

5 You wanted to play tennis but you broke your racquet.
   ....

6 You want to go swimming but you have lost your swimming costume.
   ....

7 You want to climb the mountain but you are afraid of heights.
   ....

8 You didn't set your video correctly so you didn't record the film.
   ....

9 You want to go out tonight but you haven't got enough money.
   ....

10 You want to cook an Italian meal but you have no pasta left.
   ....

179 Rewrite the text using wishes or if-clauses as in the example:

> Dear Mary,
>   I just had to write and let you know what a terrible day I've had today. As my neighbour is ill I offered to take her dog for a walk. My neighbour did warn me that he's very energetic but I didn't listen. He dragged me all around the park. What a disaster! He was so excited that he knocked another neighbour off her bicycle. Unfortunately she hurt her leg and she was very angry with me. I shouldn't have taken the dog for a walk. To make matters worse, I had forgotten to lock the front door as we'd left the house in a rush. My house was burgled. Why was I so stupid? I hadn't even renewed our house insurance. My husband keeps going on about it.
>   Well, hopefully tomorrow will be better.
>
>   With love,
>   Lisa

...*I wish I hadn't had such a terrible day today.* ...

180 *Complete the sentences using the words in bold. Use two to five words.*

1 It's a pity I can't go to the cinema today, but I have to babysit.
   could   I wish ...*I could go to the*... cinema today, but I have to babysit.
2 It's a shame we didn't go out for dinner.
   gone   I wish .... for dinner.
3 I don't have many friends here.
   had   I wish .... here.
4 It's a pity I can't go out tonight but I have to work late.
   could   I wish .... but I have to work late.
5 It's a shame we didn't go home for Christmas.
   gone   I wish .... for Christmas.
6 If it weren't raining, we could go for a walk.
   stop   I wish ....; we could go for a walk.
7 It's a pity that I wasn't given the position.
   been   I wish .... the position.
8 I've been offered a job in Spain, but I can't speak Spanish.
   speak   I wish .... because I've been offered a job in Spain.
9 If it weren't snowing, we could go for a drive.
   stop   I wish ....; we could go for a drive.
10 It's a shame we missed the beginning of the film.
   missed   I wish .... beginning of the film.

181 *Complete the following sentences.*

1 If Bob hadn't broken his leg, ...*he could have come with us*....
2 If only he hadn't lied to Sally, ...
3 If John is in trouble, ...
4 If only she had more patience, ...
5 If she had won the competition, ...
6 Ann wishes she had set the alarm, ...
7 I wish I hadn't left the oven on too long, ...
8 If only I had written down her phone number, ...
9 If she hadn't been sitting in the sun all afternoon, ...
10 Tom wishes he hadn't gambled last Sunday, ...

Unreal Past

The Past Simple can be used to talk about imaginary, unreal or improbable situations in the present and the Past Perfect can be used to talk about imaginary, unreal or improbable situations in the past. This is called Unreal Past. Unreal Past is used as follows:

Past Simple	Past Perfect
• **Conditionals Type 2 (unreal in the present)** *If I* **were** *you, I would leave now.*	• **Conditionals Type 3 (unreal in the past)** *If I* **had known** *before, I wouldn't have come.*
• **wish (present)** *I wish she* **worked** *more efficiently.*	• **wish (past)** *If only he* **hadn't lied** *to me.*
• **I'd rather/sooner sb ... (present)** *I'd rather you* **left** *the files here, please.*	• **I'd rather/sooner sb ... (past)** *I'd rather you* **had not spoken** *like that yesterday.*
• **Suppose/Supposing** *Suppose you* **won** *the lottery, what would you buy?*	• **Suppose/Supposing** *Suppose she* **hadn't reminded** *you, would you have remembered?*
• **as if/as though (untrue situation in the present)** *He acts as if he* **were** *a genius.*	• **as if/as though (untrue situation in the past)** *She looked at me as if she* **had** *never* **seen** *me before.*
• **It's (about/high) time ...** *It's about time you* **learnt** *to drive.*	

182 *Put the verbs in brackets into the correct tense.*

1 Suppose they ...*had not turned up*... (not/turn up) to meet you, what would you have done?
2 If only I .... (not/eat) so much last night.
3 If she .... (tell) me it was a secret, I wouldn't have told anyone.
4 Suppose you .... (miss) your connection, how would you have got home?
5 Suppose he .... (catch) you smoking, what would you do?
6 I'd rather we .... (leave) now.
7 If only I .... (not/stay) out so late last night.
8 It's high time you .... (take) some responsibility for your actions.
9 Supposing you .... (fail) your exams, what would you have done?
10 It's time you .... (light) the fire - it's getting very cold.
11 She spends money as if she .... (have) loads of it, but I know she's in debt.
12 If we .... (install) a burglar alarm, this wouldn't have happened.
13 I'd rather we .... (go) home now.
14 I wish she .... (study) harder instead of watching TV all the time.
15 I'd rather she .... (not/wear) my dress last night. She's ruined it.

had better = should

- **I had better + present bare infinitive (present/future reference)**
  He **had better not wait** any longer. (= He should not wait any longer.)
- **It would have been better if + Past Perfect (past reference).** *It would have been better if **he had phoned** us to tell us not to wait. (= He should have phoned us to tell us not to wait.)*

would rather = I'd prefer

when the subject of would rather is also the subject of the following verb	**I'd rather +**	**Present bare infinitive (present/future reference)** **Perfect bare infinitive (past reference)**
	*I'd rather **stay** in tonight.* *I'd rather **not have taken** the bus, but I had no choice.*	
when the subject of would rather is different from the subject of the following verb	**I'd rather sb +**	**Past Simple (present/future reference)** **Past Perfect (past reference)**
	*I'd rather **you didn't** shout so much.* *I'd rather **you had come** with me yesterday.*	

- **prefer + gerund/noun + to + gerund/noun** (general). *I prefer **watching** TV **to reading** books.*
- **prefer + full infinitive + rather than + bare infinitive** (general preference)
  *I **prefer to eat** what I want **rather than count** calories.*
- **would prefer + full infinitive + rather than + bare infinitive** (specific preference)
  *I**'d prefer to play** football **rather than watch** it.*
- **would rather + bare infinitive + than + bare infinitive.** *I**'d rather ski than skate.***

183 *Read the following situations, then make sentences using would rather or had better.*

1 You want to play tennis not squash. ...*I would rather play tennis than play squash.* ...
2 You don't want her to invite him to the party. ....
3 You want to be left alone to read and don't want to go to the cinema. ....
4 It would be more sensible for you to go and rest for an hour. ....
5 I would prefer to spend Christmas in Spain and not go home. ....
6 We should have waited for him at home. ....
7 Mary always wears horrible orange lipstick. You wish she wouldn't. ....
8 Your friend turns up late and you are angry with him. ....

184 *Put the verbs in brackets into the correct form.*

1 I'd rather ...*go*... (go) fishing this afternoon.
2 I'd rather you .... (not/wear) my red dress to the dance tonight.
3 I'd rather you .... (say) that you didn't want to come!
4 I'd rather .... (go) by plane but I couldn't afford the air fare.
5 I'd rather you .... (not/use) such bad language! It upsets people.
6 We prefer .... (watch) films to .... (watch) political programmes.
7 I'd rather you .... (not/tell) them the news yet.
8 I prefer .... (cook) dinner rather than .... (eat) in that restaurant.
9 We'd prefer .... (call) our child David, rather than .... (call) him Stephen.
10 We would rather .... (recycle) our rubbish than .... (use) non-recyclable goods.
11 He had better .... (not/tell) her or I'll be furious!
12 After a lot of thought, we've decided that we would prefer .... (get/married) in Portugal rather than in England.
13 It would have been better if she .... (give) us the information sooner.
14 You'd better .... (not/wake) her up because she hasn't slept for two days.
15 I would prefer .... (pay) in cash rather than by credit card.

185 *Fill in the gaps with the appropriate auxiliary verb.*

1 She had her hair permed and now she wishes she ...*hadn't*....
2 Her husband spends a lot of money and she wishes he ....
3 I suspect they'll be late again but I wish they ....
4 She always forgets people's names but she wishes she ....
5 He invited 20 people for dinner and now he wishes he ....
6 She doesn't know how to use a computer but she wishes she ....
7 They never ring before coming round but I wish they ....
8 You're always interfering in my affairs and I wish you ....
9 We didn't invite the Smiths but I wish we ....
10 You told them I could do the job but I wish you ....

186 *Put the verbs in brackets into the correct form.*

Dear Sarah,

I'm having an absolutely fabulous time here on Ischia! I wish you 1) ...*had decided*... (decide) to come with me. It 2) .... (be) even better if you were here. I wish I 3) .... (try) harder to persuade you to come with me. If only you 4) .... (change) your mind! I'm sure you could get time off work if you 5) .... (ask). If you can't come to Ischia, 6) .... (you/consider) meeting in Rome at the beginning of next month? Of course if you 7) .... (come) with me in the first place, we 8) .... (have) a great time right now. Anyway, if you 9) .... (give) me a ring, I 10) .... (tell) you exactly what my plans are and then you can decide what you want to do.

Love,
Julia

187 *Complete the sentences using the words in bold. Use two to five words.*

1 Jo was about to get on the train when she realised it was the wrong one.
   if   Jo would have got on the train if she ...*hadn't realised it was*... the wrong one.
2 He didn't go to the party because he didn't know where it was.
   known   If .... the party was, he would have gone.
3 I think you should have your hair cut.
   were   If .... have my hair cut.
4 You'd think she was a film star.
   though   She behaves .... a film star.
5 It would have been better if you had arrived on time.
   only   If .... on time.
6 He shouldn't have used my mug.
   used   I'd .... my mug.
7 We should leave now if we want to get the bus.
   time   It's .... if we want to get the bus.
8 It would have been better if you hadn't told her that.
   only   If .... her that.
9 It's a pity you missed the performance.
   had   I .... the performance.
10 If John doesn't turn up, we won't be able to finish the project.
   should   We won't be able to finish the project .... up.

188 *Find the word which should not be in the sentence.*

1 If you shall pay attention, maybe you'll learn something.
2 If Tom is busy, will ask Sarah to help.
3 If only she had been caught that train.
4 It's time we had announced the winner.
5 He'd better to pay off his debts before he buys a car.
6 I'd rather to write a project than sit an exam.
7 If only that I hadn't lost my traveller's cheques.
8 Suppose he had caught you stealing, what would you do?
9 Had if he known it was her birthday, he would have bought her a present.
10 Take my business card in case you will want to contact me.

1	*shall*
2	
3	
4	
5	
6	
7	
8	
9	
10	

Oral Development 10

Look at the pictures, then make sentences using conditionals or wishes to say what each child is thinking.

S1: I wish I could eat spaghetti all day. etc

189 *Look at Appendix 2, then fill in the correct particle(s).*

1 Let's **make** ...*for*... that island and wait for the storm to pass.
2 Can't you use a different pencil? I can hardly **make** .... your writing.
3 Instead of reading books to her, Mary's father used to **make** .... stories.
4 He offered to **make** .... all the inconvenience by sending them on a free holiday.
5 After shouting at each other for an hour, they decided to **make** ....
6 She **passes** .... every time she sees blood.
7 We were very sorry to hear that your grandfather **passed** .... last week.

8 "I'll **pay** you .... for that!" shouted Johnny to a friend who had played a trick on him.
9 I'll have to **pay** .... my Visa bill or I'll be charged a fortune in interest.
10 If you get caught, you'll have to **pay** .... your crime.
11 We watched the demolition men **pull** .... that old building.
12 He waited excitedly on the platform for his friend's train to **pull** ....
13 **Pull** yourself .... and stop crying.
14 The company **pulled** .... despite the economic crisis.

190 *Look at Appendix 3, then fill in the correct preposition.*

1 She has a talent ...*for*... music so we try to encourage her as much as possible.
2 Why do you waste so much money .... phone calls?
3 My season ticket is valid .... three months, so I don't have to renew it until February.
4 My student card gives me a 10% discount, but it is only valid .... certain shops.
5 She spent a lot of time .... explaining the project to us.
6 I like to spend my money .... clothes and foreign holidays.
7 Peter has terrible taste .... clothes. He wears flowery shirts with green and orange striped jeans.
8 I love the taste .... this wine - it's very dry and has a nice fruity flavour.
9 You should not worry .... your exam results. After all, there's nothing you can do now to change them.
10 I'm very suspicious .... that man in the corner - I'm sure he's been following me!
11 How is your statement relevant .... this discussion?
12 John said he would vouch .... me if anyone were to suggest that I committed the crime.

13 I was tired .... walking such a long distance.
14 I'm tired .... listening to you moaning about him all the time.
15 I feel obliged .... be nice to Jack because he's given me so much help.
16 I tried to warn you .... him but you wouldn't listen.
17 Your dress is really similar .... the one I just bought!
18 Could you please refrain .... smoking - this is a hospital!
19 Feel free to make use .... any of the books on the shelves.
20 Now that I've become used .... all the noise I quite enjoy living here.
21 If you don't stop teasing me, I'll throw this book .... you.
22 If you throw the fish .... the seals, they are sure to come to eat them.
23 You shouldn't let yourself get upset .... such silly things.
24 That comment was not worthy .... you!
25 If you subscribe .... this magazine now, you get a 30% discount.
26 It looks as though I'm going to have to deal .... all the problems myself.

191 *Complete the sentences using the words in bold. Use two to five words.*

1 She said she was sorry she had lost her temper.
 losing She ...*apologised for losing*... her temper.

2 You were wrong to keep these facts from me.
   have   You .... these facts from me.
3 They are thinking of employing extra staff this summer.
   taking   They are .... extra staff this summer.
4 We'd better leave; it's getting dark.
   time   It's ....; it's getting dark.
5 I thought that man was your father.
   for   I .... your father.
6 She regrets ever taking in lodgers.
   wishes   She .... in lodgers.
7 Has anybody told you about the problem?
   aware   Are .... the problem?
8 I changed my plans because you asked me to.
   would   If you hadn't asked me to, ... my plans.
9 His ankle was twisted during the match.
   got   He .... during the match.
10 People believe she is planning to go freelance.
   believed She .... to go freelance.
11 If there is an earthquake, you mustn't panic.
   event   In ...., you mustn't panic.
12 I think we're going to have a sunny spell.
   if   It looks .... to have a sunny spell.
13 I don't want to interfere in their business.
   rather   I .... in their business.

192 *Match the following idioms with the correct definition, then complete the sentences with an appropriate idiom from the list.*

1	dead beat	**a**	snobbish	1	....e......
2	big-headed	**b**	excited	2	....
3	loud-mouthed	**c**	stubborn	3	....
4	stuck-up	**d**	comfortably rich	4	....
5	cheesed off	**e**	exhausted	5	....
6	pigheaded	**f**	short of money	6	....
7	well off	**g**	talking too much	7	....
8	hard up	**h**	annoyed	8	....
9	full of beans	**i**	honest	9	....
10	above board	**j**	arrogant	10	....

1 The business entrepreneur assured us that the deal was ....
2 It's no good trying to persuade her to change her mind. She's too ....
3 Alan was extremely .... when Barbara cancelled their date.
4 She must be quite .... She's just bought an expensive new car.
5 You're .... this morning. You must really be looking forward to the school trip.
6 Her husband is an unpleasant, ... man who always thinks he knows best.
7 At the end of the marking weekend all of the examiners were ....
8 On a Saturday night the pub is always full of ill-mannered, ... rugby players. I find them really offensive.
9 I find Pat very difficult to get on with. She's .... and thinks she's too good for the likes of us.
10 Kevin always seems to be .... He's forever asking if he can borrow money.

143

Practice Test 8 ....

For questions 1 - 15, read the text below and decide which word A, B, C or D best fits each space. There's an example at the beginning (0).

Egyptomania

"Egyptomania" is a new art exhibition which has (0) ... at the Louvre Museum in Paris. It shows just how (1) ... images of Egypt have emerged through the (2) ... and examines why this (3) ... culture has (4) ... to have such a powerful influence on the western imagination. It has (5) ... all of the arts, from opera and cinema to architecture and furniture design. It (6) ... five years to prepare the exhibition, which (7) ... more than 300 items, many of them on (8) ... from international museums as far (9) ... as Australia. It has generally been thought that European (10) ... in Egypt started with Napoleon Bonaparte's military campaign which lasted from 1798 to 1801, but the exhibition shows that this is not the (11) ... . There are examples of Egyptian influence (12) ... back to the early 17th century. Queen Marie Antoinette, well known for her (13) ... of strange and exotic things, (14) ... an important role in starting the (15) ... for Egyptian art in France. Her bedroom ceiling in Versailles is painted with Egyptian images, and there are chairs and tables decorated with small statues of young Pharaohs.

0	A opened	B made	C launched	D come
1	A much	B lot of	C many	D every
2	A periods	B ages	C times	D history
3	A aged	B antiquated	C ancient	D antique
4	A persisted	B remained	C lasted	D continued
5	A moved	B directed	C impressed	D influenced
6	A took	B needed	C used	D was
7	A covers	B includes	C involves	D consists
8	A credit	B advance	C loan	D gift
9	A from	B away	C along	D abroad
10	A interest	B attention	C attraction	D curiosity
11	A situation	B event	C state	D case
12	A moving	B turning	C going	D coming
13	A affection	B love	C care	D like
14	A did	B had	C played	D took
15	A custom	B style	C convention	D fashion

	A	B	C	D
0	▬	☐	☐	☐
1	☐	☐	☐	☐
2	☐	☐	☐	☐
3	☐	☐	☐	☐
4	☐	☐	☐	☐
5	☐	☐	☐	☐
6	☐	☐	☐	☐
7	☐	☐	☐	☐
8	☐	☐	☐	☐
9	☐	☐	☐	☐
10	☐	☐	☐	☐
11	☐	☐	☐	☐
12	☐	☐	☐	☐
13	☐	☐	☐	☐
14	☐	☐	☐	☐
15	☐	☐	☐	☐

Part 2

For questions 16 - 30, read the text below and think of the word which best fits each space.
Use only one word in each space. Write your answers in the answer boxes provided.

The Golden Gate Bridge

The Golden Gate Bridge has linked San Francisco and the Marin Peninsula for more **(0)** .... 50 years. However, building it was no easy task. The idea of linking the two places was not a new one but it wasn't **(16)** .... 1917 that the first workable design was produced. It would **(17)** .... twenty years to complete the bridge, and from the outset there were **(18)** .... difficulties: rough waters, the often foggy conditions and the danger of earthquakes all combined to make constructing this bridge a **(19)** ....trickier business than building New York's George Washington Bridge. The Golden Gate Bridge, **(20)** .... was then the largest in the world, was finished **(21)** .... May 27th, 1937. Californians flocked to their new showpiece and walked from one end to the **(22)** .... The next day it was opened to cars. **(23)** .... the past 58 years it **(24)** .... been part of daily life for millions of commuters. Of course, its paintwork must **(25)** .... kept **(26)** .... good condition. A 28-man team is responsible for this. If you thought Michaelangelo needed a good head **(27)** .... heights to paint the Sistine Chapel ceiling, just **(28)** .... a thought for these men. The bridge stands **(29)** .... 4,200 feet. The trick, agree the painters, is never to look **(30)** .... Rather them than us!

0	than	0
16		16
17		17
18		18
19		19
20		20
21		21
22		22
23		23
24		24
25		25
26		26
27		27
28		28
29		29
30		30

Practice Test 8 ....

Part 3

For questions 31 - 40, complete the second sentence so that it has a similar meaning to the first sentence. Use the word given and other words to complete each sentence. You must use between two and five words. Do not change the word given. Write your answers in the answer boxes provided.

0 I'm sure it wasn't Jim who did it.
have
It .... Jim who did it.

0	*can't have been*	0 0 1 2

31 Take your cheque book; you may run out of cash.
case
Take your cheque book .... out of cash.

31		31 0 1 2

32 She regrets buying a light green carpet.
wishes
She .... a light green carpet.

32		32 0 1 2

33 He will probably be late for the interview.
unlikely
He is .... for the interview.

33		33 0 1 2

34 I can't see what it says here.
make
I can't .... here.

34		34 0 1 2

35 It's a two-hour drive to the seaside.
takes
It .... to the seaside.

35		35 0 1 2

36 She won't help unless you ask her.
will
Only if .... help.

36		36 0 1 2

37 The police are investigating the murder.
looking
The police .... the murder.

37		37 0 1 2

38 Sheila will pay someone to clean the pool next week.
have
Sheila .... next week.

38		38 0 1 2

39 They're advertising a new detergent these days.
is
A new detergent .... these days.

39		39 0 1 2

40 I'd prefer you to see to it personally.
rather
I .... it personally.

40		40 0 1 2

Part 4

For questions 41 - 55, read the text below and look carefully at each line. Some of the lines are correct and some have a word which should not be there. If a line is correct, put a tick (✔) by the number in the answer boxes provided. If a line has a word which should not be there, write the word in the answer boxes provided.

An unplanned pleasure

0	It seemed it was going to be having a sunny day so I
00	decided to take a walk round the city. It was my first visit,
41	and I thought that by exploring it on foot I would learn
42	more about its main attractions. I loved to visiting the
43	ancient sites and, with the help of a guidebook, I got a
44	good idea of the history and culture. I arrived at the
45	main cathedral just as it a rainstorm started. I rushed
46	inside, only intending to wait for until the weather
47	had been cleared up, but once I was inside
48	I couldn't believe that what I saw. It was the
49	most beautiful of place I had ever seen. There
50	must have been a hundred stained glass windows.
51	I found it be very peaceful, and sat for a long time
52	just relaxing and was enjoying the tranquillity.
53	In the end I was too pleased that the rain
54	had forced on me into visiting the cathedral.
55	Without planning it, I'd had a most such memorable day.

0	having	0
00	✓	00
41		41
42		42
43		43
44		44
45		45
46		46
47		47
48		48
49		49
50		50
51		51
52		52
53		53
54		54
55		55

Part 5

For questions 56 - 65, read the text below. Use the word given in capitals at the end of each line to form a word that fits in the space in the same line. Write your word in the answer boxes provided.

The Magic of Granada

You would be forgiven for mistaking the **(0)** .... city of Granada for a film set. The city's **(56)** .... hills surround a tangled network of narrow, **(57)** .... streets. The **(58)** .... Alhambra is set **(59)** .... against the Sierra Nevada, and **(60)** .... villages cluster at its feet. The "Year of Granada" is a celebration of the city's **(61)** .... into the modern capital of **(62)** .... Andalucia. Although many new buildings have been built, care has been taken to preserve the city's **(63)** .... distinction and the **(64)** .... of its style, so that new buildings fit in **(65)** .... with the old to create an enchanting whole.

MAGIC
FAME
ROMANCE
IMPRESS
DRAMA
PICTURE
TRANSFORM
SCENE

ARCHITECT
INDIVIDUAL
SYMPATHY

0	magical	0
56		56
57		57
58		58
59		59
60		60
61		61
62		62
63		63
64		64
65		65

2 Pre-Test

A **Choose the correct item.**

1 He was accused of .... from the super-market.
   A steal   C stole
   B stolen   D stealing

2 Stop .... sweets or you'll get fat.
   A to eat   C eating
   B eat   D having eaten

3 It was .... bad weather that we stayed indoors.
   A such   C such a
   B so   D that

4 I wish he .... talk to me but he never does.
   A had   C can
   B would   D will

5 Can't you work .... harder than that?
   A very   C too
   B such   D any

6 I .... my mother to sew up the hole in my shirt.
   A made   C got
   B had   D insisted

7 Unless you .... how to swim, you have to wear a life-jacket.
   A know   C don't know
   B will have known D will know

8 I don't know when she .... to you about it.
   A speaks   C had spoken
   B will speak   D has spoken

9 .... helpful people they are!
   A So   C Such
   B How   D What

10 Suppose you .... the exam, what would you do?
   A failed   C had failed
   B would fail   D have failed

11 He .... his house broken into last week.
   A had   C will have
   B has   D is having

12 The house in .... I grew up is in Brighton.
   A where   C what
   B that   D which

13 It's time the children .... to bed.
   A went   C go
   B have gone   D would go

14 She wishes she .... to see that play last night.
   A would have gone C went
   B had gone   D would go

15 I prefer watching television .... reading books.
   A than   C rather
   B from   D to

16 If he were better off, he .... a house of his own.
   A buys   C would buy
   B would have bought D will buy

17 I don't know how to .... people's fortune.
   A ask   C speak
   B tell   D say

18 If she behaved better, people .... her a lot more.
   A would like   C will like
   B would have liked D like

19 She would rather go shopping than .... at home.
   A to stay   C stay
   B to staying   D staying

20 Do you know when Sarah .... here?
   A get   C had got
   B has got   D will get

21 He goes on .... even though it annoys everyone.
   A whistling   C whistle
   B have whistled   D to whistle

22 She .... her father to collect her from school.
   A said   C talked
   B spoke   D asked

23 .... she couldn't afford it, she bought a new dress.
   A But   C Although
   B However   D Despite

24 The new theatre .... next month.
   A has been opened   C will be opened
   B is opened   D was opened

B *Fill in the gaps with the correct form of the verb in brackets.*

I wish I **1)** .... (have) more money. Life **2)** .... (be) much easier if I **3)** .... (have) some savings in the bank. If only I **4)** .... (save) my money when I was young. At the time, though, I lived only for the moment. I wish I **5)** .... (know) then what I know now. If I **6)** .... (be) careful, then I **7)** .... (make) my life much easier. If only I **8)** .... (turn) back the clock.

C *Fill in the gaps with the correct form of the verb in brackets.*

Jennifer wishes she **1)** .... (be) a vet. "If I **2)** .... (study) biology at school, maybe things **3)** .... (turn out) differently," she says. However if she **4)** .... (be) honest with herself she **5)** .... (admit) that being a vet was never a possibility. Lots of people wish they **6)** .... (do) something for which they are not qualified. If Jennifer **7)** .... (be) more realistic, she **8)** .... (tell) you that in reality she's allergic to animals.

D *Complete the sentences using the words in bold. Use two to five words.*

1 Never behave badly in class if you don't want to be sent out.
   avoid   Never behave badly in class .... sent out.
2 He regrets ever having met her.
   wishes   He .... her.
3 I didn't buy a new car because I didn't have enough money.
   would   If I had had enough money, ... a new car.
4 "I thought the food was delicious too," said Mark.
   agreed   Mark .... delicious.
5 "You never listen when I'm talking to you," said Pat.
   complained Pat .... when she talked to me.
6 My father pays someone to wash his car every week.
   washed   My father .... every week.
7 She was miserable because it had been raining all weekend.
   due   She was miserable .... it had been raining all weekend.
8 He asked the landlord to change the lock.
   had   He .... by the landlord.
9 Somebody took my car keys while I was in the shop.
   had   I .... while I was in the shop.
10 "Yes, I left the door unlocked," said Daisy.
   having   Daisy .... the door unlocked.
11 She worked hard because she wanted to be promoted.
   view   She worked hard .... promoted.
12 "Would you like me to help you with your homework?" said my mother.
   offered   My mother .... my homework.
13 She was friendly, but Peter didn't like her.
   though   Friendly ...., Peter didn't like her.
14 Mike insisted that I do the washing up.
   me   Mike .... the washing up.
15 He said he was sorry he had forgotten my birthday.
   for   He .... my birthday.
16 She wouldn't walk home alone because she was afraid of being mugged.
   fear   She wouldn't walk home alone .... mugged.
17 "Don't touch the wires; you might get electrocuted," he said to us.
   not   He .... the wires because we might get electrocuted.
18 He isn't a famous actor but he acts like one.
   though   He acts .... a famous actor.

19 Someone must have cleaned the hotel room while we were out.
   if   The hotel room looked .... cleaned while we were out.
20 She said she hadn't stolen the money.
   stealing   She .... the money.

E *Fill in the correct particle(s).*

1 The butter was left out of the fridge and now it's gone ....
2 Jake and Simon get .... well with their cousins.
3 I keep .... current affairs by reading the newspapers.
4 My grandfather was very good at making .... stories.
5 All passengers got ready to get off the train as it pulled .... to the station.
6 You mustn't give .... to temptation.
7 They were held .... by heavy traffic on the roads.
8 I want to look .... the house to see if I like it.

F *Fill in the correct preposition(s).*

1 I'm relying .... you to get the job done.
2 Students must refrain .... talking during the exam.
3 His heroic act resulted .... his being awarded a medal.
4 I can't vouch .... him; I've never met him.
5 She had no intention .... going to meet him, though she said she would.
6 They might have to operate .... him. He's very ill.
7 The soldier was presented .... a medal after the war.
8 John claimed that he was not guilty .... committing the crime.

G *Correct the following sentences by taking out the inappropriate word.*

1 I felt very too happy about passing the exam and went out to celebrate.
2 She didn't go to the work because she was ill.
3 I have had a really bad day yesterday.
4 He is likely that to be pleased with your decision.
5 The children had a great fun at the fair.
6 Jack and Mary did arrived shortly after everyone else.
7 Unless you have not tried, you don't know if you can do it.
8 This jumper it is too small for me.
9 Next the week Simon is leaving for Germany.
10 I don't know not anything about Spain; I've never been there.
11 Do you want to go for fishing with me this weekend?
12 Jenny told to me that I'd lost weight.

1	
2	
3	
4	
5	
6	
7	
8	
9	
10	
11	
12	

H *Fill in the correct word dervied from the words in bold.*

1 Trains run .... throughout the day.
2 We picked a .... spot to sit and have our picnic.
3 Our .... was cut off because we hadn't paid the bill.
4 They use very .... machinery in this factory.
5 He has changed .... since the last time I saw him.
6 Young children need their parents' ....
7 The weather is .... better today than it was yesterday.
8 He goes to the dentist ....
9 It is not .... viable to buy out that company.
10 The company's .... of shoes has doubled in the past year.
11 She listened .... to her friend's problems.
12 The new equipment they have ordered is .... advanced.

FREQUENT
SCENE
ELECTRIC
SOPHISTICATE
DRAMATIC
PROTECT
CONSIDERABLE
REGULAR
ECONOMIC
PRODUCE
SYMPATHETIC
TECHNOLOGY

Nouns

- **Nouns are: abstract** *(happiness, love etc)*, **collective** *(crowd, group etc)*, **common** *(radio, chair etc)*, **concrete** *(doctor, client etc)* **and proper** *(James, Tangiers, India etc)*.
  Gender: Nouns can be masculine (men and boys), **feminine** (women and girls) and **neuter** (inanimate things, animals and babies whose sex we do not know). When we refer to ships, vehicles (when regarded with affection or respect) and countries, we consider them feminine. Most nouns remain the same whether they are masculine or feminine *(doctor, painter etc)*. There are some nouns, though, which have different forms according to gender. These forms can be expressed in two ways:
  a. **by changing the ending** *(actor -* **actress**, *barman -* **barmaid**, *conductor -* **conductress**, *duke -* **duchess**, *emperor -* **empress**, *heir -* **heiress**, *hero -* **heroine**, *host -* **hostess**, *policeman -* **policewoman**, *prince -* **princess**, *waiter -* **waitress**, *widower -* **widow**). **In modern usage, however, many gendered forms are avoided. We use neutral forms instead.** *eg. police officer, flight attendant etc.*
  b. **by changing the word** *(bachelor -* **spinster**, *boy -* **girl**, *bridegroom -* **bride**, *father -* **mother**, *gentleman -* **lady**, *man -* **woman**, *nephew -* **niece**, *son -* **daughter**, *uncle -* **aunt** etc)*
- **Some domestic animals and wild animals have different forms according to gender:** *bull - cow, cock - hen, dog - bitch, drake - duck, gander - goose, lion - lioness, ram - ewe, stag - doe, stallion - mare, tiger - tigress, but: gorilla - gorilla etc.*

Noun Formation

- **To describe people we add -ar, -er, -ee, -or to the end of verbs, or -ian, -ist to the end of nouns or verbs making any necessary spelling changes.** *beg - begg**ar**, train - train**er**/train**ee**, invent - invent**or**, magic - magic**ian**, type - typ**ist***

Suffixes used to form nouns from verbs:

-age	*break - break**age***	**-ence**	*neglect - neglig**ence***	**-sis**	*hypnotise - hypno**sis***
-al	*remove - remov**al***	**-ion**	*inspect - inspect**ion***	**-tion**	*abolish - aboli**tion***
-ance	*attend - attend**ance***	**-ment**	*commit - commit**ment***	**-y**	*injure - injur**y***
-ation	*deprive - depriv**ation***	**-sion**	*revise - revi**sion***		

Suffixes used to form nouns from adjectives:

-ance	*tolerant - toler**ance***	**-ion**	*desperate - desperat**ion***	**-ment**	*content - content**ment***
-cy	*pregnant - pregnan**cy***	**-iness**	*happy - happ**iness***	**-ty**	*anxious - anxie**ty***
-ence	*independent - independ**ence***	**-ity**	*pure - pur**ity***	**-y**	*honest - honest**y***

193 *Fill in the correct noun.*

To be a good teacher, a teaching **(0)** ... is not all you need. Your **(1)** ... plays a big part in the **(2)** ... of your work, so it's best to make a thorough **(3)** ... of your own character before taking the **(4)** ... to take up this challenging **(5)** ... . Apart from **(6)** ..., you also need the **(7)** ... to accept others' ideas and a **(8)** ... to learn from your own mistakes. **(9)** ... to the needs of your students is also important. **(10)** ... is not enough - who you are is much more important.

QUALIFY
PERSON
EFFECTIVE
EXAMINE
DECIDE
OCCUPY
PATIENT
ABLE
WILLING
SENSITIVE
KNOW

0	qualification	
1		
2		
3		
4		
5		
6		
7		
8		
9		
10		

194 *Complete each pair below by adding the male or female equivalent.*

1	husband	...wife...	15	uncle	....
2	....	lady	16	....	niece
3	emperor	....	17	policeman	....
4	hero	....	18	....	landlady
5	count	....	19	bridegroom	....
6	....	spinster	20	....	hostess
7	father	....	21	monk	....
8	....	duchess	22	....	actress
9	heir	....	23	conductor	....
10	....	manageress	24	barman	....
11	salesman	....	25	....	stewardess
12	....	queen	26	lion	....
13	prince	....	27	....	waitress
14	....	widow	28	dog	....

The Plural of Nouns

Nouns are made plural by adding:
- **-s** to the noun. *(cat-cats etc)*
- **-es** to nouns ending in **-ch, -s, -sh, -ss, x.** *(torch - torches, bus - buses, bush - bushes, glass - glasses, fox - foxes etc)*
- **-ies** to nouns ending in **consonant + y.** *(baby - babies, lady - ladies etc)* but: **-s** to nouns ending in **vowel + y.** *(toy - toys, boy - boys etc)*
- **-es** to nouns ending in **-o.** *(tomato - tomatoes)* but: **-s** to nouns ending in: **vowel + o** *(video - videos)*, **double o** *(zoo - zoos)*, **abbreviations** *(photograph/photo - photos)*, **musical instruments** *(piano - pianos)* and **proper nouns** *(Navajo - Navajos)*. **Note that some nouns ending in -o take either -es or -s. These are: buffaloes/buffalos, mosquitoes/mosquitos, volcanoes/volcanos, zeroes/zeros, tornadoes/tornados etc.**
- **-ves** to some nouns ending in **-f/-fe.** *(self - selves but: chiefs, cliffs, roofs, safes etc)*
- **Some nouns of Greek or Latin origin form their plural by adding Greek or Latin suffixes.** *(basis - bases, crisis - crises, criterion - criteria, medium - media, terminus - termini etc)*

Compound nouns form their plural by adding -s/-es:
- **to the second noun if the compound consists of two nouns.** *(schoolboy - schoolboys)*
- **to the noun if the compound consists of an adjective and a noun.** *(frying pan - frying pans)*
- **to the first noun if the compound consists of two nouns connected with a preposition or to the noun if the compound has only one noun.** *(looker on - lookers on)*
- **at the end of the compound if this is not made up of any nouns.** *(runaway - runaways)*

Irregular Plurals: man - **men**, woman - **women**, foot - **feet**, tooth - **teeth**, louse - **lice**, mouse - **mice**, child - **children**, goose - **geese**, person - **people** (but: peoples = ethnic groups), sheep - **sheep**, deer - **deer**, fish - **fish** (also: fishes), trout - **trout**, ox - **oxen**, salmon - **salmon**, spacecraft - **spacecraft**, aircraft - **aircraft**, species - **species**, hovercraft - **hovercraft**

195 *Write the plural of the following words.*

1	day	...days...	8	church	....	15	baby	....	22	brush	....
2	box	....	9	thief	....	16	corkscrew	....	23	piano	....
3	kilo	....	10	fly	....	17	foot	....	24	child	....
4	tomato	....	11	tooth	....	18	life	....	25	cliff	....
5	knife	....	12	medium	....	19	passer-by	....	26	lady	....
6	donkey	....	13	shelf	....	20	country	....	27	wife	....
7	man	....	14	photo	....	21	steering wheel	......	28	kiss	....

Countable - Uncountable Nouns

Nouns can be countable (those that can be counted) *1 book, 2 books etc* or uncountable (those that can't be counted) *bread, wood etc.* Uncountable nouns take a singular verb and are not used with a/an. Some, any, much, no etc can be used with them. *Heavy rain caused the match to be postponed. I need to buy* **some** *food.* but: a help, a knowledge (of sth), a pity, a relief, a shame, a wonder. *What* **a relief***! What* **a pity***! What* **a shame***!*

Uncountable nouns are:

- **Mass nouns (fluids, solids, gases, particles):** *beer, blood, bread, butter, air, oxygen, corn, flour etc.*
- **Subjects of study:** *accountancy, chemistry, economics, history, literature, maths, physics etc*
- **Languages:** *Chinese, French, Italian, Japanese, Portuguese, Spanish etc*
- **Sports:** *baseball, billiards, cricket, cycling, darts, football, golf, rugby etc*
- **Diseases:** *chickenpox, flu, measles, mumps, pneumonia, tuberculosis etc*
- **Natural phenomena:** *darkness, fog, gravity, hail, snow, sunlight, shade etc*
- **Some nouns:** *accommodation, advice, anger, applause, assistance, behaviour, business, chaos, countryside, courage, dirt, education, evidence, homework, housework, information, intelligence, knowledge, luck, music, news, peace, progress, seaside, shopping, traffic, trouble, truth, wealth, work etc*
- **Collective nouns:** *baggage, crockery, cutlery, furniture, jewellery, luggage, machinery, money, rubbish, stationery etc*
  Note: With expressions of duration, distance or money meaning "a whole amount" we use a singular verb. *Five thousand pounds* **was** *too much to lose in a casino.*

Many uncountable nouns can be made countable.

a **piece** *of advice/cake/furniture/information/paper;* a **glass**/**bottle** *of beer/water/wine;* a **jar** *of jam;* a **rasher** *of bacon;* a **pint** *of beer;* a **box**/**sheet** *of paper;* a **packet** *of tea;* a **slice**/**loaf** *of bread;* a **pot** *of yoghurt;* a **pot**/**cup** *of tea;* a **kilo**/**pound** *of meat;* a **tube** *of toothpaste;* a **bar** *of chocolate/soap;* a **bit**/**piece** *of chalk;* an ice **cube***;* a **lump** *of sugar;* a **bag** *of flour;* a **pair** *of trousers;* a **game** *of soccer;* a(n) **item**/**piece** *of news;* a **drop**/**can** *of oil;* a **can** *of Coke;* a **carton** *of milk;* a **block** *of wood;* a **flash**/**bolt** *of lightning;* a **clap**/**peal** *of thunder etc*

Plural Nouns

- **objects consisting of two parts: garments** *(pyjamas, trousers etc)*, **instruments** *(binoculars, compasses etc)*, **tools** *(pliers, scissors etc)*
- **arms, ashes, barracks, clothes, congratulations, earnings, (good) looks, outskirts, people, police, premises, riches, stairs, surroundings, wages etc.** *Where* **are** *my* **clothes***?*
  Group nouns (army, audience, class, club, committee, company, council, crew, crowd, headquarters, family, jury, government, press, public, staff, team etc) can take either a singular or a plural verb depending on whether we see the group as a whole or as individuals. *The team* **was** *chosen as the most promising. (the team as a group)* *The team* **were given** *bonuses for their performance. (each member of the team separately)*
  Note how certain nouns can be used in the singular and plural with a different meaning.

Singular	Plural
She has beautiful thick brown **hair***.*	*My mother has lots of grey* **hairs***.*
Could I have a **glass** *of lemonade?*	*She bought a new pair of reading* **glasses***.*
Only people with **experience** *may apply for this job.*	*If you go travelling, you are sure to have many exciting* **experiences***.*
The face of the clock is made of **wood***.*	*I love walking in the* **woods***.*
The **rain** *is falling really heavily now.*	*The people were praying for the* **rains** *to come.*
Call me when you've finished **work***.*	*The exhibition includes many* **works** *of Boudin.*
Draw a chart on graph **paper***.*	*Many* **papers** *have been written on the subject of euthanasia.*
On a **scale** *of 1-20 I'd give that joke a 5.*	*Use these* **scales** *to weigh that - they are more accurate.*
It is not a **custom** *to kiss your friends in Japan.*	*We had nothing to declare at* **customs***.*
Take a **compass** *in case you get lost.*	*Use the* **compasses** *to make a perfect circle.*

196 *Underline the correct verb form.*

1 Chemistry are/<u>is</u> my least favourite subject.
2 Your bathroom scales is/are not very accurate.
3 £2000 is/are far too expensive for that stereo.
4 Table-tennis is/are sometimes referred to as ping-pong.
5 The police is/are coming to the rescue.
6 Paper is/are made from wood.
7 Children likes/like playing games.
8 The scissors don't/doesn't work very well.
9 These trousers is/are terribly unflattering.
10 Education are/is considered to be very important by almost everyone.
11 Most people worry/worries about the effect of pollution on the environment.
12 Water is/are necessary for plants to grow.
13 When I'm ill my hair becomes/become greasy.
14 The rubbish has/have been taken away.
15 The information is/are inaccurate.
16 Binoculars is/are needed to see that far.
17 His luggage was/were left on the platform.
18 The stairs is/are very dangerous.
19 Mumps is/are contagious.
20 The news was/were unexpected.
21 His experience of travel is/are limited.

197 *Put the verbs in brackets into the correct form.*

1 The water in this lake ...*looks*.. (look) very clean.
2 Making mistakes .... (be) only natural.
3 Maths .... (not/interest) me very much.
4 All of our furniture .... (be) brand new.
5 Sugar .... (damage) your teeth.
6 Snow rarely .... (fall) in this part of the country.
7 The applause .... (be) very loud.
8 The news they brought us .... (be) good.
9 Your trousers .... (not/match) your shirt.
10 The team .... (discuss) strategy before every game.
11 Chickenpox .... (give) you an itchy rash.
12 Billiards .... (be) his favourite game.
13 The accommodation here .... (seem) very expensive.
14 The pliers .... (be) in the tool box.
15 Knowledge of other languages .... (help) people in business.
16 Ten minutes .... (be) too little time to finish this report.
17 Every time I travel, some of my luggage .... (get) damaged.
18 Welsh .... (be) difficult to learn.
19 The staff .... (be) happy with the pay-rise.
20 Sophisticated machinery .... (cost) a lot of money.

198 *Finish the second sentence so that it has the same meaning as the first sentence.*

1 An official found her luggage near the check-in desk. Her luggage ...*was found by an official near the check-in desk*....
2 They are teaching physics in room 2A. Physics ....
3 Traditional craftsmen have used the best wood to make these ornaments. The best wood ....
4 You need to have experience if you wish to apply for this job. Experience ....
5 Rangers protect the woods. The woods ....
6 He tore his trousers in the fight. His trousers ....
7 We give exam advice at the end of the course. Exam advice ....
8 He classified the information as "Top Secret". The information ....
9 A security guard protects our property. Our property ....
10 That shop is selling wedding dresses at half price. Wedding dresses ....
11 We need new members for our tennis club. Our tennis club ....
12 You can find cheap silver jewellery in Portugal. Cheap silver jewellery ....

13 One doesn't need money to be happy. Money ....

14 He used his experiences in Africa to write his book. His experiences in Africa ....

15 The crime is being investigated by the police. The police ....

A couple of, several, a few, many, a (large/great/good) number of, both are followed by a **countable noun**. **(Too) much, a little, a great/good deal of, a large/small amount/quantity of** are followed by an **uncountable noun**. **A lot of, lots of, hardly any, some, no, plenty of** are followed by a **countable** or **uncountable noun**.

199 *Underline the correct items.*

1 We've had a great deal of, many, a few, plenty of, a little rain this year.

2 She drinks too much, several, a lot of, too many, a little cups of tea every day.

3 The proposal got a lot of, a few, some, several, a good deal of support from the public.

4 We spend a number of, several, a lot of, plenty of, many time at our country house.

5 There is many, hardly any, no, little, several milk left - could you buy some?

6 He wastes many, lots of, few, a great deal of, too much money.

7 They couldn't give us hardly any, a few, much, a lot of, a large number of evidence so we had to release the suspect.

8 She left many, plenty of, a large quantity of, a few, some jewellery to her grandchildren.

9 There were several, both, a little, a lot of, a small quantity of people at the meeting.

10 She bought a few, several, some, plenty of, lots of new cutlery.

11 I've enjoyed a number of, no, both, some, a good deal of his films.

12 He's made several, a good deal of, a little, a few, a lot of progress in his studies.

13 She always takes several, both, plenty of, a great quantity of, a number of luggage when she travels.

14 He gave us a couple of, some, no, many, plenty of useful advice.

15 There were much, a couple of, no, a good deal of, a few rooms available on the island.

A/An (indefinite article) - The (definite article)

- **A/An** is used with singular countable nouns to talk about indefinite things. *There's **a** boy leaning on the fence. (indefinite)* **Some** can be used in the affirmative with plural countable nouns or uncountable nouns and **any** in questions and negations. *There are **some** glasses on the table. There's **some** butter in the fridge. Is there **any flour** left? There aren't **any strawberries** in the fridge.*

- **The** is used with singular and plural nouns, countable and uncountable ones, to talk about something specific or when the noun is mentioned for a second time. ***The** boy in jeans is my brother. (Which boy? The one in jeans; specific.) There's a bicycle outside. **The** bicycle is Tony's.*

- **A/An or the** is used before singular countable nouns to refer to a group of people, animals or things. *A/**The** cat is a domestic animal. (We mean all cats).* **A/An or the** is never used before a noun in the plural when it represents a group. *Cats are domestic animals. (not: ~~The cats~~ are domestic animals.)*

- **A/An** can also be used meaning "per". *She goes to the cinema twice **a**/per week.* It can also be used with money *(**a**/one dollar)*, fractions *(**a**/one quarter)*, weight/measures *(**an**/one inch)*, whole numbers *(**a**/one million)*, price/weight *(£3 **a** litre)*, frequency/time *(twice **a** month)*, distance/fuel *(80 miles **a** gallon)*, distance/speed *(80 km **an** hour)* and illnesses *(**a** cold, **a** fever, **(a)** toothache, **(a)** stomach-ache, **(a)** backache etc).*

200 *Fill in: a, an, the, any or some where necessary.*

1 "Have you got ...*any*... smoked ham?" "I ordered .... last week, but .... supplier had run out so it'll be a while before I have ...." "Oh, okay. How much is .... boiled ham?"

2 When I opened ..... door this morning ..... man was standing there with ...... flowers in his hand. When I asked him if I could be of .... help he blushed, said, "I've got .... wrong house," and ran away.

3 He's been in .... country for .... six months but he can't speak .... English yet. Give him .... help with learning .... language, please.

The is used before	**The is omitted before**
• **nouns which are unique.** *the moon, the Tower of London*	• **proper nouns.** *Amy, Liverpool*
• **names of cinemas** (*The Odeon*), **hotels** (*The Ritz*), **theatres** (*The Theatre Royal*), **museums** (*The Museum of Modern Art*), **newspapers/ magazines** (*The Times*), **but:** (*Time*), **ships** (*The QE2*), **institutions** (*The Royal Academy of Art*), **galleries** (*The National Gallery*)	• **names of sports, games, activities, days, months, holidays, colours, drinks, meals and languages** (not followed by the word "language"). *I love tennis. Can you speak French?* **but: The Chinese language** *is fascinating to study.*
• **names of rivers** (*the Thames*), **seas** (*the North Sea*), **groups of islands/states** (*the Orkney Islands, the USA*), **mountain ranges** (*the Alps*), **deserts** (*the Gobi desert*), **oceans** (*the Pacific*), **canals** (*the Suez Canal*) **and names or nouns with "of".** (*the King of Spain, the Queen of England*) **Note:** *the equator, the Arctic/Antarctic, the South of France, the South/West/North/East*	• **names of countries** (*France*), **but:** *the Argentine, the Netherlands, (the) Sudan, the Hague, the Vatican,* **cities** (*Manchester*), **streets** (*Bond Street*), **but:** *the High Street, the Strand, the Mall, the A11, the M4 motorway,* **squares** (*George Square*), **bridges** (*Tower Bridge* **but:** *the Bridge of Sighs, the Forth Bridge, the Severn Bridge, the Golden Gate Bridge*), **parks** (*Central Park*), **stations** (*King's Cross Station*), **individual mountains** (*Mount Everest*), **islands** (*Corsica*), **lakes** (*Lake Geneva*), **continents** (*Africa*)
• **musical instruments, dances.** *the flute, the tango*	
• **names of families** (*the Smiths*), **nationalities ending in -sh, -ch or -ese** (*the Welsh, the Dutch, the Chinese etc*). **Other plural nationalities are used with or without "the".** (*the South Africans, the Australians etc*)	• **possessive adjectives.** *That is my book.*
	• **two-word names whose first word is the name of a person or place.** *Glasgow Airport, Edinburgh Castle* **but:** *The White House (because the first word "White" is not the name of a person or a place)*
• **titles** (*the President, the Prince of Wales, the Queen*). **"The" is omitted before titles with proper names.** *Queen Elizabeth II*	• **pubs, restaurants, shops, banks and hotels which have the name of their founder and end in -s or -'s.** *Jim's Café; Harrods; Baring's Bank* **but:** *the Queen's Arms (pub) (because "Queen's Arms" is not the name of the founder)*
• **adjectives used as plural nouns** (*the blind, the elderly, the rich, the poor etc*) **and the superlative degree of adjectives/ adverbs.** *He's* **the most intelligent** *one here.*	
• **Note:** "**most**" used as a determiner followed by a noun, does not take "the". **Most students** *pass the exams.* **but: The most interesting** *article was on Nostradamus.*	• **bed, church, college, court, hospital, prison, school, university when we refer to the purpose for which they exist.** *He goes to church every Sunday.* **but:** *We have to be at* **the church** *at 2.00 for Julie's wedding.* **Work (= place of work) never takes "the".** *I have to go to* **work** *now.*
• **the words: beach, cinema, city, coast, country(side), earth, ground, jungle, radio, pub, sea(side), sky, station, shop, theatre, village, weather, world etc but not before "man" (= people).** *I went to the* **shop** *to buy bread.* **Note:** "the" is optional with seasons. (*the*) *autumn*	• **the words home, father/mother when we talk about our own home/parents.** *Mum is at* **home** *now.*
• **morning, afternoon, evening, night.** *I'll come round in* **the** *morning.* **but: at night, at noon, at midnight, by day/night, at 5 o'clock etc**	• **means of transport: by bus/by car/by train/by plane etc but: in the car, on the bus/train etc.** *She came by* **plane.** **but:** *She was* **on the bus** *when the accident happened.*
• **historical references/events.** *the French Revolution, the Second World War* (**but:** *World War II*)	• We say: **flu/the flu, measles/the measles, mumps/the mumps but:** *He's got pneumonia.*
• **only, last, first (used as adjectives).** *As always, you are* **the first** *person to arrive.*	

201 *Fill in "the" where necessary.*

The Great Wall of China

1 ...*The*... Great Wall of China is said to be .... only man-made structure seen from .... space.

2 .... Princess of Wales visited a shelter for .... homeless yesterday.

3 .... Rock Garden café is half way up .... Queen Street, off ...... George Square.

4 .... Quins are holding a ball in .... Sherbrooke Castle Hotel on .... fifth of June.

5 When we arrived at .... Manchester Airport, Rachel was waiting for us at .... arrivals gate.

6 James went to .... hospital to pick up his wife who is a surgeon there.

7 It's interesting to look at .... old maps of .... world and see how .... borders have changed.

8 If you go to ...... New York, you must visit ...... Central Park, ... Guggenheim museum and ...... World Trade Center, but don't bother to visit ...... Times Square.

9 I was thinking of making ...... lasagne, but if you prefer we can go to ...... Queen's Arms pub for ...... lunch.

10 As soon as Jim got home from .... school he went straight to .... bed because he felt as if he had .... flu.

11 Margaret Thatcher, who was .... Prime Minister of .... Great Britain for 12 years, is now known as .... Baroness Thatcher of Kesteven.

12 We've decided to go to .... Canary Islands on holiday. Last year we went to .... Crete and liked .... people there very much.

13 I was born in .... North of England, but when I was in .... infant school we moved to .... Lewes, which is in .... East Sussex.

14 In .... office where I work .... most people have a degree in .... English, but my boss, who is .... nicest person I've ever worked for, has a PhD in .... astronomy.

15 Many people enjoy .... snowboarding and .... hiking in .... Alps and .... Pyrenees.

16 If you have .... good weather, ... summer in .... Scotland is beautiful. .... most people, however, prefer .... guaranteed sunshine of .... Mediterranean.

202 *Fill in "a/an" or "the" where necessary.*

Dear Debbie,

Thank you for 1) ...*the*... letter you sent me. I've just returned home after spending 2) ...... fabulous few weeks in 3) ...... Paris. I was staying with 4) ...... friend I told you about - Pascal. Do you remember 5) ...... French boy I told you I met on holiday in 6) ...... Greece? He has 7) ...... wonderful flat with 8) ...... good view of 9) ...... Eiffel Tower. Pascal borrowed his friend's car because I wasn't happy riding on 10) .... back of his motorbike. It was 11) .... amazing orange Citroën. He drove me around, showing me some 12) ...... places of interest, like 13) ...... Louvre, 14) ...... Pompidou Centre and 15) ...... Museum of Modern Art. I had 16) ...... really wonderful time there. Meeting lots of 17) ...... French and 18) ...... Italian friends Pascal has, and not being able to talk to them has made me anxious to start learning 19) ...... French language. Hopefully, I'll be able to afford 20) ...... private tutor for 21) ...... French when I return home. Maybe I'll be able to take 22) ...... college night course in 23) ...... Italian at the start of term as well. I've invited Pascal and some of his friends to come over for 24) ...... holiday whenever they have 25) ...... time. You really have to meet them. Please phone me when you get this letter - we can arrange to spend 26) ...... afternoon in 27) ...... town if you like!

Lots of love,
Claire

203 Fill in "a/an" or "the" where necessary.

1   On ...*the*... thirty-first of December, thousands of people gather in .... Times Square, New York, to celebrate .... coming of .... New Year.
2   Of all .... countries on .... continent of .... North America, Phil has only visited .... Canada.
3   .... universities of Oxford and Cambridge are two of .... most famous universities in .... Europe.
4   If you want to work abroad, why don't you contact .... agency I went to in .... Lamb Street?
5   .... capital city of .... Spain, ... Madrid, is to .... north of Seville.
6   .... holiday I took in .... Rome was .... best I've ever had.
7   .... Detective Sherlock Holmes and his assistant, ... Doctor Watson, solved .... lot of mysteries.
8   I would love to spend .... summer cruising in .... Caribbean.
9   Mrs Hamilton holds .... flower arranging class in .... Cathedral on .... Wednesday evenings.
10 The highest mountain in .... world, ... Mount Everest, is in .... Himalayas.
11 There is .... wonderful 1920's style restaurant-café in .... Glasgow which has some of .... most charming and helpful waiters I've ever seen.
12 Belfast is .... capital of ..... Northern Ireland and Dublin is ...... capital of....... Republic of .... Ireland.
13 .... Balearic Islands lie to .... south of Spain.
14 Julia is .... extremely patient girl - she will have no problem in her career as .... nanny.
15 Stephen has .... seminar on .... Saturday morning, so we are not able to go to .... ski-slopes until .... Sunday.
16 On Sunday we decided to go to .... beach by .... train, but by the time we got to .... station .... weather looked so threatening that we went to .... cinema instead.

204 Find the word which should not be in the sentence.

1 Susan, who is a terrible ballet dancer, is not very good at the tap-dancing either.	**1** *the*
2 They drove around the Paris in a car.	**2**
3 He travelled to Lisbon, the capital of Portugal, by a car.	**3**
4 I was invited to a dinner given to welcome the President Chirac of France.	**4**
5 Our plan was to meet him at Café Sandal and not at the home.	**5**
6 It was nice of you to invite me to go to the Malta with you.	**6**
7 She was born in the July, 1971.	**7**
8 She has got a plenty of time to reach the station.	**8**
9 Can you walk the faster?	**9**
10 Tigers are in danger of becoming an extinct.	**10**
11 I like the active holidays more than relaxing ones.	**11**
12 It is known that smoking does a damage to your health.	**12**

Oral Development 11

Look at the following list, then say each item using "the" where necessary.

British Museum, St. Pancras Station, Kew Gardens, Mendip Hills, Red Lion Square, Dutch language, King George VI, East River, High Street, Andes, Lake Windermere, Flamenco music, UNESCO, Uffizi Gallery, Macy's, Harrods, Red Sea, Duchess of Devonshire, Regents Street, Virgin Islands, Mount Etna, Charles de Gaulle Airport, Malta, Atlantic, Queen of Spain

205 Look at Appendix 2, then fill in the correct particle(s).

1 If you like, I'll **put** ...*away*... all your winter clothes for next year.
2 The army was called in to **put** .... the rebellion.
3 He **puts** his success .... being in the right place at the right time.
4 The idea Ian **put** .... is the best so far.
5 The cricket match was **put** .... until the weather had improved.
6 Over Christmas I've **put** .... at least 3 kilos.
7 At home we have two fire-extinguishers in case we have to **put** .... a fire.
8 Of course sir, I'll just **put** you .... to Mrs Thomson's office. Please hold the line.
9 After her death, a statue was **put** .... in the town square to honour her.
10 I can't stand him, but I'll have to **put** .... his being there because John likes him.
11 You'll never guess who I **ran** .... in the supermarket - your friend Tom!
12 Can you believe that he **ran** .... all our money? I didn't think he was capable of theft.
13 He **runs** people .... all the time. He never says anything nice about anyone.
14 We've **run** .. bread. Go and get some, please!

206 Look at Appendix 3, then fill in the correct preposition.

1 ...*At*... the age of eight months I took my first steps, much to everyone's amazement.
2 .... the top of the street there's a baker's that sells the most delicious bread.
3 .... the beginning we got along very well, but now all we seem to do is fight and argue.
4 .... the end of the story the murderer was caught.
5 We had decided to go to France, but .... the end we went to Rome.
6 .... first I thought he was very rude, but now I quite like him.
7 The computer chooses data .... random, so that there is no bias or discrimination involved.
8 .... my request, they ordered me a taxi.
9 "................ popular request, I proudly present comedian Dave Jones," said the announcer.
10 Our baby-sitter lives close .... hand, so it's no problem calling her at a moment's notice.
11 When Chris met Ann it was love ..... first sight.
12 .... the top of this hill there is a casino.
13 Put your essay .... top of that pile over there.
14 The sports shop is .... 31, Pine Street.
15 .... all accounts she was a well-behaved little girl.
16 We decided to go .... bus, but we had to wait for an hour at the bus-stop. The next time we go, we'll go .... taxi for sure.
17 I was sitting .... the bus, reading my book, when Dave sat down beside me.
18 We saw her sitting .... the taxi and waved at her, but she didn't notice us.
19 He must have reached Israel .... now.
20 Don't worry, I won't post it. I'll make sure the letter is delivered .... hand.
21 The teacher asked the children to learn the poem .... heart.
22 Although she seems to be a selfish old woman she must be kind .... heart.
23 I'm sorry, but I did the wrong exercise for home-work .... mistake.
24 We took him .... surprise by arranging a party for his 50th birthday.
25 She told me that she had sent the letter .... post a week ago.
26 The ship was lost .... sea.

207 Complete the sentences using the words in bold. Use two to five words.

1 Shall I help you with the cooking?
   like   Would ...*you like me to help*... you with the cooking?
2 Raymond started driving ten years ago.
   been   Raymond .... ten years.
3 She decided to buy herself a new coat for Christmas.
   treat   She decided .... a new coat for Christmas.

4 I'm sure she is working hard.
be She .... hard.

5 Mary can't see at all without her glasses.
blind Mary is .... without her glasses.

6 The thief wore gloves in order not to leave fingerprints.
that The thief wore gloves .... leave fingerprints.

7 She wished she had left earlier.
having She .... earlier.

8 She never seems to have the time to write letters.
round She never seems .... letters.

9 She has such a big house that you can get lost in it.
so Her .... you can get lost in it.

10 It's the first time she's ever been on a plane.
never She .... plane before.

11 "No, I didn't take the money from the till," he said.
taken He .... from the till.

12 I won't stand for any more of this nonsense.
put I .... any more of this nonsense.

208 Explain the meaning of the idioms in bold.

1 She is **head and shoulders above** her colleagues, which is why she is soon to be made a company director.
2 Even with five children and two dogs to take care of, Margaret's house is always **spic and span**.
3 She was very embarassed when she realised she had gone to the party with her pullover on **inside out**.
4 The new house has its problems, but **by and large** it's an improvement on the old one.
5 Even though the carpet was well made, after ten years it was unable to stand up to the **wear and tear** of continual use.
6 I'm **sick and tired** of listening to his excuses.
7 After falling off her horse Laura was **black and blue** all over.
8 The nervous customer paced **back and forth** outside the bank manager's office.
9 The student was only pretending to read - he was holding his book **upside down**.
10 The footballer was covered in mud **from head to foot**.

209 Choose the correct item.

1 When you .... the traffic lights turn left!
A arrive **B** reach **C** get **D** come

2 My favourite .... of car is the Ferrari.
A style **B** make **C** trademark **D** model

3 This shirt will .... if you wash it with bleach.
A fade **B** lighten **C** waken **D** faint

4 It's very rude to .... at people.
A gaze **B** glance **C** glimpse **D** stare

5 With lots of time and patience you can .... dogs to be obedient.
A guide **B** instruct **C** learn **D** train

6 Could you leave me ....? I have to study.
A alone **B** only **C** single **D** lonely

7 From my point of .... there is no benefit in remaining here.
A idea **B** opinion **C** view **D** belief

8 His injuries turned out to be .... - he died the day after the accident.
A fatal **B** final **C** solemn **D** lethal

9 I'm really .... about this situation; I hope we can find a solution.
A anxious **B** careful **C** watchful **D** afraid

10 She .... all her classmates and finished the race first.
A beat **B** earned **C** gained **D** won

Practice Test 9

Part 1

For questions 1 - 15, read the text below and decide which word A, B, C or D best fits each space. There's an example at the beginning (0).

Panama Hats

When summer **(0)** ... and the sun appears, it's **(1)** ... to have a hat. Many people have traditionally **(2)** ... for the panama hat. Stylish, light and cool on the head, these palm leaf hats are flexible enough to roll up and **(3)** ... in a pocket or bag. Nowadays panamas can be found in fashionable shops **(4)** ... over the world, sometimes at exorbitant **(5)** ... . However the hat itself originated in rather humble **(6)** ... in the jungles of South America. In a long tradition **(7)** ... down from generation to generation, the palm leaves are **(8)** ... by the men and the hats are woven by the women. It can **(9)** ... up to 12 palm leaves to make a **(10)** ... quality hat. Each leaf is split up to 25 times to obtain a straw that is fine enough to be woven into a hat. The women's job is dictated by the weather and visibility: there must be enough light for them to **(11)** ... the fine straw, but the air must be moist enough for it to **(12)** ... flexible. This means that the women can usually only work in the **(13)** ... morning. **(14)** ... panama hats are expensive, back in the villages the craftsmen and women are struggling to keep the tradition **(15)** ... and often receive only a fraction of the price you pay in the shops.

0	**A** gets	**B** comes	**C** reaches	**D** becomes
1	**A** well	**B** right	**C** good	**D** functional
2	**A** sought	**B** asked	**C** gone	**D** tried
3	**A** put	**B** add	**C** locate	**D** insert
4	**A** on	**B** at	**C** throughout	**D** all
5	**A** tags	**B** amounts	**C** prices	**D** costs
6	**A** parts	**B** areas	**C** surroundings	**D** environments
7	**A** handed	**B** past	**C** given	**D** delivered
8	**A** gathered	**B** congregated	**C** grouped	**D** massed
9	**A** need	**B** be	**C** take	**D** want
10	**A** great	**B** top	**C** class	**D** grade
11	**A** watch	**B** see	**C** discern	**D** attend
12	**A** continue	**B** endure	**C** persist	**D** remain
13	**A** prompt	**B** early	**C** soon	**D** fast
14	**A** Although	**B** Still	**C** But	**D** Even
15	**A** live	**B** existing	**C** alive	**D** lively

	A	B	C	D
0		■		
1				
2				
3				
4				
5				
6				
7				
8				
9				
10				
11				
12				
13				
14				
15				

Practice Test 9 ··

For questions 16 - 30, read the text below and think of the word which best fits each space.
Use only one word in each space. Write your answers in the answer boxes provided.

Cyprus

With **(0)** .... warm sunshine, sparkling seas and serene landscapes, Cyprus offers **(16)** .... of reasons to escape the grey winter days. Cyprus has so **(17)** .... attractions as a holiday island. The sun shines most days of the year and even in the **(18)** .... of winter the days are warm and inviting. The shoreline of rough cliffs, sandy beaches and old harbours is washed **(19)** .... the Mediterranean. Inland, you **(20)** .... discover another world of ancient mountains and green valleys with neat fields, orange and lemon groves, vineyards and old villages built out **(21)** .... stone. Legend has it that Cyprus was the place **(22)** .... the ancient Greek goddess of love, Aphrodite, **(23)** .... born. The exact spot is **(24)** .... to be the Rocks of Romiou, a beautiful beach just **(25)** .... the coast from the old port and town of Paphos. This is **(26)** .... largest town in Cyprus and is located **(27)** .... the south western part of the island. Paphos has developed **(28)** .... a thriving modern city and is a large tourist resort, but even **(29)** ...., it has managed to preserve its ancient past. The old harbour is still the central part of the town with tavernas lining the waterside. **(30)** .... are also excellent bars, clubs and restaurants in the modern part of town where visitors can enjoy traditional food and entertainment.

0	*its*	0 ▬
16		16
17		17
18		18
19		19
20		20
21		21
22		22
23		23
24		24
25		25
26		26
27		27
28		28
29		29
30		30

Part 3

For questions 31 - 40, complete the second sentence so that it has a similar meaning to the first sentence. Use the word given and other words to complete each sentence. You must use between two and five words. Do not change the word given. Write your answers in the answer boxes provided.

0 I'm sure it wasn't Jim who did it.
have
It .... Jim who did it.

0	*can't have been*	0 0 1 2

31 Famous as he was, I didn't recognise him.
his
Despite ...., I didn't recognise him.

31		31 0 1 2

32 Unless he apologises, I'll punish him.
apologise
If ...., I'll punish him.

32		32 0 1 2

33 He doesn't like riding a bicycle as much as walking.
prefers
He .... a bicycle.

33		33 0 1 2

34 She had to take care of her mother after her father died.
look
She .... her mother after her father died.

34		34 0 1 2

35 "Let's go to the cinema," he said.
going
He .... the cinema.

35		35 0 1 2

36 But for the help of my friends I'd never have survived.
helped
If .... me, I'd never have survived.

36		36 0 1 2

37 Would you prefer to stay here or leave?
rather
Would you .... leave?

37		37 0 1 2

38 She tried to pay the rent on time.
fall
She tried .... the rent.

38		38 0 1 2

39 The Smiths will ask someone to fix the door tomorrow.
fixed
The Smiths .... tomorrow.

39		39 0 1 2

40 One has to hear it to appreciate it.
heard
It has .... appreciated.

40		40 0 1 2

Practice Test 9 ....

Part 4

For questions 41 - 55, read the text below and look carefully at each line. Some of the lines are correct and some have a word which should not be there. If a line is correct, put a tick (✔) by the number in the answer boxes provided. If a line has a word which should not be there, write the word in the answer boxes provided.

Morning Mischief

0	I was in the middle of a marvellous dream when
00	the alarm clock it went off. Friday morning, seven thirty.
41	"Ten more minutes," I muttered and then promptly fell
42	back to sleep. I woke me up suddenly, knowing that I
43	had slept for more over than ten minutes. A quick
44	glance at the alarm clock confirmed my whole fears.
45	Quarter past eight. I jumped out of bed and
46	ran into the bathroom. There was no any time to
47	wait for the water to warm itself up so I had to
48	have a cold shower. There wasn't time still for
49	breakfast or to iron my clothes. By twenty-five
50	past eight I was been dressed in creased
51	clothes, was cold, hungry and hadn't even
52	had a cup of tea drunk. As I ran out of the house
53	my neighbour shouted good morning to me and
54	added, "Where are you going in on a Sunday?" I
55	couldn't believe it - I don't work on the Sundays.

0	✓	0
00	it	00
41		41
42		42
43		43
44		44
45		45
46		46
47		47
48		48
49		49
50		50
51		51
52		52
53		53
54		54
55		55

Part 5

For questions 56 - 65, read the text below. Use the word given in capitals at the end of each line to form a word that fits in the space in the same line. Write your word in the answer boxes provided.

The Lake District

The **(0)** .... mountains and charming valleys of the Lake District have made the region one of Britain's most **(56)** .... tourist areas. It is, however, still possible to experience **(57)** .... walking among the **(58)** .... landscapes. The eastern hills are more **(59)** .... than their westerly neighbours, and are full of **(60)** .... interest. Really **(61)** .... walkers can spot wildlife such as deer and eagles, while everyone can enjoy the **(62)** .... scenery. Other **(63)** .... features include quaint little villages and pubs where the **(64)** .... poets like Wordsworth and Coleridge used to sit and write their famous **(65)** .... .

IMPRESS		
CROWD		
SOLITARY		
MOUNTAIN		
PEACE		
HISTORY		
OBSERVE		
BEAUTY		
INTEREST		
ROMANCE		
POET		

0	impressive	0
56		56
57		57
58		58
59		59
60		60
61		61
62		62
63		63
64		64
65		65

Determiners are: indefinite article (a/an), definite article (the), demonstratives (this-these/that-those), possessive adjectives (my, your, his etc), quantifiers (some, any, no, every, both, each, either, neither, a lot of, many, much, enough, several, all, most etc) and numbers (one, two etc).

Demonstratives (this - these / that - those)

This/These are used

- **for people or things near us.** *This dress is mine.*
- **for present/future situations.** *I'm seeing George this Friday.*
- **when the speaker is in or near the place he/she is referring to.** *This statue was made in 40 AD. (The speaker is near the statue.)*
- **to introduce people or to identify ourselves on the phone.** *"Liz, this is Mary."*

That/Those are used

- **for people or things not near us.** *That woman over there is the director.*
- **for past situations.** *That month was the best.*
- **to refer back to something mentioned before.** *"We're getting engaged in June." "That's marvellous."*
- **when speaking on the phone to ask who the other person is.** *"Hello. This is James Smythe. Who's that, please?"*

This/These - That/Those are not always followed by nouns. *That's how* he survived the shipwreck.

210 *Fill in: this, these, that or those.*

1. Look at ...*those*... hot air balloons. Aren't they spectacular?
2. James and Claire have decided to get married .... year.
3. Look! .... is the fabric I want for our bedroom curtains.
4. .... people over there come from Swansea.
5. .... girl over there is going to move in next door.
6. ....buildings in the centre of town need to be pulled down. They are an eyesore.
7. "...................... were the best days of my life!" grandpa said.
8. "Is your sister in, Jane? .... is Diana speaking."
9. "Marilyn and Ian are engaged!" "Isn't .... brilliant!"
10. "Rachel, let me introduce you to Stephen. Stephen, ... is Rachel."
11. I wish I'd bought one of .... jackets we saw last week.
12. "I'll take .... earrings." "............... is a good choice. The others don't really suit you."
13. .... car parked over there belongs to my boss.
14. "...................... is one of his earlier works," explained the guide as we all looked at the painting.
15. Do you know .... boy who has just walked past?
16. "Did you know that the director earns over £500,000 a year?" "...................... is scandalous!"
17. .... peaches were extremely juicy, weren't they?
18. "Jason and Caroline were chosen for the lead roles." "...................... is impossible!"
19. Do you remember our holiday in Spain? .... was one of the best times of my life.
20. Could you take .... bags? I'm about to drop them.
21. "So you see, ... is how we met," she explained as she reached the end of her story.
22. Hello, ... is Stephen. Can I speak to your mother, please?
23. "............... is the house where Wordsworth lived," said the guide as she stood outside the front door.
24. .... curry we had last night was delicious, wasn't it?
25. Can you reach .... jars on the top shelf?

A lot of - many - much - (a) few - (a) little

	countables	uncountables	
Positive	a lot (of)/lots of/ many (formal)	a lot (of)/lots of/ much (formal)	There are **a lot of** books in the library. There is **a lot of** salt in this omelette.
Interrogative	many	much	Are there **many** paintings in the museum? Did you have **much** time to talk to him?
Negative	many	much	There aren't **many** tickets left. I can't buy this. I don't have **much** money.
	a few (= some)/ (very) few (= not many, not enough)	a little (= some)/ (very) little (= not much, not enough)	**A few** people were invited to the party. **Very few** people are billionaires. **A little** sugar will make the pie sweeter.

- **A lot (of)/Lots of** are followed by countable or uncountable nouns and are normally used in positive sentences. *There were **a lot of** people at the reception. He's got **lots of** patience.* **A lot of** can also be used in questions and negations in informal English. *Were there **a lot of** arguments caused by the election?*
- **Many** is followed by countable nouns and **much** is followed by uncountable nouns. They are normally used in negations or questions. *There isn't **much** sugar left. Are there **many** boxes?* **Many** and **much** are often used in positive sentences after **how, so, too** or in formal English. *He didn't realise **how much** food he had eaten. You should go on a diet. You're eating **too much**.*
- **A few** (= some, a small number) is followed by countable nouns. **A little** (= some, a small amount) is followed by uncountable nouns. Both **a few** and **a little** have a positive meaning. *Ann has **a little** flour left so she'll make **a few** cakes.*
- **Few** (= not many, almost none) is followed by countable nouns. **Little** (= not much, almost none) is followed by uncountable nouns. Both **few** and **little** have a negative meaning and are rather formal. **Very few/very little, only a few/only a little** are more usual. *Few people are allowed to meet the Queen. I've had **very little** response to my offer. She had **few** doubts about marrying him even though she had known him only **a little** while.*
- **Many, much, (a) few, (a) little, most, all, some, any, several, both, one, two** etc are followed by **of** when a noun follows, preceded by possessives or words such as: **this, that, these, those, the** or **a.** *How **much of** the money you earn do you need for food? I have lent her so **many of** my books that I have nothing to read.*

211 *Fill in: a lot (of), much or many.*

1 Not ...*many*... children believe in Father Christmas any more.
2 It takes .... hard work to get a university degree.
3 I haven't got ... money at the moment so I can't go shopping.
4 He ate too .... food last night so today he's not feeling well.
5 I have too .... books to carry so my bag is very heavy.
6 He must have .... money if he has a big car like that.
7 I haven't got .... time, so please hurry up.
8 There were too .... misprints in the letter.
9 Have you invited .... guests to your dinner party?
10 She doesn't have ..... of an appetite - that's why she's so thin.
11 Are there .... English people living in Germany?
12 How .... milk do you need?
13 She's working overtime as she's got so .... to do.
14 The house isn't finished yet; there's still ....work to be done.
15 There was so .... traffic that we were delayed for an hour.

212 *Underline the correct item.*

1 There are much/many/a lot skyscrapers in Chicago.
2 We spent a lot of/many/few money on holiday.
3 A lot/Much/Few visitors are disappointed by our hotel.
4 If you add a little/a few/many salt, it will taste better.
5 There are much/a lot of/little people on this bus.
6 We've had many/little/too many rain this winter.
7 Few/Much/A little people are as pretty as she is.
8 There's been few/very little/a few news about the earthquake.
9 You must pay many/lots of/few attention to understand this.
10 Lots of/Much/Little flowers were planted in the garden.
11 A few /A little/Little students here have passed the exam.
12 There was many/few/much annoyance caused by her outbreak of anger.

Some - Any - No

	Adjectives	Pronouns		Adverbs
		people	things	places
Positive	some any	someone/somebody anyone/anybody	something anything	somewhere anywhere
Interrogative	any	anyone/anybody	anything	anywhere
Negative	no/not any	no one/not anyone nobody/not anybody	nothing not anything	nowhere not anywhere
Positive/Negative/ Interrogative	every	everybody (all people) everyone	everything (all things)	everywhere (in all places)

● **Some** is used before countable or uncountable nouns. *I want **some** strawberries. She asked for **some** help.* **Some** and **its** compounds (someone, something etc) are normally used in positive sentences. They can also be used in questions to make an offer, a request or when we expect a positive answer. *There's **someone** in the kitchen. (positive) Would you like **something** to drink? (offer) Can I have **something** to eat? (request) Is there **someone** in the garden? (I expect there is.) but: Is there **anyone** in the garden? (I'm asking in general.)*

● **Every** is used before singular nouns. ***Every** candidate has to complete a form. (= all the candidates)* **Every** and **its** compounds take a verb in the singular. ***Everything** he does is wrong. (= all the things) **Every** person working in the laboratory **has** to wear a uniform. (= all persons)*

● **Any** is used before countable or uncountable nouns. *Are there **any** apples left? Is there **any** milk in the fridge?* **Any** and **its** compounds (anyone, anything etc) are normally used in questions. *Is there **anything** for me?* They can also be used in positive sentences meaning "It doesn't matter how/what/when/where/which/who." *Take **anything** you like.* **Any** and **its** compounds can be used after **if** in a positive sentence. ***If** you let **anyone** in, you'll be in trouble.*

● **No/not any** can be used before countable and uncountable nouns. *There are **no** pens in the drawer. There's **no** news from him.* **No/not any** and **their** compounds (no one/not anyone, nothing/not anything etc) are used in negations. *He did **nothing** to help me. He didn't do **anything** to help me.* **Any** and **its** compounds are used with negative words (hardly, never, without, seldom, rarely etc). *She **seldom** goes **anywhere** these days. (not: She ~~seldom goes nowhere~~ these days.)*

10 Determiners / Pronouns

213 Underline the correct item.

1 Don't worry, I said nothing/anything.
2 Pete didn't see anyone/no one come out of the building.
3 We need to take some/any food with us.
4 It took him any/some time to recover from his illness.
5 Anybody/Everybody was pleased with their exam results.
6 Is there any/some sugar in this coffee? It's very bitter.
7 We didn't go nowhere/anywhere this year.
8 Can I have some/any water please?
9 The doctor told her there was anything/nothing wrong with her.
10 He does his homework any/every evening before dinner.

214 Fill in: some, any, no, every or their compounds.

1 Ron knows ...*everything*... there is to know about computers.
2 .... knows Charlie but .... really likes him.
3 We could hardly see .... in the dark.
4 I'm so tired! I just want to go .... to relax for a few days.
5 I've never been .... more exciting than London.
6 Are you doing .... at the moment? I need to ask you ....
7 Michael never does .... without asking .... first.
8 Is there ....milk in the fridge or shall I go and get ....?
9 ....was very pleased with their results; .... was disappointed.
10 Has ....told you .... about what you have to do?
11 There is ....that .... can say to make me feel better.
12 They looked ....for Helen but they couldn't find her.
13 .... is wondering why .... noticed .... before.
14 I want to go .... this weekend. I haven't been .... for ages.
15 Has .... seen my pen? I've looked for it .... but it's .... to be found.

- **Both** refers to two people or things. It has a positive meaning and takes a verb in the plural. It is the opposite of **neither/not either**. *James and Robin are students.* **Both** *James and Robin are students.* **They** *are* **both** *students.* **Both** *of them* *are students.* **Both** *boys* **are** *students.*

- **All** refers to more than two people or things. It has a positive meaning and takes a verb in the plural. It is the opposite of **none**. *All the children laughed.* **All of them** *laughed. They* **all** *laughed.* **All three of them** *laughed.*
  All + that-clause (= the only thing) takes a singular verb. **All that** *she did was to stare at him without speaking.*

- **None** refers to more than two people or things. It has a negative meaning and isn't followed by a noun. *"Are there any biscuits left?"* No, **none.**"
  None of is used before nouns or object pronouns followed by a verb either in the singular or plural. It is the opposite of **all**. *None of the four boys/them know(s) how to ride a bike.* **Note: no + noun.** *There's* **no place** *safer than one's own house.*

- **Either** (= any one of two) / **Neither** (= not one and not the other) refer to two people or things and are used before singular countable nouns. **Neither boy** *likes spaghetti.* **Neither of/Either of** take a verb either in the singular or plural. **Neither of them is/are** *married.*

- **Every** is used with singular countable nouns. It refers to a group of people or things and means "all", "everyone", "everything" etc. *She cooks lunch* **every** *day.*

- **Each** is used with singular countable nouns. It means "one by one", considered individually. **Each** *student* **was** *awarded a diploma.*
  Note that **every one** and **each one** have of constructions. **Every one of/Each one of** *the workers will be given a bonus.*

- **Whole** (= complete) is used with countable nouns. We always use **a, the, this, my** etc + **whole + countable.** *the whole morning = all morning*

- **One/Ones** are used to avoid repetition of a countable noun. *"Which car is yours?" "That* **one.**"

215 *Underline the correct item.*

1 Both/All Margo and Steve are models.
2 Neither/Either Julie nor Lucy enjoyed the film.
3 He goes to the gym either/every day.
4 Both/Neither Rebecca and Charlie are teachers.
5 You will have to talk to each/both person alone to find out what happened.
6 All/Each eight men are working really hard.
7 None/Every of the applicants he interviewed were suitable for the job.
8 Every/All that he needs is a good rest. He's very tired.
9 Neither/Either the bride nor the groom arrived on time. They were all/both late.
10 There's no/none need to do the washing up. The maid will do it.
11 He spent whole/all the evening studying for the exam.
12 Jim speaks neither/either French nor German. He only speaks English.
13 There was a good film on television yesterday but all/none of us saw it.
14 Sam plays football nearly each/every day.
15 I like both of these skirts but I'll take this ones/one because it's cheaper.
16 Each/All flat will have central heating installed before November.
17 Sally and Andrew all/both enjoyed themselves.
18 Jane did not utter a single word the whole/all time she was here.
19 Annette takes the bus to work neither/every day.
20 Either/Neither you start doing some work or I'll fire you.
21 "Do you like these trousers?" "No, I prefer those ones/one actually."
22 I spent all/whole day answering the phone and had no time to do anything else.
23 All of/None of us wanted to go to the party, but we couldn't refuse the invitation.
24 Joe had no/none time to waste; the boat was leaving in five minutes.
25 Both/Either Sonia and Rachel are nurses.
26 A teacher should know the names of every/all his students.
27 None of/All of us eat meat so we went to a vegetarian restaurant.
28 Each/Both time I try to call Jenny her phone is engaged.
29 "Which perfume do you like best?" " I don't really like either/neither of them."
30 The twins' grandfather gave them all/each five pounds for their birthday.

> **Both ... and ... + plural verb** *Both Frank and Terry* **enjoy** *scuba diving.*
> **Either ... or ... Neither ... nor ... / Not only ... but also + singular** or **plural verb depending on the subject which follows or, nor, but also.** *Neither Paula nor Sue and Clare are in the office at the moment.*

216 *Rewrite the sentences using both ... and, neither ... nor, either ... or, not only ... but also.*

1 Joe likes swimming and so does Tom. ...*Both Joe and Tom like swimming*....
2 Molly is going to the cinema tomorrow; so are the Smiths. ....
3 James and Alex like riding horses. ....
4 Jane has never been on an aeroplane and Victoria hasn't either. ....
5 Nick worked late; so did Sue and Fiona. ....
6 Dr Green will see you or else Dr Howe will. ....
7 Daniel is going to Brighton by train and so is Guy. ....
8 Justin doesn't watch television. Andrew doesn't either. ....
9 Katie will give you directions or else Paula will. ....
10 Pete is a lawyer and so is Kathy. ....
11 Paul works as a cashier; so does Bob and Fred..
12 Jill is having her hair cut; so are Sally and Lynn. ....
13 Cath could give us a lift or else Laura could. ....

217 *Complete the sentences using the words in bold. Use two to five words.*

1 My father doesn't like cheese and neither does my brother.
  nor   Neither my father ...*nor my brother like(s)*... cheese.
2 William is a dentist; John is too.
  are   Both .... dentists.
3 Debbie enjoys scuba diving and so does her husband.
  enjoy   Both Debbie .... scuba diving.
4 Sandra can speak Portuguese and Spanish.
  only   Sandra ....; she can also speak Spanish.
5 You can ask Tim for a lift to work or you can ask Sam.
  either   You can .... for a lift to work.
6 It is believed that Jack is guilty and that Pam is too.
  both   It is believed that .... guilty.
7 We didn't realise that Tina wasn't there and that Ann wasn't either.
  nor   We didn't realise that .... there.
8 The bank manager explained that Terry could co-sign the account or else Janet could.
  either   The bank manager explained that .... co-sign the account.
9 He told me that Chester is worth a visit and so is York.
  and   He told me that .... worth a visit.
10 Did you know that Carole is getting married this year and so is Amanda?
  not   Did you know that .... Amanda is getting married this year?

> **Ever** can be added to **question words** to mean **"any"**. These are: however (= in any way that),
> whatever (= anything that), whenever (= any time that), wherever (= any place that), whichever
> (= any of), whoever (= anyone who). **Whoever** *did this must be punished. (= anyone who did it)*

218 *Fill in: whatever, whichever, whenever, wherever, whoever or however.*

1 My dog follows me ...*wherever*... I go. He never leaves my side.
2 That chair is going to break again ....well you fix it.
3 .... happens I'll still be his friend.
4 .... I try to talk to Kate she just ignores me.
5 The bus is leaving. ....wants a ticket must buy one now.
6 Sam has a Spanish friend. .... he goes to Spain he stays with him.
7 .... hard I try, I can't seem to forget that awful night.
8 .... we go to the cinema Julie pays for me.
9 He dresses smartly. ....he goes he makes a good impression.
10 I won't accept that behaviour from anyone, ... they may be.

> ● **Else** (= more; different) is followed by a singular verb and can be used with **indefinite pronouns**
>   and words such as **everyone, something, nobody** etc. *eg. I don't really like Pam and I don't think*
>   *anyone else does either.* **Else** can also be used with **what, where, who** and **how** to refer to people,
>   places , things etc. *Who else can work on the project?*
> ● **Else** forms its possessive case with **'s**. *That notebook isn't yours, it's **someone else's**.*
> ● **Or else** means "otherwise". *Get a taxi **or else** you'll be late.*

219 *Complete the blanks using "else" constructions.*

1 I'd better get some money out of the bank ....*or else*.......... I won't be able to pay the rent.
2 Someone told me that Jim was leaving and then .... told me that he wasn't.
3 I went shopping on my own because .... wanted to come with me.
4 You'd better be in bed by ten o'clock .... there'll be trouble.
5 Why don't you agree with this plan? .... does.

6   We always go to Nice on holiday; can't we go ....
    this year?
7   I'm afraid I can't answer that question. You'd better ask ....
8   Why did they put a parking ticket on my car? ....has one.
9   You'd better write your essay ....you'll be in trouble.
10 That bag isn't mine - it must belong to ....

"Other" structures

the other(s) = the rest	*Only those books are mine;* **the others** *are from the library.*
others = several more apart from the ones already mentioned	*At weekends some people like to go out and dance, while* **others** *prefer to stay at home and relax.*
each other = one another	*Her two small children are always fighting with* **each other**.
every other = alternate	*I clean the house* **every other** *day.*
the other day = a few days ago	*I saw Joe* **the other day.** *I went to his house for dinner.*
the other one(s) = not this/these but something else	*I quite like this dress, but I liked the* **other one** *better.*
another = one more apart from those already mentioned **Another can be used with expressions of distance, money and time.**	*May I have* **another** *slice of cake please?* *It will take us* **another** *two hours before we get to Plymouth.*

220 *Fill in: (the) other(s), each other, every other or another.*

1   Lisa goes riding ...*every other*... week.
2   I need .... pair of shoes; these are falling apart.
3   There was a good film on TV .... night. Did you see it?
4   We're leaving now; .... will join us later.
5   My mother telephones .... day to see how I am.
6   He has to write .... two pages before the article is finished.
7   Have you got .... book I can read? I've finished mine.
8   Some couples are very dependent on .... for companionship.
9   I was the only one who liked the film; .... hated it.
10 It'll be .... few weeks before I see my brother again.
11 Although they work together, they don't get on with ....
12 Sue has to go to the supermarket .... day to buy food.
13 Simone came to see us .... day; she looked very well.
14 There's only .... week to go before the summer holidays begin.
15 This was the only house that we could afford; all .... were too expensive.

221 *Replace the underlined words with an expression containing other/another.*

1   He plays football <u>once a fortnight</u>. ...*He plays football every other week*....
2   I would like <u>one more piece</u> of meat please. ....
3   Sam left <u>a few days ago</u>. ....
4   I've only got these two dresses with me - <u>the rest</u> are at home. ....
5   This car is certainly value for money but I'd prefer <u>something else</u>. ....
6   Some guests turned up with presents while <u>several more</u> came empty handed. ....
7   The Butlers went to Ohio <u>a few weeks ago</u>. ....
8   Do you think I could borrow <u>£5 more</u> this week, please? ....
9   Pat visits her mother <u>on alternate days</u>. ....
10 I would like Gill and Tom to stay behind after class, <u>the rest of you</u> can go home. ....

In Other Words

- Sally, Sue and Liz work as secretaries.
  All three of them work as secretaries.
- Jim, Ted and Phil hate squash.
  None of them like/likes squash.
- There isn't anyone in the room.
  There is no one in the room.
- He's the best dancer of all.
  No one dances as well as he does.

- Lynn is an actress. Sharon is an actress too.
  Both Lynn and Sharon are actresses.
- Sheila doesn't like milk. Paula doesn't like milk either. Neither of them like(s) milk.
  Neither Sheila nor Paula like(s) milk.
- Nothing can be compared to this.
  There isn't anything that/which can be compared to this.

222 *Complete the sentences using the words in bold. Use two to five words.*

1 Bob speaks French. Sam speaks French too.
  speak   Both ...*Bob and Sam speak*... French.
2 No one knows what the outcome will be.
  anyone   There .... what the outcome will be.
3 There isn't anything to watch on television tonight.
  nothing   There .... on television tonight.
4 The girls all dislike playing tennis.
  likes   None .... playing tennis.
5 Lucy is a doctor. Fiona is a doctor too.
  are   Both .... doctors.
6 There isn't anything I would like better.
  is   There .... like better.
7 No one knows the way to the airport.
  anyone   There .... the way to the airport.
8 These exercises are not hard to do.
  of   None .... hard to do.
9 Tony lives abroad. Sylvia does too.
  live   Both .... abroad.
10 There isn't anything Joanne can do to help me.
  nothing   There .... to help me.

Oral Development 12

Use both, all, neither and none as well as the cues below to compare the three animals.
You can use ideas of your own.
tails, legs, ears, teeth, horns, paws, furry skin, fly, walk, talk, run fast, mammals,
carnivorous, small, big etc

eg. All three animals have tails. etc.

Pronouns

Personal pronouns		Possessive adjectives	Possessive pronouns	Reflexive-Emphatic pronouns
before verbs as subjects	after verbs as objects	followed by nouns	not followed by nouns	
I	me	my	mine	myself
you	you	your	yours	yourself
he	him	his	his	himself
she	her	her	hers	herself
it	it	its	---	itself
we	us	our	ours	ourselves
you	you	your	yours	yourselves
they	them	their	theirs	themselves

 223 *Fill in the correct pronouns or possessives.*

Dear Mary,

1) ...We... 're having a marvellous time here in Rhodes. The island is absolutely beautiful. 2) .... is a lot bigger than 3) .... expected. 4) .... hired a car for the first week so 5) .... visited all the interesting places on the island, which was fabulous - if a little tiring. 6) .... was well worth getting a car. 7) .... intend to relax for the rest of 8) .... holiday.

The children have been behaving 9) ...., and there's a children's representative based at the resort so 10) .... takes care of all the children for 4 hours each morning. 11) .... is a lovely girl and the children are mad about 12) .... At least that gives James and 13) .... the morning to 14) .... The hotel is great and the staff are really friendly. 15) .... appreciate 16) .... attempts to speak the Greek language. The weather is great and 17) .... are getting a lovely tan. That's all 18) .... news. 19) .... will see you when 20) .... get back. Take care and thanks again for looking after 21) .... pets.

Love,
Samantha, James & the kids

● **We use the instead of a possessive adjective with parts of the body after prepositions. Verbs used in this pattern include: bite, hit, kiss, pat, punch, slap, sting, touch etc.** *He punched his opponent on the nose. (not: on his nose)*

● **Possessive adjective + own is used to emphasise the fact that something belongs to one person and no one else.** *They've got their **own** house. or They've got a house **of their own.***

224 *Fill in the blanks with "the" or "(own +) possessive adjective".*

1 The boxer was disqualified after kicking his opponent in ...the... leg.
2 The mother hugged .... son as he left for school.
3 Someone hit him in .... face on his first day of school.
4 She kissed .... father on .... cheek before she went to bed.
5 A bee stung her on .... arm while she was sunbathing.
6 A dog bit Sharon on .... leg.
7 He used to share a room with .... brother but now he has .... room.
8 A brick fell and hit her on .... head so she had to spend two weeks in hospital.
9 She patted her daughter on .... back and told .... not to worry.
10 She hasn't got a car .... so she has to borrow her mother's.

10 Determiners / Pronouns

225 Fill in: of one's own, on one's own or one's own.

1 She enjoys being ...*on her own*... .
2 I can borrow my father's car but I'd really love to have .... car.
3 He couldn't afford to rent a flat .... so he had to share with a friend.
4 He's quite a sociable person, but there are times when he really wants to spend some time ....
5 I'd love to set up .... business one day. I think I'd find it very challenging.
6 Thank you for your offer of help, but this is my problem and I shall handle it ....
7 He couldn't paint the house .... so he asked his brother to help him.
8 I offered to help her as she wouldn't have been able to prepare all that food ....
9 They're saving all their money so they can buy a car ....
10 She started .... hairdressing business when she was only sixteen.

Reflexive - Emphatic Pronouns (myself - yourself etc)

- **Reflexive pronouns** are used after certain verbs (**behave, burn, cut, enjoy, hurt, kill, look at** etc) when the subject and the object of the verb are the same. *Did you enjoy* ***yourself***? They can also be used after **be, feel, look, seem** to describe emotions or states. *She doesn't seem* ***herself*** *these days.* **Reflexive pronouns can be used after prepositions but not after prepositions of place.** *He is ashamed of* ***himself***. *but: She looked in front of her. (not: ~~in front of herself~~)*
  Certain verbs (wash, shave, dress, undress, meet, rest, relax, stand up, get up, sit down, wake up etc) **do not normally take a reflexive pronoun.** *She sat down and relaxed. (not: She sat down and relaxed* ~~*herself*~~*.)* **Wash** or **dress** can be used with a reflexive pronoun to talk about young children or animals. *The little boy is trying to* ***dress himself***. *The cat is* ***washing itself***.

- **Emphatic pronouns** have the same form as reflexive pronouns but a different meaning. They give emphasis to the noun, or the fact that a certain person performs an action. *She* ***herself*** *booked everything.* They can also mean "without help". *He repaired the car* ***himself***. *(without help)*

- Note these idioms: **Enjoy yourselves!** (= Have a good time!) **Behave yourself!** (= Be good!) **He likes being by himself.** (= He likes being alone.) **He lives by himself.** (= He lives on his own.) **By myself, by yourself, by himself** etc (= on my own, on your own, on his own etc) **Help yourself to tea.** (= You're welcome to take some tea if you want some.) **Do it yourself.** (= Do it without being helped.) **Make yourself at home!** (= Feel comfortable.) **Make yourself heard.** (= Speak loudly enough to be heard by others.) **Make yourself understood.** (= Make your meaning clear.)

- Note: **each other** means "one another". Compare: *Brothers and sisters look after* ***each other***. *Children without brothers or sisters have to look after* ***themselves***.

---

226 Fill in the correct pronoun, then identify them: reflexive or emphatic.

1 There was nobody to help me so I had to do all the cleaning ...*myself*... . *(emphatic)*
2 If you don't behave ...., I shall put you all to bed early.
3 The music in the club was so loud that I had to shout to make .... heard.
4 The teacher tried to make .... understood but she failed to get the class to understand.
5 We painted the room ....
6 She was very pleased with .... when she got such a good job.
7 My mother warned my brother to behave .... at the wedding.
8 I think I'll get a cat. They're very clean animals which are always washing ....
9 She prepared all the food by ....
10 I think I'd go back to Austria. We really enjoyed .... there.
11 My sister is very vain. She never stops looking at .... in the mirror.
12 I don't feel .... today. I don't know what's wrong with me.
13 My father decorated the house ....

There - It

- **There + be** is used for something mentioned for the first time or to say that someone or something exists. *There are several parcels to be delivered before noon.*
  We use a **personal pronoun + be/other verb** to give more details about someone or something already mentioned. *There's someone in the waiting room.* *He wants to give you something.*
- **It + be** is used for identification. *There's someone in the sitting room.* *It's your aunt.*
- **It + be ... to-inf/that-clause** is used to begin a sentence. *It's such a pleasure to see you after so long.* It can also be used for distance, temperature, time expressions, weather and in the following expressions: It appears that, It seems that, It looks like, It is said that, It doesn't matter etc.
  It is 25˚C today. *It's another twenty miles to Edinburgh.* *It seems that there is a problem with the figures.* (but we also say): *There seems to be a problem with the figures.*

 Fill in: there or it.

1 ...*It*...'s such a pity you can't come with us. .... is said that Rome is beautiful at this time of the year.
2 ....'s such a lovely day today - let's go for a picnic. ....'s a good picnic site only 5 kms from here.
3 We'd better take our anoraks. .... are lots of clouds in the sky. .... looks like it's going to rain.
4 Let's go by car. ....will only take us 2 hours to drive there.
5 ....'s nothing on the television tonight. ......'s a shame we didn't go to the cinema.
6 Mum, ...'s a man at the door. He wants to talk to you.
7 ....'s so nice to see you. .... seems that we haven't had a proper chat in ages.
8 ....'s a pity you can't come to the cinema tonight. ....'s a new film on.
9 ....'s someone waiting to see you.
10 .... are some new magazines on your desk.
11 .... appears that she has quit her job.
12 This fax machine doesn't work properly. .... seems to be faulty.
13 .... seems to be heavy traffic. We may be late.
14 ....'s a shame he lied to you.
15 .... are several letters for you on your desk.
16 ....'s another thirty miles to Brighton.

Fontana di Trevi - Rome

Possessive case

's / s' (people or animals)	**of (inanimate things)**
- **singular noun + 's** *the girl's skirt,the dog's teeth, my mother-in-law's flat*	- **of + inanimate thing/abstract noun** *the heel of the shoe, the top of the stairs*
- **regular plural noun + '** *the farmers' tractors*	- **of + possessive case/pronoun when there is a determiner (this, any etc) before the noun** *Listen to this record of Jo's. (one of Jo's records), a hat of hers (one of her hats)*
- **irregular plural noun not ending in -s + 's** *the women's department, the children's bedroom*	
- **compound noun + 's** *a police officer's duty*	- **of + people (in longer phrases)** *She's the mother of one of my friends.*
- **'s after the last of two or more names to show common possession** *Jane and George's house (they share the same house) but: Jane's and George's houses (each one has got a house)*	- **'s/of to talk about places or organisations** *Britain's history/the history of Britain*

phrases of place + 's *(at the dentist's)* **time/distance expression + 's/'** *(last month's issue, three months' work)*

10 Determiners / Pronouns ....

228 Rewrite the following in the correct possessive form.

1 the child - the toys ...*the child's toys*...
2 the women - the clothes ....
3 the cats - the kittens ....
4 the fridge - the door ....
5 my parents - the car ....
6 the roof - the house ....
7 the man - the trousers ....
8 the dogs - the kennels ....
9 the teachers - the room ....
10 the woman - the money ....
11 the men - the changing rooms ....
12 the train - the windows ....
13 the old man - the wheelchair ....
14 the rules - the club ....
15 the girl - the eyes ....

16 the temperature - the water ....
17 Brian and Jack - the father ....
18 Katy and Sarah - the cars ....
19 a flight - eight hours ....
20 Emily - the hair ....
21 the doctors - the conference ....
22 the lid - the box ....
23 the twins - the mother ....
24 my father-in-law - the garden ....
25 the yacht - my brother's friend ....
26 the boy - the shirt ....
27 my sister's husband - the office ....
28 the apples - the price ....
29 the old woman - the umbrella ....
30 a walk - two miles ....

229 Complete the following sentences using the words in bold. Use two to five words.

1 In the company where I work, Mr Jones is the boss.
of   Mr Jones ...*is the boss of*... the company where I work.
2 This jumper used to belong to my mother.
was   This .... jumper.
3 It takes twelve hours to drive to Scotland.
hour   It is .... to Scotland.
4 I know that John dislikes playing golf and so does Simon.
nor   I know that .... playing golf.
5 In the USA the President lives in the White House.
of   The... in the White House.
6 Are you sure that you can drive to London on your own next week?
yourself Are you sure you can .... next week?
7 There are only a few people here tonight.
not   There .... tonight.
8 She wanted to sit down but another person had taken her seat.
someone   She wanted to sit down .... her seat.
9 He doesn't know very much about cars.
knowledge He .... cars.
10 I enjoy being alone sometimes.
by   I .... sometimes.
11 He enjoys reading books as well as going to the cinema.
both   He .... going to the cinema.
12 Bob doesn't like playing football and Sam doesn't either.
likes   Neither .... playing football.
13 You must do the work on your own if you want to pass the exam.
yourself You must .... if you want to pass the exam.
14 She waited all evening for him to come.
whole   She .... for him to come.
15 She had done everything except the ironing.
thing   The .... done was the ironing.
16 The journey to France takes four hours.
is   It .... to France.
17 At my school, Mrs Forrester is the headmistress.
of   Mrs Forrester .... my school.

176

18 There were very few guests at Sharon's wedding.
   many   There .... at Sharon's wedding.
19 She went alone to see the film.
   own   She .... to see the film.
20 They just sat on the beach all day.
   nothing   They .... on the beach all day.
21 She spent all evening at her friend's house.
   whole   She .... at her friend's house.
22 You are free to leave at any time you choose.
   whenever   You are free .... you choose.
23 He has been to every continent except Asia.
   continent   The .... been to is Asia.
24 We could go to Holland. Alternatively, we could stay in England.
   or   We could .... stay in England.
25 I was supposed to meet Tony a few days ago but he didn't turn up.
   the   I was supposed to meet .... but he didn't turn up.
26 We haven't had any time to see each other.
   no   We .... to see each other.
27 He invited both his parents and his friends to the party.
   only   He .... but also his friends to the party.
28 She finished the book in one night.
   whole   She .... in one night.
29 She drank from another person's cup by mistake.
   someone   She drank .... by mistake.

230 *Find the word which should not be in the sentence.*

1	us
2	
3	
4	
5	
6	
7	
8	
9	
10	
11	
12	
13	
14	
15	
16	
17	
18	
19	
20	
21	
22	
23	
24	
25	

1 We all us went to see a film last night.
2 She always enjoys buying them gifts for her family.
3 They admire each the other a lot.
4 They are both of very happy about the news.
5 Every one child has to be at school by nine o'clock.
6 She stood herself up and went to the front of the classroom.
7 Jenny hadn't realised how far away her own friend lived.
8 I spent the whole of day writing letters.
9 My brother he works in a bank.
10 She likes being by herself own more than being with others.
11 If anyone person calls, tell them to call back in an hour.
12 This shirt is nice but and the other one is nicer.
13 There are a lot of much animals to see in the zoo.
14 Somebody or else will show you how to do it.
15 Whoever he gave you those instructions was mistaken.
16 I don't know how much about Physics.
17 He hates waking up himself early in the morning.
18 My uncle he owns a large restaurant.
19 All of runners must take their places for the race to begin.
20 The only else thing he could do was refuse the offer.
21 Joe is so busy that he has a very little time to do anything.
22 She is too much young to get married.
23 There was not someone in the room.
24 She turned herself round to see who was behind her.
25 She took someone else's books instead of her own one.

Guidelines on how to treat error correction exercises

- Read the text carefully line by line trying to identify the unnecessary words. Such words can be: participles, articles, conjunctions, prepositions, determiners, quantifiers, parts of tense constructions, pronouns, linking words, adjectives, modals, relatives etc.
- When you have completed the exercise, read the text carefully to see if it makes sense. Keep in mind that some lines are correct.

Study the following examples:

Having been invited him to the party, you'd better be nice to him. (**been**; *participle in the active voice - not in the passive*)

He started work in the September. (**the**; *misuse of article - proper nouns do not take "the"*)

He gave me such a useful information. (**a**; *misuse of article - uncountable nouns do not take "a/an"*)

I had no sooner entered the house that than the bell rang. (**that**; *we say: no sooner..than - that isn't necessary*)

Despite of the cold weather, she went out. (**of**; *"despite" isn't followed by "of"*)

There were a lots of children at the party. (**a**; *"lots of" doesn't take "a" whereas we say: a lot of*)

She went to home. (**to**; *we say: go home*)

He's going to ask her to marry with him. (**with**; *we say: marry someone*)

Each of flat has its own balcony. (**of**; *we say: each flat*)

John is being talking to Ann now. (**being**; *Present Continuous is formed with be + verb -ing*)

Tell them as soon as they will arrive. (**will**; *Future tense is never used after time words such as: as soon as, when etc*)

Let me to go out. (**to**; *"let" takes an infinitive without to*)

This it is Anna speaking. (**it**; *we use "this is" to identify ourselves on the phone*)

I would love reading novels. (**would**; *"would love" takes an infinitive with to - "love" takes an -ing form*)

She's more happier than ever. (**more**; *two syllable adjectives form their comparative with -(i)er, not "more"*)

I usually relax myself by taking a hot bath. (**myself**; *relax isn't followed by a reflexive pronoun*)

You needn't to worry. (**to**; *"needn't" is followed by an infinitive without to; misuse of the infinitive*)

Which one boy hit you? (**one**; *we say "which one" when it is not followed by a noun*)

He's the man I spoke to him last week. (**him**; *repetition of the object*)

He has taken after of his mother. (**of**; *the phrasal verb is "take after"; misuse of the preposition*)

She'd rather you have gone by car. (**you**; *the subject of "would rather" and "go" is the same, otherwise we should read: She'd rather you had gone by car.*)

 231 *Find the odd word out.*

0	Arriving in a foreign country for the first time can be	
00	extremely nerve racking. Even if you are on the holiday	
1	with a large group of friends or with a tour guide to help you	
2	out, you never know what it might happen. Firstly	
3	there is the worry of hearing a language which you really	
4	don't understand at the all. If you are ever in a situation	
5	where you have to be communicate with someone in a	
6	foreign language, you may become panic. It never	
7	really seems to matter that though, because I find	
8	that sign language always gets me by in these situations.	
9	For an example, you can use your fingers to show how	
10	many of items you want from a shop. In a hotel you can	
11	act out your requests to use the telephone, to eat a dinner	
12	and take a shower or bath. In fact you could to say that	
13	this aspect of holidaying at abroad makes it all	
14	much the more entertaining. After all, it would be very boring	
15	if the whole world spoke with the same language.

0	✔	□ ⁰ ■
00	*the*	□ ⁰⁰ ■
1		□ ¹ □
2		□ ² □
3		□ ³ □
4		□ ⁴ □
5		□ ⁵ □
6		□ ⁶ □
7		□ ⁷ □
8		□ ⁸ □
9		□ ⁹ □
10		□ ¹⁰ □
11		□ ¹¹ □
12		□ ¹² □
13		□ ¹³ □
14		□ ¹⁴ □
15		□ ¹⁵ □

232 Look at Appendix 2, then fill in the correct particle(s).

1 My brother left for France last night so the whole family went to the airport to **see** him ...*off*... .

2 "The butler will **see** you ....," said Lord Thornton to his visitor as he stood up to leave.

3 We asked if we could **see** .... the vacant house, thinking we might want to buy it.

4 "I'm going to **see** .... it that you never work in this town again!" shouted John's boss.

5 James was not fooled by Helen's charm. He could **see** right .... her.

6 "Don't worry about your university fees. We've got some money **set** .... for your education," said David to his son.

7 It took only a few weeks to **set** .... the business.

8 We **set** .... at 6.00 a.m. in order to reach Birmingham by lunchtime.

9 In the north of Scotland, once bad weather **sets** .... it's bound to last for a long time.

10 A problem at the Nantes office has **set** the programme .... by about three months.

11 It wasn't his fault that he lost his job - somebody had **set** him ....

12 If we want to get this done by five o'clock, we'd better **set** .... immediately.

13 He said he would **set** his dogs .... the boys if they came into his garden again.

233 Look at Appendix 3, then fill in the correct preposition.

1 I won the competition more ...*by*... luck than ...*by*... skill.

2 Jane's bad behaviour left everyone.............. a loss for words.

3 The old building was .... danger of collapsing.

4 We must catch this man .... all costs! He is armed and dangerous.

5 "............... once in your life think of someone besides yourself!" said Tom to his brother.

6 My name's William but people call me Bill .... short.

7 Before a plan is carried out, it must be studied .... detail to make sure everyone knows what they have to do.

8 The sign by the beach said "Motorboats and jet-skis .... hire".

9 When Jenny went to buy the dress she had been saving up for, she was disappointed to find that the shop did not have her size .... stock.

10 It was only .... chance that Kathy learned about her friend's wedding.

11 "I wonder if we could discuss my salary .... private," said Bob to his boss.

12 I've never been introduced to Patricia but I know her .... sight.

13 In our hi-tech world there are many things that we take .... granted.

14 Ann collapsed .... tears upon hearing of her grandfather's death.

15 Why don't we do something else .... a change? I'm sick and tired of going to the cinema every Saturday.

16 When the teacher opened the door to the class-room he was pleased to see all the pupils hard .... work.

17 As the time came for Daniel and Jessica to part, they promised each other that they would stay .... touch.

18 "I pushed Sarah over............ accident. I didn't mean to hurt her," cried Tina.

19 "You'll be .... charge of the children until 12.00 when we get back," I told the babysitter.

20 This diet seems to work fine. Take Mrs Jones, ... instance. She has lost three kilos in a week.

21 When I went to make a phone call all the tele-phones were .... use, so I had to wait.

22 "This time I'm back .... good. I'm never going back to Australia again," Nick's brother assured him.

23 Jane was .... a hurry and didn't notice she had dropped her purse.

24 Dora was still .... pain after her operation; she couldn't even get out of bed.

25 "Until I know .... certain that I've passed my driving test I won't buy a car."

26 The room was .... a mess because the cleaners had not had time to clear it up.

27 I would like to see your proposal .... writing before I make a decision.

28 She's staying with her aunt .... the time being, until she finds a flat.

29 Most shops sell goods .... a profit because they have bought them very cheaply.

234 *Complete the sentences using the words in bold. Use two to five words.*

1   "You ruined my dress!" she said to me.
    of   She ...*accused me of ruining*... her dress.
2   I've never driven such a fast car.
    ever   This is the .... driven.
3   VIP means "very important person".
    for   VIP .... "very important person".
4   It was reported that the demonstrators were taken away by the police.
    been   The demonstrators were .... away by the police.
5   He was evicted from his flat for not paying the rent.
    turned   He .... flat for not paying the rent.
6   Perhaps he has forgotten our date.
    have   He .... our date.
7   I'm sure he invented the story about the stolen jewellery.
    up   He .... the story about the stolen jewellery.
8   Police are diverting the traffic.
    diverted   The traffic .... the police.
9   She got someone to check the security system last Monday.
    checked   She .... last Monday.
10 The piano is too heavy for us to lift.
    so   The piano is .... lift it.
11 I'd love to come with you next weekend!
    only   If .... you next weekend!
12 The police are investigating the blackmail attempt.
    into   The police .... the blackmail attempt.
13 It's a pity I left the door unlocked.
    only   If .... the door unlocked.
14 Can you please close the window?
    closing   Would .... the window?
15 He hates people not taking him seriously.
    taken   He .... seriously.

235 *Complete the sentences below using an appropriate idiom from the list, then explain the idioms.*

at a loose end	from scratch	for donkey's years
on all fours	on the house	out of the blue
over the moon	under the thumb	for a song
down the drain		

1   When the model fell to pieces Mary had to build it again ...*from scratch (from the beginning)*... .
2   That's the second bad film we've seen in two weeks. Another £5 ....
3   He bought the house .... ten years ago before property prices started to rise.
4   Please get what you want from the bar. Drinks are .... tonight.
5   I haven't heard from Diane .... I wonder where she may be.
6   The news of the wedding came quite .... Everyone thought they had split up.
7   When Pauline finally retired she felt .... as she didn't know what to do all day.
8   Cath was .... when her team won the championship.
9   Charlie is really .... of his wife. He does whatever she says.
10 I entered the room to find my husband .... searching for his wedding ring.

Practice Test 10

Part 1

For questions 1 - 15, read the text below and decide which word A, B, C or D best fits each space. There's an example at the beginning (0).

The Great Outdoors

Climbing Everest and walking up a mountain in Scotland may seem **(0)** ... completely **(1)** ... activities, but both require **(2)** ... preparation. **(3)** ... injury and even death can occur, even on an apparently easy route if a few **(4)** ... guidelines are not followed. Firstly, and perhaps most importantly, **(5)** ... the weather forecast before you **(6)** ..... . If you have any doubts at all, **(7)** ... your trip until conditions improve. Ensure that you have the **(8)** ... equipment. Your list should **(9)** ... a good pair of walking boots, a thick jumper and a good **(10)** ... waterproof jacket. Be **(11)** ... to take food supplies in case you **(12)** ... against problems on the mountainside and **(13)** ... having to spend the night there. An emergency first aid kit, a torch and a whistle are also **(14)** ..... . As long as you are **(15)** ..., the great outdoors has a lot to offer.

0	**A** if	**B** as	**C** like	**D** so		**0**	A ☐ B ☐ **C** ■ D ☐
1	**A** different	**B** awkward	**C** unlike	**D** various		**1**	A ☐ B ☐ C ☐ D ☐
2	**A** exact	**B** carefree	**C** careful	**D** cautious		**2**	A ☐ B ☐ C ☐ D ☐
3	**A** Important	**B** Emergency	**C** Urgent	**D** Serious		**3**	A ☐ B ☐ C ☐ D ☐
4	**A** basic	**B** base	**C** plain	**D** bottom		**4**	A ☐ B ☐ C ☐ D ☐
5	**A** hear	**B** check	**C** listen	**D** examine		**5**	A ☐ B ☐ C ☐ D ☐
6	**A** set up	**B** set to	**C** set off	**D** set down		**6**	A ☐ B ☐ C ☐ D ☐
7	**A** put off	**B** put down	**C** put up	**D** put on		**7**	A ☐ B ☐ C ☐ D ☐
8	**A** needed	**B** accurate	**C** specific	**D** proper		**8**	A ☐ B ☐ C ☐ D ☐
9	**A** involve	**B** include	**C** entail	**D** insert		**9**	A ☐ B ☐ C ☐ D ☐
10	**A** make	**B** brand	**C** quality	**D** mark		**10**	A ☐ B ☐ C ☐ D ☐
11	**A** definite	**B** sure	**C** able	**D** clever		**11**	A ☐ B ☐ C ☐ D ☐
12	**A** come on	**B** come down	**C** come up	**D** come through		**12**	A ☐ B ☐ C ☐ D ☐
13	**A** end up	**B** cut off	**C** pick up	**D** get out		**13**	A ☐ B ☐ C ☐ D ☐
14	**A** essential	**B** needy	**C** wanted	**D** in need		**14**	A ☐ B ☐ C ☐ D ☐
15	**A** senseless	**B** sensitive	**C** sensual	**D** sensible		**15**	A ☐ B ☐ C ☐ D ☐

Part 2

For questions 16 - 30, read the text below and think of the word which best fits each space.
Use only one word in each space. Write your answers in the answer boxes provided.

Power Dressing

Fashion designers have finally realised that working women are **(0)** .... main customers. Well-made clothes for the office rather **(16)** .... high glamour are now top priority. This season's designs show that the working woman has **(17)** .... very important to a wide range of fashion designers, with garments being made to **(18)** .... not only the body **(19)** .... the lifestyle as well. **(20)** .... years, plain-coloured basic suits were the only thing business women **(21)** .... wear, but today's woman isn't happy wearing what is no more than a version of a man's business suit. She wants her clothes to be elegant, modern and dynamic - and good **(22)** .... for money. While few big names in fashion have **(23)** .... their attention to the office, a new group of designers is emerging, **(24)** .... main goal is to dress city women in style. Collections are **(25)** .... designed with the **(26)** .... of providing easy, comfortable, all-purpose clothes **(27)** .... will free women from thinking only in **(28)** .... of the usual blouse, jacket and skirt. For **(29)** ...., a long black fitted jacket worn over a simple but beautifully cut dress would **(30)** .... a woman to go from the office to a cocktail party with elegant ease.

0	*their*	0 ▬
16		16
17		17
18		18
19		19
20		20
21		21
22		22
23		23
24		24
25		25
26		26
27		27
28		28
29		29
30		30

Part 3

For questions 31 - 40, complete the second sentence so that it has a similar meaning to the first sentence. Use the word given and other words to complete each sentence. You must use between two and five words. Do not change the word given. Write your answers in the answer boxes provided.

0 I'm sure it wasn't Jim who did it.
have
It .... Jim who did it.

| 0 | *can't have been* | 0 0 1 2 |

31 "Shall I call them later?" he asked himself.
whether
He .... later.

| 31 | | 31 0 1 2 |

32 The shoes we bought John no longer fit him.
grown
John .... the shoes we bought him.

| 32 | | 32 0 1 2 |

33 It's time they stopped fighting over this issue.
gave
It's time they .... over this issue.

| 33 | | 33 0 1 2 |

34 Why don't you go to Hungary this year?
could
You .... this year.

| 34 | | 34 0 1 2 |

35 She had no one who could help her.
turn
She .... for help.

| 35 | | 35 0 1 2 |

36 They pay someone to mow the lawn every week.
mowed
They .... every week.

| 36 | | 36 0 1 2 |

37 They bought a large house because they planned to start a family.
view
They bought a large house .... a family.

| 37 | | 37 0 1 2 |

38 He doesn't mind if he is asked to work late.
being
He .... to work late.

| 38 | | 38 0 1 2 |

39 Everyone did the exercise except Ann.
only
The .... do the exercise was Ann.

| 39 | | 39 0 1 2 |

40 He broke their agreement at the very last minute.
went
He .... at the very last minute.

| 40 | | 40 0 1 2 |

Part 4

For questions 41 - 55, read the text below and look carefully at each line. Some of the lines are correct and some have a word which should not be there. If a line is correct, put a tick (✔) by the number in the answer boxes provided. If a line has a word which should not be there, write the word in the answer boxes provided.

Working on a Ship

0	It has always been my own ambition to travel, so when	**0**	*own*
00	I was offered a job on a cruise ship last winter,	**00**	✓
41	I jumped out at the chance to fulfill my dream.	**41**	
42	I was been told that the ship I would be working on	**42**	
43	would be to sailing in the exotic waters of the Caribbean,	**43**	
44	so I made it sure to pack plenty of light clothes.	**44**	
45	However, when I arrived at the port of Southampton,	**45**	
46	where the ship would be leaving from, I discovered	**46**	
47	from a one of my fellow employees that we would	**47**	
48	actually be cruising in the freezing waters of the	**48**	
49	English Channel, in between from the Channel Islands.	**49**	
50	I had also been told that I would be supervising	**50**	
51	the ship's restaurant, but since as soon as we started	**51**	
52	sailing I was ordered to start serving food to people!	**52**	
53	By this time I knew about that I had been misled	**53**	
54	about the job. There it was nothing I could do, except	**54**	
55	wish that I had checked lot more carefully before taking it.	**55**	

Part 5

For questions 56 - 65, read the text below. Use the word given in capitals at the end of each line to form a word that fits in the space in the same line. Write your word in the answer boxes provided.

Eat, Drink and Be Merry

The **(0)** .... of festive periods like Christmas, brings with it a greater **(56)** .... of sweet treats. **(57)** .... believe that it is not just the flavour which makes us feel such **(58)** .... for certain foods. Western **(59)** .... eat more than two million tons of chocolate a year. There are many theories to explain the **(60)** .... of chocolate.
(61) .... have found that chocolate contains endorphins, which make people more **(62)** .... yet, in large amounts, cause **(63)** .... . Chocolate also contains caffeine, which is **(64)** .... . Whatever the theories, most chocaholics would say that eating chocolate is simply **(65)** .... .

ARRIVE	**0**	*arrival*
CONSUME	**56**	
PSYCHOLOGY	**57**	
FOND		
EUROPE	**58**	
	59	
POPULAR	**60**	
SCIENCE	**61**	
ENERGY	**62**	
RELAX		
ADDICT	**63**	
	64	
COMFORT	**65**	

Questions - Short Answers

Yes/No questions (questions which require Yes/No in the answer) are formed by putting the auxiliary or modal verb (be, can, have etc) before the subject. *She can do it.* ➡ *Can she do it?* With all other verbs we form Yes/No questions with **Do/Does** (Present Simple) or **Did** (Past Simple). *He works hard.* ➡ *Does* he work hard? Yes/No questions are asked with a rising intonation. *Did you like the party?* ↗

Wh-questions begin with a question word (**what, which, when, where, who, why, how** etc) *Who* is he? When there is a verb followed by a preposition, the preposition usually goes at the end of the question. In formal English it can be put before the question word. *Who* did she get married *to*? *(more usual)* *To whom* did she get married? *(formal English)*

We use questions to ask for information or permission. We can also use them to make offers, requests, suggestions or invitations. *Do you know* what time the train leaves? (information), *May I* see the manager? (permission), *Would you like me* to do the ironing? (offer), *Could you* show me how to fix the tap? (request), *Shall we* go to the opera? (suggestion), *Would you like* to have dinner with me? (invitation)

236 *Form questions, then identify the speech situation for each question.*

1 (you/pick up children from school?)   *Could you pick up the children from school? (request)*
2 (I/use the car today?)   ....
3 (you/like/come over to my house?)   ....
4 (you/do my shopping tomorrow?)   ....
5 (what time/shops close today?)   ....
6 (we go/concert this evening?)   ....
7 (I borrow/some money?)   ....
8 (we/go/the cinema tonight?)   ....
9 (you like/go to the beach tomorrow?)   ....
10 (I use/your pen for a minute?)   ....

We normally use the following question words to ask about:

people	animals/things	place	time	quantity	manner	reason
What	What	Where	How long	How many	How	Why
Which (of)	Which (of)		How often	How much		
Who			What time			
Whose (possession)			When			

- **Who** is used to ask about people. *"Who is the author of this book?"*
- **Whose** is used to express possession. *"Whose is this car?" "It's Paul's."*
- **Which** is used for people, animals or things, alone or before **nouns, one/ones** or **of**. *Which bag is yours? Which of these books do you want?* **Which** is normally used when there is a **limited choice**. *"Which is your car - the Mercedes or the Volvo?"* (there are only two cars we are talking about - limited choice.) It can also be used with the **comparative** and **superlative**. *"Which is faster, a Ferrari or a Porsche?" "Which is the tallest building in America?"*
- **What** is used alone or before a noun to ask about things. *"What can I say?" "What books do you enjoy reading?"* **What** is used when there is an **unlimited choice**. *"What kind of food do you enjoy eating?"* (there are many kinds of food to choose from - unlimited choice) **What** can also be used in the following expressions: **What ... look like?** (asking for a description of physical appearance), **What ... for?, What colour ...?, What size?, What kind/sort?, What time?, What is he like?** (asking for a description of character), **What is it used for?** etc *"What is your brother like?" "He's very nice." "What does Jack look like?" "He's very tall and thin." "What colour is his hair?" "Dark brown."*
- **What** and **which** are sometimes both possible. *What/Which fruit shall we have for dessert?*

237 Fill in: who, whose, which, what, where, how long, how often, what time, when, how many, how much, how or why.

1 "...*What*... does she do for a living?" "She's a florist."
2 "..................... bag is this?" "It's Mary's."
3 "..................... skirt do you prefer, the long one or the short one?"
"The short one."
4 "..................... people work in this office?" "Thirty."
5 "..................... is your mother coming back?" "Next week."
6 "..................... didn't you tell me that you were leaving?" "I forgot."
7 "..................... does a ticket to Edinburgh cost?" "£50."
8 "..................... have you been living in London?" "Three years."
9 "..................... times a week do you go to the gym?" " Four."
10 "..................... car is that parked outside?" "John's."
11 "..................... bus goes to the airport?" " The number 24."
12 "..................... were you born?" "In Brighton."
13 "..................... does the plane arrive at Heathrow?"
"Twelve o'clock."
14 "..................... don't you come with us to the theatre?" "I'd love to."
15 "..................... do you get to work?" "By bus."
16 "..................... is that tall man over there?" "My uncle."
17 "..................... times have you been to France?" "Three."
18 "..................... is the cheapest way to get to Liverpool, by bus or by train?" "By bus."
19 "..................... do you see your parents?" "Every month."
20 "..................... kind of films do you like?" "Adventure stories."

Subject/Object Questions

If what, which or who are the subject of the question, the word order is the same as in statements (subject questions). If they are the object of the question, the verb is in question form (object questions).

subject		object		subject		object
Ian	met	Sally.		Sally	met	David.

Who met Sally? (not: ~~Who did meet Sally?~~)   **Who did** Sally **meet?**

 238 Write questions for the sentences below. The words in bold should be the answer.

1 **James** arrived late. ...*Who arrived late?*...
2 **Tina** cooked the food. ....
3 She likes **ice skating**. ....
4 **My father** drove me to school. ....
5 It was **Ann's** fault. ....
6 He bought **a new tie**. ....
7 **Shakespeare** wrote that play. ....
8 Daniel shouted at **Sarah**. ....
9 **Sheila** didn't talk to Diane. ....
10 Henry arrived **at ten o'clock**. ....
11 **My sister** had a baby. ....
12 Paul gave the parcel to **Mary**. ....

13 **Anita** opened the window. ....
14 The car belongs to **Barbara**. ....
15 I have **five** brothers. ....
16 The ticket cost **£5**. ....
17 Nick lives in **London**. ....
18 My favourite food is **pizza**. ....
19 **Simon** likes Julie. ....
20 Dennis was born in **1970**. ....
21 My favourite pet is **the cat**. ....
22 Tom is getting married to **Lisa**. ....
23 Paul gave the parcel to **Barbara**. ....
24 The film lasted **three hours**. ....

Negative Questions

- **Negative questions** are formed with **not**, but there is a difference in word order for the short and full form.
  (short form) **auxiliary + n't + subject + verb** ***Haven't they reached*** Hawaii yet? *(everyday speech)*
  (full form) **auxiliary + subject + not + verb** ***Have they not reached*** Hawaii yet? *(emphatic)*
- **Negative questions** are used to express: **annoyance/sarcasm** (***Hasn't she*** come back yet?), **surprise** (***Don't you*** know she was fired?), **a wish to persuade someone** (***Won't you*** help me do the exercises?) and **expectation of a "Yes" - answer** (***Don't you*** know they got engaged?).

239 *Use the prompts below to make a negative question, then give a suitable reply.*

1 A: Why didn't you come to school yesterday? ...*Weren't you feeling well*...? (you/feeling well)
  B: ...*No*,... I wasn't.
2 A: There was a good film on TV last night. ....? (you/watch it)
  B: ...., I was too tired.
3 A: The meeting's been cancelled, Mr Bright. ....? (anyone/tell you)
  B: ...., they didn't.
4 A: It's getting late. ....? (he/should be here by now)
  B: ...., he should.
5 A: You look very tired. ....? (you/sleep well last night)
  B: ...., I'm afraid not.
6 A: Why is John at home today? ....? (he/should be working)
  B: ...., he has the day off.
7 A: Why weren't you at the party last night? ....? (you/be invited)
  B: ...., but I didn't feel like going.

Question Tags

- **Question tags** are short questions added to the end of a statement to ask for **confirmation** of, or **agreement** with, the statement. They are formed with an auxiliary verb and the appropriate personal pronoun. They take the same auxiliary verb as in the statement if there is one, otherwise they take **do/does** (Present S.) or **did** (Past S.). *He is in hospital, **isn't he**? She didn't come, **did she**?*
- **Question tags** can be said with a **rising intonation** when we are not sure and expect an answer, or a **falling intonation** when we are sure and don't really expect an answer.
  *She is lying, **isn't she?*** *(not sure) He bought a new car, **didn't he**? (sure)*
- A positive statement is followed by a negative question tag, and a negative statement is followed by a positive question tag. *She sings well, **doesn't she**? He won't tell, **will he**? Note that **everyone/someone/anyone/no one** form their question tags with an **auxiliary verb + they**. Everyone attended the meeting, **didn't they**?*
- Study the following question tags.

"I am"	"aren't I?"	*I am shorter than you, aren't I?*
"I used to"	"didn't I?"	*He used to be your best friend, didn't he?*
Imperative	"will you/won't you?" "can you/could you?"	*Write to me, will you?/won't you?/ can you?/could you?*
"Let's"	"shall we?"	*Let's go for a walk, shall we?*
"Let me/him" etc	"will you/won't you?"	*Let her come with us, will you/won't you?*
"Don't" (negative imperative)	"will you?"	*Don't forget to call me, will you?*
"I have" (= possess)	"haven't I?"	*He has a nice house, hasn't he?*
"I have" (idiomatic use)	"don't I?"	*She had dinner, didn't she?*
"There is/are"	"isn't/aren't there?"	*There is room for me, isn't there?*
"This/That is"	"isn't it?"	*This is your pen, isn't it?*

240 *Fill in the appropriate question tag.*

1 You have got enough money, *..haven't you..?*
2 He will be on time, ...?
3 There is enough food for everyone, ...?
4 She used to fight with her brother, ...?
5 Everyone felt embarrassed, ...?
6 I am dressed smartly enough, ...?
7 That's your car, ...?
8 You will pick me up, ...?
9 Let's eat dinner now, ...?
10 Don't leave without me, ...?

11 You have been invited, ...?
12 There are a lot of people here, ...?
13 She left an hour ago, ...?
14 He hates pizza, ...?
15 That was your father, ...?
16 Tell me, ...?
17 Let me know, ...?
18 Ann can't speak French, ...?
19 She has a brother, ...?
20 I am older than you, ...?

- **Question tags can also be affirmative-affirmative. If said with a rising intonation, we ask for more information.** *She is always late, is she?* **If said with a falling intonation, we express negative feelings such as disappointment or disapproval. We don't expect an answer.** *He'll be angry, will he?*

- **Echo tags are a response to an affirmative or negative sentence. They are used in everyday speech to ask for more information or to show anger, concern, confirmation, interest, surprise etc.**
  Affirmative: *He left. - **He did, didn't he**? (confirmation) He left. - **He did**?/**Did he**? (surprise)*
  Negative: *He didn't come. - **He didn't, did he**? (confirmation) He didn't come. - **He didn't**? (surprise)*

241 *Add an appropriate response expressing disappointment, disapproval, surprise or confirmation.*

1 "He is in India." "*...He is...?*" (surprise)
2 "It is very cold today." "...........................?" (confirmation)
3 "It's five o'clock already." "...........................?" (surprise)
4 "She failed the exam." "...........................?" (disappointment)
5 "Mary's ill." "...........................?" (surprise)
6 "He missed the bus." "...........................?" (disappointment)
7 "Jack's her cousin." "...........................?" (confirmation)
8 "I haven't read that book." "...........................?" (surprise)
9 "He's a very quiet child." "...........................?" (confirmation)
10 "She's very rude." "...........................?" (disapproval)

India

Short Answers

Short answers are used to avoid repetition of the question asked before. Positive short answers are formed with Yes + personal pronoun + auxiliary verb (do, can, have, will etc).
"Did he do it?" "Yes, he did." **Negative short answers are formed with No + personal pronoun + negative auxiliary verb.** *"Did she see you?" " No, she didn't."*

242 *Add question tags and short answers to the following.*

1 "You used to play the piano, *...didn't you...?*" "Yes, *...I did... .*"
2 "She's got a loud voice, ... ?" "Yes, ..."
3 "Walk a bit slower, ... ?" "No, ..."
4 "He works for Laura, ... ?" "No, ..."
5 "You've been to Japan, ... ?" "Yes, ..."
6 "You're coming to the party tonight, ... ?" "No, ..."
7 "They had been told about it, ... ?" "Yes, ..."
8 "Don't repeat what I told you, ... ?" "No, ..."

9 "They won't be very happy, ...?" "No, ..."
10 "You have an appointment this morning, ...?" "Yes, ..."
11 "They bought that car last year, ...?" "Yes, ..."
12 "He's going to be surprised, ...?" "Yes, ..."

Oral Development 13

Look at the pictures, then make sentences using question tags and short answers.

S1: He seems to be working hard, doesn't he?
S2: Yes, he does.

So - Neither/Nor - But

- **So + auxiliary verb + personal pronoun/noun (positive addition to a positive sentence).** *She plays tennis.* **So do I.** *(I play tennis too.) Sarah went to university.* **So did Bill.** *(Bill went to university too.)*
- **Neither/Nor + auxiliary verb + personal pronoun/noun (negative addition to a negative sentence).** *James can't swim.* **Neither/Nor can Jim.** *(not: So can't Jim.)*

- **But + personal pronoun/noun + affirmative auxiliary verb (positive contrast to negative statement)** *Daniel hasn't seen that film,* **but I have.** *He hasn't read that book,* **but she has.**
- **But + personal pronoun/noun + negative auxiliary verb (negative contrast to positive statement)** *Mike looks sad,* **but Jim doesn't.** *He has been to Paris,* **but she hasn't.**

243 *Rephrase the sentences using so, neither/nor or but as in the example:*

1 Both Simon and Joe play football. ...*Simon plays football. So does Joe.*...
2 Peter can't drive and I can't either. ....
3 I've been to America. David hasn't. ....
4 Sally and Ann don't want to come. ....
5 Both Mary and Sam are at school. ....
6 Mark doesn't speak French and Tim doesn't either. ....
7 Jane saw the play. Kate did too. ....
8 I don't like watching cricket - Daniel does. ....
9 Sean hasn't done his homework. Pam hasn't either. ....
10 I passed the exam. My friend didn't pass. ....
11 Both Peter and I are going to the concert. ....
12 I don't approve of gambling. My friends don't either. ....
13 Paul has been informed. Louise has too. ....
14 Tom doesn't like Thai food. His wife does. ....
15 Charlie won't come and Dan won't either. ....
16 I can play the violin. My brother can't. ....

11 Questions / Short Answers

When we wish to express surprise at what somebody has said we use so + subject + auxiliary verb.
*George: Mary looks upset. Ann: **So she does**!*

244 *Add an appropriate response to the following sentences.*

1 That's Harry over there! (surprise) ...*So it is!*...
2 She's found a job! (surprise) ....
3 George doesn't like strawberries. (addition - I) ....
4 Diana has gone on holiday. (addition - Alice) ....
5 Rebecca doesn't like Caroline. (addition - I) ....

So - Not

So and not can be used in short answers after: think, hope, expect, suppose, I'm afraid, guess, it seems, say, tell sb, it appears, believe or imagine.

I'm afraid so - I'm afraid not
It appears so - It doesn't appear so/It appears not
I believe so - I don't believe so/I believe not
I expect so - I don't expect so/I expect not
I guess so - I guess not
I hope so - I hope not

I imagine so - I don't imagine so/I imagine not
He says so/He said so - He didn't say so
It seems so - It doesn't seem so/It seems not
I suppose so - I don't suppose so/I suppose not
He told me so - He didn't tell me so
I think so - I don't think so/I think not

*"Will she marry him?" **I think so**." "Shouldn't he have been here by now?" **"I don't think so**."*

245 *Fill in the blanks using the verb in brackets and so or not.*

1 A: Will Bill come to the races? (think)
  B: ...*I don't think so*... . He's not very well.
2 A: Will you go away for Christmas? (hope)
  B: .... I need a rest.
3 A: Will your grandmother have to go into hospital? (afraid)
  B: .... She's very sick.
4 A: How do you know that John will be late? (tell)
  B: .... He mentioned it before leaving.
5 A: Are you going shopping tomorrow? (suppose)
  B: .... There's no food in the house.
6 A: Is the whole family invited to the reception? (appear)
  B: .... The hall is too small.
7 A: Will you be at home this evening? (expect)
  B: .... I haven't made any plans.
8 A: Do you think Caroline likes Hugh? (imagine)
  B: .... They don't seem to get on very well together.
9 A: Can you lend me some money? (afraid)
  B: .... I haven't been paid yet.
10 A: Do you think it will rain tomorrow? (hope)
  B: .... I want to go on a picnic.
11 A: Will he approve of the plan? (expect)
  B: .... He's accepted all our ideas so far.
12 A: Will you be at the wedding? (afraid)
  B: .... I'll be in Glasgow that weekend.

Asking for permission / Making requests	Giving/Refusing Permission / Answering requests
Can I/Could I have something to eat? I'm starving. **May I/Might I** borrow your rubber?	Yes, you can./Yes, of course (you can)./No, you can't. Yes, you may./Yes, of course (you may)./No, you may not./I'd rather you didn't./I'm afraid not.

Making suggestions/invitations	Answering suggestions/invitations
Will you/Would you/Would you like to go for a coffee? **Shall we** go to the cinema?	I'd like to./I'd love to./Yes, all right./I'm afraid I can't./ I'd love to but I can't./I'm sorry, I can't.

Making offers	Answering offers
Shall I/we, Can I/we, Would you like me to come with you?	Yes, please./No, thank you./No thanks.

246 *Fill in short answers as in the example:*

1 A: Shall we go rafting this Sunday?
  B: ...*Yes, of course*... . I'm sure we'll have a nice time.
2 A: Would you like another cup of coffee?
  B: .... I'm very thirsty.
3 A: Shall I wash your shirt for you?
  B: .... I'll do it later.
4 A: Will you be able to drive me to work?
  B: .... The car's broken down.
5 A: Shall we go out for a meal tonight?
  B: .... We haven't been out for ages.
6 A: Would you and Bill like to come over on Saturday night?
  B: .... We've been invited to a party.
7 A: Could you go and buy some fruit?
  B: .... I have nothing to do at the moment.
8 A: Can I wear your blue jumper today?
  B: .... I'm going to wear it.
9 A: May I borrow this book?
  B: .... I've read it already.
10 A: Will you be coming tomorrow?
  B: .... I have to go to the dentist.

247 *Find the word which should not be in the sentence.*

1 John goes jogging every morning, doesn't he go?
2 Would you mind to picking some things up at the supermarket?
3 That's your car, isn't it this?
4 How long have you be lived in London?
5 There is a problem with the photocopier again, isn't it there?
6 Don't forget to ring the dentist, will you not?
7 How long time does it take to get there?
8 Would you to like a cup of coffee?
9 Didn't you not see him yesterday?
10 She used to be a flight attendant, didn't use she?
11 Who did told you about the problem?
12 How long is it the film?
13 Could you mind copy these notes for me?
14 What Tom did he say about the assignment?

1	*go*
2	
3	
4	
5	
6	
7	
8	
9	
10	
11	
12	
13	
14	

248 Look at Appendix 2, then fill in the correct particle(s).

1 Don't worry, I'll **stand** ...*by*... you whatever problems you may have.

2 Even though they knew he was innocent, no one **stood** .... him.

3 Tom's **taken** .... fishing; it's a very relaxing pastime.

4 Joanna really **stands** .... with her red hair.

5 You **take** ...... your father; you're a lot like him.

6 Their business is being **taken** ...... by a bigger company.

7 Simon is too young to **take** .... such a big responsibility.

8 RAC **stands** .... Royal Automobile Club.

9 Everyone was **taken** .... when the manager stood up and walked out of the meeting.

10 As the plane **took** .... we had a wonderful view of Hong Kong.

11 Why don't you **take** some time ....? You look exhausted.

12 One of my colleagues was ill yesterday so I **stood** .... her.

13 I **was taken** .... by her; she fooled me completely.

14 She had to **take** her skirt .... because she had lost a lot of weight.

15 This is quite complicated, so you might not **take** .... all the information the first time.

16 Work is going well; we've **taken** .... a lot of new clients.

17 Military nurses were told to **stand** .... in case of an attack.

18 I don't know why she **stands** .... that sort of behaviour. I wouldn't tolerate it.

19 If washing powder doesn't **take** that spot ......, maybe bleach will.

20 When we heard he had no place to stay, we offered to **take** him ....

249 Look at Appendix 3, then fill in the correct preposition(s).

1 The miners are ...*on*... strike again. They want better pay.

2 He hid the file .... purpose so that no one would find it.

3 When Tom is .... duty he does a lot of sport to relax.

4 She accepted the prize .... behalf of her father, who was abroad.

5 The drinks machine is .... order; you'll have to go out and buy something.

6 Everything is .... control. There is no need to panic.

7 The plate fell on the floor and smashed .... little pieces.

8 I'm sorry, but that item is .... stock. We have sold them all.

9 Don't buy those shoes now - wait till they're .... sale.

10 I see their house is .... sale - they must be planning to move away.

11 .... regard to your question, the answer is "yes".

12 I was .... the impression that you like football, but I was wrong.

13 He discovered, ... his surprise, that it was already ten o'clock.

14 There are a lot of animals .... our farm in Devon.

15 I'm telling you this .... the record, so you mustn't print it.

16 Suddenly, ... warning, a car pulled out from a side road and crashed into her car.

17 The house is .... fire! Call the fire brigade!

18 This information is .... limits to all but authorised personnel.

19 The police officer said, "You are .... arrest."

20 Welcome .... board this flight to Rome.

21 Strawberries are .... season at the moment, so they're very expensive.

22 It is .... the law to sell alcohol to children.

23 We sat down .... a field to have our picnic.

24 We live .... the outskirts of town, not .... the centre.

25 I am not .... good terms with my brother; we're always fighting.

26 I've heard this song so many times that I know it .... heart.

27 The bridge is .... repair; it collapsed last night.

28 You're getting .... the point; that's not what we're talking about.

29 He started .... scratch and built up an empire.

30 I was late for work .... account of the bus strike.

250 *Complete the sentences using the words in bold. Use two to five words.*

1 This is the best stew she has ever eaten.
   better   She has never ...*eaten better stew than*... this.
2 You always notice Josh in a crowd.
   out   Josh .... a crowd.
3 "Don't forget to unplug the TV," Mum said to us.
   reminded Mum .... the TV.
4 Someone has spilt ink on the tablecloth.
   had   The tablecloth .... on it.
5 That cheese will spoil unless it's put in the fridge.
   off   That cheese .... it's put in the fridge.
6 People considered Mozart to be a prodigy.
   looked   Mozart .... a prodigy.
7 You should have dressed smartly.
   better   It .... you had dressed smartly.
8 He cooked too much food which was not necessary.
   have   He .... much food.
9 I'm sure Tony invented that story.
   made   Tony .... that story.
10 There is only a little money left.
   not   There .... left.
11 Laura can't eat chocolate because she's on a diet.
   not   If Laura .... she could eat chocolate.
12 Parking in this road is not allowed.
   park   You .... in this road.
13 Do you know where Larry has gone?
   idea   Do you .... where Larry has gone?

251 *Replace the underlined words in each sentence with a suitable idiom that includes the word in bold.*

1 Jill and her husband are always quarrelling. They never seem to agree about anything.
   (loggerheads) ....
2 I kept my daughter at home yesterday because she wasn't feeling very well. **(sorts)**
   ....
3 The minister has a reputation for understanding things and reacting quickly. **(ball)**
   ....
4 Peter heard from someone who has secret information about the factory's financial situation.
   (know) ....
5 I think David's version of what happened was a bit of an exaggeration. **(top)**
   ....
6 Felicity asked to leave early because she felt slightly unwell. **(weather)**
   ....
7 Gillian felt slightly annoyed when she wasn't asked to speak at the conference. **(cheesed)**
   ....
8 Nobody has told me we are moving offices. I was told nothing about it. **(dark)**
   ....
9 This essay will have to be rewritten. It isn't good enough. **(mark)**
   ....
10 After Peter failed to meet the deadline he was thought poorly of at the office. **(cloud)**
   ....

Practice Test 11 ....

Part 1

For questions 1 - 15, read the text below and decide which word A, B, C or D best fits each space. There's an example at the beginning (0).

Art in Amsterdam

One of the world's most radical museums, which can be (0) ... in Amsterdam, has recently reached the great (1) ... of 100. The Stedelijk Museum first opened its (2) ... on 14 September, 1895 and it was controversial from the start. The French poet Appolinaire (3) ... it as "the only place in the (4) ... where you can see truly modern art". From the (5) ... its main (6) ... was to display the best of new art whether it was accepted by the establishment or not. Back in 1905, its decision to show the work of Van Gogh (7) ... a problem with city authorities, as his work was "little valued" at the time. But the (8) ... trouble started after the War when they decided to exhibit even more experimental work. Rudi Fuchs, the (9) ... director of the museum, has decided to be a bit more (10) ... in his choice of exhibits, as (11) ... to previous directors. He believes it is his (12) ... to care for the old collection of paintings as well as to continue encouraging new art. As (13) ... as the future is concerned, he has decided to display a (14) ... collection of modern classics, including art dating back to the 19th century, but he will also continue to (15) ... for more unusual and daring work to display at the Stedelijk.

0	A found	B discovered	C traced	D detected
1	A era	B birth	C age	D period
2	A doors	B hands	C entrance	D gates
3	A illustrated	B defined	C characterised	D described
4	A earth	B continent	C world	D Europe
5	A introduction	B origin	C beginning	D commencement
6	A cause	B purpose	C reason	D view
7	A made	B did	C brought	D caused
8	A real	B true	C apparent	D virtual
9	A topical	B present	C now	D contemporary
10	A constant	B steady	C stuck	D cautious
11	A different	B contrasted	C opposed	D unlike
12	A duty	B charge	C intention	D aim
13	A long	B far	C much	D though
14	A continual	B constant	C fixed	D permanent
15	A view	B search	C investigate	D explore

	A	B	C	D
0	▬	☐	☐	☐
1	☐	☐	☐	☐
2	☐	☐	☐	☐
3	☐	☐	☐	☐
4	☐	☐	☐	☐
5	☐	☐	☐	☐
6	☐	☐	☐	☐
7	☐	☐	☐	☐
8	☐	☐	☐	☐
9	☐	☐	☐	☐
10	☐	☐	☐	☐
11	☐	☐	☐	☐
12	☐	☐	☐	☐
13	☐	☐	☐	☐
14	☐	☐	☐	☐
15	☐	☐	☐	☐

Part 2

For questions 16 - 30, read the text below and think of the word which best fits each space.
Use only one word in each space. Write your answers in the answer boxes provided.

Keeping Warm In Winter

Do you feel the cold? If the answer is "yes", then **(0)** .... not try a cold bath or shower? This unusual advice **(16)** .... from a natural health therapist in Germany **(17)** ...., for the last 30 years, has **(18)** .... studying the effects of cold water. Most people are brought **(19)** .... to believe that it's important to **(20)** .... warm during the cold weather, with extra clothing and heaters, **(21)** .... research shows that the opposite is true. At a German health centre, hundreds of visitors follow this advice by taking their first cold bath at 6 am, and come out feeling **(22)** .... more relaxed. This is **(23)** .... to the fact that the cold water increases blood sugar levels, the heart beat and breathing rate. New research at the medical centre of Hanover has **(24)** .... that those taking daily cold baths have 50% **(25)** .... colds and breathing problems than those who don't. Studies **(26)** .... London have also proven that **(27)** .... treatment will help protect **(28)** .... heart attacks. For those people who find the idea of such behaviour unthinkable, then regular exercise such **(29)** .... running or cycling is a good alternative. So, next time you're suffering from the cold, don't sit and complain, **(30)** .... action!

0	*why*	0
16		16
17		17
18		18
19		19
20		20
21		21
22		22
23		23
24		24
25		25
26		26
27		27
28		28
29		29
30		30

Part 3

For questions 31 - 40, complete the second sentence so that it has a similar meaning to the first sentence. Use the word given and other words to complete each sentence. You must use between two and five words. Do not change the word given. Write your answers in the answer boxes provided.

0 I'm sure it wasn't Jim who did it.
have
It .... Jim who did it.

0	*can't have been*	0 **0** 1 2

31 You had better see a doctor.
were
If .... see a doctor.

31		31 **0** 1 2

32 "Why don't we go to the zoo?" said Billy.
going
Billy .... the zoo.

32		32 **0** 1 2

33 They managed to find someone to replace John.
in
They managed to find .... John.

33		33 **0** 1 2

34 Mark will possibly be back next Monday.
may
Mark .... next Monday.

34		34 **0** 1 2

35 You need to calm down or you'll fail the exam.
not
Unless you .... pass the exam.

35		35 **0** 1 2

36 I'd prefer not to go out tonight.
rather
I .... tonight.

36		36 **0** 1 2

37 They were forced to postpone the meeting.
off
They had .... the meeting.

37		37 **0** 1 2

38 "I didn't steal your wallet," he said.
stolen
He .... my wallet.

38		38 **0** 1 2

39 John plays polo well and so does Greg.
play
Both .... well.

39		39 **0** 1 2

40 She didn't want to be identified so she used a pen name.
being
She used a pen name .... identified.

40		40 **0** 1 2

Part 4

For questions 41 - 55, read the text below and look carefully at each line. Some of the lines are correct and some have a word which should not be there. If a line is correct, put a tick (✔) by the number in the answer boxes provided. If a line has a word which should not be there, write the word in the answer boxes provided.

Mountain Climbing

0	The most frightening experience in my life happened	**0**	✓
00	to me a few years ago while I was been at university. I was	**00**	*been*
41	a member of the rock climbing club, and every weekend	**41**	
42	we would go for climbing in the Welsh mountains. One	**42**	
43	Saturday we set off in fine spirits - the sun was shining	**43**	
44	and there it was not a cloud in the sky. We began to climb	**44**	
45	the mountain, and by lunchtime we had being managed to	**45**	
46	get at least halfway that up. While we were eating our	**46**	
47	sandwiches and mint cake we noticed some dark clouds	**47**	
48	forming up in the distance. We weren't worried,	**48**	
49	however, so we continued on with our way. This turned out	**49**	
50	to be a big mistake - the clouds got more closer and closer,	**50**	
51	then it began to snow. We tried to get down the mountain,	**51**	
52	but the snowstorm became so much bad that we got stuck.	**52**	
53	Eventually we were rescued, but not before that we had spent	**53**	
54	half the night up there, cold, miserable and sure about that	**54**	
55	we were all going to die. I hope it will never happens again.	**55**	

 Part 5

For questions 56 - 65, read the text below. Use the word given in capitals at the end of each line to form a word that fits in the space in the same line. Write your word in the answer boxes provided.

Credit Cards

The first **(0)** .... step towards creating a credit card was taken by a US company in 1914. They issued an **(56)** .... metal token to their customers, allowing them to defer their bills. But **(57)** .... half a century was to pass before the **(58)** .... of establishing a **(59)** .... credit card would be taken **(60)** .... . France was the **(61)** ...., creating the "Carte Bleue". Barclays bank in Britain **(62)** .... followed. When the Visa system was developed in 1977, credit rose, with most card holders joining this **(63)** .... credit network. By 1994 the Visa system had a credit total of $207.4 billion in 2.8 million **(64)** .... in Europe. The credit card has **(65)** .... become international.

EXPERIMENT	**0** *experimental*	
	56	
SOPHISTICATED	**57**	
NEAR	**58**	
POSSIBLE	**59**	
UNIVERSE	**60**	
SERIOUS	**61**	
LEAD	**62**	
QUICK		
	63	
GLOBE	**64**	
LOCATE	**65**	
TRUE		

12 Inversion / Emphatic Structures

Inversion

We can invert the subject and the auxiliary verb in the sentence to give emphasis. If there is no auxiliary verb, we use **do/does** (Present S.) or **did** (Past S.) in the interrogative. This happens:

- after certain expressions when they are placed at the beginning of a sentence. These are: Barely, Hardly (ever) ... when, In no way, In/Under no circumstances, Little, Never (before), Nor/Neither, No sooner ... than, Not even once, Not only ... but also, Not since, Not till/until, Nowhere, Only by, Only in this way, On no account, On no occasion, Only then, Rarely, Scarcely (ever) ... when, Seldom etc. *Under no circumstances should you open* the door. *Seldom do we see* him these days. **Only after, only by, only if, only when, not since, not till/until** used at the beginning cause inversion of the subject and the auxiliary verb in the main clause. *Only when* they had left, *did he burst* into tears.
- in conditionals when **should, were, had** (Past Perfect) are placed at the beginning of the sentence. Note that "if" is omitted. *Should you come* early, we'll go to the theatre. (If you should come, .. - Type 1) *Were I* you, I would see a doctor. (If I were you, ... - Type 2) *Had he* been asked, he would have helped. (If he had been asked, ... Type 3)
- after **so, such, to such a degree** (in result clauses) placed at the beginning of a sentence. *So* short *is she* that she can't reach the shelf.
- after **as, neither/nor, so** to express agreement. *"He likes trout." "So does his wife."* ("So" is used to agree with an affirmative sentence) *"She doesn't like fish." "Neither/Nor do I."* ("Neither/Nor" are used to agree with a negative statement) His schoolmates admire him, *as do* his teachers.

In the following structures we invert the subject and the main verb.
- after **adverbs of place.** *Here comes Ann!* (but: Here she comes!) Here *is her bag!* (but: Here it is!)
- in **Direct Speech** when the reporting verb comes after the quote and the subject is a noun. *"What awful weather!" said Mary.* ("Mary said" is also possible). (but: What awful weather!" she said.)

252 *Complete the sentences using the words in bold. Use two to five words.*

1 We can get into the house only if you have a key.
   can   Only if ...*you have a key can*... we get into the house.
2 If the weather gets any colder, we'll turn on the heating.
   get   Should ...., we'll turn on the heating.
3 He had just entered when the telephone rang.
   sooner   No .... the telephone rang.
4 He visits us so rarely that I can hardly remember what he looks like.
   visit   So .... that I can hardly remember what he looks like.
5 Mark works so hard that I'm sure he'll be promoted soon.
   does   So .... that I'm sure he'll be promoted soon.
6 If you had been there, you would have enjoyed it.
   been   Had .... would have enjoyed it.
7 He spoke to me only after I spoke to him.
   speak   Only after I spoke to him .... to me.
8 Janet won't get on a plane under any circumstances.
   will   Under .... on a plane.
9 I realised who she was only after a few minutes.
   realise   Only after a few minutes .... she was.
10 She didn't know that her wish would come true.
   did   Little .... her wish would come true.
11 He didn't laugh once all evening.
   did   Not .... all evening.
12 They scarcely talk to each other any more.
   do   Scarcely .... each other any more.
13 This restaurant rarely gets so crowded.
   get   Seldom .... so crowded.

14 If he had left earlier, he would have been on time.

he   Had .... have been on time.

15 She was so happy that she decided to celebrate.

she   So .... she decided to celebrate.

16 This is the only way that we can be sure we are right.

in   Only .... be sure that we are right.

17 If he notices anything, we'll be in trouble.

notice   Should ...., we'll be in trouble.

18 Sarah forgot to take her purse and her handbag too.

did   Sarah didn't remember to take her purse; .... to take her handbag.

19 He was so scared that he could hardly breathe.

fear   Such .... he could hardly breathe.

20 She performed so well that she won an Oscar.

perform   So .... that she won an Oscar.

21 Thailand is warmer and cheaper than England.

only   Not .... than England, it's cheaper too.

22 If I were you, I would try calling her again.

you   Were ...., calling her again.

23 The weather hasn't been this warm since last summer.

has   Not since last summer .... this warm.

24 You must not miss the plane on any account.

no   On .... the plane.

25 She had just left when the boss asked to see her.

sooner   No .... the boss asked to see her.

26 You will only understand him if you speak French.

will   Only .... you understand him.

27 If you don't apologise, he will never forgive you.

not   Should ...., he will never forgive you.

---

253 *Rewrite the sentences using "so" or "such" at the beginning of the sentence.*

1 The weather was so bad that they stayed at home. So ...*bad was the weather that they stayed at home.*...

2 The house was so big that he almost got lost. So ....

3 He was so surprised to see her he could hardly speak. Such ....

4 She was so bored by the play that she fell asleep. So ....

5 He was so angry that he shouted at everyone. Such ....

254 *Fill in "so", "neither/nor" and the appropriate verb.*

1 "I'd like to go to Belgium one day."

"...*So would I.* ... I've never been there."

2 "I really enjoyed that film last night."

"............................. . It's one of the best I've ever seen."

3 "I've used up all my money."

"....................................... . My purse is empty."

4 "We didn't like the food they served yesterday."

"....................................... . It was overcooked."

5 "I feel like going to the beach today."

"....................................... . Let's go!"

6 "I can't remember how to make soufflé."

"............................. . Let's look in the recipe book."

7 "I don't believe he's telling the truth."

"............................... . The facts don't add up."

Brussels - Belgium

Emphatic Structures

Emphatic structures are used to emphasise a particular part of a sentence.

- **it is/was (not) + subject/object + who(m)/that** (used in statements and negations)
  It **wasn't John who/that** *called last night. It* **wasn't her bicycle that** *was stolen.*
  It **was his house that** *was burgled. It's* **David who** *is modelling for Fendi.*

- **is/was it + subject/object + who(m)/that** (used in questions)
  Was it my fault that *it happened?* **Was it her sister who** *got a first at university?*

- **that is/was + question word** (statements) **That's why** *she left the party so early.*

- **is/was that + question word** or **question word + is/was it + that** (questions)
  Was that why *she was crying?* **Why was it that** *he got so angry?*

- **question word + subject + verb + is/was** (used in statements) **What I need** *is some time alone.*

- **We can use do/does/did + bare infinitive** in the Present Simple, Past Simple or Imperative to give emphasis. *I* **do hope** *he will be all right.* **Do have** *another piece of pie. You* **do look** *well today.*

- To express **admiration, anger, concern** etc we use question words with **ever.**
  Whatever *shall I do?* **Whoever** *is that?*

255 *Rewrite the sentences as in the example giving emphasis to the words in bold.*

1 **Mary** sent this card. ...*It was Mary who sent this card....*
2 **Judy** baked the cake. ....
3 Did **you** lock the front door? ....
4 You need **a long rest**. ....
5 Johnny needs **a new pair of shoes**. ....
6 **Mary** came round last night. ....
7 **Where** did you go on holiday last year? ....
8 **Why** are you always biting your nails? ....
9 It doesn't matter **what** he does, he always makes mistakes. ....
10 He **bought** a new ring for her. ....
11 Are you angry with **Jim**? ....
12 **Mr Brown** called the police. ....
13 **When** are you moving house? ....
14 Jane needs **a lot of support** at the moment. ....
15 **How** will I get there so early in the morning? ....

256 *Complete the sentences using the words in bold. Use two to five words.*

1 You haven't paid last month's phone bill.
   that   It ...*is you that/who hasn't*... paid last month's phone bill.
2 Mr Jones is the manager of the supermarket.
   is   It .... the manager of the supermarket.
3 Did you go to the Caribbean for Christmas?
   you   Was .... the Caribbean for Christmas?
4 The bus driver himself doesn't want to let any more passengers on board.
   who   It .... doesn't want to let any more passengers on board.
5 Julie doesn't want to invite Malcolm to her party.
   is   It .... doesn't want to invite to her party.
6 My father didn't let me go out last night.
   who   It .... didn't let me go out last night.

7 Mum, you promised to buy me a new pair of jeans.

did Mum, ... buy me a new pair of jeans.

8 She said that she might be late for dinner.

say She .... might be late for dinner.

9 You were the one who wanted to come here.

was It .... to come here.

10 Did he fail his driving test?

failed Was .... his driving test?

257 *Complete the sentences using the words in bold. Use two to five words.*

1 You should never press the red button on the telephone.

circumstances Under ...*no circumstances should you*... press the red button on the telephone.

2 He didn't know that Jack had planned a surprise party.

did Little .... Jack had planned a surprise party.

3 Tom is the person who made all this possible.

who It .... all this possible.

4 He seldom goes out at the weekends.

go Seldom .... at the weekends.

5 I won't be at home before Monday.

after Only .... at home.

6 Why were you late for work today?

that Why .... were late for work today?

7 It is impossible for him to find £50,000 to pay the ransom.

can On no account .... to pay the ransom.

8 You'll only find a good job if you're lucky nowadays.

will Only if .... find a good job nowadays.

9 His father cooked the dinner on Thursday night.

who It .... the dinner on Thursday night.

10 He met his wife while on holiday in Italy.

that It was while he was .... he met his wife.

258 *Find the word which should not be in the sentence.*

1	*did*
2	
3	
4	
5	
6	
7	
8	
9	
10	
11	
12	
13	
14	
15	
16	
17	
18	

1 Only when did he turned around was he able to see properly.

2 It was only last week who that they got married.

3 Please, do you help yourself to another piece.

4 I can't drive and neither does can my mother.

5 So long was the journey that I did fell asleep.

6 Not once did she to regret having come.

7 Why is it that she does always looks unhappy?

8 What he needs it is a long holiday.

9 It was Claire who she left work early yesterday.

10 Whoever disagrees should they raise their hand.

11 So much hard was the exam that everyone failed.

12 Mark likes sailing and so too do I.

13 Little did she not know that James would be there.

14 If you talk in class, you will to be punished.

15 Were I be you, I'd apologise.

16 No sooner had he left than that the bomb exploded.

17 Only by he studying will John be successful.

18 What the school does needs is a new canteen.

259 *Look at Appendix 2, then fill in the correct particle.*

1 We weren't expecting Bob to **turn** ...*up*... so we were very surprised when he did.
2 He's **turning** .... work of a very high standard these days.
3 I'm going to **turn** .... now; I have to get up early tomorrow.
4 Please **turn** .... the lights when you leave.
5 The new detergent is claimed to **work** .... even the most difficult stains.
6 I'm sure you'll be able to **work** .... your problems with each other.
7 There's no one else I can **turn** .... - you're my last hope.
8 The lettering on the monument has been **worn** .... by acid rain.
9 You'll get **worn** .... if you don't stop working so hard.
10 I couldn't **turn** .... his offer; it was too good to refuse.
11 I felt sick yesterday morning but the feeling had **worn** .... by lunchtime.
12 Please **turn** .... and do the exercise on the next page.

260 *Complete the sentences using the words in bold. Use two to five words.*

1 I have no doubt that she was lying about her intentions.
   been She ...*must have been lying about*... her intentions.
2 The residents of the area found the proposed changes alarming.
   were The residents of the area .... proposed changes.
3 It's a pity you didn't come to the opening ceremony.
   have You .... the opening ceremony.
4 She enrolled in an evening class because she wanted to study art.
   so She enrolled in an evening class .... art.
5 He felt strongly about local issues.
   strong He .... local issues.
6 I'll ask the secretary to book us two tickets.
   have I'll .... two tickets.
7 Peter suggested that idea.
   forward It was .... that idea.
8 "You mustn't open the window," the nurse told us.
   forbade The nurse .... the window.
9 I'm sure he didn't know what the consequences would be.
   of I'm sure he .... consequences.
10 My mother became extremely angry when she saw the size of the phone bill.
   roof My mother .... she saw the size of the phone bill.
11 "You must read the form carefully," John said to me.
   reading John .... the form carefully.
12 The accountant changed the figures to conceal the fact that money had gone missing.
   books The accountant .... the fact that money had gone missing.

261 *Explain the meaning of the idioms in bold.*

1 Our grandmother is nearly 95 years old but she is still **alive and kicking.**
2 They could come to an agreement only if there was a bit more **give and take**.
3 She knew that her husband was a devoted man who would stay with her **through thick and thin.**
4 There was nothing dishonest about the deal. I told you **fair and square** what the terms were.
5 I don't need to know all the details, so try to keep your explanation **short and sweet.**
6 I'm afraid that since you've broken several terms of the contract, it is now **null and void.**
7 After a week in bed with flu Sandra is now **up and about** again.
8 He can't be eating properly; he's all **skin and bone.**

262 *Fill in the correct prepositions of place or movement.*

between, down, on top of, over, in/inside, above, in front of, past, up, among, next to/ by/ beside, from...to, through, under, below, behind, along, opposite, at, round/around, near,outside, on, against, onto, out of, across, to/towards/in the direction of, into

   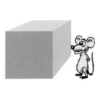 

1 .....*in/inside*.... 2 .... 3 .... 4 .... 5 .... 6 ....

    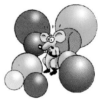 

7 .... 8 .... 9 .... 10 .... 11 .... 12 ....

13 .... 14 .... 15 .... 16 .... 17 .... 18 ....

19 .... 20 .... 21 .... 22 .... 23 .... 24 ....

25 .... 26 .... 27 .... 28 .... 29 ....

Practice Test 12 ....

For questions 1 - 15, read the text below and decide which word A, B, C or D best fits each space. There's an example at the beginning (0).

Aristotle

Aristotle lived (0) ... the time when Philip of Macedonia was conquering areas of Greece such as Attica. Aristotle (1) ... to Athens when he was 17 to study philosophy. He became a student of Plato, only (2) ... the academy after Plato's death. After a period of (3) ..., Aristotle decided to (4) ...with his former teacher's views on philosophy. In 343 BC he was employed as a tutor for Alexander the Great, whom he taught for four years. Aristotle (5) ... the Lyceum, which was well known for its zoo and library, a public garden and a gymnasium, which was (6) ... to Apollo. Aristotle lectured to his students there, and it (7) ... an educational institution for 800 years. After Alexander's death, anti-Macedonian feeling (8) ... Aristotle to escape to the north where he lived for one year, (9) ... his death at the age of 62. Unfortunately, only a fifth of his writings have (10) ... . These works are mostly (11) ... up of those discovered in a cellar in 100 BC. There are 60 (12) ... works and 20 pseudonymous (13) ... ones. Since the time of the find, philosophers have argued about the value and meaning of his writings. For example, in Italy in the 1500's there was a reaction against his ideas, which were (14) ... as unnecessarily complicated. In spite of this, his influence as a philosopher has continued to the (15) ... day.

0	**A** on	**B** throughout	**C** during	**D** over
1	**A** reached	**B** arrived	**C** landed	**D** went
2	**A** abandoning	**B** escaping	**C** deserting	**D** leaving
3	**A** travel	**B** trip	**C** journey	**D** voyage
4	**A** stop	**B** separate	**C** break	**D** oppose
5	**A** formed	**B** founded	**C** based	**D** imposed
6	**A** offered	**B** devoted	**C** dedicated	**D** given
7	**A** endured	**B** lasted	**C** remained	**D** kept
8	**A** forced	**B** made	**C** kicked	**D** pushed
9	**A** since	**B** at	**C** to	**D** until
10	**A** traced	**B** survived	**C** rescued	**D** saved
11	**A** held	**B** kept	**C** made	**D** turned
12	**A** genuine	**B** real	**C** pure	**D** true
13	**A** wrong	**B** false	**C** artificial	**D** fake
14	**A** declared	**B** seen	**C** observed	**D** noticed
15	**A** current	**B** now	**C** present	**D** close

	A	B	C	D
0	☐	☐	■	☐
1	☐	☐	☐	☐
2	☐	☐	☐	☐
3	☐	☐	☐	☐
4	☐	☐	☐	☐
5	☐	☐	☐	☐
6	☐	☐	☐	☐
7	☐	☐	☐	☐
8	☐	☐	☐	☐
9	☐	☐	☐	☐
10	☐	☐	☐	☐
11	☐	☐	☐	☐
12	☐	☐	☐	☐
13	☐	☐	☐	☐
14	☐	☐	☐	☐
15	☐	☐	☐	☐

Part 2

For questions 16 - 30, read the text below and think of the word which best fits each space.
Use only one word in each space. Write your answers in the answer boxes provided.

Fatal Frogs

Across South America one can find a variety of frog unlike **(0)** .... found in Europe. Apart **(16)** .... being different colours, such as yellow and blue, these frogs are poisonous. Some of them are **(17)** .... poisonous that even touching **(18)** .... can be fatal. The Embera Choco people of Colombia have **(19)** .... using toxins from frogs for many years in **(20)** .... to hunt. However, since the arrival of other types of weapons in the rainforest, the art of making dart guns **(21)** .... started to disappear. However, it is still possible to find craftsmen making dart guns **(22)** .... the trunks of palm trees. The actual dart is covered **(23)** .... poison from the frog's skin. The poison will remain strong **(24)** .... to kill animals for more **(25)** .... a year. About 55 of the 135 species of South American frogs are toxic. The frogs are brightly coloured to warn predators not to touch them. Some species of frogs produce toxins **(26)** .... may be useful for mankind as painkillers. A number of species are **(27)** .... bred by researchers in the States to investigate the possibility of using toxins for **(28)** .... benefit. By licking the frog's skin scientists **(29)** .... judge the level of toxins. There is no danger of being poisoned, though, as frogs in captivity gradually become **(30)** .... poisonous.

0	those/any	0
16		16
17		17
18		18
19		19
20		20
21		21
22		22
23		23
24		24
25		25
26		26
27		27
28		28
29		29
30		30

Part 3

For questions 31 - 40, complete the second sentence so that it has a similar meaning to the first sentence. Use the word given and other words to complete each sentence. You must use between two and five words. Do not change the word given. Write your answers in the answer boxes provided.

0 I'm sure it wasn't Jim who did it.
have
It .... Jim who did it.

| 0 | *can't have been* | 0 **0** 1 2 |

31 He didn't have the chance to see George.
opportunity
He had .... George.

| 31 | | 31 **0** 1 2 |

32 We couldn't stop ourselves laughing at the clown.
help
We .... at the clown.

| 32 | | 32 **0** 1 2 |

33 He had never before met with such hostility.
before
Never .... such hostility.

| 33 | | 33 **0** 1 2 |

34 I advise you to book tickets early this year.
had
You .... this year.

| 34 | | 34 **0** 1 2 |

35 He was fired because he was late for work too often.
sack
He .... late for work too often.

| 35 | | 35 **0** 1 2 |

36 He got all the benefit he could out of his holiday.
made
He .... his holiday.

| 36 | | 36 **0** 1 2 |

37 We were surprised by his impolite behaviour.
aback
We .... his impolite behaviour.

| 37 | | 37 **0** 1 2 |

38 However hard you try, you won't convince her.
how
No ...., you won't convince her.

| 38 | | 38 **0** 1 2 |

39 He tried to attract the waiter's attention without success.
eye
He tried .... without success.

| 39 | | 39 **0** 1 2 |

40 I'd prefer you to work on this.
rather
I .... on this.

| 40 | | 40 **0** 1 2 |

Part 4

For questions 41 - 55, read the text below and look carefully at each line. Some of the lines are correct and some have a word which should not be there. If a line is correct, put a tick (✔) by the number in the answer boxes provided. If a line has a word which should not be there, write the word in the answer boxes provided.

Adventure Holidays

0	Nowadays it seems as that not everybody	**0**	*as*
00	wants to go on holiday to relax. Although	**00**	✓
41	most of us are quite enough happy to go	**41**	
42	somewhere warm and lie on to a beach all day,	**42**	
43	there are some people who can't sit still for	**43**	
44	more than an hour without be getting bored.	**44**	
45	These are the kind of people who they are now	**45**	
46	choosing to go on adventure holidays,	**46**	
47	where there are almost too many of things	**47**	
48	to do! Activities on offer include the horse-riding,	**48**	
49	rock-climbing, windsurfing and scuba diving,	**49**	
50	depending on where the holiday centre is being.	**50**	
51	The price for a holiday of this kind is usually	**51**	
52	about the just same as that of a "normal"	**52**	
53	holiday, but to be warned - adventure holidays are	**53**	
54	only recommended for those who want to return from	**54**	
55	their holiday bit more exhausted than when they left.	**55**	

Part 5

For questions 56 - 65, read the text below. Use the word given in capitals at the end of each line to form a word that fits in the space in the same line. Write your word in the answer boxes provided.

Dream Machine

In an era when family cars are about as **(0)** .... as fridges, Volkswagen has taken the most **(56)** .... car of all time, the "Beetle", back to the **(57)** .... board and given it a **(58)** .... look. Its return promises to be one of the greatest comebacks of all time. The **(59)** .... say the new model will pay tribute to the original, which epitomised **(60)** .... and mobility. Emphasis will be put on fuel **(61)** .... and low emissions, the main selling point being its ecological **(62)** .... . The engine will switch off **(63)** .... when not being used. Due to go into **(64)** .... within a year, the car will be very different to the one that served so many **(65)** .... in the past.

	CHARISMA
	SUCCESS
	DRAW
	FUTURE
	MANUFACTURE
	INDIVIDUAL
	EFFICIENT
	FRIENDLY
	AUTOMATIC
	PRODUCE
	MOTOR

0	*charismatic*
56	
57	
58	
59	
60	
61	
62	
63	
64	
65	

3 Pre-Test

A *Choose the correct item.*

1 Let's go round to Duncan's house, ...?
  A **will we**
  B **do we**
  C **shall we**
  D **may we**

2 He spent the .... evening studying.
  A **all**
  B **whole**
  C **each**
  D **every**

3 There was hardly .... wine left.
  A **every**
  B **no**
  C **some**
  D **any**

4 It is said that .... Harrods is one of the best shops in the world.
  A **an**
  B **a**
  C **-**
  D **the**

5 .... purse is this? I must have picked it up by mistake.
  A **What**
  B **Which**
  C **Who**
  D **Whose**

6 No sooner .... his umbrella than it began to rain again.
  A **had he closed**
  B **has he closed**
  C **will he close**
  D **does he close**

7 My house .... at the moment.
  A **will be painted**
  B **is being painted**
  C **was painted**
  D **has been painted**

8 The tourists were given a guided tour of .... Houses of Parliament.
  A **an**
  B **a**
  C **the**
  D **-**

9 No one enjoyed the show very much, ...?
  A **had they**
  B **hadn't they**
  C **didn't they**
  D **did they**

10 She liked .... of the two presents I gave her.
  A **either**
  B **both**
  C **all**
  D **none**

11 Peter is my oldest friend - I met him a long time ....
  A **before**
  B **until**
  C **ago**
  D **yet**

12 Tommy is very spoilt and is used .... his own way.
  A **getting**
  B **get**
  C **to get**
  D **to getting**

13 My father .... China but I haven't.
  A **has been to**
  B **has gone in**
  C **has been in**
  D **has gone at**

14 He swims .... a fish and is only five years old.
  A **as**
  B **like**
  C **similar**
  D **same**

15 .... of these two records do you like best?
  A **Which**
  B **Who**
  C **What**
  D **Whose**

16 Don't forget to call Jenny, ...?
  A **shall you**
  B **do you**
  C **don't you**
  D **will you**

17 .... shall we do this evening?
  A **Who**
  B **Where**
  C **What**
  D **Which**

18 "I don't like chocolate ice-cream." "........ do I."
  A **But**
  B **Nor**
  C **Either**
  D **So**

19 We all failed the exam because .... of us had studied for it.
  A **both**
  B **either**
  C **neither**
  D **none**

20 She spends .... money on clothes.
  A **a large amount of**
  B **a couple of**
  C **a great number of**
  D **several**

21 I prefer eating out .... cooking at home.
  A **than**
  B **from**
  C **to**
  D **of**

22 .... seem to be a lot of people here today.
  A **They**
  B **There**
  C **It**
  D **These**

23 Her condition is .... better than it was yesterday.
  A **many**
  B **very**
  C **far**
  D **any**

24 Hurry. There is very .... time left.
  A **little**
  B **few**
  C **several**
  D **many**

B *Complete the sentences using the words in bold. Use two to five words.*

1 She started taking French lessons two weeks ago.
 been She .... French lessons for two weeks.

2 The holiday was too expensive for me to book.
 that The holiday .... I didn't book it.

3 I found his account of the accident very confusing.
 confused I .... of the accident.

4 She regrets inviting him to her party.
 wishes She .... him to her party.

5 There wasn't anything we could do to improve the situation.
 nothing There .... to improve the situation.

6 This is her landlady. She came back from Mexico last week.
 who This is her landlady, ... last week.

7 I haven't seen her for two months.
 time The last .... two months ago.

8 Despite being hungry, he didn't have anything to eat.
 was He didn't have anything to eat .... hungry.

9 John fixed the leaking tap for me yesterday.
 had I .... by John yesterday.

10 Jim and Brian went to the same school.
 as Jim went to .... Brian.

11 It wasn't necessary for her to ask my permission to do that.
 asked She .... my permission to do that.

12 I'll take a towel because we might go for a swim.
 case I'll take a towel .... for a swim.

13 All the members agreed with the changes.
 disagreed None .... the changes.

14 A girl from the beauty salon does my nails every week.
 done I .... every week.

15 "Why don't you stay for dinner, Ann?" said Martin.
 suggested Martin .... for dinner.

16 She had never been so offended.
 before Never .... so offended.

17 This is Paul's problem. He should deal with it himself.
 whose Paul, ..., should deal with it himself.

18 This crossword is very easy, but I can't complete it.
 though Easy .... I can't complete it.

19 "Don't forget to buy some milk, Cathy," said Angela.
 reminded Angela .... some milk.

20 Bella is saving up her money because she wants to buy a car.
 view Bella is saving up her money .... a car.

21 It would be better for you to come with me tomorrow.
 rather I .... with me tomorrow.

22 Michael is so unreliable that he can't be trusted to deliver important messages.
 too Michael is .... to deliver important messages.

23 "It wasn't me who broke the vase," said Mary.
 broken Mary .... the vase.

24 It is likely that she'll be home late tonight.
 to She .... late tonight.

25 I don't like rock music so I'm not going to the Rolling Stones' concert.
 liked If ...., I would go to the Rolling Stones' concert.

26 He discovered that someone had gone through his files while he was out.
 been He discovered that his .... while he was out.

27 He prefers relaxing to going out at the weekends.
 to He prefers .... out at the weekends.

28 I've never met such a rude person before.
   ever   He is the .... met.
29 They give information at the front desk.
   given   Information .... at the front desk.
30 Somebody set the museum on fire last night.
   was   The museum .... last night.
31 Henry regretted not asking for some help with the job.
   wishes   Henry .... some help with the job.
32 The brown bag is more expensive than the blue one.
   much   The blue bag doesn't .... the brown one.
33 She will not leave the baby unattended on any account.
   no   On .... the baby unattended.
34 James was late for work because his car broke down.
   have   James .... for work if his car hadn't broken down.
35 "You haven't done your homework, Jim," said Sandra.
   accused   Sandra .... his homework.
36 The authorities are investigating conditions in the prison.
   investigated   Conditions in the prison .... by the authorities.

C *Fill in the correct particle(s).*

1 Last night I saw my friend .... at the airport.
2 She didn't turn .... at work until lunchtime.
3 I ran three miles and now I'm worn ....
4 Mary is always running people ....
5 They set .... at four o'clock.
6 Meg stood .... Billy throughout the trial.
7 The firemen quickly put .... the fire.
8 UN stands .... United Nations.

D *Fill in the correct preposition(s).*

1 He was sacked .... account of stealing.
2 I'm afraid these jumpers are .... stock.
3 There's a house .... sale near here.
4 He's .... the impression that you like him.
5 .... his surprise, he won first prize.
6 The house is still .... fire.
7 The policeman placed the suspect ..... arrest.
8 Last night I broke a vase .... mistake.

E *Correct the following sentences by taking out the inappropriate word.*

1 I've seen nothing but of the first draft.
2 I am make sure you will enjoy yourself.
3 It's about time to you went home.
4 She won from a radio in a competition.
5 Cooking it is something that I really enjoy.
6 Paul and Sally are getting married to next week.

7 I never thought of he would say that.
8 If you will want to go out, you must tell me first.
9 Tom hired a too luxurious yacht while on holiday.
10 I would like to learn about to speak Italian.
11 Michael has been sold his old car.
12 Their wedding took the place last Sunday.

F *Fill in the correct word derived from the words in bold.*

1 He is .... sorry for everything he did and wants you to forgive him.   **TRUE**
2 Mr Jones is at risk of having a heart attack and must reduce his ...... of fatty foods.   **CONSUME**
3 The Eiffel Tower is a .... landmark in Paris.   **FAME**
4 Thailand is a .... country which is well worth visiting.   **BEAUTY**
5 Buses run .... between Little Compton and Newholt.   **FREQUENT**
6 The .... seems to be working - Sandra's getting better!   **TREAT**
7 Many .... are working on finding a cure for cancer.   **SCIENCE**
8 The bus was very .... - I couldn't find a seat anywhere.   **CROWD**
9 .... should reduce their speed when driving in fog.   **MOTOR**
10 Caffeine is very ...., which is why people drink so much coffee.   **ADDICT**
11 The police responded .... to the emergency call.   **QUICK**
12 Many buildings in Rome are of great .... interest.   **HISTORY**

Further Practice Sections

Section A

1 Multiple Choice Questions

Read the sentences below and decide which answer A, B, C or D best fits each blank.

1 I found a wonderful Persian rug in the .... market the other day.
   A archaic   B old
   C antique   D antiquated

2 Mr Jackson needs a .... of the report first thing Monday morning.
   A copy   B print
   C image   D reproduction

3 Helen and George are expecting .... at the end of winter.
   A sets   B twins
   C couples   D pairs

4 My son wants to .... a doctor when he's older.
   A change   B develop
   C turn   D become

5 The computer course .... of ten two-hour lessons over six months.
   A composes   B consists
   C makes up   D contains

6 The lecture was so boring that I had a very difficult time paying .... and almost fell asleep.
   A attention   B notice
   C warning   D interest

7 Authorities are investigating the .... of the fire.
   A reason   B manner
   C cause   D way

8 This shop has everything .... from exotic spices to designer clothes.
   A stocking   B ranging
   C varying   D extending

9 He was .... to the amount of money he could spend on holiday.
   A bounded   B fixed
   C set   D limited

10 Please, ... once in your life, try not to be late tomorrow.
   A for   B at
   C by   D upon

11 Of course I .... you! We went to school together, didn't we?
   A consider   B see
   C recognize   D hold

12 His .... of confidence resulted in him not getting the job.
   A losing   B lack
   C failure   D missing

13 I heard a loud bang and the .... thing I knew, police were everywhere.
   A future   B after
   C following   D next

14 Please .... me to cancel my dentist's appointment on Tuesday.
   A remind   B retain
   C remember   D recall

15 We never would have guessed who had .... the crime.
   A committed   B done
   C had   D caused

16 I called the plumber to get a(n) .... on how much a new shower would cost.
   A guess   B estimate
   C number   D count

17 The Smiths have their piano tuned on a .... basis.
   A right   B normal
   C regular   D proper

18 She cut the cake into eight .... after she had blown out the candles.
   A portions   B sizes
   C parts   D figures

19 Ben has just bought a house, so he can't .... to go on holiday this year.
   A afford   B cost
   C price   D budget

20 The company will .... a new line of cosmetics onto the market this autumn.
   A put   B bring
   C introduce   D commence

Further Practice Sections

2 Open Cloze Text

Read the text below and think of the word which best fits each space. Use only one word in each space. There is an example at the beginning (0).

Home Education

For many people, the choice **(0)** *of* school is just a matter of public or private. However, for a rapidly growing **(1)** .... of parents and children, school has nothing to **(2)** .... with classrooms, teachers or school uniforms. For them, there is simply no place **(3)** .... home when it comes to education. These people feel that their children **(4)** .... not receive satisfactory education at school. As a result, they **(5)** .... to teach their child in the comfort of their own home and at the same **(6)** .... have some control **(7)** .... the teaching process. Indeed, home schooling has many benefits. Children can work **(8)** .... their own pace, **(9)** .... to their own abilities. They are not **(10)** .... back by slower students or worried **(11)** .... being slow themselves. They can study what they are interested **(12)** .... and learn to work on their own, **(13)** .... prepares them for further education. They also have fewer behavioural **(14)** .... and are less dependent and **(15)** .... mature.

3 Key-word Transformation Sentences

Read the sentences below and complete the second sentence so that it has a similar meaning to the first one, using the word given. Do not change the word given. You must use between two and five words, including the word given. Study the example (0).

0 "Are you coming to John's party tonight?" he asked Carol.
   whether   He asked *Carol whether she was going* to John's party that evening.

1 Most children do not think documentaries are interesting.
   interested   Most children .... documentaries.

2 I would rather you didn't turn on the television.
   sooner   I .... not turned on.

3 "You should apologise to Bill for breaking his favourite mug", she said.
   had   "You .... to Bill for breaking his favourite mug," she said.

4 Young people usually get bored very easily.

likely   Young people .... get bored very easily.

5 "Don't you think you're too young to go on holiday alone?" said his father.

enough   I don't think .... go on holiday alone," said his father.

6 Despite being rather old, Mr Brown is still very energetic.

although   Mr Brown is still very energetic .... rather old.

7 "You should go out more often," said Anne.

suggested   Anne .... out more often.

8 The graduation ceremony was held in the school hall.

took   The graduation ceremony .... in the school hall.

9 I wish I had not given up my previous job.

had   If .... given up my previous job.

10 Philip suggested that I take up a sport.

good   Philip told me that it would .... take up a sport.

11 If you don't ask somebody the way, you might get lost.

otherwise   You'd better ask somebody the way .... get lost.

12 It took the artist three years to finish his work.

years   The artist .... to finish his work.

13 I have never been to a football match before.

ever   It's the first .... to a football match.

14 John spent a lot of money buying that car.

fortune   John .... that car.

15 Mary has lived in Milan for two years but she is thinking of going back to London.

been   Mary .... Milan for two years
                but she is thinking of going back to London.

16 Mike doesn't like rafting and neither does Sue.

nor   Neither .... rafting.

17 When did George buy a new boat?

ago   How .... a new boat?

18 Charles regretted having lied to his brother.

wished   Charles .... to his brother.

19 You should have come with us to the theatre.

pity   What .... come with us to the theatre.

20 The plane couldn't land because of the strong wind.

from   The strong wind .... landing.

Further Practice Sections

4 Multiple Choice Cloze

Read the text below and decide which answer A, B, C or D best fits each space. There is an example at the beginning (0).

Valley of the Kings

The valley of the Kings is a small **(0)** *area* located four miles from modern Luxor, in Egypt, where **(1)** .... 1539 and 1078 BC, some of the world's most **(2)** .... kings were buried. The valley is well-known for its **(3)** .... art, although not all the tombs are decorated. Archaeologists believe that there are still many things **(4)** .... in the valley and until recently

(5) .... were still going on. However, Egyptian **(6)** .... have decided to close down the digs in order to **(7)** .... them. The reason this decision has been taken is because the tombs are under serious **(8)** .... caused by the weather, man and animals. For example, floods have severely damaged the tombs and have knocked down pillars and destroyed wall paintings. Also, the **(9)** .... winds that sweep through the valley are extremely harmful to the tombs as they make the paint **(10)** .... quicker. Tourists are also to **(11)** .... They visit the tombs in large **(12)** ...., touching the walls and using cameras, although this is **(13)** .... Another problem is that the tombs are **(14)** .... to thousands of bats which cause a great **(15)** .... of damage to the ancient wall paintings.

0 Ⓐ area	**B** part	**C** setting	**D** landscape
1 A in	**B** at	**C** between	**D** before
2 A public	**B** efficient	**C** trustworthy	**D** famous
3 A awful	**B** spectacular	**C** handsome	**D** pretty
4 A buried	**B** immersed	**C** concealed	**D** covered
5 A tests	**B** excavations	**C** expeditions	**D** exams
6 A bosses	**B** authorities	**C** presidents	**D** leaders
7 A protect	**B** care	**C** defend	**D** keep
8 A warning	**B** risk	**C** threat	**D** hazard
9 A sturdy	**B** intense	**C** firm	**D** strong
10 A fade	**B** faint	**C** weaken	**D** dull
11 A accuse	**B** answer	**C** blame	**D** charge
12 A groups	**B** sets	**C** teams	**D** bunches
13 A banned	**B** outlawed	**C** restricted	**D** forbidden
14 A nest	**B** home	**C** house	**D** residence
15 A share	**B** number	**C** deal	**D** portion

Section B

1 Multiple Choice Questions

Read the sentences below and decide which answer A, B, C or D best fits each blank.

1 During the carnival, the streets were .... with people from all over the world.
   A crowded   B full
   C congested   D occupied

2 The total .... of money needed for this project is over one million pounds.
   A mass   B amount
   C number   D bulk

3 He has a .... of looking at life that is very refreshing.
   A method   B way
   C mean   D plan

4 James has had an argument .... Tina and is not speaking to her.
   A in   B of
   C by   D with

5 My morning .... never changes – I wake up, take a shower, have a cup of coffee and go to work.
   A routine   B custom
   C practice   D time

6 I'll never be .... to understand what she saw in him!
   A capable   B probable
   C able   D possible

7 The hotel .... free accommodation for children under the age of ten.
   A provides   B assists
   C makes   D does

8 Air pollution has .... to an increase in breathing disorders.
   A directed   B guided
   C led   D brought

9 Sally is so sensitive that she cries .... she watches a sad film.
   A whenever   B however
   C whichever   D how

10 Don't worry! The instructions are very .... to follow.
   A natural   B ordinary
   C easy   D casual

11 Even though my grandfather is 87 years old, he's as .... as a fiddle.
   A healthy   B fit
   C happy   D slim

12 Don't .... the chance to visit the Museum of Fine Arts when you're in town.
   A miss   B omit
   C forget   D look over

13 How long was it before you .... that your purse was missing?
   A viewed   B noticed
   C faced   D witnessed

14 If you have an alibi, it will .... that you were nowhere near the scene of the crime.
   A prove   B say
   C clear   D find

15 Alison .... most of her pocket money on CD's.
   A throws   B spends
   C exploits   D buys

16 Mary .... her own business when she was only 20 years old.
   A did up   B made out
   C set up   D brought on

17 The only reason why he .... the crash was because he was wearing his seatbelt.
   A saved   B endured
   C lasted   D survived

18 One of the most .... rules of tennis is to always keep your eye on the ball.
   A basic   B weighty
   C significant   D extreme

19 I'm sorry, but without the .... the shop will not be able to give you a refund.
   A recipe   B formula
   C receipt   D prescription

20 The only .... of living in a flat is that it is a cheaper than living in a house.
   A advantage   B asset
   C gain   D plus

Further Practice Sections

2 Open Cloze Text

Read the text below and think of the word which best fits each space. Use only one word in each space. There is an example at the beginning (0).

The Mind of a Dog

For thousands **(0)** *of* years, dogs have worked with us, eaten with us and lived with us. In fact, in **(1)** .... years, evidence has proved that dogs and humans have been living **(2)** .... for much longer than anyone **(3)** .... expected. General research suggests that we began to domesticate dogs **(4)** .... we were still hunter-gatherers **(5)** .... in caves. Scientists are starting to reveal **(6)** .... this strange partnership has influenced the **(7)** .... dogs think and behave. They claim that a dog's natural habitat is the human family or **(8)** .... other human setting. It is widely **(9)** .... that domestication has, in **(10)** ...., increased the dog's abilities. They can learn and **(11)** .... rules. Dogs understand these rules through games and **(12)** .... observing other dogs or humans. Furthermore, they can **(13)** .... sense when a person or another dog is in danger and "feel compassion" **(14)** .... other dogs are sad or ill. Finally, researchers actually argue that dogs **(15)** .... teach us a lesson about love and sympathy.

3 Key-word Transformation Sentences

Read the sentences below and complete the second sentence so that it has a similar meaning to the first one, using the word given. Do not change the word given. You must use between two and five words, including the word given. Study the example (0).

0 There are more boys than girls in our class.
   as   There are *not as many girls as* boys in our class.

1 I wish I had not given up without an effort.
   had   If .... without an effort.

2 Sarah's teacher is such a nice person that all his students love him.
   so   Sarah's teacher is .... that all his students love him.

3 Pam thought the tall man was her sister's friend.
   mistook   Pam .... a friend of her sister's.

4 I prefer skating to cycling.

  rather I .... than cycling.

5 When did George buy his new car?

  long How .... a new car?

6 Use this door only in an emergency.

  should Only in an emergency .... this door.

7 Was this the warmest sweater you could find?

  than Couldn't you find a .... this one?

8 Paul is said to be looking for a new house to move into.

  is They .... for a new house to move into.

9 She started taking Italian lessons five years ago.

  has She .... Italian lessons for five years.

10 Eva hasn't been abroad for many years.

  ages It's .... abroad.

11 Lock the door when you leave the house.

  had You .... when you leave the house.

12 Peter drove so carelessly that he got a fine.

  such Peter .... that he got a fine.

13 Bill didn't take part in the golf tournament because he had sprained his wrist.

  due Bill didn't take part in the golf tournament .... he
  he had sprained his wrist.

14 "You had better not go out in this weather!" said Kay.

  advised Kay .... out in that weather.

15 I haven't got much information on vacancies at the moment.

  little I .... on vacancies at the moment.

16 I'd love to buy that dress but I can't afford it.

  as Much .... to buy that dress, I can't afford it.

17 I had no idea that she was a newspaper editor.

  little Little .... that she was a newspaper editor.

18 Mrs Jones found her son's school report rather disappointing.

  disappointed Mrs Jones .... her son's school report.

19 He woke up early because he wanted to be on time for the interview.

  so He woke up early .... on time for the interview.

20 Those shoes you are wearing are not very fashionable anymore.

  fashion Those shoes you are wearing have been .... quite some time.

Further Practice Sections ·

4 Multiple Choice Cloze

Read the text below and decide which answer A, B, C or D best fits each space. There is an example at the beginning (0).

An Arctic Ice Palace

A new **(0)** *kind* of hotel has emerged **(1)** .... the snowy landscape within the Arctic Circle, the Ice Palace. A **(2)** .... in such a hotel is surely one you will not forget. A **(3)** .... deal of work goes into designing, building and decorating these hotels, **(4)** .... can only be used five months out of the year. The palaces are **(5)** .... up of connecting arched hallways **(6)** .... solid walls and the ceilings are **(7)** .... by thick columns of ice. Guests can **(8)** .... a night in an ice palace to be cold, as **(9)** .... inside are about -6˚C. What is **(10)** ...., everything is made of ice – the walls, windows, floors and even the beds! However, the exquisite beauty of an ice palace will make guests **(11)** .... the cold. The magnificent colours of the ice **(12)** .... from transparent to various shades of green to black, **(13)** .... on the thickness of the ice. Moreover, along the corridors and in the rooms, visitors can **(14)** .... ice sculptures, which are so beautiful that they would enrich even the **(15)** .... museums of the world.

0	Ⓐ kind	**B** brand	**C** set	**D** species
1	**A** at	**B** of	**C** from	**D** next
2	**A** safari	**B** holiday	**C** festival	**D** carnival
3	**A** plenty	**B** much	**C** many	**D** great
4	**A** which	**B** who	**C** where	**D** those
5	**A** developed	**B** build	**C** formed	**D** made
6	**A** in	**B** from	**C** with	**D** behind
7	**A** supported	**B** held	**C** maintained	**D** carried
8	**A** hope	**B** anticipate	**C** expect	**D** wait
9	**A** temperatures	**B** conditions	**C** circumstances	**D** positions
10	**A** else	**B** more	**C** many	**D** most
11	**A** forget	**B** remember	**C** realise	**D** remind
12	**A** reach	**B** run	**C** range	**D** extend
13	**A** relying	**B** trusting	**C** confiding	**D** depending
14	**A** worship	**B** admire	**C** adore	**D** respect
15	**A** brilliant	**B** superior	**C** greatest	**D** important

Section C

1 Multiple Choice Questions

Read the sentences below and decide which answer A, B, C or D best fits each blank.

1 Mrs James had difficulty in controlling the class, ... though she was an experienced teacher.
   A indeed   B even
   C just   D exactly

2 There are many ways .... which you can make food tasty and attractive to children.
   A over   B of
   C in   D among

3 Jim Perkins was .... to be the only suitable candidate for the job.
   A imagined   B hoped
   C designed   D considered

4 He walked slowly although he was .... late for his appointment.
   A extremely   B ultra
   C highly   D intensely

5 Frieda is always .... a very warm welcome whenever she visits her cousins.
   A saved   B reserved
   C performed   D guaranteed

6 The increase of traffic in cities has resulted .... more people suffering from breathing problems.
   A to   B in
   C of   D towards

7 The man was eventually .... by the police to come out from his hiding place.
   A persuaded   B arranged
   C suggested   D made

8 Your work falls well .... the required standard.
   A under   B below
   C short   D lower

9 Jane's .... told her that something had happened to her twin sister.
   A affinity   B aptitude
   C flair   D intuition

10 "You can always be .... of our support," my parents told me when I left home.
   A count   B depend
   C sure   D rely

11 For a long time, he has been .... by bad luck.
   A dogged   B bugged
   C doomed   D haunted

12 As the policeman handed me a speeding ticket he said that nobody was .... the law.
   A beyond   B above
   C over   D under

13 Everyone's attention was drawn .... the noise in the street.
   A to   B by
   C on   D for

14 Many species of fish are in danger of being .... by increasing levels of sea pollution.
   A finished off   B wiped out
   C dried up   D wore off

15 Many people never .... to be amazed by the records athletes set each year.
   A stop   B end
   C cease   D finish

16 The manager told the workers that he had every .... in their ability.
   A confidence   B trust
   C belief   D feeling

17 The school sets a very high .... for all its pupils.
   A shaped   B spirit
   C standard   D term

18 This neighbourhood looks a little .... these days.
   A well-heeled   B run-down
   C well-off   D down-and-out

19 Don't you think it would be a good idea to try and .... our problem?
   A work out   B polish off
   C do up   D wear off

20 The young boy .... to taking the bicycle.
   A agreed   B denied
   C accepted   D confessed

Further Practice Sections

2 Open Cloze Text

Read the text below and think of the word which best fits each space. Use only one word in each space. There is an example at the beginning (0).

Hanging by a Thread

So you think you **(0)** *would* like to try bungee jumping? **(1)** .... starting, let me tell you **(2)** .... an incident that might convince you otherwise. On January 8, 1999 a sixteen year old Korean girl decided she wanted **(3)** .... excitement in her life, so thought she would give bungee jumping a **(4)** .... She jumped **(5)** .... a 15 metre high platform and everything **(6)** .... normal. The problem was **(7)** .... because of the cold, a support wire had frozen and she couldn't **(8)** .... brought down.

She had to hang upside **(9)** ...., ten metres from the ground until firemen came to her rescue, four hours **(10)** .... On investigating the incident, **(11)** .... was discovered that the owner of the platform had ignored the cold weather conditions. Furthermore, **(12)** .... of the operators of the bungee jump had any safety or rescue training. **(13)** .... asked to comment, the owner stated, "Frankly, I don't know **(14)** .... about a bungee. I just want to **(15)** .... money."

3 Key-word Transformation Sentences

Read the sentences below and complete the second sentence so that it has a similar meaning to the first one, using the word given. Do not change the word given. You must use between two and five words, including the word given. Study the example (0).

0 Sue doesn't want to go out tonight because she's tired.
 would   Sue *would rather stay in* tonight because she's tired.

1 Jill may go to Austria for a holiday.
 thinking   Jill .... to Austria for a holiday.

2 It wasn't necessary to buy all those tomatoes. I only asked for a kilo.
 need   You .... all those tomatoes. I only asked for a kilo.

3 My grandparents 50th wedding anniversary is on 30th March.
 married   By 30th March my grandparents .... for 50 years.

4   Leslie hasn't read a book since September.
   last   Leslie .... in September.

5   Our car really needs repairing.
   should   We really .... repaired.

6   With the exception of Rosie, all the pupils went on the trip.
   only   Rosie .... didn't go on the trip.

7   The government hasn't done anything about the environment.
   something   It's time .... about the environment.

8   It is a nine-hour flight from here to New York.
   takes   It .... from here to New York.

9   Mat tried as hard as he could to pass the exam.
   did   Mat .... to pass the exam.

10 The film was too sad for her to watch to the end.
   such   It was .... she couldn't watch it to the end.

11 Kate tried very hard but she couldn't find the answer.
   hard   However ...., she couldn't find the answer.

12 You are not required to bring your passport.
   have   You .... your passport.

13 She never introduced herself to me.
   me   She never .... name.

14 "Don't forget to water the plants, Alex," said Mum.
   reminded   Mum .... the plants.

15 This has nothing to do with you.
   none   This .... business.

16 Our flat badly needs redecorating.
   up   We really ought .... our flat.

17 Ian is supposed to be here by now.
   been   Ian .... here by now.

18 I thought the novel would be better than it was.
   as   The novel .... I thought it would be.

19 I spoke loudly so that everybody could here me.
   be   I spoke loudly, ... by everybody.

20 "Well done Peter, you played wonderfully," said his teacher.
   congratulated Peter's teacher .... wonderfully.

Further Practice Sections

4 Multiple Choice Cloze

Read the text below and decide which answer A, B, C or D best fits each space. There is an example at the beginning (0).

Fast Food

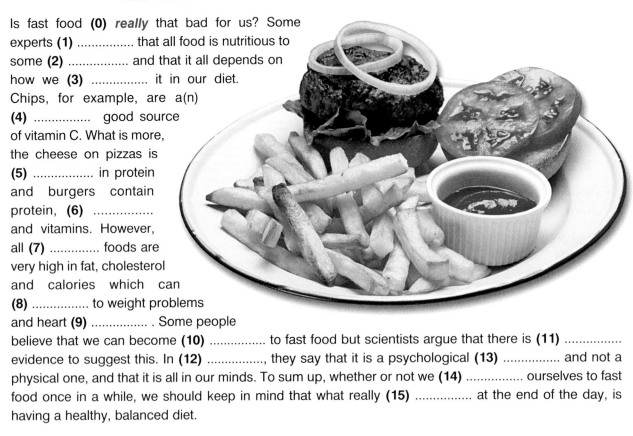

Is fast food **(0)** *really* that bad for us? Some experts **(1)** .... that all food is nutritious to some **(2)** .... and that it all depends on how we **(3)** .... it in our diet. Chips, for example, are a(n) **(4)** .... good source of vitamin C. What is more, the cheese on pizzas is **(5)** .... in protein and burgers contain protein, **(6)** .... and vitamins. However, all **(7)** .... foods are very high in fat, cholesterol and calories which can **(8)** .... to weight problems and heart **(9)** .... Some people believe that we can become **(10)** .... to fast food but scientists argue that there is **(11)** .... evidence to suggest this. In **(12)** ...., they say that it is a psychological **(13)** .... and not a physical one, and that it is all in our minds. To sum up, whether or not we **(14)** .... ourselves to fast food once in a while, we should keep in mind that what really **(15)** .... at the end of the day, is having a healthy, balanced diet.

0	**A** certainly	**B** plainly	**C** truthfully	**(D)** really
1	**A** request	**B** claim	**C** ask	**D** demand
2	**A** way	**B** standard	**C** degree	**D** part
3	**A** enclose	**B** involve	**C** encircle	**D** include
4	**A** fairly	**B** enough	**C** too	**D** much
5	**A** great	**B** big	**C** high	**D** tall
6	**A** iron	**B** steel	**C** gold	**D** silver
7	**A** this	**B** much	**C** that	**D** these
8	**A** pilot	**B** lead	**C** guide	**D** steer
9	**A** illness	**B** sickness	**C** disease	**D** infection
10	**A** effected	**B** addicted	**C** dependent	**D** dedicated
11	**A** small	**B** few	**C** tiny	**D** little
12	**A** truth	**B** fact	**C** data	**D** actual
13	**A** need	**B** necessity	**C** demand	**D** want
14	**A** entertain	**B** please	**C** enjoy	**D** treat
15	**A** says	**B** notes	**C** signifies	**D** matters

Section D

1 Multiple Choice Questions

Read the sentences below and decide which answer A, B, C or D best fits each blank.

1 The accountant was asked to go .... the document very carefully.
   A of   B at
   C over   D for

2 Their goal had always been to reach the .... of Mount Everest.
   A crown   B summit
   C point   D head

3 These workshops are designed to .... listening and speaking skills.
   A grow   B develop
   C create   D plant

4 Many patients complained that they didn't receive the proper medical .... they needed.
   A behaviour   B attitude
   C action   D treatment

5 Mary decided to consider the proposal that was put .... to her a few days ago.
   A forward   B first
   C front   D ahead

6 The police are still .... the cause of the explosion which damaged five cars.
   A investigating   B researching
   C considering   D exploring

7 Not .... is John a good writer, he is also a good singer.
   A simply   B even
   C just   D only

8 He decided to invest the .... of his money in property.
   A remains   B others
   C rest   D all

9 The book discusses how we could be more .... in managing our time.
   A effective   B adequate
   C energetic   D able

10 His job .... spending a lot of time travelling.
   A involves   B implies
   C covers   D consists

11 Some companies offer courses as a .... of training their staff.
   A pattern   B type
   C means   D design

12 She did not want him to jump .... the conclusion that it was all her fault.
   A to   B for
   C of   D at

13 This amazing collection of poems first saw the .... of day in 1980.
   A morning   B light
   C broad   D break

14 I started typing my paper and the .... thing I knew, my computer broke down.
   A next   B following
   C additional   D previous

15 Maria Callas became one of the best .... opera singers of her day.
   A understood   B known
   C liked   D popular

16 She was looking .... the mail when the phone rang.
   A towards   B up
   C through   D on

17 Everybody, myself ...., had been looking forward to the concert.
   A also   B included
   C involved   D too

18 He works here temporarily but has plans to .... open his own business.
   A finally   B eventually
   C soon   D really

19 Airline fares have been .... as much as 25% since January.
   A discounted   B decreased
   C lessened   D cut

20 All track events will be .... in the new Olympic stadium.
   A stored   B kept
   C made   D held

Further Practice Sections

2 Open Cloze Text

Read the text below and think of the word which best fits each space. Use only one word in each space. There is an example at the beginning (0).

The Importance of the Dinner Table

Not too long **(0)** *ago*, the dinner table was the centre **(1)** .... family life. Parents and children would **(2)** .... around the table, enjoy a good home-made **(3)** .... and discuss the day's events. Nowadays, **(4)** ...., the family dinner table has become a **(5)** .... of the past. The reason for this is the **(6)** .... that parents don't spend as much time with their children as they once **(7)** .... to. In most households, both parents **(8)** .... and are simply too tired to organise meals **(9)** .... other domestic matters. Nevertheless, many experts insist **(10)** .... time spent at the family dining table is essential to the well-being of the family unit. Gathering for meals gives children a **(11)** .... of security and helps them understand and appreciate family life. Experts also claim that children not **(12)** .... get a nourishing meal but they also get emotional, intellectual and spiritual nourishment. So, **(13)** .... it is once a month or once a week, busy parents should **(14)** .... aside a few hours of their time to organise a family meal and spend quality time with their children. **(15)** .... all, the family that eats together stays together.

3 Key-word Transformation Sentences

Read the sentences below and complete the second sentence so that it has a similar meaning to the first one, using the word given. Do not change the word given. You must use between two and five words, including the word given. Study the example (0).

0 I have always admired my grandmother.
   look   I *have always looked up to* my grandmother.

1 You should have seen her on stage.
   see   It's a pity .... her on stage.

2 She felt strongly about the issue of using animals in experiments.
   strong   She .... on the issue of using animals in experiments.

3 I'll ask Peter to help me move the furniture.
   have   I'll .... me move the furniture.

4   This book is so old that it's coming to pieces.
    apart   This book .... because it's so old.

5   It's not much good inviting her out for dinner. She turns everybody down.
    use   It's .... for dinner because she will only turn you down.

6   They had just fallen asleep when the baby started crying.
    than   No sooner .... the baby started crying.

7   He hardly goes out anymore.
    go   Hardly .... anymore.

8   Every student in my class loves basketball.
    students   All .... basketball.

9   Mrs Brown gave a detailed description of the robbery.
    described   Mrs Brown .... detail.

10 Tom accused the little boy of breaking his bedroom window.
    blamed   Tom .... breaking his bedroom window.

11 Has Martin decided to move yet?
    made   Has Martin .... moving yet?

12 It must have been somebody else you saw because Stella is still in Belgium.
    have   It .... you saw because she is still in Belgium.

13 Perhaps he's in the bathroom, that's why he's not answering the phone.
    be   He .... a bath and that's why he's not answering the phone.

14 It is forbidden to take photographs inside this museum.
    take   You .... inside this museum.

15 Could you pass me the sugar, please?
    mind   Would .... the sugar?

16 It was difficult for me to walk in such a tight pair of shoes.
    hardly   I .... my shoes were too tight.

17 She wanted to be home in time for her favourite TV programme so she caught a taxi.
    miss   She caught a taxi .... her favourite TV programme.

18 Experts claim that climate changes are caused by global warming.
    to   Climate changes are caused by global warming .... experts.

19 Although he lives in Spain, Jack can't speak a word of Spanish.
    of   In spite ...., Jack can't speak a word of Spanish.

20 Why didn't you tell me that it was your birthday yesterday?
    wish   I .... it was your birthday yesterday.

Further Practice Sections ....

4 Multiple Choice Cloze

Read the text below and decide which answer A, B, C or D best fits each space. There is an example at the beginning (0).

Where Love Lives

Researchers at University College, London **(0)** *conducted* a unique test to highlight areas of the brain **(1)** .... to love. Volunteers **(2)** .... recruited by posters in the college. The test **(3)** .... two brain scans. The first was taken **(4)** .... the volunteers gazed **(5)** .... photos of their loved ones; the second while they looked at a friend of the same gender **(6)** .... their partner. Looking at pictures of their partners **(7)** .... activity in two areas of the volunteers' brains. One of them is **(8)** .... linked to 'gut feelings', and the other often **(9)** .... with feelings of euphoria. These areas both **(10)** .... neutral when the volunteers looked at a friend.

There were no **(11)** .... differences between the brain activities of men and women. Larger scale tests will be **(12)** .... to confirm the findings. Dr Bartels, who supervised the project, is **(13)** .... that the research could **(14)** .... to "a test for true love." However, he does point **(15)** .... that it would not be cheap.

0	**A** made	**(B)**	conducted	**C**	did	**D**	finished
1	**A** linked	**B**	tied	**C**	joined	**D**	fixed
2	**A** were	**B**	are	**C**	have	**D**	being
3	**A** included	**B**	contained	**C**	consisted	**D**	composed
4	**A** and	**B**	so	**C**	while	**D**	during
5	**A** in	**B**	at	**C**	for	**D**	on
6	**A** with	**B**	to	**C**	like	**D**	as
7	**A** caused	**B**	resulted	**C**	completed	**D**	made
8	**A** really	**B**	commonly	**C**	likely	**D**	soon
9	**A** relates	**B**	transmits	**C**	associates	**D**	transforms
10	**A** remained	**B**	continued	**C**	kept	**D**	ended
11	**A** more	**B**	main	**C**	significant	**D**	less
12	**A** made	**B**	asked	**C**	realized	**D**	required
13	**A** said	**B**	convinced	**C**	believed	**D**	thought
14	**A** lead	**B**	conclude	**C**	end	**D**	finish
15	**A** at	**B**	out	**C**	of	**D**	forward

Section E

1 Multiple Choice Questions

Read the sentences below and decide which answer A, B, C or D best fits each blank.

1 He gained .... experience working as a volunteer in Africa.
   A deserving   B admirable
   C worthy   D invaluable

2 It never .... to amaze me how babies learn to communicate.
   A stops   B ceases
   C ends   D finishes

3 Those old buildings are dangerous and should be .... down.
   A knocked   B pushed
   C brought   D wrecked

4 It is a fact that this kind of snake bite rarely .... fatal.
   A grows   B emerges
   C turns   D proves

5 Eating a large breakfast allowed her to go .... lunch.
   A up   B without
   C away   D off

6 There is very little .... that he will pass the exam.
   A opportunity   B chance
   C opening   D probability

7 What she likes .... about travelling is meeting new people.
   A great   B much
   C most   D a lot

8 "What .... of shampoo do you use?" Martha asked Jan.
   A brand   B mark
   C label   D tag

9 Julia shares all the .... with her husband, including the cooking and the ironing.
   A household   B homeland
   C housework   D homework

10 It was such a small car that it could only .... two people.
   A include   B contain
   C embrace   D hold

11 When my sister and I were young children, our father used to .... us on his shoulders.
   A carry   B bring
   C take   D uphold

12 Do not .... the opportunity to see Hamlet at the National Theatre.
   A fail   B lose
   C miss   D forget

13 My .... to London was delayed so I had to hang around the airport for three hours.
   A ride   B flight
   C tour   D voyage

14 He asked his friends to .... a good dentist.
   A recommend   B advise
   C prescribe   D counsel

15 Becky mentioned something about setting .... her own catering company.
   A up   B off
   C in   D around

16 The police have been trying for months to .... the whereabouts of the kidnapper.
   A stalk   B trace
   C detect   D follow

17 The .... of the television set goes back more than 50 years.
   A legend   B history
   C story   D age

18 This year's winter fashion .... to women of all ages.
   A attracts   B takes
   C calls   D appeals

19 I know for a .... that Pam hates Chinese food.
   A fact   B sure
   C certain   D truth

20 We will .... your order before sending the goods.
   A deal   B measure
   C process   D operate

Further Practice Sections

2 Open Cloze Text

Read the text below and think of the word which best fits each space. Use only one word in each space. There is an example at the beginning (0).

Gibraltar

Gibraltar is probably the most famous rock in the **(0)** *world*. It is not an island as many people **(1)** .... but actually a small country that is connected to the Spanish mainland. Gibraltar is also perfectly located as it **(2)** .... Europe from Africa and the Atlantic Ocean from the Mediterranean **(3)** .... It is not **(4)** .... big though, and only a few **(5)** .... live there.

Finding somewhere to **(6)** .... in Gibraltar can be difficult so it's a good **(7)** .... to book a hotel before you go. Some of the hotels have their own gardens and swimming **(8)** .... The first **(9)** .... you should do when you arrive is to go on a tour of the rock. There is a cable car which will take you to the **(10)** ...., where the view is absolutely beautiful. If you are interested in caves, then Gibraltar is just the **(11)** .... for you, as it is **(12)** .... of them. **(13)** ...., if you are looking for a different **(14)** .... of holiday or you want to go on a day trip **(15)** .... you are in Spain, then come to Gibraltar.

3 Key-word Transformation Sentences

Read the sentences below and complete the second sentence so that it has a similar meaning to the first one, using the word given. Do not change the word given. You must use between two and five words, including the word given. Study the example (0).

0 What about going for a walk in the countryside?
like   Do *you feel like going* for a walk in the countryside?

1 She is always complaining about how much work she has.
never   She .... much work she has.

2 When I first came to England, I had difficulty driving on the left.
used   When I first came to England, I .... to driving on the left.

3 Mary bought more eggs than she needed for the cake.
many   Mary .... for the cake.

4 I went to Oxford to take a summer course in English.

view I went to Oxford .... taking a summer course in English.

5 Can you look after the baby for a while, Sandra?

keep Can you .... the baby for a while, Sandra?

6 The clients arrived before I reached the office.

already The clients .... I reached the office.

7 Each wedding guest was given a small gift.

were The .... a small gift.

8 Please do not approach the counter all together.

one Please approach the counter .... time.

9 We had to complete a form when we arrived at the employment agency.

in We .... a form when we arrived at the employment agency.

10 Shall I carry your shopping for you?

to Would .... your shopping?

11 Perhaps he is the new headmaster.

be He .... headmaster.

12 The National Museum exhibits many interesting objects.

display Many interesting objects .... the National Museum.

13 She completely agreed with the decision I made.

total She was .... the decision I made.

14 Stop doing that or you'll land yourself in trouble.

give Unless .... that, you'll land yourself in trouble.

15 It was wrong of you to reveal my secret under any circumstances.

given You shouldn't .... my secret under any circumstances.

16 He wouldn't have started writing if his wife hadn't encouraged him.

up Had it not been for his wife's encouragement, he .... writing.

17 Many people have a tendency to catch colds during the winter.

prone Many people are .... during the winter.

18 I'm sure you forgot to tell Mrs Burns that you'd be late today.

must I'm sure you .... tell Mrs Burns that you'd be late today.

19 There is only a very small amount of sugar in the bowl.

hardly There is .... the bowl.

20 She spoke loudly so as to be heard at the back of the auditorium.

order She spoke loudly .... at the back of the auditorium.

4 Multiple Choice Cloze

Read the text below and decide which answer A, B, C or D best fits each space. There is an example at the beginning (0).

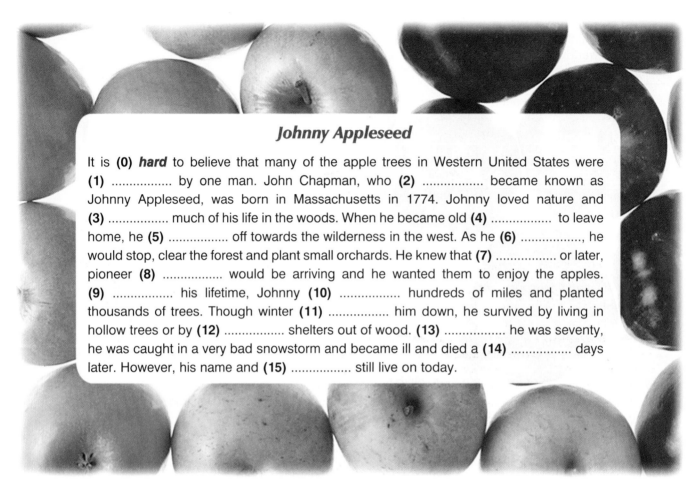

Johnny Appleseed

It is **(0) hard** to believe that many of the apple trees in Western United States were **(1)** .... by one man. John Chapman, who **(2)** .... became known as Johnny Appleseed, was born in Massachusetts in 1774. Johnny loved nature and **(3)** .... much of his life in the woods. When he became old **(4)** .... to leave home, he **(5)** .... off towards the wilderness in the west. As he **(6)** ...., he would stop, clear the forest and plant small orchards. He knew that **(7)** .... or later, pioneer **(8)** .... would be arriving and he wanted them to enjoy the apples. **(9)** .... his lifetime, Johnny **(10)** .... hundreds of miles and planted thousands of trees. Though winter **(11)** .... him down, he survived by living in hollow trees or by **(12)** .... shelters out of wood. **(13)** .... he was seventy, he was caught in a very bad snowstorm and became ill and died a **(14)** .... days later. However, his name and **(15)** .... still live on today.

0	Ⓐ hard	**B**	tough	**C**	complicated	**D**	complex
1	**A** made	**B**	harvested	**C**	planted	**D**	farmed
2	**A** after	**B**	later	**C**	next	**D**	following
3	**A** used	**B**	played	**C**	stayed	**D**	spent
4	**A** adequate	**B**	plenty	**C**	enough	**D**	fairly
5	**A** set	**B**	went	**C**	moved	**D**	made
6	**A** moved	**B**	travelled	**C**	crossed	**D**	toured
7	**A** longer	**B**	shorter	**C**	earlier	**D**	sooner
8	**A** families	**B**	relations	**C**	relatives	**D**	pairs
9	**A** Within	**B**	Through	**C**	During	**D**	Continuing
10	**A** crawled	**B**	jogged	**C**	ran	**D**	walked
11	**A** delayed	**B**	slowed	**C**	quietened	**D**	sped
12	**A** forming	**B**	establishing	**C**	starting	**D**	building
13	**A** What	**B**	When	**C**	While	**D**	As
14	**A** few	**B**	some	**C**	lot	**D**	little
15	**A** notoriety	**B**	fable	**C**	legend	**D**	fiction

Present Forms

Present Simple	Present Continuous	Present Perfect	Present Perf. Continuous
Affirmative	**Affirmative**	**Affirmative**	**Affirmative**
I cook You cook He cook**s** etc	I **am** cook**ing** You are cooking He is cooking etc	I **have** cook**ed** You have cooked He **has** cook**ed** etc	I **have been** cook**ing** You have been cooking He **has been** cook**ing** etc
Negative	**Negative**	**Negative**	**Negative**
I **don't** cook You don't cook He **doesn't** cook etc	I'm not cooking You aren't cooking He isn't cooking etc	I haven't cooked You haven't cooked He hasn't cooked etc	I haven't been cooking You haven't been cooking He hasn't been cooking etc
Interrogative	**Interrogative**	**Interrogative**	**Interrogative**
Do I cook? Do you cook? **Does** he cook? etc	Am I cooking? Are you cooking? Is he cooking? etc	Have I cooked? Have you cooked? Has he cooked? etc	Have I been cooking? Have you been cooking? Has he been cooking? etc
permanent situations or states *He **lives** in a mansion.* **permanent truths or laws of nature** *Water **boils** at 100˚C.*	**temporary situations** *She **is staying** with Pam at the moment.* **changing or developing situations** *He **is getting** fatter and fatter.*	**recently completed actions** *She **has cooked** dinner.* (The action is complete. Dinner is now cooked. - evidence in the present)	**actions started in the past and continuing up to the present.** *He **has been digging** in the garden for an hour.* (He started an hour ago and he's still digging it.)
repeated/habitual actions (especially with frequency adverbs: often, usually, always etc) *He **always is** on time.* (Here "always" means every day.)	**frequently repeated actions with always, constantly, continually expressing annoyance or criticism** *He's **always biting** his nails.* (Here "always" means constantly.)	**complete past actions connected to the present with stated or unstated time reference** *He **has bought** a house.* (Now he has a house.) *He **has just entered**.* (stated time reference)	**past actions of certain duration having visible results or effects in the present** *He **has been walking** in the rain. That's why he's wet.*
reviews/sports commentaries/ dramatic narrative *Ford **acts** brilliantly in this film.*	**actions happening at or around the moment of speaking** *The police **are investigating** the case of the murder.*	**personal experiences/ changes which have happened** *She **has grown** her hair long recently.*	**to express anger, irritation, annoyance, explanation or criticism** *Someone **has been sleeping** in my bed.* (annoyance)
timetables/programmes (future meaning) *The match **starts** at 5.00.* **in exclamatory sentences** *Here **comes** George!*	**fixed arrangements in the near future** *I'm **seeing** Greg on Monday.*	**emphasis on number** *He **has checked** three hotels this week.* *She **has been** to the shop twice this morning.*	**Present Perfect Continuous is normally used with for, since or how long to put emphasis on duration** *She **has been working** since 8 o'clock.*

Time expressions usually used with Present Forms

Present Simple	Present Continuous	Present Perfect & Present Perfect Continuous
every day/week/month/ year, usually, sometimes, always, rarely, never, often, in the morning/ evening/afternoon, at night, on Mondays etc	now, at the moment, at present, nowadays, today, tonight, always, still etc	just, ever, never, already, yet (negations & questions), always, how long, so far, recently, since (= from a starting point in the past), for (= over a period of time), today, this week/month etc **For** and **since** are usually used with Present Perfect Continuous to emphasise the duration of an action

Appendix

Past Forms

Past Simple	Past Continuous	Past Perfect	Past Perf. Continuous
Affirmative I cook**ed** You cooked He cooked etc	**Affirmative** I **was** cook**ing** You **were** cook**ing** He was cooking etc	**Affirmative** I **had** cook**ed** You had cooked He had cooked etc	**Affirmative** I **had been** cook**ing** You had been cooking He had been cooking etc
Negative I **didn't** cook You didn't cook He didn't cook etc	**Negative** I wasn't cooking You weren't cooking He wasn't cooking etc	**Negative** I hadn't cooked You hadn't cooked He hadn't cooked etc	**Negative** I hadn't been cooking You hadn't been cooking He hadn't been cooking etc
Interrogative **Did** I cook? Did you cook? Did he cook? etc	**Interrogative** Was I cooking? Were you cooking? Was he cooking? etc	**Interrogative** Had I cooked? Had you cooked? Had he cooked? etc	**Interrogative** Had I been cooking? Had you been cooking? Had he been cooking? etc
past actions which happened one immediately after the other She **put on** her clothes, **took** her bag and **left** the house.	**action in the middle of happening at a stated past time** I **was travelling** this time last year.	**past action which occurred before another action or before a stated past time** He **had finished** the report by the end of the day.	**action continuing over a period up to a specific time in the past** She **had been trying** to get hold of David for months before he called her.
past habit or state He **used to walk**/**walked** to work every day. **complete action or event which happened at a stated past time** She **quit** her job **last week**. ("When?" "Last week" - stated past time)	**past action in progress interrupted by another past action. The longer action is in the Past Continuous, the shorter action is in the Past Simple.** I **was watching** TV when the lights went off.	**complete past action which had visible results in the past** He was desperate because he **had lost** his dog.	**past action of certain duration which had visible results in the past** Her feet hurt because she **had been walking** all day.
complete past actions not connected to the present with a stated or implied time reference Coleridge **wrote** lots of poems. (Coleridge is dead; he won't write poems any more. - period of time now finished - implied time reference)	**two or more simultaneous past actions of certain duration** He **was reading** his paper while she **was doing** her nails. **or background description to events in a story/description** They **were walking** in the park ...	**the Past Perfect is the past equivalent of the Present Perfect** There was no milk left; she **had drunk** it all. (Present Perfect: There's no milk left; she has drunk it all.)	**the Past Perfect Cont. is the past equivalent of the Present Perfect** He was exhausted that day because he **had been driving** all day long. (Present Perfect: He's exhausted today because he's been driving all day long.)

Time Expressions usually used with Past Forms

Past Simple	Past Continuous	Past Perfect	Past Perf. Continuous
yesterday, last week etc, (how long) ago, then, just now, when, in 1992 etc	while, when, as, the moment that etc	for, since, already, after, just, never, yet, before, by, by the time etc	for, since

Future Forms

Future Simple

Affirmative

I **will** cook
You will cook
He will cook etc

Negative

I **won't** cook
You won't cook
He won't cook etc

Interrogative

Shall/Will I cook?
Will you cook?
Will he cook? etc

decisions taken at the moment of speaking (on-the-spot decisions)
It's hot in here. I'll open the window.

hopes, fears, threats, offers, promises, warnings, predictions, requests, comments etc, esp. with: expect, hope, believe, I'm sure, I'm afraid, probably etc *I'm afraid he won't come.*

actions or predictions which may (not) happen in the future
She'll probably call.
or actions which we cannot control and will inevitably happen
Their baby will be born in the summer.

things we are not yet sure about or we haven't decided to do yet
Maybe I'll go out later.
Note: Shall is used with I/we in questions, suggestions, offers or when asking for advice
Shall we have lunch?

Be going to

Affirmative

I **am going to** cook
You are going to cook
He is going to cook etc

Negative

I'm not going to cook
You're not going to cook
He's not going to cook etc

Interrogative

Am I going to cook?
Are you going to cook?
Is he going to cook? etc

actions intended to be performed in the near future
I'm going to visit Joanne next week.

planned actions or intentions
Now that she has finished school, she's going to search for a job.

evidence that something will definitely happen in the near future *It looks like the bus is going to be late. Be careful! You're going to have an accident.*

things we are sure about or we have already decided to do in the near future *They are going to have extra personnel for the summer. (It has been decided.)*

Future Continuous

Affirmative

I **will be** cook**ing**
You will be cooking
He will be cooking etc

Negative

I **won't** be cooking
You won't be cooking
He won't be cooking etc

Interrogative

Will I be cooking?
Will you be cooking?
Will he be cooking? etc

actions in progress at a stated future time
I'll be working in Plymouth this summer.

actions which are the result of a routine (instead of Present Continuous)
We'll be going to the zoo tomorrow. (We go there every Sunday - it's part of our routine)

when we ask politely about people's arrangements to see if they can do sth for us or because we want to offer to do sth for them. Will you be going to town today?
Can I come with you?

Future Perfect

Affirmative

I **will have** cook**ed** etc
Negative
I **won't** have cooked etc
Interrogative
Will I have cooked? etc

Future Perfect Cont.

Affirmative
I **will have been** cook**ing** etc
Negative
I won't have been cooking etc
Interrogative
Will I have been cooking? etc

Future Perfect

action finished before a stated future time *They will have got married by May.*

Note: by or not ... until/till are used with Future Perf. Until/till are normally used with Future Perfect only in negative sentences. *She will have finished it by next week. (not: till/until) She won't have finished until tomorrow.*

Future Perfect Cont.

duration of an action up to a certain time in the future
By this time next week he will have been working here for 3 years.

Present Simple with future meaning	Present Continuous with future meaning
timetables/programmes *The train leaves at 7 o'clock in the evening.*	**fixed arrangement in the near future** *I'm spending the weekend with the Smiths. (It's planned.)*

Shall is used:	Will is used:
with I/we in questions, suggestions, offers or when asking for advice. **Shall** we play tennis? Where **shall** I go?	to express offers, threats, promises, predictions, warnings, requests, hopes, fears, on-the-spot decisions, comments (mainly with: think, expect, believe, I'm sure, hope, know, suppose and probably). **I'm sure** Mary **will accept** his proposal.

Time Expressions used with :

Future Simple & Be going to	Future Perfect	Future Perfect Cont.
tomorrow, tonight, next week/month, in two/three etc days, the day after tomorrow, soon, in a week/month etc	before, by, by then, by the time, (until is used only in negative sentences with this tense)	by ... for

Spelling Rules

1 -(e)s ending
   a. words ending in -s, -ss, -ch, -x, -sh, -z, -o * add -es

   bus -buses, compass - compasses, watch - watches, box - boxes, dish - dishes, do - does, piano - pianos

   b. nouns ending in vowel + o, double o, short forms/ musical instruments/proper nouns ending in -o add -s

   zoo - zoos, video - videos - hello - hellos, Eskimo - Eskimos

2 -f/-fe ending
   nouns ending in -f/-fe drop -f/-fe and add -ves

   thief - thieves, wife - wives

3 -y ending
   a. words ending in consonant + y drop -y and add -ies, -ied, -ier, -iest, -ily

   study - studies - studied, pretty - prettier - prettiest, pretty - prettily

   b. words ending in consonant + y add -ing

   study - studying

   c. words ending in vowel + y add -s, -ed, -ing, -er, -est

   employ -employs - employed - employing, grey - greyer - greyest

4 -ie ending
   words ending in -ie change -ie to -y before -ing

   die - dying

5 dropping -e
   a. words ending in -e drop -e and add -ing, -ed, -er, -est

   save - saving - saved (but: be - being)
 late - later - latest

   b. adjectives ending in -e add -ly to form their adverbs

   rare - rarely, mere - merely (but: whole - wholly)

   c. adjectives ending in -le change -le to -ly to form their adverbs

   incredible -incredibly

   d. verbs ending in -ee add -ing

   see - seeing

Pronunciation

Pronunciation of -(e)s ending (noun plurals and the 3rd person singular of verbs in the Present Simple)

/s/ after /f/, /t/, /p/, /k/	/ɪz/ after /z/, /dʒ/, /tʃ/, /s/, /ʃ/	/z/ after /b/, /g/, /m/, /d/, /l/, /n/, /v/ or any vowel sound
laughs, hits, hops, talks	*poses, dodges, watches, kisses, rushes*	*stabs, sags, steams, descends, falls, retains, saves, delays*

Pronunciation of -ed ending

/ɪd/ after /t/, /d/	/t/ after /k/, /tʃ/, /f/, /s/, /ʃ/, /p/	/d/ after /b/, /dʒ/, /m/, /v/, /g/, /l/, /n/, /z/, vowel + /r/
wasted, landed	*poked, watched, laughed, rinsed, dashed, stopped*	*grabbed, dodged, slammed, saved, hugged, killed, stained, squeezed, soared*

Phrasal Verbs

Be

be about to = (int) be on the point of *He was about to leave when the phone rang.*

be after = (tr) chase *The police were after the thief.*

be down with = (tr) be ill with; **go down with** *John is down with the flu.*

be for = (tr) be in favour of (opp: **be against**) *They are(all) for the proposal to build a leisure centre.*

be in for = (tr) expect sth, usu bad *We are in for bad weather.*

be off = (tr) be absent from school/work *John isn't in his office. He's off for two days.*

be on = (tr) be shown on TV, at the cinema/theatre etc *There's a good film on at the Metro.*

be out = 1) (int) be unfashionable *Long skirts are out this season.*
2) (int) (of light/fire) have stopped burning. *The fire is out - that's why it's cold in here.*

be over = (int) have come to an end *The film starts at 8.00 and will be over at 10.00.*

be through with = (int) have ended a relationship/job etc *I'm through with Tom; he's so selfish.*

be up to = 1) (tr) be capable of *Let's take the train - I don't think I'm up to driving so far.*
2) (tr) feel like doing sth usu sth wrong *The children must be up to something - they're very quiet.*

Break

break down = 1) (int) (of machinery) stop working *The car broke down so we missed the ferry.*
2) (int) (of a person) lose control of feelings. *She broke down when she was told her father was dead.*
3) (int) fail (talks/negotiations etc) *Negotiations broke down and war was declared.*
4) (tr) separate under headings *He broke the list down into categories.*

break in = (int) enter by force or illegally *Burglars broke in and stole my jewellery.*

break into = 1) (tr) enter by force *He broke into the villa and stole some money.*
2) (tr) interrupt *He broke into their conversation to ask something.*

break off = (tr) end a relationship/agreement *Sue broke off her relationship with Jim.*

break out = (int) begin suddenly (war etc) *War broke out between the two countries.*

break through = (int) advance (in spite of opposition) *The soldiers broke through the enemy lines.*

break to = (tr) tell (usu bad news) to sb in a kind way *He had to break the bad news to John.*

break up = 1) (int) stop for holidays (school etc) *Schools break up on the 23rd for Christmas.*
2) (int) end a relationship *Sue and Paul are no longer together; they broke up last week.*

Bring

bring about = (tr) cause to happen *The end of the war brought about great changes.*

bring back = (tr) cause to recall *This smell brings back childhood memories.*

bring down = (tr) cause to fall *The measures brought down the government.*

bring forward = (tr) move sth to an earlier date or time *The exam date was brought forward by a week.*

bring in = (tr) create profit/money *His plan brought in lots of money.*

bring on = (tr) cause, usu sth unpleasant *The damp weather brought on his cold.*

bring out = (tr) put on the market *The new shampoo will be brought out next March.*

bring round = 1) (tr) cause to regain consciousness; **bring to** *They poured cold water on his face to bring him round.*
2) (tr) persuade; **bring over (to)** *He tried to bring him round to his point of view.*

bring up = 1) (tr) raise a child *She was brought up by her grandmother as her parents were abroad.*
2) (tr) mention/introduce a subject *You shouldn't have brought that matter up in front of everyone.*

Call

call for = (tr) need *The situation calls for immediate action.*

call in = (int) visit briefly *She called in last Monday to see our new house.*

call off = (tr) cancel *The match was called off due to bad weather.*

call on sb = (tr) visit formally *Our representative will call on your company next Tuesday.*

call out = (tr) order to come to sb's help *All firefighters were called out to save the burning building.*

call up = (tr) order to join the army *Thousands of young men were called up during World War I.*

Carry

be carried away = be very excited *They were all carried away by his performance.*

carry off = (tr) handle a difficult situation successfully *She carried her speech off well.*

carry on (with) = (tr) continue with *Carry on with your work while I am out.*

carry out = (tr) conduct an experiment *They carried out some tests to see the effects of the new drug.*

carry through = complete successfully *I don't think anyone but Matt can carry this project through.*

Come

come across = (tr) find/meet by chance *I came across this ring in an antique shop.*

come by = (tr) obtain *Everybody wonders how he came by so much money.*

come down to = (int) be passed on to sb by inheritance *This house came down to me after my aunt died.*

come down with = (tr) become ill; **go down with** *I'm sure I'm coming down with the flu.*

come into = (tr) inherit *He came into a large sum of money after his grandfather died.*

come off = (int) succeed *Despite all his planning the deal didn't come off.*

come out = 1) (int) (of flowers) begin to blossom *Roses come out in summer.*
2) (int) be published *When does her new book come out?*
3) (int) (of stains) be able to be removed *This wine stain will come out if you let it soak in warm water.*

come round = 1) (int) visit casually *Come round any time for coffee.*
2) (int) recover consciousness *To the doctors' surprise the patient came round quickly.*

come to = (tr) amount to a total *The bill came to £50.*

come up = 1) (int) be mentioned *Your name came up in the conversation.*
2) (tr) arise; occur *Such an opportunity comes up once in a lifetime.*

come up to = 1) (tr) approach *A strange man came up to me and asked me for money.*
2) (tr) equal; be up to (expectations) *He failed to come up to his parents' expectations.*

come up with = (tr) find (an answer, solution etc) *He came up with a brilliant plan to save the company.*

Cut

cut across = (tr) take a shorter way *Cut across this field if you're in a hurry.*

cut back (on) = (tr) reduce (expenses, production); **cut down on** *We must cut back on eating out; we just can't afford it.*

cut in = 1) (int) move suddenly in front of another car *A car cut in and forced us to slow down.*

2) (int) interrupt *Would you mind not cutting in until I've finished speaking?*

cut into = (tr) interrupt *The children kept cutting into our conversation.*

cut off = 1) (tr) disconnect *Our electricity was cut off as we didn't pay the bill on time.*
2) (tr) isolate (usu places) *The flood cut off the village for a week.*

cut out = (tr) omit *Your article is fine provided you cut out the third paragraph.*

be cut out for/to be = be suited for (a profession) *I don't think I'm cut out for teaching/to be a teacher - I haven't got enough patience.*

cut up = (tr) cut into small pieces *Cut up the meat for Johnny - otherwise he won't be able to eat it.*

Do

do away with = (tr) abolish *Most countries have done away with capital punishment.*

do down = (tr) speak badly of sb *Nobody likes him because he is always doing people down.*

do in = (tr) kill *He threatened to do her in if she didn't cooperate*

do up = (tr) fasten; tie *Do up your jacket; it's cold.*

do with = (tr) want *I could do with a cup of tea.*

do without = (tr) live or continue without having sth/sb *There's no Coke left - we'll have to do without.*

Draw

draw back = 1) (tr) be unwilling to fulfil a promise; **pull back** *Although he had promised to help us, he drew back at the last minute.*
2) (int) move away *On seeing the snake she drew back in terror.*

draw in = (int) (of a bus/train) arrive at a station; **pull in** *The train drew in and the passengers began to get off.*

draw out = 1) (tr) encourage sb to be less shy *He's very shy; someone should draw him out.*
2) (tr) take money out of a bank account *He drew out some money to pay his rent.*

draw up = 1) (of a vehicle) stop *The limo drew up outside the mansion and the millionaire got out.*
2) (tr) write out (will, list, contract etc) *My grandfather had a solicitor draw up his will last year.*

Fall

fall apart = (int) come to pieces *This book is so old that it's falling apart.*

fall back on = turn to sb/sth for help when other plans have failed *Keep some money in the bank to fall back on in case something goes wrong.*

fall behind = (int) fail to keep up with *The company cancelled my credit card when I fell behind with my payments.*

fall for = 1) (tr) fall in love with sb *George fell for Mary at first sight.*
2) (tr) be deceived *Everybody fell for the conman's lies.*

fall in = (int) collapse *I'm afraid the roof will fall in if an earthquake hits the area.*

fall in with = (tr) agree with *All members of the committee fell in with his suggestion to build a new hospital.*

fall into = (tr) 1) be divided into (categories) *This novel falls into the category of historical adventure.*
2) (tr) begin; enter a state *I fell into conversation with an interesting man on the train.*

fall on = 1) (tr) attack *The raider fell on the policeman.*
2) (tr) eat hungrily *The children fell on the cake and ate all of it.*

fall out (with) = quarrel *She fell out with Peter because he came home late.*

fall through = (int) fail to be completed *Our plans fell through due to lack of money.*

Get

get across = (tr) successfully communicate ideas *The teacher got his message across by using diagrams and photographs.*

get along = (int) continue despite difficulties *She is getting along fine despite all her problems.*

get along with = (tr) be on friendly terms; **get on with** *They get along with each other despite their differences.*

get at = (int) mean *I don't know what you're getting at by saying such things.*

get away with = (tr) escape punishment for a wrongful, illegal act *He got away with a fine of only £5.*

get back = (tr) recover possession of *She managed to get back the ring she had lost two months before.*

get down = 1) (tr) swallow with difficulty *I can't get this steak down. It's very tough.*
2) (tr) depress *This rainy weather gets me down.*

get down to = (tr) start doing sth seriously *It's time you got down to looking for a better job.*

get on = 1) (tr) enter (bus, train etc) *Get on the bus before it starts.* 2) (int) make progress *He's getting on well at school.*

get on with = (tr) be on good terms with *She gets on well with her friend Lucy.*

get out = (int) (of news) become known *How did the news of his promotion get out?*

get over = (tr) recover from *He's trying hard to get over the death of his wife.*

get round = (tr) persuade; **bring round** *We eventually got him round to our point of view.*

get round to (tr) = find time to do sth *I haven't got round to writing that letter yet.*

get through = 1) (tr) finish (a piece of work) *I've got to get through this chapter before I go out.*
2) (int) go on living through difficult times *How can old people get through the cold winters?*

get through to = (tr) reach by phone *Did you get through to your dentist or will you call him later?*

get up = (int) rise from bed *What time did you get up today?*

Give

give away = 1) (tr) reveal *Promise not to give away my secret.*
2) (tr) give sth free of charge *She gave away most of her clothes to the poor.*

give back = (tr) return *Give me back the money or I'll sue you.*

give in = (int) surrender; yield *He finally gave in and admitted he was wrong.*

give off = (tr) emit (smells, heat, fumes etc) *The radiators give off lots of heat.*

give out = 1) (int) come to an end *Their supplies gave out halfway through the climb.*
2) (tr) distribute *They were giving out free samples of the new shampoo at the supermarket.*

give up = 1) (tr) abandon an attempt/habit *He gave up smoking last year and hasn't smoked since.*
2) (tr) surrender *The thieves gave themselves up to the police.*

Go

go after = (tr) pursue *The policeman went after the thief and caught him.*

go ahead = (int) be allowed to happen *Although several members were absent, the board meeting went ahead as planned.*

go away = (int) stop; cease *If you take an aspirin, your headache will go away.*

go back on = (tr) break a promise/agreement *Although he had promised to help us, he went back on his word.*

go by = (tr) base one's ideas on *You shouldn't go by what he says - he always exaggerates.*

go down with = (tr) become ill *John has gone down with the flu.*

go for = 1) (tr) attack *A big Alsatian went for my little dog.*
2) (tr) apply for (a job) *Why don't you go for this marketing job? You may get it.*

go in for = (tr) take part in (a competition) *She went in for the baking competition and won first prize.*

go off = 1) (int) explode (bomb) *The bomb went off, killing 10 people.*
2) ring (alarm) *When the alarm went off she woke up and got out of bed.*
3) (int) (of food) spoil *The milk has gone off; it smells terrible.*
go on = 1) (int) continue; **carry on** *Go on, finish what you were saying.*
2) (int) happen *A large crowd gathered to see what was going on.*
go out = (int) stop burning *Put some coal on the fire before it goes out.*
go over = 1) (tr) examine details; **go through** *The police went over/through the evidence many times trying to come up with something.*
2) (tr) repeat *Go over the details again please. I wasn't following you.*
go round = 1) (int) be enough for everyone to have a share *There's enough food to go round.*
2) (int) (news/disease) spread; circulate; **get round** *The news went round very quickly.*
go through = 1) (tr) experience *She went through a painful time when her mother died.*
2) (int) (of a deal/arrangement) be completed with success *Has the sale of your flat gone through yet?*
3) (tr) discuss in detail *They went through his suggestions again before making a decision.*
go up = (int) rise (price) *The price of cigarettes went up again yesterday.*
go with = (tr) match *This jumper really goes with your skirt.*
go without = (tr) endure the lack of sth; **do without** *Since they had run out of lemonade, they had to go without.*

Hold

hold back = 1) (tr) control (tears, laughter) *She tried to hold back her tears and not cry in front of her mum.*
2) (int) hesitate *Don't hold back; take the opportunity while it's there.*
hold in = (tr) restrain *He held his anger in and didn't shout at the boy.*
hold off = (int) keep at a distance *The police held off the crowd until the troops arrived.*
hold on = (int) wait (esp on the phone) *Please hold on; Mr Mathews is on the other line.*
hold out = 1) (int) last *The food supplies won't hold out until Monday so we'll have to find some food before then.*
2) (int) persist *The miners held out for 18 months before they called off the strike.*
hold to = (tr) follow exactly; keep to (a promise etc) *Whatever you say, I'll hold to my opinion.*
hold up = 1) (tr) delay *Sorry we're late; we were held up in traffic.*
2) (tr) use violence in order to rob *The robbers held up the train and stole £22,000.*

Keep

keep after = (tr) continue to pursue *The police kept after the escaped prisoners until they caught them.*
keep away (from) = (tr) stay away *She had to be kept away from school as she had measles.*
keep back = (tr) conceal *How did she manage to keep back her true feelings?*
keep down = (tr) cause to remain at a lower level *The government is trying to keep prices down.*
keep in = (tr) make sb stay indoors (as punishment) *The teacher kept us in for misbehaving in class.*
keep off = (tr) stay away from; avoid *Keep off the benches. The paint is wet.*
keep on = (int) continue despite difficulties *Although he failed his test, he kept on studying and retook it in May.*
keep out = (tr) exclude sb/sth *He locked the gate to keep out unwanted visitors.*
keep up (with) = (tr) stay at the same level as sb/sth *Despite being ill he kept up with his work and passed the exam.*
keep up with = (tr) continue to be informed *He reads a newspaper every day to keep up with the news.*

Let

let down = 1) (tr) (of clothes) lengthen (opp: **take up**) *I need to let down my skirt; it's too short.*
2) (tr) disappoint *He let me down by lying to me.*
let in(to) = allow sb to enter a place *They let us into the room after we showed them our invitation card.*
let off = (tr) not to punish *The policeman let him off without arresting him.*
let on = (int) reveal a secret *He let on that she had stolen the money.*
let out = 1) (tr) release *He was let out of prison after 10 years.*
2) (tr) (of clothes) make larger (opp: **take in**) *I have to have my trousers let out; I've gained several kilos.*
let up = (int) become less strong *The boats won't sail until the strong winds let up.*

Look

look after = (tr) take care of *My mother looks after my son when I'm working.*
look back (on) = (tr) consider the past *My grandfather looks back on his army days with pleasure.*

look down on = (tr) despise (opp: **look up to**) *She looks down on John because he isn't rich.*

look forward to = (tr) anticipate with pleasure *I'm really looking forward to my brother's wedding.*

look in on sb = (tr) pay a short visit to *I'll look in on my mother on my way home.*

look into = (tr) investigate *The police are looking into the case of the smuggled diamonds.*

look on = (int) observe *He was just looking on while the other two were playing.*

look out = (int) be careful *Look out! There's a car coming.*

look out for = (tr) be alert in order to see/find sb/sth *When you're cleaning the flat, please look out for my silver earring. I lost it somewhere.*

look over = (tr) examine carefully; **go through** *The judge looked over the evidence before passing judgement.*

look round = (tr) inspect a place *He looked round many houses before he settled on this one.*

look through = (tr) look at quickly *Look through these books and see if you want any of them.*

look up = (tr) look for sth in an appropriate book/list *Get the telephone directory and look up the number of the shop.*

Make

be made for = suit exactly *Buy this dress - it's simply made for you.*

make for = (tr) go towards *It's late. Let's make for home as quickly as possible.*

make out = 1) (tr) distinguish *I can't make out what the name on the bell is.*

2) (tr) write out; fill in *Please make the cheque out to Norman Brothers Ltd.*

make over = (tr) give possession of sth to sb else *Before their uncle died he made over his whole estate to them.*

make up = 1) (tr) invent *That is not true; she made the whole thing up.*

2) (tr) put cosmetics on *She made herself up before she went out.*

3) (int) reconcile *Thank goodness they've made up after their quarrel.*

make up for = compensate *The good summer weather is making up for the bad winter.*

make up one's mind = decide *She can't make up her mind whether to go to Turkey or India.*

Pass

pass away = (int) die *I'm sorry to tell you your aunt passed away last night.*

pass off as = (tr) pretend to be sth/sb else successfully *She passed herself off as a police officer*

in order to get into the building.

pass out = (int) lose consciousness *He passed out from the fumes, and it took them some time to bring him round.*

Pay

pay back = 1) (tr) return money owed *I promise I'll pay you back as soon as I get paid.*

2) (tr) take revenge on sb *I promise I'll pay you back one day for what you did to my family.*

pay down = (tr) pay part of the price for sth and the rest over a period of time *We paid £100 down and the balance over a period of 6 months.*

pay for = (tr) receive punishment *All criminals should pay for their crimes.*

pay off = (tr) pay sb to leave employment *They paid off all their senior management in an attempt to restructure the company.*

pay up = (tr) pay (a debt) in full *As I hadn't paid my monthly instalments the company requested me to pay up the balance.*

Pull

pull down = (tr) demolish *They pulled down the old building as it was dangerous.*

pull in = (int) (of trains) arrive (opp: **pull out**) *The train from Dublin is due to pull in at 5.30 pm.*

pull oneself together = bring one's feelings under control *Although she was tired, she pulled herself together and continued working.*

pull through = (int) succeed despite difficulties *If all employees work harder, the company will definitely pull through.*

pull up = stop *The jockey pulled the horse up as it had an injured leg.*

Put

put aside/by = (tr) save *He puts aside £50 a month for his summer holidays.*

put across = (tr) communicate successfully; **get across/over** *The lecturer managed to put his ideas across to the audience.*

put away = 1) (tr) store *Put the toys away in the cupboard. We're expecting guests tonight.*

2) (tr) put sb into prison/mental hospital *The murderer was put away for 10 years.*

put down = 1) (tr) write down; **take down** *Make sure you take down everything said at the meeting.*

2) (tr) suppress forcibly *The police try to put down rioting at football matches.*

put down to = (tr) attribute to *She puts her recent success down to hard work and dedication.*

put forward = (tr) propose *He put forward a new plan to help decrease unemployment.*

put off = (tr) postpone *The meeting was **put off** due to the president's illness.*

put on = 1) (tr) dress oneself in *Put on your coat and come with me.*

2) (tr) increase (in weight) *He has **put on** weight since he stopped smoking.*

3) (tr) cause to take place (show/performance) *They **are putting on** "My Fair Lady" on Broadway next month.*

put out = (tr) extinguish (fire etc) *The firefighters **put out** the fire quickly.*

2) cause trouble *I hope I'm not **putting** you **out** by asking you to do this.*

be put out = be annoyed *She **was put out** by his bad behaviour.*

put through = (tr) connect by phone *Can you put me **through** to Mr Jones, please?*

put up = 1) (tr) erect; build *They've **put up** a statue in the square.*

2) (tr) offer hospitality *When you are in town, I'll **put** you **up** in my flat.*

3) (tr) show in a public place *The WWF has **put up** posters all round the city.*

put up with = (tr) tolerate *I won't **put up with** such rude behaviour any longer.*

Run

run across/into = (tr) meet/find by chance *She **ran across** an old friend while on holiday.*

run after = (tr) chase *The dog **ran after** the cat.*

run away with = (tr) steal *The thieves **ran away with** £15,000,000 from the bank.*

run down = 1) (tr) knock down (with a vehicle); **run over** *The old man was **run down/over** by a bus.*

2) (tr) speak badly of sb *You shouldn't **run down** your sister; you've got no reason to criticise her.*

run in = (tr) bring a new car engine into full use (by driving it slowly for a set period) *I can't go any faster; I'm **running** the car **in**.*

run off = (tr) make prints/copies *Can you please **run off** 100 copies for me?*

run out of = (tr) no longer have a supply *We've **run out of** coffee. Could you buy some when you go out?*

run through = 1) (tr) use up *It's unbelievable; he has **run through** all his money already.*

2) (tr) rehearse, check or revise quickly *Let's **run through** the last scene once more.*

run up = (tr) accumulate *He **ran up** a huge debt on his credit card which he couldn't pay off.*

run up against = (tr) encounter (difficulties/opposition) *He **ran up against** difficulties when he tried to enter the country without a visa.*

See

see about = (tr) deal with; **see to** *I'll see about* the food if you get the table ready.

see off = (tr) accompany a traveller to his/her plane, train etc *When she left for Berlin her parents **saw** her **off** at the station.*

see out = (tr) accompany sb to the door/exit of a house/building *Don't bother to **see** me **out**, I can find my own way.*

see over = (tr) inspect a place; **look round** *Can I **see over** the flat before I make my decision?*

see through = (tr) not be deceived *He was such a poor liar that they **saw through** him at once.*

Set

set about = (tr) begin to do *He **set about** fixing the door while she cleaned the house.*

set aside = 1) (tr) save for a special purpose *She **sets aside** £20 a week to buy a car.*

2) (tr) stop sth for some time; **set by** *She had to **set** the report **aside** until she had dealt with the correspondence.*

set back = 1) move the hands of a clock/watch to show an earlier time *We usually **set** the clocks **back** one hour at the beginning of autumn.*

2) (tr) hinder *The fire has **set** our plans **back**.*

set in = (int) (of weather) start and seem likely to continue *The rain seems to have **set in**.*

set off/out = (int) start a journey *We'll **set off/out** for the airport at 6 am.*

set on = (tr) (cause to) attack *He threatened to **set** the dogs **on** us if we didn't leave.*

set sb up = (tr) cause sb to receive blame *Although he knew someone had **set him up**, he couldn't prove it.*

set to = (int) begin working hard *Get the duster and **set to**; there's lots of work to do before our visitors arrive.*

set up = 1) (tr) start a business *He left his job to **set up** his own business.*

2) (tr) establish (a record etc) *He **set up** a new record time for the men's championship.*

Stand

stand by = 1) (tr) support sb, esp in difficulties *I'll **stand by** you, whatever happens.*

2) (int) be ready for action *The army was **standing by** in case war broke out.*

stand for = 1) (tr) represent *Do you know what UFO **stands for**?*

2) (tr) tolerate; **put up with** *We won't **stand for** his rude behaviour any longer.*

stand in for = (tr) replace sb temporarily *Since John is ill I'll **stand in for** him tonight at work.*

stand out = (int) be noticeable *She really **stands out** wearing that pink suit.*

stand up = 1) (int) rise to one's feet *Stand up and come over here.*

2) (tr) fail to meet *We were supposed to meet at 11.00 but he stood me up.*

stand up for = (tr) support *You ought to stand up for your friends when people criticise them.*

stand up to = (tr) resist *The building has been reinforced to stand up to earthquakes.*

Take

take after = (tr) resemble *She takes after her mother. She looks and acts just like her.*

take away = (tr) remove *May I take away the dirty dishes now?*

take back = (tr) apologise *He took back his remarks about her cooking because she was obviously upset.*

take for = (tr) identify wrongly *Sorry, I took you for your brother. I always mix you up.*

take in = 1) (tr) give accommodation *Seaside villagers often take in tourists as paying guests.*

2) (tr) make clothes narrower (opp: **let out**) *Now that I've lost weight I should take my clothes in.*

3) (tr) fully understand *Did you take in what I said or should I repeat it?*

take off = 1) (tr) remove clothes (opp: **put on**) *Take off this dirty dress and I'll wash it for you.*

2) (int) (of planes) leave the ground (opp: **come down**) *We saw the plane take off and disappear into the clouds.*

3) (tr) imitate *He's good at taking off famous people.*

4) (tr) (of time) take time as a holiday *He took three days off work to go and see his parents.*

take on = 1) (tr) undertake work/responsibility *He took on an extra class as the previous teacher had quit.* 2) (tr) employ *They decided to take on two extra assistants during the Christmas rush.*

take out = 1) (tr) remove *The dentist took out my bad tooth.*

2) (tr) clean (mark, dirt) *Use this spray to take out the stain.*

take over = (tr) gain control of sth *She'll take over the company when her father retires.*

take to = 1) (tr) begin a habit *I don't know why she's taken to biting her nails.*

2) (tr) like *She has really taken to her nephew and always buys him expensive presents.*

take up = 1) (tr) begin a hobby, sport, job *When he retired, he took up sailing as a hobby.*

2) (tr) fill (time, space) *This sofa takes up most of the living room.*

be taken aback = be strongly surprised *We were taken aback when they said they were getting married. No one expected it.*

be taken in = (tr) be deceived *She was taken in by the conman and bought a fake insurance policy.*

Turn

turn away = (tr) refuse admittance *They tried to enter the pub but they were turned away at the door.*

turn down = 1) (tr) refuse an offer *He proposed to her but she turned him down.*

2) (tr) reduce loudness (opp: **turn up**) *Could you turn down the radio a little? I can't hear him on the phone.*

turn in = 1) (int) go to bed *It's late and I'm tired. I'd better turn in.*

2) (tr) give to the police *They turned the fugitive in to the police.*

turn off = (tr) switch off (opp: **turn on**) *Turn off the oven before you leave.*

turn out = 1) (tr) produce *Our factory turns out 100 cars a day.*

2) (int) prove to be *He turned out to be the one who had stolen the money.*

turn over = (int) turn to a new page; change the TV channel *Now children, turn over to the next page.*

turn to = 1) (tr) go to sb for help/advice *When I'm in trouble I always turn to my brother.*

2) (tr) begin (a way of life or doing sth) *Why did he turn to drinking in the first place?*

turn up = 1) (int) arrive or appear (unexpectedly) *He finally turned up at the meeting an hour late.*

2) (int) (of an opportunity) arise *When a better job turned up she seized the chance and applied for it.*

Wear

wear away = (tr) (of wood/stone) reduce gradually *We couldn't make out the names on the gravestone because the letters had been completely worn away.*

wear down = (tr) reduce opposition gradually *A few weeks in solitary confinement will wear down the prisoner's resistance.*

wear off = (int) stop gradually *Your nervousness will wear off when the exams are over.*

wear out = 1) (tr) exhaust *I've worked so hard today, I'm worn out.*

2) (int) use until no longer serviceable *We'll have to replace this plug - it is completely worn out.*

Work

work on = (tr) have an effect on *We have to check this new drug to see how it works on animals.*

work out = 1) (tr) find a solution to a problem by reasoning or calculation *I'm sure we can work out our problems if we talk about them.*

2) (int) develop successfully *I hope things will work out well for you in your new job.*

work up = (tr) develop *I've been walking all day so I've worked up a really good appetite.*

Verbs, Adjectives, Nouns with Prepositions

A

abide by (v)
absent from (adj)
abstain from (v)
accompanied by (adj)
according to (prep)
account for (v)
accuse sb of (v)
accustomed to (adj)
acquainted with (adj)
addicted to (adj)
adequate for (adj)
adjacent to (adj)
advantage of (n)
(but: there's an **advantage in** - (have) an **advantage over** sb)
advice on (n)

afraid of (adj)
agree to/on sth (v)
agree with sb (v)
ahead of (prep)
aim at (v)
allergic to (adj)
amazed at/by (adj)
amount to (v)
amused at/with (adj)
angry at what sb does (adj)
angry with sb about sth (adj)
angry with sb for doing sth (adj)
annoyed with sb about sth (adj)
(in) answer to (n)
anxious about sth (adj)
(be) anxious for sth to happen (adj)
apologise to sb for sth (v)
(make an) appeal to sb for sth (n)

appeal to/against (v)
apply to sb for sth (v)
approve of (v)
argue with sb about sth (v)
arrest sb for sth (v)
arrive at (a small place) (v)
arrive in (a town) (v)
ashamed of (adj)
ask for (v) (but: **ask sb a question**)
assure (sb) of (v)
astonished at/by (adj)
attached to (adj)
attack on (n)
attend to (v)
(un)aware of (adj)

B

bad at (adj) (but: He was very **bad to** me.)
base on (v)
basis for (n)
beg for (v)
begin with (v)
believe in (v)
belong to (v)

benefit from (v)
bet on (v)
beware of (v)
(put the) blame on sb (n)
blame sb for sth (v)
blame sth on sb (v)

boast about/of (v)
bored with/of (adj)
borrow sth from sb (v)
brilliant at (adj)
bump into (v)
busy with (adj)

C

call at/on (phr v)
call for (= demand) (phr v)
campaign against/for (v)
capable of (adj)
care about (v)
care for sb (v) (= like)
(take) care of (n)
care for sth (v) (= like to do sth)
careful of (adj)
careless about/with (adj)
cause of (n)
certain of (adj)
change into (v)
characteristic of (n/adj)
charge for (v)
charge sb with (v)
cheque for (n)
choice between/of (n)
clever at (adj) (but: It was very **clever of** you to buy it.)
close to (adj)
coax sb into (v)
coincide with (v)

collaborate with (v)
collide with (v)
comment on (v)
communicate with (v)
compare with (v) (how people and things are alike and how they are different)
compare to (v) (show the likeness between sb/sth and sb/sth else)
comparison between (n)
complain of (v) (= suffer from)
complain to sb about sth (v) (= be annoyed at)
compliment sb on (v)
comply with (v)
conceal sth from sb (v)
concentrate on (v)
(have) confidence in sb (n)
confine to (v)
confusion over (n)
congratulate sb on sth (v)
connection between (n) (but: **in connection with**)
conscious of (adj)
connect to/with (v)

consist of (v)
contact between (n) (but: **in contact with**)
content with (adj)
contrary to (prep)
contrast with (v)
contribute to (v)
convert to/into (v)
cope with (v)
correspond to/with (v)
count against (v)
count on sb (phr v)
cover in/with (v)
covered in/with (adj)
crash into (v)
(have) a craving for sth (n)
crazy about (adj)
crowded with (adj)
cruel to (adj)
cruelty towards/to (n)
cure for (n)
curious about (adj)
cut into (phr v) (= interrupt sb/a conversation)

Verbs, Adjectives, Nouns with Prepositions

D

damage to (n)
date back to (v)
date from (v)
deal with (v)
dear to (adj)
decide on/against (v)
decrease in (n)
dedicate to (v)
deficient in (adj)
definition of (n)
delay in (n)
delight in (v)
delighted with (adj)
demand for (n)
demand from (v)
depart from (v)
departure from (n)

depend on/upon (v)
dependent on (adj)
deputise for (v)
descended from (adj)
describe sb/sth to sb else (v)
description of (n)
die of/from (v)
die in an accident (v)
differ from (v)
(have) difference between/of (n)
different from (adj)
difficulty in/with (n)
disadvantage of (n) (but: **there's a disadvantage in doing sth**)
disagree with (v)
disappointed with/about (adj)
disapprove of (v)

discharge sb from (v)
discouraged from (adj)
discussion about/on (n)
disgusted by/at (adj)
dismiss from (v)
dispose of (v)
disqualified from (adj)
dissatisfied with (adj)
distinguish between (v)
divide between/among (v)
divide into/by (v)
do sth about (v)
doubtful about (adj)
dream about (v)
dream of (v) (= imagine)
dressed in (adj)

E

eager for (adj)
economise on (v)
efficient at (adj)
(put) effort into sth (n)
emphasis on (n)
engaged to sb/in sth (adj)
engagement to sb (n)
enter into (= start) (v)
enthusiastic about (adj)
envious of (adj)

equal to (adj)
escape from/to (v)
example of (n)
excellent at (adj)
exception to (n)
(make an exception of sth/sb = treat sth/sb as a special case
take exception to sth = object to sth)
exchange sth for sth else (v)
excited about (adj)
exclaim at (v)
excuse for (n)
excuse sb for (v)

exempt from (adj)
expel from (v)
experienced in (adj)
experiment on/with (v)
expert at/in (sth/doing sth) (n)
(= person good at)
expert at/in/on (sth/doing sth) (adj)
(= done with skill or involving great knowledge)
expert with sth (n) (= good at using sth)
expert on (n) (= person knowledgeable about a subject)

F

face up to (phr v)
fail in an attempt (v)
fail to do sth (v)
failure in (an exam) (n)
failure to (do sth) (n)
faithful to (adj)
fall in (n)
familiar to sb (= known to sb) (adj)

familiar with (= have knowledge of) (adj)
famous for (adj)
fed up with (adj)
fill sth with sth else (v)
finish with (v)
fire at (v)
flee from (v)
fond of (adj)

forget about (v)
forgive sb for (v)
fortunate in (adj)
friendly with/to (adj)
frightened of (adj)
full of (adj)
furious with sb about/at sth (adj)

G

generosity to/towards (n)
genius at (n)
glance at (v)
glare at (v)

good at (adj) (but: He was very **good to** me.)
grateful to sb for sth (adj)
grudge against (n)

guess at (v)
guilty of (adj) (but: he felt **guilty about** his crime)

H

happen to (v)
happy about/with (adj)
harmful to (adj)
hear about (v) (= be told)
hear from (v) (= receive a letter)

hear of (v) (= learn that sth or sb exists)
heir to (n)
hinder from (v)
hint to sb about sth (v) (but: **hint at sth**)

hope for (v)
hope to do sth (v)
(no) hope of (n)
hopeless at (adj)

Verbs, Adjectives, Nouns with Prepositions

I
idea of (n)
identical to (adj)
ignorant of/about (adj)
ill with (adj)
impact on (n)
impressed by/with (adj)
(make an) impression on sb (n)
improvement in/on (n)
incapable of (adj)
include in (v)

increase in (n)
independent of (adj)
indifferent to (adj)
indulge in (v)
inferior to (adj)
information about/on (n)
(be) informed about (adj)
inoculate against (v)
insist on (v)
insure against (v)
intelligent at (adj)

intent on (adj)
(have no) intention of (n)
interest in (n)
interested in (adj)
interfere with/in (v)
invasion of (n)
invest in (v)
invitation to (n)
invite sb to (v)
involve in (v)
irritated by (adj)

J
jealous of (adj)

join in (v)

joke about (v)

K
knock at/on (v)
know about/of (v)
keen on sth (adj)

keen to do sth (adj)
kind to (adj)

key to (n)
knowledge of (n)

L
lack in (v)
lack of (n)
laugh at (v)
lean on/against (v)

leave for (v) (= head for)
lend sth to sb (v)
listen to (v)
live on (v)

long for (v)
look after (phr v) (= take care of)
look at (v)
look for (= search for) (phr v)

M
married to (adj)
marvel at (v)

mean to (adj)
mention to (v)

mistake sb for (v)
mix with (v)

N
name after (v)
necessary for (adj)
need for (n)
neglect of (n)

nervous about (adj)
new to (adj)
nice to (adj)

nominate sb (for/as sth) (v)
(take) (no) notice of (n)
notorious for doing sth (adj)

O
obedient to (adj)
object to (v)
objection to (n)
obliged to sb for sth (adj)

obvious to (adj)
occur to (v)
offence against (n)

operate on (v)
opinion of/on (n)
opposite of/to (n)

P
part with (v)
patient with (adj)
pay by (cheque) (v)
pay for (v) (but: **pay a bill**)
pay in (cash) (v)
peculiar to (adj)
persist in (v)
(but: **insist on**)
(take a) photograph of (n)
picture of (n)
pity for (n)
take pity on sb (exp)
pleasant to (adj)

pleased with (adj)
(take) pleasure in (n)
(have the) pleasure of (n)
point at/to (v)
(im)polite to (adj)
popular with (adj)
praise sb for (v)
pray for sth/sb (v)
prefer sth to sth else (v)
(have a) preference for (n)
prepare for (v)
present sb with (v)
prevent sb from (v)

(take) pride in (n)
pride oneself on sth/on doing (v)
prohibit sb from doing sth (v)
prone to (adj)
protect against/from (v)
protection from (n)
protest about/at (v)
proud of (adj)
provide sb with (v)
punish sb for (v)
puzzled about/by (adj)

Q
quarrel about sth/with sb (v/n)

qualified for (adj)
quick at (adj)

quotation from (n)

Verbs, Adjectives, Nouns with Prepositions

R

rave about (v)
react to (v)
reaction to (n)
ready for (adj)
reason for (n)
reason with (v)
rebel against (v)
receive from (v)
(keep) a record of (n)
recover from (v)
reduction in (n)
refer to (v)
(in/with) reference to (n)
refrain from (v)
regard as (v)

regardless of (prep)
related to (adj)
relationship between (n) (but: a **relationship with** sb)
relevant to (adj)
rely on (v)
remind sb of/about (v)
remove from (v)
replace sth with sth else (v)
reply to (n/v)
report on (n/v)
reputation for/of (n)
research on/into (n)
respect for (n)
respected for (adj)

respond to (v)
responsiblity for (n)
responsible for (adj)
result from (v) (= be the consequence of)
result in (v) (= cause)
result of (n)
resulting from (adj)
rhyme with (v)
rich in (adj)
(get) rid of (phr)
rise in (n)
(make) room for (n)
rude to (adj)
run into (phr v)

S

safe from (adj)
same as (adj)
satisfied with/by (adj)
save sb from (v)
scared of (adj)
search for (v/n)
(be) in search of (n)
sensible of sth (adj) (= aware of sth)
sensitive to (adj)
sentence sb to (v)
separate from (v)
serious about (adj)
share in/of sth (n)
shelter from (v)
shocked at/by (adj)
shoot at (v)
short of (adj)
shout at (v)

shy of (adj)
sick of (adj)
silly to do sth (adj) (but: it was **silly of** him)
similar to (adj)
skilful/skilled at (adj)
slow in/about doing sth/to sth (adj)
smell of (n/v)
smile at (v)
solution to (n)
sorry about (adj) (= feel sorry for sb) (but: I'm **sorry for** doing sth)
speak to/with sb about (v)
specialise in (v)
specialist in (n)
spend money on sth (v)
spend time in/doing sth (v)
split into/in (v)
spy on (v)

stand for (phr v)
stare at (v)
strain on (n)
subject to (adj/v)
submit to (v) (but: **submit sth for** publication)
subscribe to (v)
succeed in (v)
suffer from (v)
sufficient for sth/sb (adj)
superior to (adj)
sure of/about (adj)
surprised at/by (adj)
surrender to (v)
surrounded by (adj)
suspect sb of (v)
suspicious of (adj)
sympathetic to/towards (adj)
sympathise with (v)

T

take sth to sb/sth (v)
talent for sth (n)
talk to sb about sth (v)
(have) taste in (n)
taste of (v)
terrible at (adj)
terrified of (adj)

thank sb for (v)
thankful for (adj)
think about/of (v)
threat to sb/sth/of sth (n)
threaten sb with sth (v)
throw at (v) (in order to hit)
throw to (v) (in order to catch)

tire of (v)
tired of (adj) (= fed up with)
translate from ... into (v)
tread on (v)
trip over (v)
trouble with (n)
typical of (adj)

U

unaware of (adj)
understanding of (n)

uneasy about (adj)
upset about/over sth (adj)

(make) use of (n)
used to (adj)

V

valid for (length of time) (adj)

valid in (places) (adj)
value sth at (v)

vote against/for (v)
vouch for (v)

W

wait for (v)
warn sb against/about/of (v)
waste (time/money) on (v)

weak in/at (adj)
wink at (v)
wonder about (v)
worry about (v)

worthy of (adj)
write to sb (v)
wrong about (adj)

Prepositional Phrases

At

at the age of
at the airport
at an auction
at the beginning of (when sth started) (but: **in the beginning** = originally)
at one's best
at breakfast/lunch etc
at the bottom of
at the bus stop
at church
at the corner/on the corner
at all costs
at the crossroads
at dawn
at one's desk
at the door
at ease
at the end (= when sth is finished) (but: **in the end** = finally; at all events)
at fault
at first

at first hand
at first sight
at a glance
at a guess
at hand
at heart
at home
at/in a hotel
at ... km per hour
at large
at last
at the latest
at least
at length
at liberty
at a loss
at the match
at midnight
at the moment
at most
at night (but: **in the** night)
at noon
at once

at peace/war
at present
at a profit
at the prospect
at random
at any rate
at one's request
at the same time
at school
at sea
at the seaside
at short notice
at/in the station
at sunset
at the table
at the time
at times
at the top of (but: **on top of**)
at university
at the weekend
at work
at 23 Oxford St.

By

by accident
by all accounts
by appointment
by the arm/hand
by auction
by birth
by bus/train/plane/ helicopter/taxi/ coach/ ship/boat/sea/air/car etc (but: **on a/the** bus/plane/ train/coach/ship/boat **in a** taxi/car/helicopter/ plane)
by chance
by cheque

by correspondence
by day/night
by degrees
by the dozen
by far
by force
by hand
by heart
by invitation
by land/sea/air
by law
by luck
by marriage
by means of
by mistake

by nature
by now
by oneself
by order of
by phone
by post/airmail
by profession
by request
by (the/one's) side
by sight
by surprise
by the time
by the way
by oneself
by one's watch

For

for ages
for breakfast/lunch/dinner
for certain
for a change
for ever
for fear (of)
for fun (= for amusement)
for good
for granted

for hire
for keeps
for instance
for luck
for life
for love
for nothing
for once
for the rest of

for safe keeping
for one's sake
for the sake of
for sale (= to be sold)
for short
for the time being
for a visit/holiday
for a walk
for a while

Prepositional Phrases

In

in action
in addition to (+ -ing form)
in advance (of)
in agreement (with)
in aid of
in all (= all in all)
in answer to
in an armchair
in a bad temper
in bed
in the beginning
(= originally)
in blossom
in a book
in brief
in any case
in cash
in the centre of
in charge (of)
in cities
in code
in colour
in comfort
in common
in comparison with
in conclusion (to)
in (good/bad) condition
in confidence
in control (of)
in the country
in danger
in the dark
in debt
in demand
in detail
(be) in difficulty
in the direction of
in doubt
in a ... dress
in due course
in the end (= finally)
in exchange for
in existence
in fact
in fashion
in favour of/with
in flames
in the flesh
in focus
in one's free time
in full swing
in fun

in future
in gear
in general
in good time
in half
in hand
in haste
in good/bad health
in hiding
in honour of
in the hope of
in hospital
in a hotel
in a hurry
in ink/pencil/pen
in sb's interest
in length/width etc
in all sb's life
in the limelight
in a line
in the long run
in love (with)
in luxury
in the meantime
in a mess
in the middle of
in a mirror
in moderation
in a moment
in a good/bad mood
in the mood
in the morning
in mourning
in name only (= not in reality)
in need of
in the news
in a newspaper
in the name of (= on behalf of)
in the nick of time
in the north/south
in a nutshell
in oils
in the open
in one's opinion
in orbit
in order of/to
in other words
in pain
in pairs
in the park
in particular
in the past

in person
in pieces
in place of
in politics
in pounds
in practice/theory
in principle
in prison
in private/public
in all probability
in progress
in a queue
in reality
in return
in the right/wrong
in a row/rows
in ruins
in safety
in season
in secret
in self-defence
in short
in sight (of)
in the sky
in some respects
in stock
in the streets
in succession
in the suburbs
in the sun/shade
in good/bad taste
in tears
in theory
in a tick
in time
in no time
in touch
in town
in tune (with)
in turn
in two/half
in uniform
in use
in vain
in view of
in a loud/low voice
in a way (= in a manner)
in the way
in writing
in a word

Prepositional Phrases

On

on account of
on a ... afternoon/
evening
on the agenda
on the air
on approval
on arrival
on average
on bail
on balance
on the beach
on behalf of
on one's birthday
on board
on the border
on business
on call
on a campsite (at a
campsite)
on the coast
on condition
on the contrary
on credit
on a cruise/excursion/
trip/tour
on (a ...) day
on demand
on a diet
on the dole

on duty
on earth
on edge
on an expedition
on a farm (but: **in a field**)
on fire
on the (4th) floor (of)
on the floor
on foot
on the one hand
on the other hand
on holiday
on horseback
on impulse
on the increase
on an island (but: **in the
mountains**)
on a journey
on one's knees
on leave
on the left
on loan
on the market (= available to the
public)
on one's mind
on that morning
on the move
on New Year's Day
on the news

on order
on the outskirts
on one's own
on page ...
on parade
on the pavement
on the phone
on a platform
on principle
on purpose
on the radio/TV
on the right
on the River Seine
on sale (sold at reduced price)
(but: for sale = to be sold)
on schedule
on the screen
on second thoughts
on sight
on the sofa
on this street/on the street(s)
on strike
on good/bad terms
on time
on top of
on the trail of
on a trip
on the way (to) (= as I was going)
on the whole

Out of

out of breath
out of character
out of condition
out of control
out of danger
out of date
out of debt
out of doors
out of fashion

out of focus
out of hand
out of luck
out of order
out of the ordinary
out of place
out of practice
out of print
out of the question

out of reach
out of season
out of sight
out of step
out of stock
out of tune
out of turn
out of use
out of work

Off

off the air
off colour
off duty
off limits

off the map
off the peg
off the point

off the record
off the road
off school/work

Under

under age
under arrest
under one's breath
under control

under discussion
under the impression
under orders

under pressure
under repair
under the weather

Against	against the law
Ahead	ahead of schedule, ahead of one's time
Before	before long
Behind	behind schedule, behind the times
From	from time to time, from now on, from experience, from memory, from scratch
Into	into pieces
To	to one's astonishment, to one's surprise, to this day, to some extent
With	with regard to, with a view to (+ -ing form)
Within	within minutes
Without	without delay, without fail, without success, without warning

Prepositions of Time

AT	IN	ON
at 10.30	in the morning/evening/afternoon/night	on Monday
at Christmas/Easter	in the Easter/Christmas holiday(s)	on Easter Sunday etc
at noon/night/midnight	in January (months)	on Christmas Day
at lunch/dinner/breakfast (time)	in (the) winter (seasons)	on Friday night
at that time	in 1992 (years)	on July 30th
at the moment	in the 19th century	on a summer afternoon
at the weekend (on the weekend: Am. English)	in two hours (two hours from now)	on that day

We never use **at**, **in** or **on** before **yesterday**, **tomorrow**, **next**, **this**, **last**, **every**. *He's coming **next** Monday.*

Concrete noun	Abstract noun	Verb	Adjective
	(in/dis)ability	disable, enable	able, disabled
	acceptance, acceptability	accept	acceptable
	accident		accidental
	achievement	achieve	achievable
actor, actress	action, act, activity, acting, activation	activate, act	active
admirer	admiration	admire	admiring, admirable
admission	admittance, admission	admit	admissible
adventurer	adventure		adventurous
adviser	advice, advisability	advise	advisable, advisory
alarm	alarm	alarm	alarming, alarmed
analyst	analysis	analyse	analytic(al)
	anxiety		anxious
applicant, applicator	application	apply	applicable, applied
artist	art, artistry		artistic
	assumption	assume	
attendant	attendance, (in)attention	attend	attendant, (in)attentive
beginner	beginning	begin	beginning
behaviourist	behaviour, behaviourism	behave	behavioural
benefit, benefactor, beneficiary	benefit	benefit	beneficial
	breath, breathing	breathe	breathless, breathy, breathtaking, (un)breathable
calculator	calculation	calculate	calculating, calculable
celebrity	celebration	celebrate	celebrated
centre	centre	centralise, centre	central
character, characteristic	character, characterisation	characterise	characteristic, characterless
child	childhood, childbirth		childless, childish, childlike
	choice	choose	choos(e)y
	classification	classify	classified, classifiable
collection, collector	collection	collect	collected, collective
comforter	comfort	comfort	comfortable, comfortless, comforting
	commitment, committal	commit	committed
	communication	communicate	communicable, communicative
competitor	competition	compete	competitive
	complaint	complain	
	completeness, completion	complete	complete
confidant(e)	confidence, confidentiality	confide	confident, confidential, confiding
	consciousness		conscious
	conservation	conserve	conservative
	(in)consideration	consider	considerable, considerate
construction, constructor	construction	construct	constructive
correction	(in)correctness, correction	correct	correct, corrective
correspondent, correspondence	correspondence	correspond	corresponding
creation, creator, creature	creation, creativeness, creativity	create	creative

Concrete noun	Abstract noun	Verb	Adjective
cure	cure	cure	curable, curative
	curiosity		curious
	danger	endanger	dangerous, endangered
daily	day, daylight		daily
	decision, (in)decisiveness	decide	decided, decisive
demonstrator	demonstration	demonstrate	demonstrative
	depression	depress	depressed, depressing, depressive
	depth, deepness	deepen	deep
	description	describe	describable, descriptive
	despair, desperation	despair	despairing, desperate
destroyer	destruction, destructiveness	destroy	destructible, destructive
	determination	determine	determined
discovery, discoverer	discovery	discover	discoverable
dramatist	drama	dramatise	dramatic
	ease	ease	easy
economist	economy, economics	economise	economic, economical
educator	education	educate	educated, educational
elector	election	elect	elective, electoral
electrician	electricity, electrocution	electrify, electrocute	electric, electrical
employer, employee	(un)employment	employ	employed, employable
	encouragement	encourage	encouraging
end	end, ending	end	endless
	energy	energise	energetic
	enjoyment	enjoy	enjoyable
enthusiast	enthusiasm	enthuse	enthusiastic
	envy	envy	envious, envied, enviable
escapee, escapist	escape, escapism	escape	
	exactness, exactitude	exact	exact, exacting
examiner, examinee	exam(ination)	examine	
	excitement	excite	exciting, excited, excitable
exhaust	exhaustion	exhaust	exhausted, exhausting, exhaustive
	existence	exist	existent, existing
	expectation, expentancy	expect	expected, expectant
expenses	expense, expenditure	expend	expensive, expendable
	explanation	explain	explanatory
	fame		famed, famous, infamous
	fascination	fascinate	fascinating
	fashion	fashion	fashionable
	fault	fault	faulty, faultless
finance, financier	finance	finance	financial
	fluency		fluent
fortune	fortune, misfortune		fortunate

4 Appendix

Concrete noun	Abstract noun	Verb	Adjective
	(in)frequency	frequent	frequent
	generalisation, generality	generalise	general, generalised
globe	globalisation	globalise	global
government, governor	government, governance	govern	governing, governmental
guide	guidance	guide	guided, guiding
	happiness		happy
	health, healthiness		healthy
	honesty		honest
host, hostess	hospitality	host	hospitable
human, humanist, humanity	humanisim, humanity, inhumanity		human, humanly, humane, humanitarian
	idiom		idiomatic
	illness, ill		ill
image	imagination, image, imagery	imagine	imaginary, imaginable, imaginative
	importance		important
	impression	impress	impressive, impressionable
	inspiration	inspire	inspirational, inspired, inspiring
insurance, insurer	insurance	insure	insured
intelligence	intelligence		intelligent
	interest	interest	interested, interesting
interpreter	interpretation	interpret	
	introduction	introduce	introductory
intruder	intrusion	intrude	intrusive
investigator	investigation	investigate	investigative, investigatory
invitation	invitation	invite	inviting, invited
	isolation	isolate	isolated, isolating
jewel, jeweller, jewellery			jewelled
learner	learning	learn	learned
	likelihood		likely
likeness	likeness	liken	like, alike
	loudness		loud
luxuriance	luxury	luxuriate	luxurious, luxuriant
	madness	madden	mad
	majority		major
medicine	medicine, medication		medical, medicated, medicinal
(im)mortal	(im)mortality	immortalise	mortal
mover	movement, move, motion	move	moving, movable, motionless
musician	music, musical		musical
	mystification, mystery, mysteriousness	mystify	mysterious
nature	nature	naturalise	natural
necessaries	necessity	necessitate	necessary
nerve	nerve, nervousness	nerve	nervous, nerveless, nervy

Concrete noun	Abstract noun	Verb	Adjective
	norm, normal, normality, normalisation	normalise	(ab)normal
operator	operation	operate	operable, operational, operative
opportunist	opportunity, opportunism		opportune
	option	opt	optional
organisation, organiser	organisation	organise	organised
	(im)patience		(im)patient
	peace, peacefulness		peaceful, peaceable
	percent, percentage		
perfectionist	(im)perfection, perfectionism	perfect	perfect, perfectible
performer	performance	perform	
personality, person, personnel	personality, personification	personalise, personify	personal
pessimist	pessimism		pessimistic
	pleasure, pleasantness	please	pleasant, pleasurable, pleased, pleasing
politician	policy, politics	politicise	political
pollutant	pollution	pollute	polluted, polluting
population	popularity	populate	popular
	possibility		possible
	power	empower, power	powerful, powered, powerless
practitioner	practicality, practice	practise	practical, practicable
	prevention	prevent	preventable, preventive
	privacy, privatisation	privatise	private
	probability		probable
product, produce, producer, productivity	production, productivity	produce	productive
professional	profession		professional
promoter	promotion	promote	promotional
	proposal, proposition	propose	proposed
protector	protection	protect	protective, protected
psychologist	psychology, psyche, psychosis	psych(e)	psychological, psychic, psychotic
public	publicity	publicise	public
pursuer	pursuit	pursue	
qualification	qualification	(dis)qualify	qualified, unqualified, disqualified
realist	reality, realism, realisation	realise	real, realistic
	recognition	recognise	recognisable
reference	reference	refer	referable
reject	rejection	reject	reject, rejecting
relation, relative	relation, relationship, relativity,	relate	related, relative
	relaxation	relax	relaxing, relaxed
	reliability, reliance	rely	(un)reliable, reliant

Concrete noun	Abstract noun	Verb	Adjective
repeater	repetition, repeat	repeat	repeatable, repetitive
replacement	replacement	replace	(ir)replaceable
	requirement	require	
response	response, responsiveness	respond	responsive
	(ir)responsibility		(ir)responsible
	restriction, restrictiveness	restrict	restricted, restrictive
safe, saver, saviour, savings	safety	save	safe
	(dis)satisfaction	satisfy	(dis)satisfied, satisfactory, satisfying
scenery	scene		scenic
scientist	science		scientific
	security	secure	secure
sense, sensor	sense, sensation, sensitivity, sensibility	sense	sensible, sensitive, sensory, sensational, senseless
	skill		skilled, skillful
spectacles, spectator	spectacle	spectate	spectacular
	starvation	starve	starving, starved
stranger	strangeness		strange
	stress	stress	stressful
	success	succeed	successful
suit	suit	suit	suitable, suited
	suggestion	suggest	suggestive, suggestible
summary	summary	summarise	summary
	surprise	surprise	surprising, surprised
surroundings		surround	surrounding
sympathiser	sympathy	sympathise	sympathetic
tempter	temptation	tempt	tempting, tempted
	tendency	tend	
	threat	threaten	threatening
trainer, trainee	training	train	trained, training
	trend	trend	trendy
	truth		true, truthful
type	type		typical
	understanding	understand	understandable, understanding
valuer	value, valuation	value	valuable, valueless, invaluable
variety	variety, variation, variability	vary	various, varied, variable
warmer	warmth, warm	warm	warm
westerner, west	west	westernise	western, west, westerly, westward
watch, watcher	watch	watch	watchful
worker, work	work	work	workable, working

Irregular Verbs

Infinitive	Past	Past Participle	Infinitive	Past	Past Participle
be	was	been	lie	lay	lain
bear	bore	born(e)	light	lit	lit
beat	beat	beaten	lose	lost	lost
become	became	become	make	made	made
begin	began	begun	mean	meant	meant
bite	bit	bitten	meet	met	met
blow	blew	blown	pay	paid	paid
break	broke	broken	put	put	put
bring	brought	brought	read	read	read
build	built	built	ride	rode	ridden
burn	burnt	burnt	ring	rang	rung
burst	burst	burst	rise	rose	risen
buy	bought	bought	run	ran	run
can	could	(been able to)	say	said	said
catch	caught	caught	see	saw	seen
choose	chose	chosen	seek	sought	sought
come	came	come	sell	sold	sold
cost	cost	cost	send	sent	sent
cut	cut	cut	set	set	set
deal	dealt	dealt	sew	sewed	sewn
dig	dug	dug	shake	shook	shaken
do	did	done	shine	shone	shone
draw	drew	drawn	shoot	shot	shot
dream	dreamt	dreamt	show	showed	shown
drink	drank	drunk	shut	shut	shut
drive	drove	driven	sing	sang	sung
eat	ate	eaten	sit	sat	sat
fall	fell	fallen	sleep	slept	slept
feed	fed	fed	smell	smelt	smelt
feel	felt	felt	speak	spoke	spoken
fight	fought	fought	spell	spelt	spelt
find	found	found	spend	spent	spent
fly	flew	flown	spill	spilt	spilt
forbid	forbade	forbidden	split	split	split
forget	forgot	forgotten	spoil	spoilt	spoilt
forgive	forgave	forgiven	spread	spread	spread
freeze	froze	frozen	spring	sprang	sprung
get	got	got	stand	stood	stood
give	gave	given	steal	stole	stolen
go	went	gone	stick	stuck	stuck
grow	grew	grown	sting	stung	stung
hang	hung	hung	strike	struck	struck
have	had	had	swear	swore	sworn
hear	heard	heard	sweep	swept	swept
hide	hid	hidden	swim	swam	swum
hit	hit	hit	take	took	taken
hold	held	held	teach	taught	taught
hurt	hurt	hurt	tear	tore	torn
keep	kept	kept	tell	told	told
know	knew	known	think	thought	thought
lay	laid	laid	throw	threw	thrown
lead	led	led	understand	understood	understood
learn	learnt	learnt	wake	woke	woken
leave	left	left	wear	wore	worn
lend	lent	lent	win	won	won
let	let	let	write	wrote	written

The author and publishers wish to thank the following who have kindly given permission for the use of copyright material:

The European for *Counterfeits* by Claudia Flisi on p. 19, *You Eat What You Are* by Darius Sanai on p. 25, *Laughter* by Tessa Thomas on p. 49, *Saving Europe's Woodlands* by Michael Bond on p. 94, *Wake Up, It's Summer* by Barbara Rowlands on p. 95, *Egyptomania* by Julie Stree on p. 144, *Power Dressing* by Mary Gallagher on p. 182, *Eat, Drink and Be Merry* by Tessa Thomas on p. 184, *Art in Amsterdam* by Mindy Ran on p. 194, *Keeping Warm in Winter* by Tessa Thomas on p. 195, *Credit Cards* on p. 197, *Dream Machine* by Tony Lewin on p. 207; Focus magazine for *Easter Island* on p. 51, *Toys* on p. 97, *Art Goes Audio* on p. 128, *Panama Hats* on p. 161, *the Lake District* on p. 164; Best magazine for *Caravanning in Wales* on p. 20, *Live Your Life* on p. 48, *Flight to Disaster* on p.69, *Tasty Snacks* on p. 114; National Geographic for *Water* on p. 66, *Fatal Frogs* on p. 205; The Greek News for *Coping with Shyness* on p. 67; Time magazine (c) 1991 Time Inc for *Cars on Display* on p. 97; Bella magazine for *Healthy Teeth for Life* on p. 131; British Airways Highlife magazines for *The Magic of Granada* on p. 147; Woman's Own for *Cyprus* on p. 162; Philosophy Now for *Aristotle* on p. 204.

Photographs: IDEAL PHOTO for the pictures on pages 16, 35, 43, 45, 51, 119, 135 and 141.

Every effort has been made to trace all the copyright holders but if any have been inadvertently overlooked, the publishers will be pleased to make the necessary arrangement at the first opportunity.

ACKNOWLEDGEMENTS